GREAT DUBLIN STREET ATLAS

GW00420178

Contents

Key to map symbols

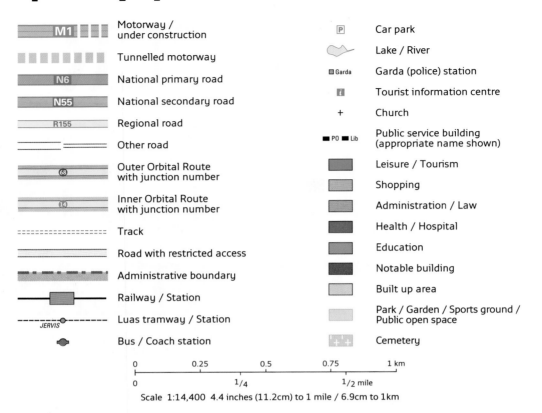

- M1 Motorway / under construction
- Tunnelled motorway
- N6 National primary road
- N55 National secondary road
- R155 Regional road
- Other road
- 68 Outer Orbital Route with junction number
- 14 Inner Orbital Route with junction number
- Track
- Road with restricted access
- Administrative boundary
- Railway / Station
- JERVIS Luas tramway / Station
- Bus / Coach station
- P Car park
- Lake / River
- Garda Garda (police) station
- i Tourist information centre
- + Church
- PO Lib Public service building (appropriate name shown)
- Leisure / Tourism
- Shopping
- Administration / Law
- Health / Hospital
- Education
- Notable building
- Built up area
- Park / Garden / Sports ground / Public open space
- Cemetery

0 0.25 0.5 0.75 1 km

0 1/4 1/2 mile

Scale 1:14,400 4.4 inches (11.2cm) to 1 mile / 6.9cm to 1km

Key to map symbols (pages 4-7)

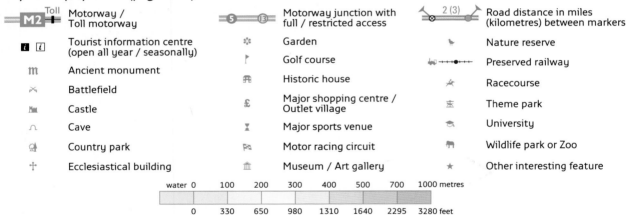

- M2 Toll Motorway / Toll motorway
- Tourist information centre (open all year / seasonally)
- Ancient monument
- Battlefield
- Castle
- Cave
- Country park
- Ecclesiastical building
- 5 13 Motorway junction with full / restricted access
- Garden
- Golf course
- Historic house
- Major shopping centre / Outlet village
- Major sports venue
- Motor racing circuit
- Museum / Art gallery
- 2 (3) Road distance in miles (kilometres) between markers
- Nature reserve
- Preserved railway
- Racecourse
- Theme park
- University
- Wildlife park or Zoo
- Other interesting feature

water	0	100	200	300	400	500	700	1000 metres
	0	330	650	980	1310	1640	2295	3280 feet

Published by Collins
An imprint of HarperCollins Publishers
77-85 Fulham Palace Road, Hammersmith, London W6 8JB

www.collinsbartholomew.co.uk

Mapping generated from Collins Bartholomew digital databases

Based on Ordnance Survey Ireland by permission of the Government of Ireland.
Ordnance Survey Ireland Permit No. 8045

Printed in China

Imp 002 (DUN) Imp 001 (TRADE)

e-mail: roadcheck@harpercollins.co.uk

Key to map pages

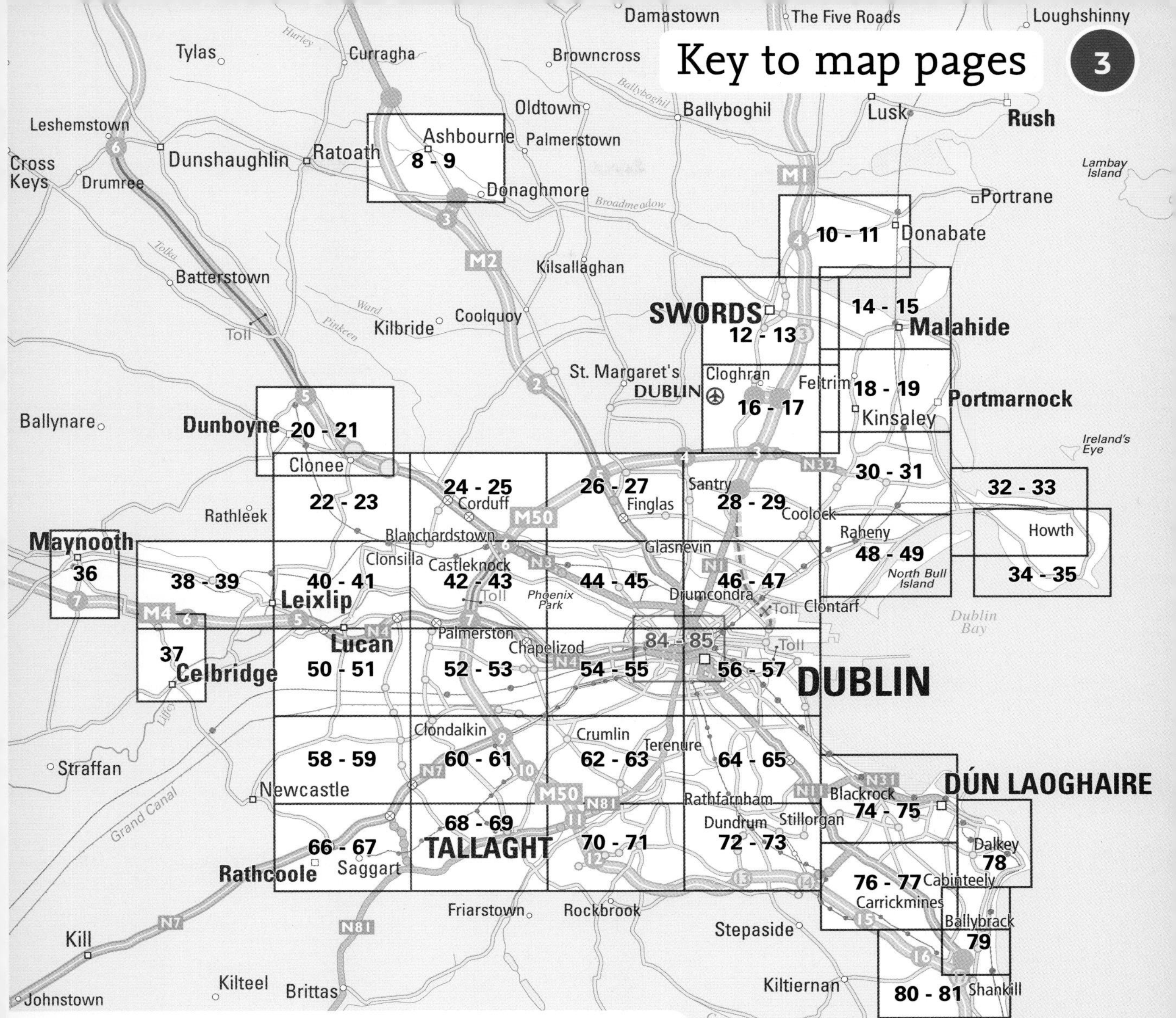

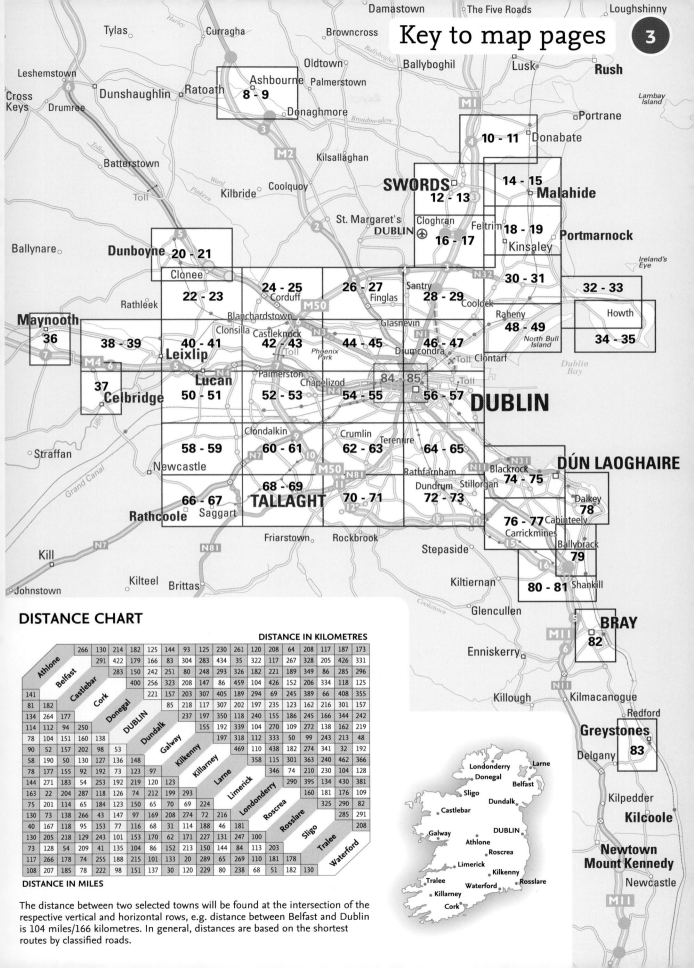

DISTANCE CHART

DISTANCE IN KILOMETRES

	Athlone	Belfast	Castlebar	Cork	Donegal	DUBLIN	Dundalk	Galway	Kilkenny	Killarney	Larne	Limerick	Londonderry	Roscrea	Rosslare	Sligo	Tralee	Waterford
Athlone		266	130	214	182	125	144	93	125	230	261	120	208	64	208	117	187	173
Belfast	141		291	422	179	166	83	304	283	434	35	322	117	267	328	205	426	331
Castlebar	81	182		283	150	242	251	80	248	293	326	182	221	189	349	86	285	296
Cork	134	264	177		400	256	323	208	147	86	459	104	426	152	206	334	118	125
Donegal	114	112	94	250		221	157	203	307	405	189	294	69	245	389	66	408	355
DUBLIN	78	104	151	160	138		85	218	117	307	202	197	235	123	162	216	301	157
Dundalk	90	52	157	202	98	53		237	197	350	118	240	155	186	245	166	344	242
Galway	58	190	50	130	127	136	148		155	192	339	104	270	109	272	138	162	219
Kilkenny	78	177	155	92	192	73	123	97		197	318	112	333	50	99	243	213	48
Killarney	144	271	183	54	253	192	219	120	123		469	110	438	182	274	341	32	192
Larne	163	22	204	287	118	126	74	212	199	293		358	115	301	363	240	462	366
Limerick	75	201	114	65	184	123	150	65	70	69	224		346	74	210	230	104	128
Londonderry	130	73	138	266	43	147	97	169	208	274	72	216		290	395	134	430	381
Roscrea	40	167	118	95	153	77	116	68	31	114	188	46	181		160	181	176	109
Rosslare	130	205	218	129	243	101	153	170	62	171	227	131	247	100		325	290	82
Sligo	73	128	54	209	41	135	104	86	152	213	150	144	84	113	203		285	291
Tralee	117	266	178	74	255	188	215	101	133	20	289	65	269	110	181	178		208
Waterford	108	207	185	78	222	98	151	137	30	120	229	80	238	68	51	182	130	

DISTANCE IN MILES

The distance between two selected towns will be found at the intersection of the respective vertical and horizontal rows, e.g. distance between Belfast and Dublin is 104 miles/166 kilometres. In general, distances are based on the shortest routes by classified roads.

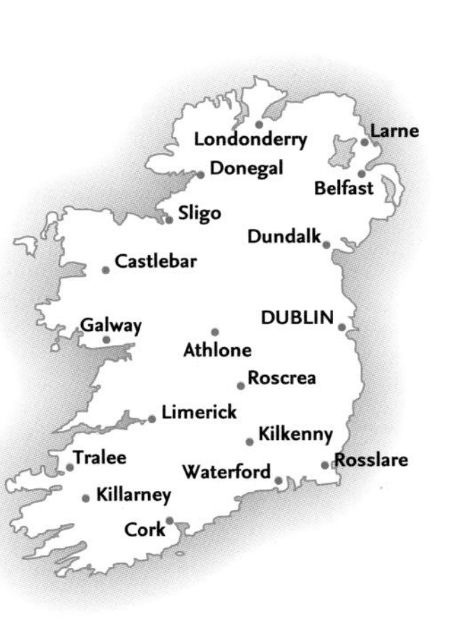

4 Route planning map

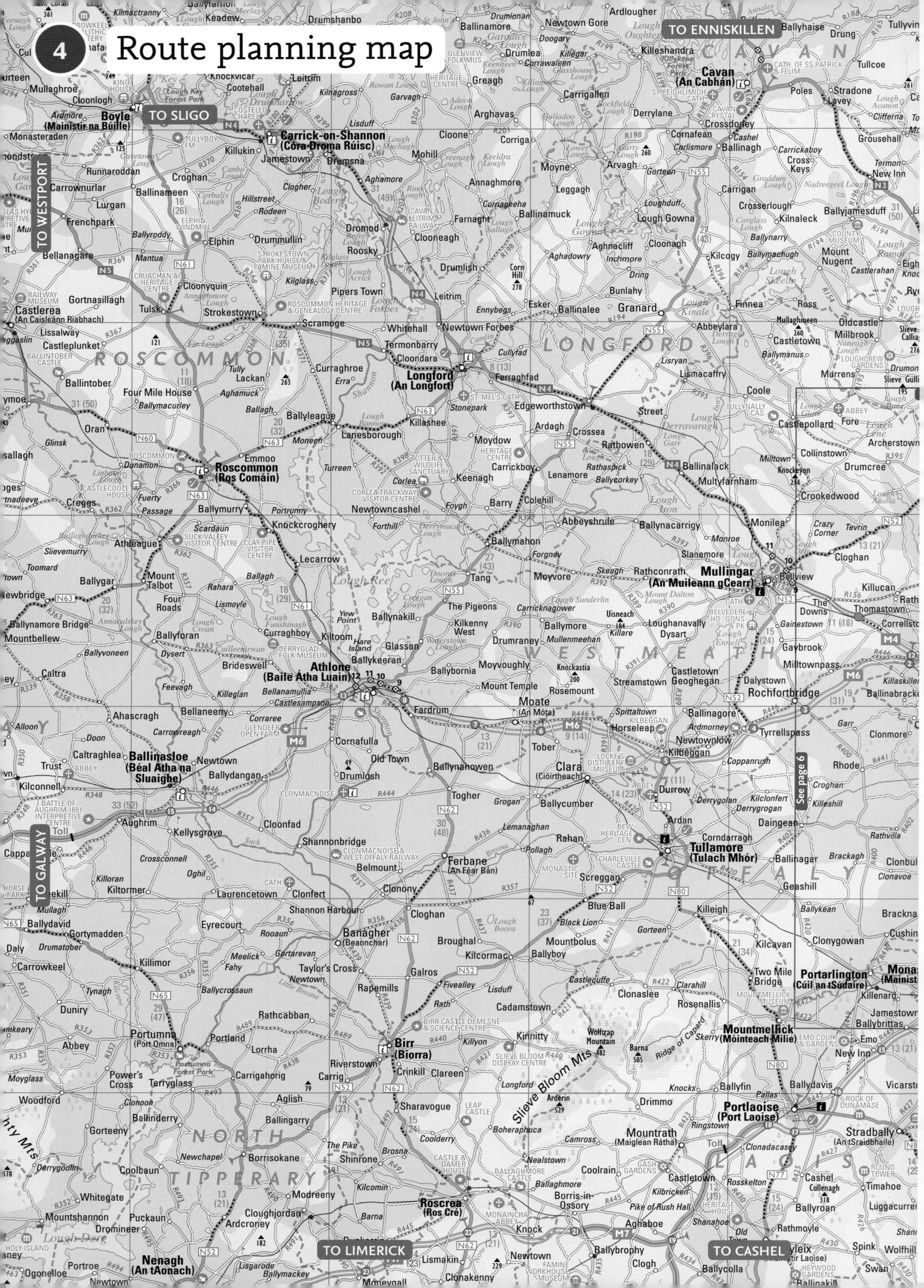

TO MONAGHAN
TO NEWRY
DUNDALK
(DÚN DEALGAN)
Kilkeel
Carlingford
Greenore
Cooley Point
Dundalk Bay
Grange
Ravensdale
Jenkinstown
Castletown
South Marsh
Sandymount
Blackrock
Haggardstown
Knockbridge
Inishkeen
Mullabohy
Ballybarrack
Kilcurly
Lough Eglish
Broomfield
Shantonag
Donaghmoyne
Drumbroagh
Corduff
Shercock
Carrickmacross
(Carrig Mhachaire)
Northlands
Corcreeghagh
Louth
Magheracloone
Carrickashedoge
Drumanespick
Bailieborough
(Coillan Chollaigh)
Moyer
341
Kingscourt
(Dún an Rí)
Ballynamona
Tallanstown
Mansfieldstown
Readypenny
Dromiskin
Castlebellingham
Kilsaran
Annagassan
Dunany Point
Ardee
(Baile Átha Fhirdhia)
Stabannan
Dromin
Drumcar
Dunleer
(Dún Léire)
Grangebellow
Hoathstown
Teevurcher
Kilmainhamwood
Drumcondra
Virginia
Nobber
Mullagh
Woodtown
Lisduff
Moynalty
Lobinstown
Mount Oriel
246
Monasterboice
Collon
Newtown Monasterboice
Clogher Head
Clogherhead
Termonfeckin
Castletown
Derver
Carnaross
Kells
(Ceannanus Mór)
Carlanstown
Rathkenny
Ballymakenny
Baile Órthai
(Oristown)
Wilkinstown
Tullyallen
Moneymore
DROGHEDA (DROICHEAD ÁTHA)
Baltray
Mornington
Donacarney
Bettystown (Baile an Bhiataigh)
Ballinlough
Crossakeel
Kilberry
Slane
Stackallan
Newgrange
Dowth
Donore
Laytown
Julianstown
Mosney
Gormanston
See page 6
See page 7
Kilskeer
Baile Ghib
(Gibstown)
Cortown
Clonmellon
Fordstown
Navan
(An Uaimh)
Blackcastle
Athlumney
Rathdrinagh
Duleek
(Damhliag)
Bellewstown
Stamullen
Balscaddan
Balbriggan
(Baile Brigín)
Bohermeen
Ballinlig
Athboy
(Baile Átha Buí)
Kilcarn
Johnstown
Kentstown
Greenanstown
Garlowcross
Balrath
Ardcath
Delvin
Dunderry
Robinstown
Rathfeigh
Hawkinstown
Balrothery
Skerries (Na Sceirí)
Bective
Screen
Clonalvy
Naul
Kildalkey
Tara
Garristown
Damastown
The Five Roads
Trim
(Baile Átha Troim)
Kilmessan
Baldwinstown
Loughshinny
Ballivor
Laracor
Dunsany
Tylas
Curragha
Ashbourne
(Cill Dhéagláin)
Oldtown
Lusk
(Lusca)
Rush (An Ros)
Raharney
Leshemstown
Dunshaughlin
Ratoath
Palmerstown
Cross Keys
Drumree
Donaghmore
Portrane (Port Reachrann)
The Nose
Lambay I.
Donabate
Hill of Down
Castlerickard
Rathmolyon
Summerhill
Moynalvy
Fairyhouse
Kilsallaghan
Togher
Coolquoy
SWORDS
(SORD)
Malahide (Mullach Íde)
Kinnegad
Clonard
Longwood
Kilmore
Agher
Garadice
Batterstown
Mullagh
Kilbride
Feltrim
Rathcore
Bunglass
Moyvalley
Dunboyne
(Dún Búinne)
St. Margaret's
Cloghran
Portmarnock (Port Mearnóg)
Ireland's Eye
Kinsaley
Ballynadrumny
Enfield
Cloncurry
Kilcock
(Cill Choca)
Ballynare
Clonee
Castlejordan
Cadamstown
Kilshanchoe
Johnstown Bridge
Newtown
Maynooth
(Maigh Nuad)
Rathleek
Mulhuddart
Blanchardstown
Finglas
Coolock
Raheny
Howth
Nose of Howth
North Bull Is.
Leixlip
(Léim an Bhradáin)
Castleknock
Phoenix Park
Palmerstown
Drumcondra
Clontarf
DUBLIN CITY
M50 Dublin Port Tunnel:
Toll for non-HGV traffic only
DOUGLAS
(Apr-Sept)
HOLYHEAD
LIVERPOOL
Grange
Mucklon
Laragh
Celbridge
(Cill Droichid)
Lucan (Leamhcán)
DUBLIN (BAILE ÁTHA CLIATH)
(see p29 for key to ref. nos)
Dublin Bay
Carbury
Derrinturn
Timahoe
Donadea
Edenderry
(Éadan Doire)
Staplestown
Mainham
Adamstown
Clondalkin
Crumlin
Ballyfore
Straffan
Milltown
Newcastle
(An Caisleán Nua)
TALLAGHT
Blackrock
DÚN LAOGHAIRE
HOLYHEAD
Killinagh
Coolearagh
Allenwood
Prosperous
Clane
(Claonadh)
Rathcoole
(Ráth Cúil)
Saggart
Rathfarnham
Dundrum
Stillorgan
Dalkey
Bog of Allen
Lullymore
Robertstown
Rockbrook
Mount Seskin
397
Friarstown
Stepaside
DÚN LAOGHAIRE-RATHDOWN
Kilmeague
Allen
Sallins
Kill (An Chill)
Brittas
Kiltiernan
Killinthomas
Carragh
Johnstown
Kilteel
Glendoo Mountain
584
Glencullen
Shankill
Rathangan
(Ráth Iomgháin)
Milltown
Naas
(An Nás)
Rathmore
Enniskerry
(Áth an Sceire)
BRAY (BRÉ)
Bray Head
Dunmurry Hill
234
Newbridge
(Droichead Nua)
Kilbride
Oldcourt
Kippure
754
Killough
Kilmacanogue
Redford
Kildare
(Cill Dara)
Lackagh
Cherryville
The Curragh
Athgarvan
Two Mile House
Blessington
(Baile Coimín)
Tonduff
642
Djouce Mountain
725
Great Sugar Loaf
Greystones (Na Clocha Liathe)
Wicklow Mountains National Park
Curragh Camp
Kilcullen
(Cill Chuillin)
Ballymore Eustace
Lackan
Pollaphuca Reservoir
Sally Gap
Delgany
Brannockstown
Milemill
Valleymount
Kilpedder
Kilcoole (Cill Chomhghaill)
Suncroft
Old Kilcullen
Hollywood
Ballynockan
Mullaghcleevaun
850
Lough Dan
Newtown Mount Kennedy
(Baile an Chinnéidigh)
Nurney
Ballyshannon
Calverstown
Kilgowan
Wicklow Mountains
Roundwood
Newcastle
Boley
Tonelagee
819
Cloney
Fontstown
Narraghmore
Dunlavin
Granabeg
Tomdarragh
Kilberry
Colbinstown
Donard
Camaderry
699
Glendalough
Annamoe
Killiskey
Ardscull
Crookstown
Freynestown
Rathnew
(Ráth Naoi)
Churchtown
Athy
(Baile Átha Í)
Ballitore
Grange Con
Camenabologue
758
Laragh
Ashford
Carrick Mountain
382
Castleruddery
Knockanarrigan
Wicklow Mountains National Park
Wicklow (Cill Mhantáin)
Wicklow Head
Ballintubbert
Timolin
Stratford
Glenmalure
Lugnaquilla
926
Glenealy
Ballyroe
Moone
Keadeen Mountain
653
Ballinderry
Kilkea
Ballylynan
Kilmorony
Baltinglass
(Bealach Conglais)
Greenan
Rathdrum
(Ráth Droma)
Kilbride
Ardmore Point
Ballinacor
Maganey
Talbotstown
Rathdangan
Aghavannagh
664
Castledermot
Kilmurry
Kiltegan
Ballinaclash
Brittas Bay
Arless
TO CARLOW
Graney
TO ARKLOW
Ballickmoyler
Knocknacree
Rathvilly
Sheeanamore
Cushbawn
402
Knockananna
0 2 4 6 miles
0 2 4 6 8 10 km
DUBLIN PLACES OF INTEREST
1 BOOK OF KELLS
2 CHRIST CHURCH CATHEDRAL
3 CROKE PARK & GAA MUSEUM
4 DUBLIN CASTLE
5 DUBLINIA
6 GUINNESS STOREHOUSE
7 IRISH MUSEUM OF MODERN ART
8 OLD JAMESON DISTILLERY
9 ST. MARY'S CATHEDRAL
10 ST. PATRICK'S CATHEDRAL

6 Dublin approaches

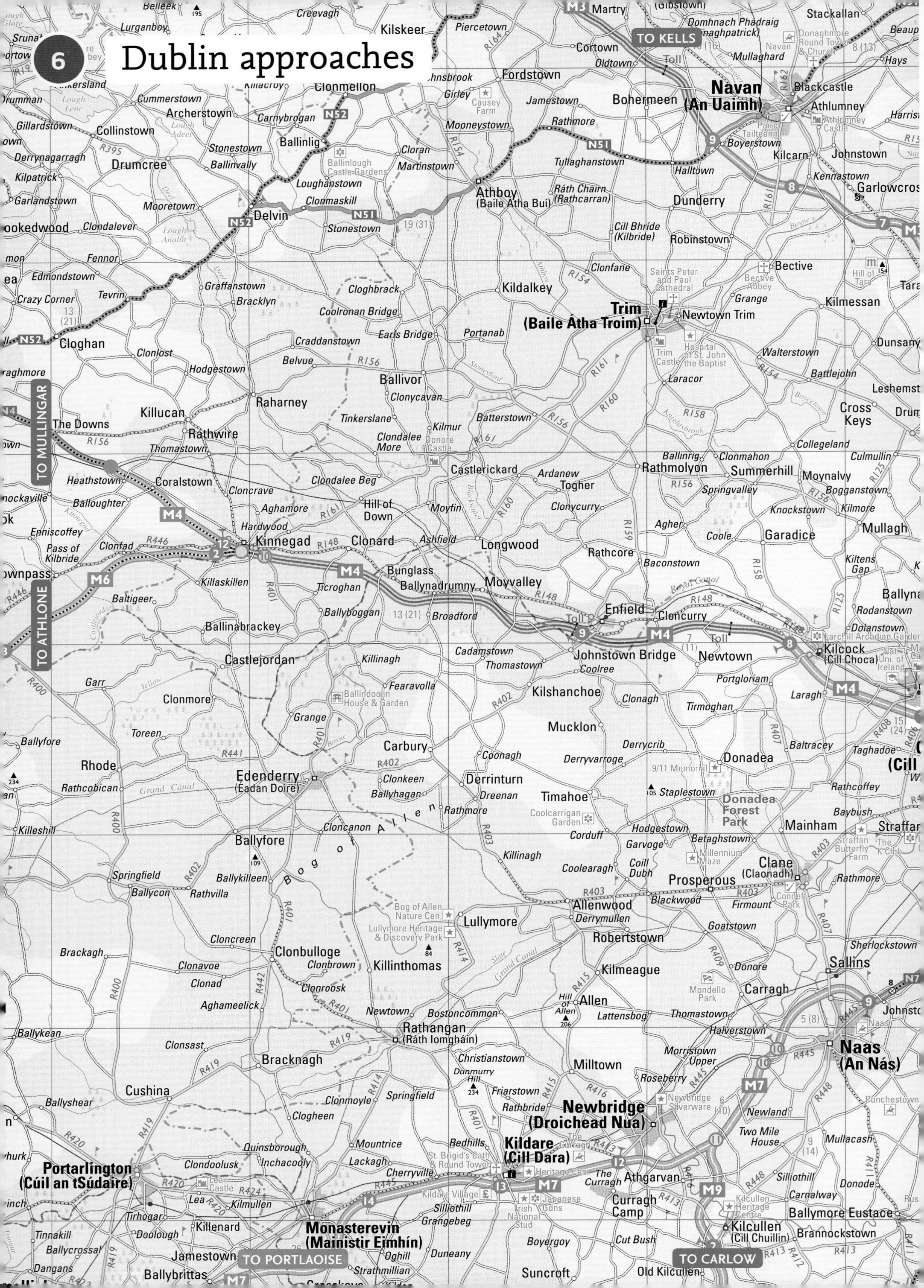

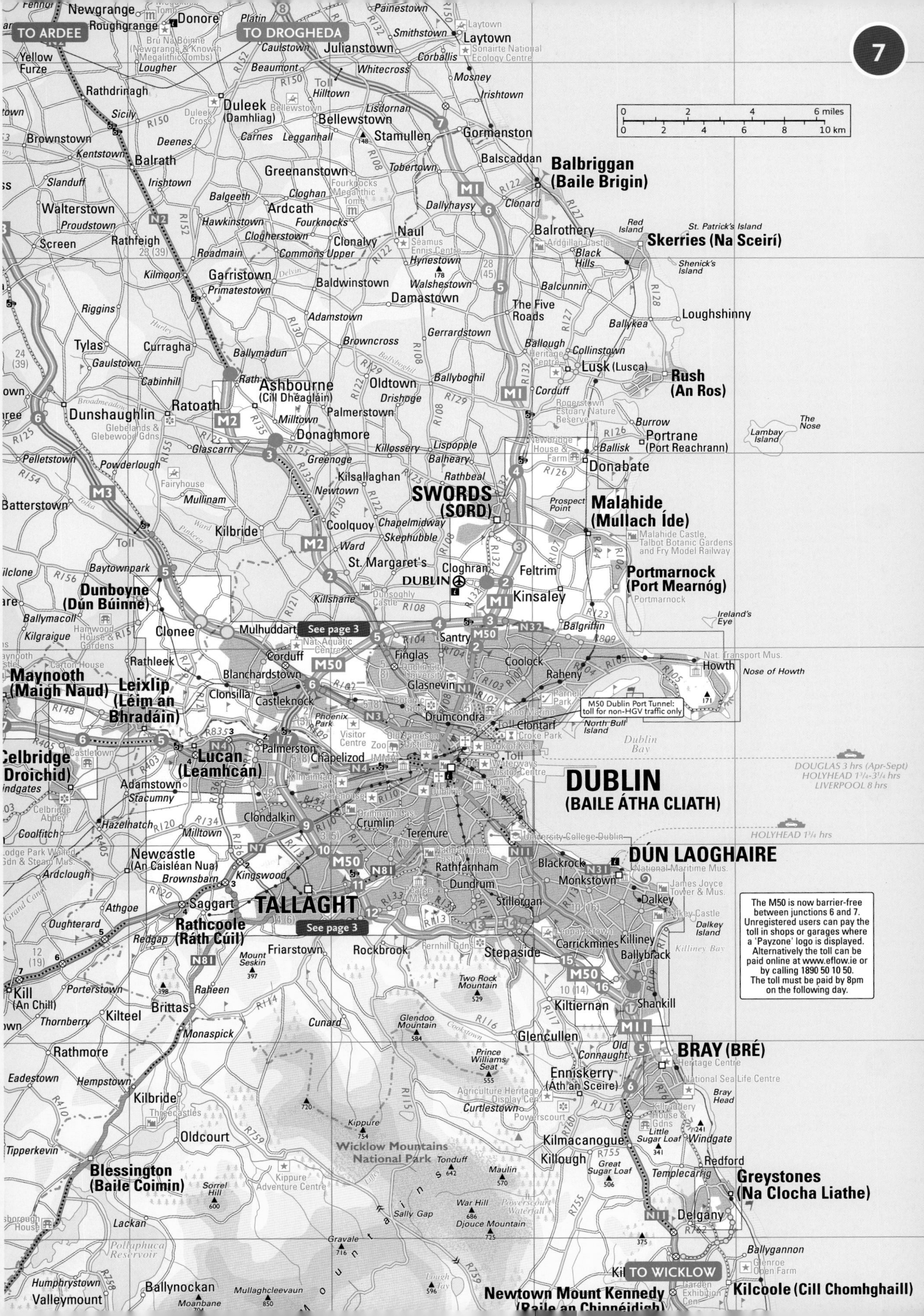
TO ARDEE
TO DROGHEDA
TO WICKLOW
0 2 4 6 miles
0 2 4 6 8 10 km
Newgrange
Roughgrange
Donore
Brú Na Bóinne (Newgrange & Knowth Megalithic Tombs)
Platin
Painestown
Smithstown
Laytown
Sonairte National Ecology Centre
Caulstown
Julianstown
Corballis
Yellow Furze
Lougher
Beaumont
Whitecross
Mosney
Toll
Hilltown
Irishtown
Rathdrinagh
Duleek (Damhliag)
Bellewstown
Lisdornan
Sicily
Duleek Cross
Brownstown
Deenes
Carnes
Legganhall
Stamullen
Gormanston
Kentstown
Balrath
Balscaddan
Balbriggan (Baile Brigin)
Greenanstown
Tobertown
Slanduff
Irishtown
Fourknocks Megalithic Tomb
Walterstown
Balgeeth
Cloghan
Dallyhaysy
Clonard
Ardcath
Proudstown
Hawkinstown
Fourknocks
Balrothery
Ardgillan Castle
Red Island
St. Patrick's Island
Skerries (Na Sceirí)
Screen
Rathfeigh
Clogherstown
Clonalvy
Naul
Séamus Ennis Centre
Black Hills
Roadmain
Commons Upper
Hynestown
Shenick's Island
Kilmoon
Garristown
Delvin
Walshestown
Balcunnin
Primatestown
Baldwinstown
Damastown
The Five Roads
Riggins
Adamstown
Loughshinny
Ballykea
Gerrardstown
Tylas
Curragha
Browncross
Ballough Heritage Centre
Collinstown
Gaulstown
Ballymadun
Lusk (Lusca)
Rush (An Ros)
Cabinhill
Rath
Ashbourne (Cill Dhéagláin)
Oldtown
Ballyboghil
Drishoge
Corduff
Ratoath
Milltown
Palmerstown
Rogerstown Estuary Nature Reserve
Dunshaughlin
Glebelands & Glebewood Gdns
Donaghmore
Burrow
Lambay Island
The Nose
Portrane (Port Reachrann)
Glascarn
Killossery
Lispopple
Ballisk
Newbridge House & Farm
Pelletstown
Powderlough
Greenoge
Balheary
Donabate
Fairyhouse
Kilsallaghan
Rathbeal
Newtown
SWORDS (SORD)
Prospect Point
Malahide (Mullach Íde)
Batterstown
Mullinam
Chapelmidway
Kilbride
Coolquoy
Skephubble
Malahide Castle, Talbot Botanic Gardens and Fry Model Railway
Toll
Ward
St. Margaret's
Cloghran
Feltrim
Baytownpark
DUBLIN
Portmarnock (Port Mearnóg)
Dunboyne (Dún Búinne)
Killshane
Dunsoghly Castle
Kinsaley
Portmarnock
Ballymacoll
Hamwood House & Gardens
Clonee
Mulhuddart
See page 3
Nat. Aquatic Centre
Santry
Balgriffin
Ireland's Eye
Kilgraigue
Corduff
Finglas
Coolock
Raheny
Nat. Transport Mus.
Howth
Nose of Howth
Carton House
Rathleek
Dublin City University
Maynooth (Maigh Nuad)
Leixlip (Léim an Bhradáin)
Blanchardstown
Glasnevin
Clonsilla
Castleknock
Botanic Gdns
Parnell Park
M50 Dublin Port Tunnel: toll for non-HGV traffic only
Phoenix Park
Drumcondra
Casino Marino
Clontarf
North Bull Island
Visitor Centre
Zoo
Old Jameson Distillery
Croke Park
Dublin Bay
Celbridge (Droichid)
Castletown
Palmerston
Book of Kells
Lucan (Leamhcán)
Chapelizod
IMMA
Toll
Waterways Visitor Centre
DOUGLAS 3 hrs (Apr-Sept)
HOLYHEAD 1¾-3¼ hrs
LIVERPOOL 8 hrs
Windgates
Adamstown
Kilmainham Gaol
DUBLIN (BAILE ÁTHA CLIATH)
Stacumny
Storehouse
Dublin Civic Mus.
Celbridge Abbey
Hazelhatch
Drimnagh Cas.
Clondalkin
Crumlin
Coolfitch
Milltown
Terenure
University College Dublin
HOLYHEAD 1¾ hrs
Lodge Park Walled Gdn & Steam Mus.
Newcastle (An Caisléan Nua)
Rathfarnham Castle
DÚN LAOGHAIRE
Kingswood
Blackrock
National Maritime Mus.
Ardclough
Brownsbarn
Rathfarnham
Monkstown
Dundrum
James Joyce Tower & Mus.
Athgoe
Saggart
TALLAGHT
Pearse Mus.
Stillorgan
Dalkey
Dalkey Castle
Oughterard
Rathcoole (Ráth Cúil)
See page 3
Leopardstown
Dalkey Island
Redgap
Killiney
Friarstown
Rockbrook
Fernhill Gdns
Stepaside
Carrickmines
Ballybrack
Killiney Bay
Mount Seskin
The M50 is now barrier-free between junctions 6 and 7. Unregistered users can pay the toll in shops or garages where a 'Payzone' logo is displayed. Alternatively the toll can be paid online at www.eflow.ie or by calling 1890 50 10 50. The toll must be paid by 8pm on the following day.
Kill (An Chill)
Porterstown
Raheen
Two Rock Mountain
Shankill
Thornberry
Kilteel
Brittas
Kiltiernan
Cunard
Glendoo Mountain
Monaspick
Glencullen
Rathmore
Prince Williams Seat
Old Connaught
BRAY (BRÉ)
Heritage Centre
Eadestown
Hempstown
Enniskerry (Áth an Sceire)
National Sea Life Centre
Kilbride
Agriculture Heritage Display Cen.
Bray Head
Threecastles
Curtlestown
Powerscourt
Killruddery House & Gdns
Oldcourt
Kippure
Kilmacanogue
Little Sugar Loaf
Windgate
Tipperkevin
Wicklow Mountains National Park
Killough
Great Sugar Loaf
Redford
Blessington (Baile Coimin)
Sorrel Hill
Kippure Adventure Centre
Tonduff
Maulin
Templecarrig
Greystones (Na Clocha Liathe)
War Hill
Powerscourt Waterfall
Sally Gap
Djouce Mountain
Delgany
Lackan
Pollaphuca Reservoir
Gravale
Ballygannon
Glenroe Open Farm
Humphrystown
Lough Tay
Ballynockan
Valleymount
Mullaghcleevaun
Moanbane
Newtown Mount Kennedy
Kilcoole (Cill Chomhghaill)

A
B
C
1
2
3
4
M2
R135
R125
Dunreagh
1916 Rebellion Mon.
Cookstown
Rath Cross Roads
ASHBOURNE INDUSTRIAL PARK
RATH LODGE
RACE HILL LODGE
RACE HILL LANE
RACE HILL PK
RACE HILL MANOR
RACE HILL CRES
RACE HILL RD
RACE HILL CL.
THE ASHES
WEST. GRN
WEST. VW
ST. JOHNS WD. CT
BRINDLEY PK GDN.
BRI. PK SQ
BRI. PK CRES
ST. JOHNS WD. PK
ST. JOHNS WD.
ST. JOHNS WD. DR
TUDOR
TUDOR CRES
GROVE
TUDOR GRO
TUDOR HTS
Sch
HUNTERS LANE
HUNTSGROVE
BROOKVILLE
KILDERRY HA.
RISE
CLUAIN
Health Centre
Shopping Centre
KILLEGLAND PARK
KIL. CT
Lib
PO
FREDERICK STREET
CEM
Garda
Milltown
ASHDALE CRES
MAPLE GRO
MILLTOWN ESTATE
THE HAWTHORNS
PINE CT
Spo Grou
BALLYBIN ROAD
COOKSTOWN BRIDGE
Ballybin
ASHBOURNE
BROAD MEADOW CASTLE
BACHELORS WK
BRIDGE ST
CASTLE STREET
MEAD. BR. CT
CRESTWOOD ROAD
CRESTWOOD GREEN
CRESTWOOD AVE
CRESTWOOD PARK
CASTLE
THE GREEN
PARK
CASTLE WAY
CASTLE CRES
CASTLE CL.
DEERPARK
ALDERBROOK GLEN
DUBLIN ROAD
ALD. VALE
Killegland
BROAD MEADOW RIVER
BOURNE VIEW
WESTV
THE BAILEY
Sch
KILLEGLAND RD
KILL. RISE
BOURNE AVENUE
PARK HI
BOUR CT
LINDS. MWS
BROADMEADOW RD
GREEN GRO
TARA PL
TARA CL
ALDERBROOK RISE
ALDERBROOK DOWN
ALDERBROOK RD
ALD. PK
BROADMEADOW GREEN
CHERRY LANE
THE BRIARS
HICKEY'S LANE

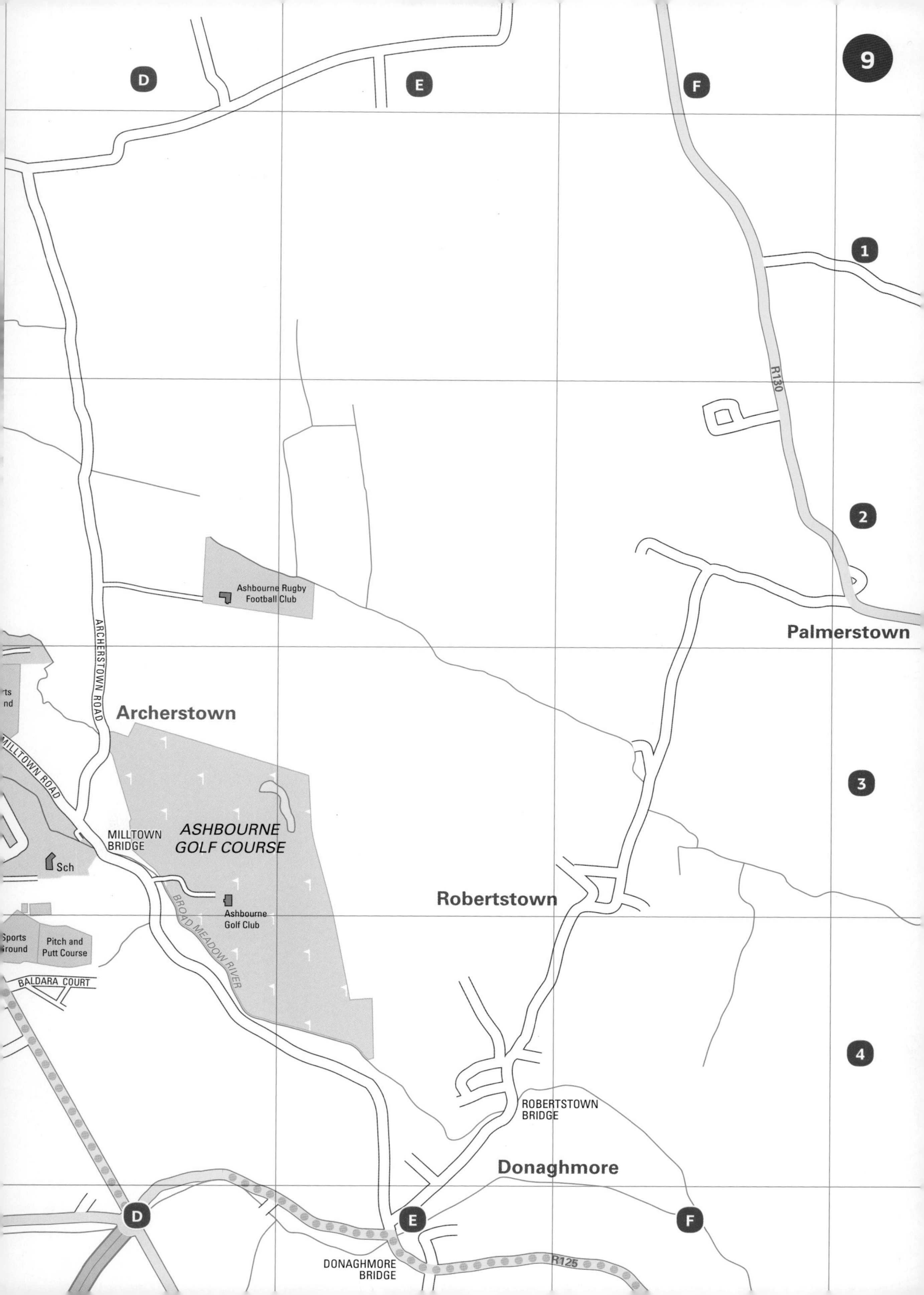
9
D
E
F
1
2
3
4
R130
Palmerstown
Ashbourne Rugby Football Club
ARCHERSTOWN ROAD
Archerstown
MILLTOWN ROAD
MILLTOWN BRIDGE
ASHBOURNE GOLF COURSE
Sch
Ashbourne Golf Club
BROAD MEADOW RIVER
Pitch and Putt Course
BALDARA COURT
Robertstown
ROBERTSTOWN BRIDGE
Donaghmore
DONAGHMORE BRIDGE
R125

10
A
B
C
Staffordstown Turvey
Turvey
TURVEY BRIDGE
TURVEY BUSINESS PARK
TURVEY BUSINESS CENTRE
Club House
TURVEY AV
M1
1
Belinstown
DISTRIBUTION CENTRE
2
Lissenhall Little
R132
Lanestown
M1
R126 HEARSE ROAD
Junction 4
3
SUNDAY WELL BRIDGE
Lissenhall Great
Ballymadrough
R132
4
ESTUARY BUSINESS PARK
LISSENHALL BRIDGE
Lissen Hall
HUTCHINSONS
ESTUARY ROAD
BALLYMADROUGH ROAD
Newport House
ROAD COVERED AT HIGH TIDE
Wastewater Treatment Plant
13
14
A
B
C
Seapoint
STRAND
ROAD COVERED AT HIGH TIDE
GARTAN DRIVE
GARTAN CT
SEATOWN
THE GREEN
THE CT
NEWCOURT
NEW MEWS

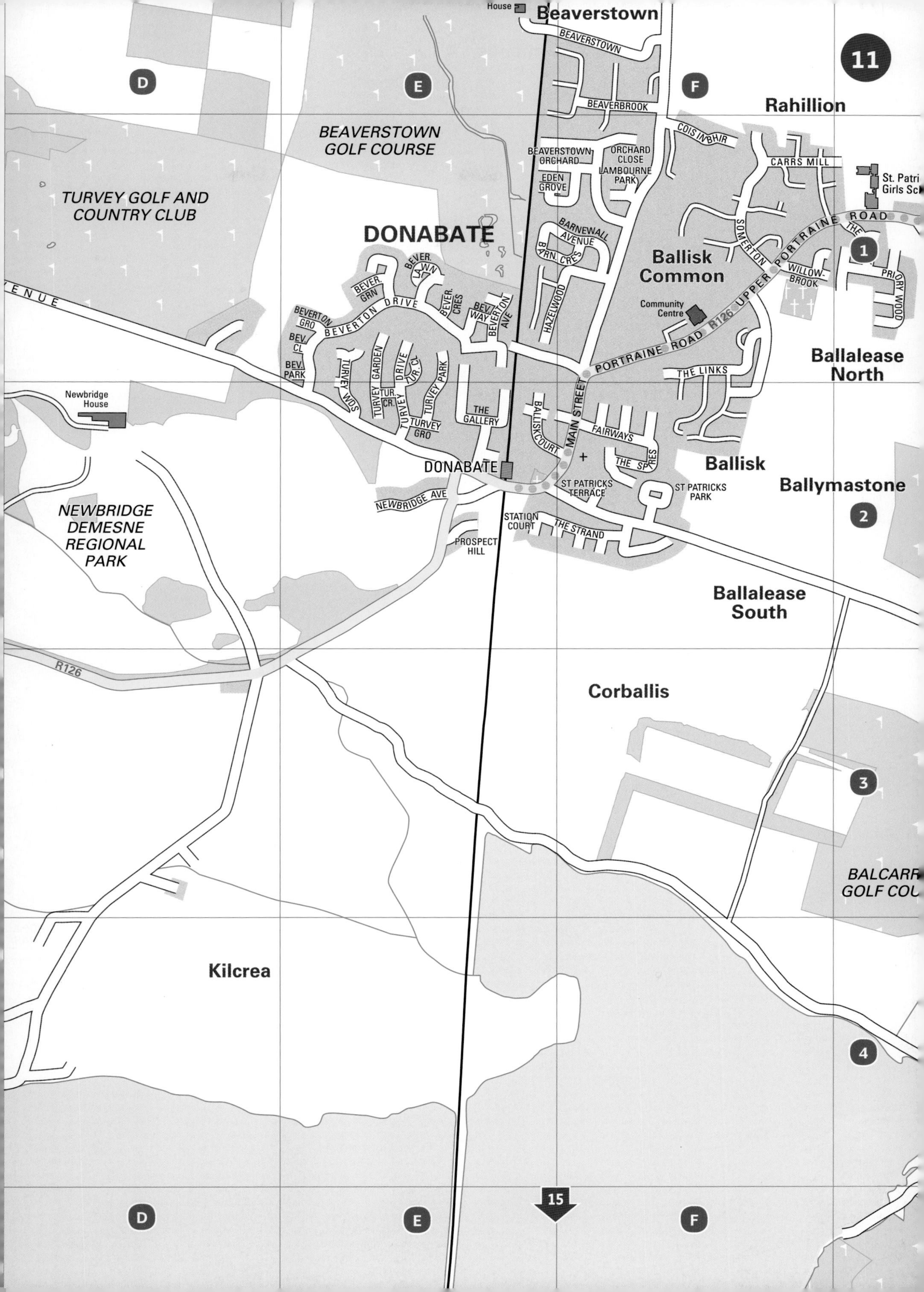
11
Beaverstown
House
BEAVERSTOWN
BEAVERBROOK
COIS INBHIR
Rahillion
CARRS MILL
St. Patri
Girls Sc
BEAVERSTOWN GOLF COURSE
BEAVERSTOWN ORCHARD
ORCHARD CLOSE
LAMBOURNE PARK
EDEN GROVE
TURVEY GOLF AND COUNTRY CLUB
DONABATE
BARNEWALL AVENUE
BARN. CRES
HAZELWOOD
Ballisk Common
SOMERTON
UPPER PORTRAINE ROAD
R126
PORTRAINE ROAD
THE
WILLOW-BROOK
PRIORY WOOD
Community Centre
BEVER. LAWN
BEVER. GRN
BEVERTON DRIVE
BEVER. CRES
BEV. WAY
BEVERTON AVE
BEVERTON GRO
BEV. CL
BEV. PARK
TURVEY WDS
TURVEY GARDEN
TUR. CR.
TURVEY DRIVE
TUR. CL
TURVEY PARK
TURVEY GRO
THE GALLERY
MAIN STREET
BALLISK COURT
FAIRWAYS
THE SPIRES
THE LINKS
Ballalease North
Newbridge House
DONABATE
Ballisk
Ballymastone
ST PATRICKS TERRACE
ST PATRICKS PARK
NEWBRIDGE AVE
STATION COURT
THE STRAND
PROSPECT HILL
NEWBRIDGE DEMESNE REGIONAL PARK
Ballalease South
R126
Corballis
BALCARR
GOLF COU
Kilcrea
D
E
F
1
2
3
4
15

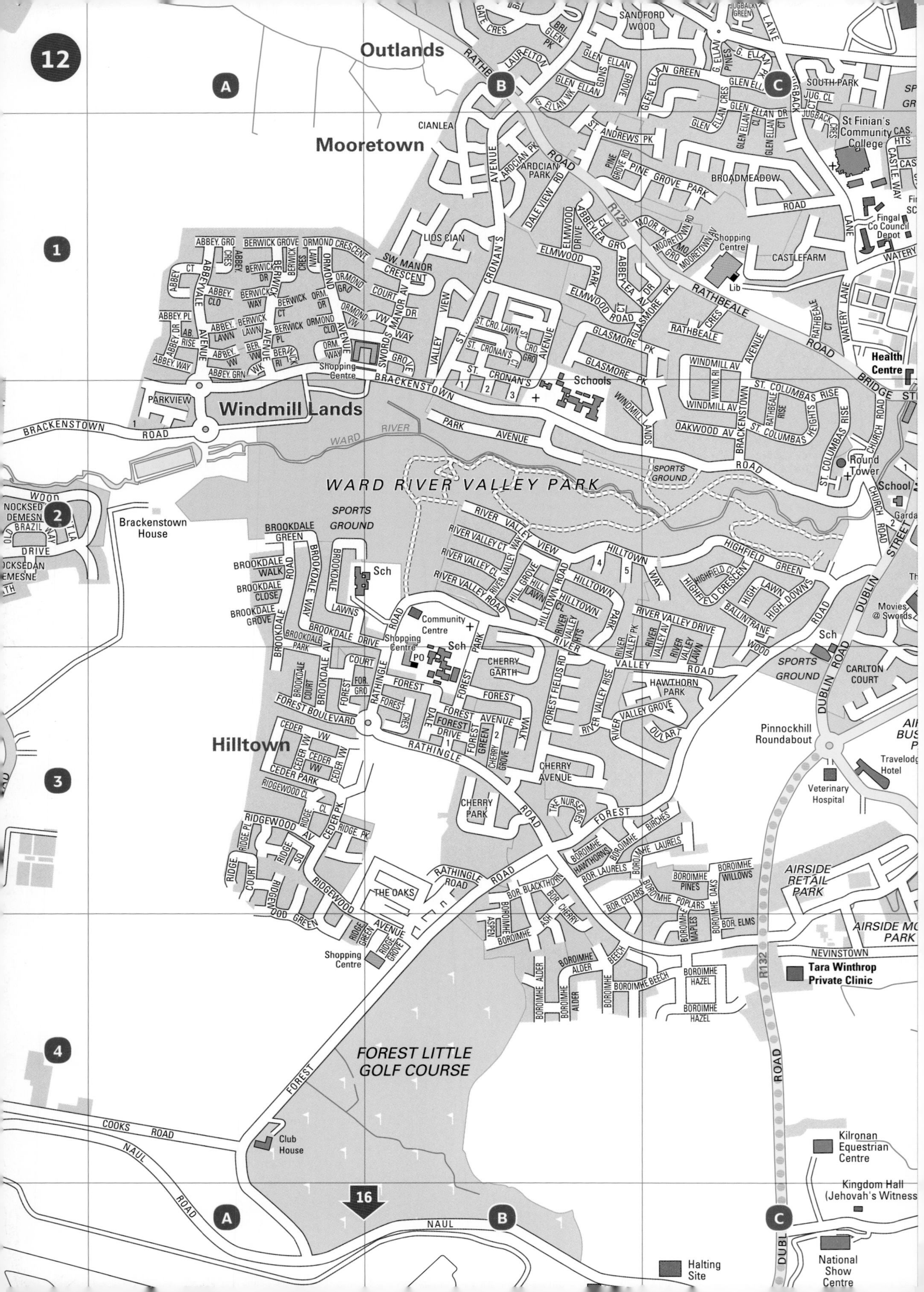
Outlands
Mooretown
Windmill Lands
WARD RIVER VALLEY PARK
Hilltown
Brackenstown House
SPORTS GROUND
Shopping Centre
Schools
Community Centre
St Finian's Community College
Fingal Co Council Depot
Health Centre
Round Tower
Movies @ Swords
Pinnockhill Roundabout
Veterinary Hospital
Travelodge Hotel
AIRSIDE RETAIL PARK
Tara Winthrop Private Clinic
FOREST LITTLE GOLF COURSE
Club House
Kilronan Equestrian Centre
Kingdom Hall (Jehovah's Witness
National Show Centre
Halting Site
16

10
17
18
14
D
E
F
1
2
3
4
Seapoint
Newport House
Lissen Hall
LISSENHALL BRIDGE
HUTCHINSONS
ESTUARY
ESTUARY BUSINESS PARK
LAWLESS MEMORIAL PARK
FB
Estuary Roundabout
Wastewater Treatment Plant
STRAND
ROAD COVERED AT HIGH TIDE
ROAD COVE
Prospect Point
ESTUARY ROAD
Seatown House
BALHEARY ROAD
NORTH STREET BUSINESS PARK
Fire Station
SEATOWN
SEATOWN ROAD
NEWCOURT
NEW MEWS
THE GREEN PK
THE CT
THE CRESCENT
THE AVENUE
THE DRIVE
AVE
PARK
LISSEN HALL DR
GARTAN DRIVE
GARTAN
GARTAN CT
ESTUARY CT
R132
SEATOWN VILLAS
MANTUA PARK
Fingal Community College
Lib
NORTH STREET
Swords Castle
Court House
Seatown Roundabout
SEATOWN TERRACE
SWORDS BUSINESS PARK
TIONSCAIL INDUSTRIAL ESTATE
M1
Castle Shopping Centre
Council Offices
ST. COLUMCILLS PARK
Schs
SEATOWN WALK
CHAPEL LANE
OAKLANDS PK
OAKLANDS AVENUE
CASTLE DR
CASTLE AVENUE
CASTLE PK
MAIN ST
PO
The Plaza Shopping Centre
LONGLANDS
ASHLEY AV
CAS. GRO
The Pavilions Shopping Centre
R106
Malahide Roundabout
MALAHIDE ROAD
SEAMOUNT VIEW
FOXWOOD
CLIFFORDS LANE
MONT. VW
MILESIAN GRO
ST. WERBURGHS
MILESIAN LAWN
MILESIAN AV
MILESIAN CT
DRYNAM ROAD
DRYNAM CT
SWORDS
R132
LAKESHORE DRIVE
LAKEVIEW DR
WATER. DR
WATER. AV
WATER. WK
WATER. CRES
WATERSIDE DRIVE
WATERSIDE LWN
WATERSIDE CLO
WATERSIDE GRN
WATERSIDE CT
WATERSIDE PARK
WATERSIDE
SPORTS GROUND
SEABURY GARDENS
SEABURY WOOD
SEABURY MEADOWS
SEABURY HEIGHTS
SEABURY PARK
SEABURY DALE
SEABURY ORCHARD
SEABURY AV
SEABURY ROAD
SEABURY VIEW
CASTLE LNS
LISSADEL CRES
LISSADEL GROVE
LISSADEL PARK
LISSADEL WOOD
SEABURY LA
ESTUARY WALK
THE WARREN
SWORDS ROAD
GAINS. CRES
GAINSBOROUGH
GAINS. GREEN
GAINS. LAWN
GAINS. DOWNS
GAINS. CT
GAINSBOROUGH PARK
TALBOT RD
FELTRIM INDUSTRIAL PARK
FELTRIM HALL
School
Shopping Centre
ASPEN DR
ASPEN PK
ASPEN
KINSEALY COURT
BIRCHDALE RD
BIRCHDALE CLOSE
BIRCHDALE DRIVE
BIRCHDALE PK
ASHDALE CLOSE
ASHDALE RD
THE CLOSE
THE LAWN
THE RISE
THE GREEN
MELROSE PARK
MOUNT D.
MOUNT D. WK
MOUNT DRINAN PK
MOUNT DRINAN AV
KINSEALY DOWNS
THE DRIVE
THE VILLA
THE AVENUE
THE PARK
HOLYWELL SQUARE
HOLYWELL VIEW
HOLY AVE
GARDENS
HOL VW GRO
HOLYWELL
HOLY. WOOD
HEATH RD
HOL WK
HOLYWELL PK
HOLYWELL WAY
HOLY. RISE
HOLY. ROW
CRES
R125
THE GROVE
THE HEIGHTS
THE WK
THE CRES
MOUNT
DRYNAM DRIVE
DRYNAM CRESCENT
DRYNAM GRO
DRYNAM SQUARE
DRYNAM RISE
DRYNAM PL
Junction 3
KETTLES LANE
FELTRIM
REAMSTOWN
LANE

A
B
C
10
Lissenhall Great
Ballymadrough
Kilcrea
1
BALLYMADROUGH ROAD
Newport House
10
Seapoint
STRAND
ROAD COVERED AT HIGH TIDE
ROAD COVERED AT HIGH TIDE
Prospect Point
2
ESTUARY ROAD
Seatown House
SPORTS GROUND
Swords Sailing & Boating Club
Malahide Yacht Club
3
SEABURY GARDENS
SEABURY WOOD
SEABURY MEADOWS
SEABURY HEIGHTS
SEABURY PARK
SEABURY GLEN
SEABURY VALE
SEABURY ORCHARD
SEABURY AV
SEABURY ROAD
SEABURY VIEW
CASTLE LNS
LISSADEL CRES
LISSADEL WOOD
LISS. GROVE
LISSADEL PARK
SEABURY PARADE
SEABURY GREEN
SEABURY CRESCENT
SEABURY DR
OLD YELLOW WALLS ROAD
CASTLE COVE
C. DOWN GROVE
CASTLE DOWN RD
SEABURY CLOSE
SEABURY WALK
SEABURY DOWNS
SEABURY PLACE
SEABURY LANE
ESTUARY ROAD
ESTUARY WALK
THE WARREN
KILLEEN
KILLEEN AV
KILLEEN CRES
KILLEEN PK
MILFORD
Cross
Band Room
School
STRAND ROAD
SEA ROAD
INBHIR IDE
INBHIR IDE CLOSE
INBHIR IDE DRIVE
SONESTA
LANE
BISSE
THE HAVE
CHALF
CHALFONT P
CHALFONT PK
CHALFONT ROAD
TEXAS LANE
YELLOW WALLS ROAD
MILLVIEW CT
MILLVIEW LAWNS
MILLVIEW ROAD
MILLVIEW
Yellow Walls
ARD NA MARA
MCCREADIES LANE
Burial Ground
School
DUBLIN ROAD
LAHIDE ROAD
13
WATER. DR
WATER. AV
WATER. WK
WATER. CRES
WATERSIDE
WATERSIDE CT
WATERSIDE PARK
SWORDS ROAD
R106
4
GAINS. CRESCENT
GAINS. GREEN
GAINSBOROUGH
GAINS. LAWN
GAINS. DOWNS
GAINS. CT
GAINS. PARK
GAINSBOROUGH AVE
TALBOT RD
TALBOT PK
TALBOT AV
CASTLE HEATH
GAYBROOK LAWNS
LAWSON SPINNEY
CASTLEVIEW PARK
PAR 3 GOLF COURSE (9 HOLE)
Sports Pavilion
PITCH & PUTT
TALBOT BOTANIC GARDENS
Yourell's Well
GRAVE YARD
Malahide Castle
School
Shopping Centre
ASPEN
ASPEN DR
ASPEN PK
ASPEN ROAD
KINSEALY COURT
BIRCHDALE RD
BIRCHDALE DRIVE
BIRCHDALE CLOSE
BIRCHDALE PK
ASHDALE RD
ASHDALE CLOSE
MOUNT DRINAN AV
MOUNT DRINAN PK
KINSEALY DOWNS
DRIVE
A
18
ABINGTON
B
AUBURN GROVE
Auburn
ROAD
C
Malahide Demesne

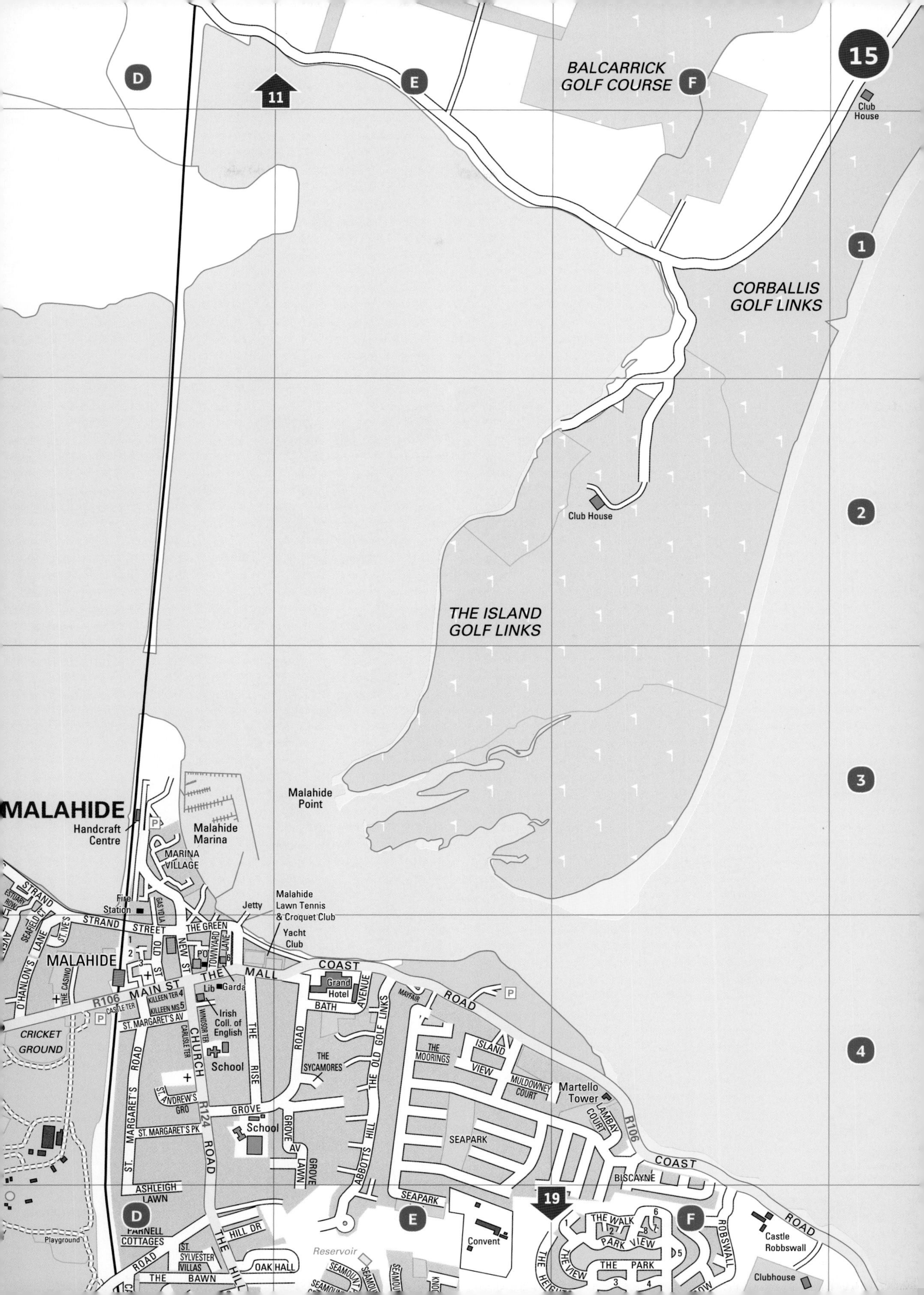
D
E
F
11
BALCARRICK
GOLF COURSE
Club
House
1
CORBALLIS
GOLF LINKS
2
Club House
THE ISLAND
GOLF LINKS
3
Malahide
Point
MALAHIDE
Handcraft
Centre
Malahide
Marina
MARINA
VILLAGE
Fire
Station
Jetty
Malahide
Lawn Tennis
& Croquet Club
Yacht
Club
STRAND
ESTUARY
ROW
SEAFIELD CT
LANE
ST. IVE'S
STRAND
STREET
GAS YD LA
OLD
ST
NEW
ST
THE GREEN
TOWNYARD
LANE
PO
THE
MALL
COAST
MALAHIDE
O'HANLON'S
THE CASINO
MAIN ST
R106
CASTLE TER
KILLEEN TER
KILLEEN MS
Lib
Garda
Irish
Coll. of
English
ST. MARGARET'S AV
WINDSOR TER
CARLISLE TER
CHURCH
Grand
Hotel
BATH
AVENUE
MAYFAIR
ROAD
4
CRICKET
GROUND
THE
RISE
ROAD
THE
SYCAMORES
THE OLD GOLF LINKS
THE
MOORINGS
ISLAND
VIEW
MULDOWNEY
COURT
Martello
Tower
LAMBAY
COURT
R106
School
ST. ANDREW'S
GRO
R124
GROVE
School
GROVE
AV
LAWN
GROVE
ST. MARGARET'S PK
ROAD
ST. MARGARET'S
ROAD
ABBOTTS
HILL
SEAPARK
COAST
BISCAYNE
ASHLEIGH
LAWN
SEAPARK
19
THE WALK
PARK VIEW
Convent
ROBSWALL
Castle
Robbswall
ROAD
PARNELL
COTTAGES
Playground
HILL DR
ST.
SYLVESTER
VILLAS
THE
HILL
ROAD
THE
BAWN
OAK HALL
Reservoir
SEAMOUNT
THE VIEW
THE
PARK
Clubhouse

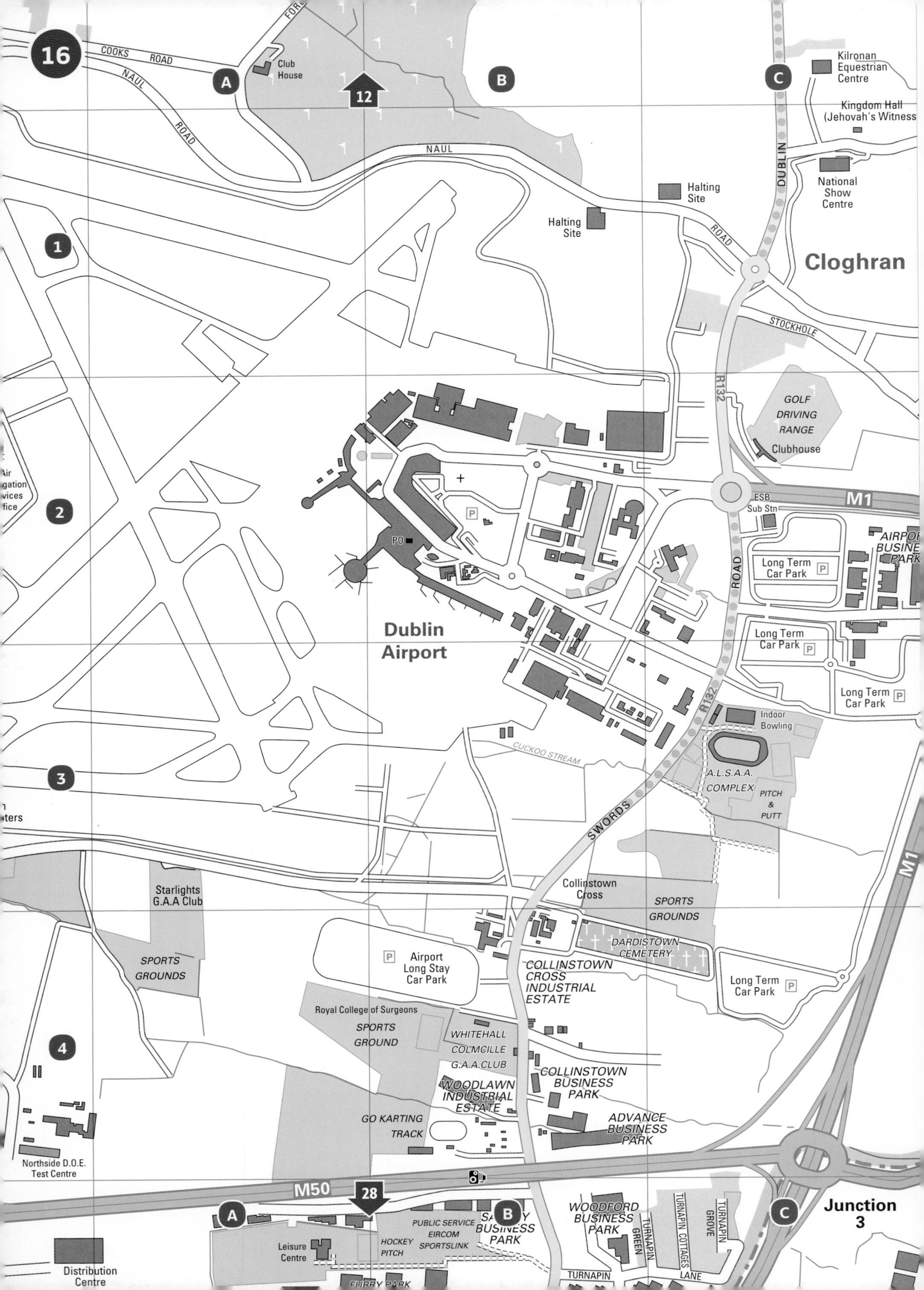
COOKS ROAD
NAUL ROAD
Club House
12
Kilronan Equestrian Centre
Kingdom Hall (Jehovah's Witness)
NAUL
DUBLIN
National Show Centre
Halting Site
Halting Site
ROAD
Cloghran
STOCKHOLE
R132
GOLF DRIVING RANGE
Clubhouse
M1
ESB Sub Stn
PO
AIRPORT BUSINESS PARK
Long Term Car Park
ROAD
Long Term Car Park
Dublin Airport
Long Term Car Park
R132
Indoor Bowling
CUCKOO STREAM
A.L.S.A.A. COMPLEX
PITCH & PUTT
SWORDS
M1
Starlights G.A.A Club
Collinstown Cross
SPORTS GROUNDS
DARDISTOWN CEMETERY
SPORTS GROUNDS
Airport Long Stay Car Park
COLLINSTOWN CROSS INDUSTRIAL ESTATE
Long Term Car Park
Royal College of Surgeons SPORTS GROUND
WHITEHALL COLMCILLE G.A.A.CLUB
COLLINSTOWN BUSINESS PARK
WOODLAWN INDUSTRIAL ESTATE
GO KARTING TRACK
ADVANCE BUSINESS PARK
Northside D.O.E. Test Centre
M50
28
WOODFORD BUSINESS PARK
TURNAPIN GREEN
TURNAPIN COTTAGES
TURNAPIN GROVE
Junction 3
PUBLIC SERVICE EIRCOM SPORTSLINK
BUSINESS PARK
Leisure Centre
HOCKEY PITCH
Distribution Centre
TURNAPIN
LANE
FURRY PARK

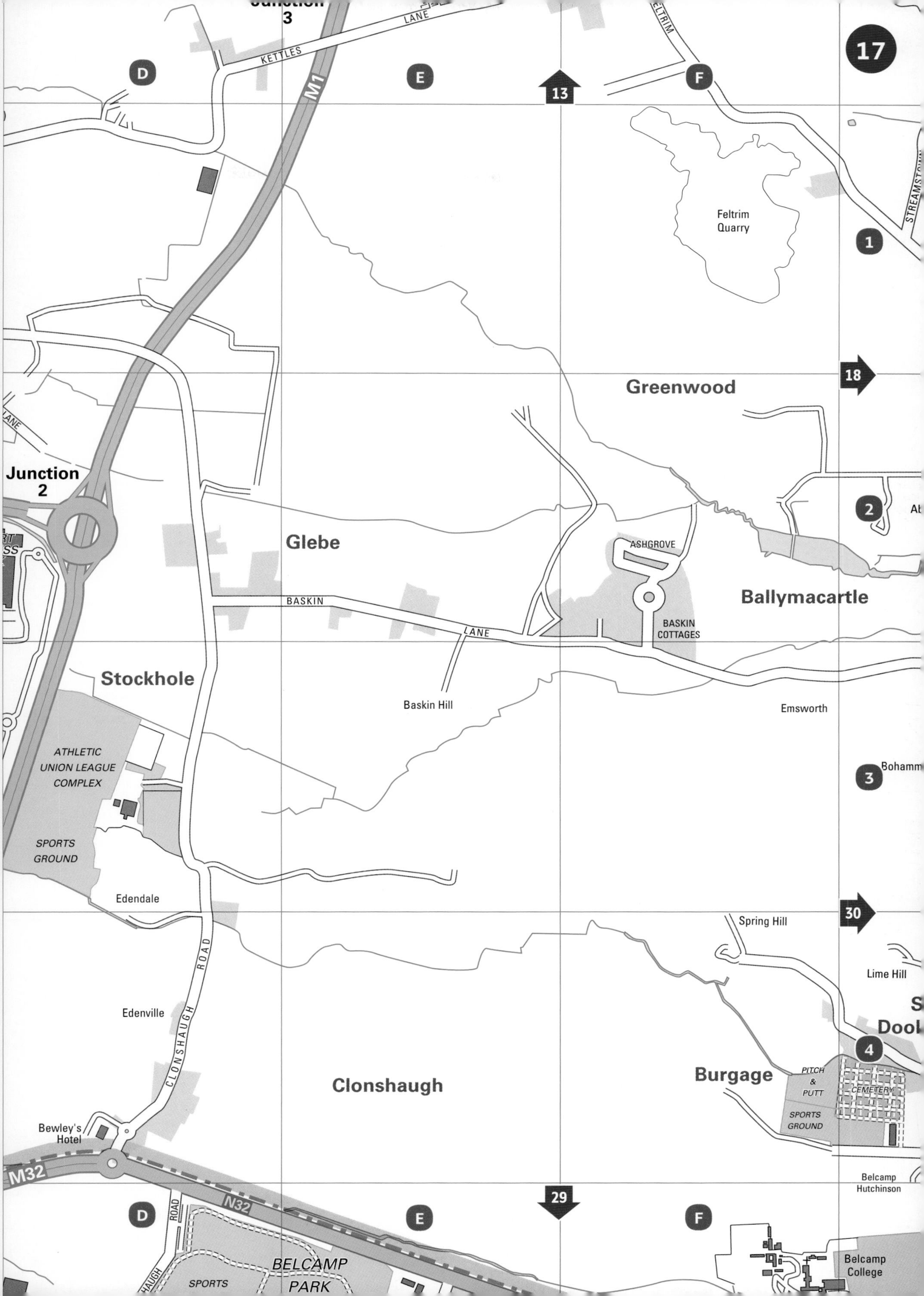
Junction
3
KETTLES
LANE
M1
D
E
F
13
FELTRIM
STREAMSTOWN
Feltrim
Quarry
1
18
Greenwood
LANE
Junction
2
2
Glebe
ASHGROVE
Ballymacartle
BASKIN
LANE
BASKIN
COTTAGES
Stockhole
Baskin Hill
Emsworth
ATHLETIC
UNION LEAGUE
COMPLEX
3
Bohamm
SPORTS
GROUND
Edendale
30
Spring Hill
Lime Hill
CLONSHAUGH
ROAD
Edenville
Dool
4
Clonshaugh
Burgage
PITCH
&
PUTT
CEMETERY
SPORTS
GROUND
Bewley's
Hotel
M32
N32
Belcamp
Hutchinson
29
D
E
F
ROAD
BELCAMP
PARK
SPORTS
Belcamp
College

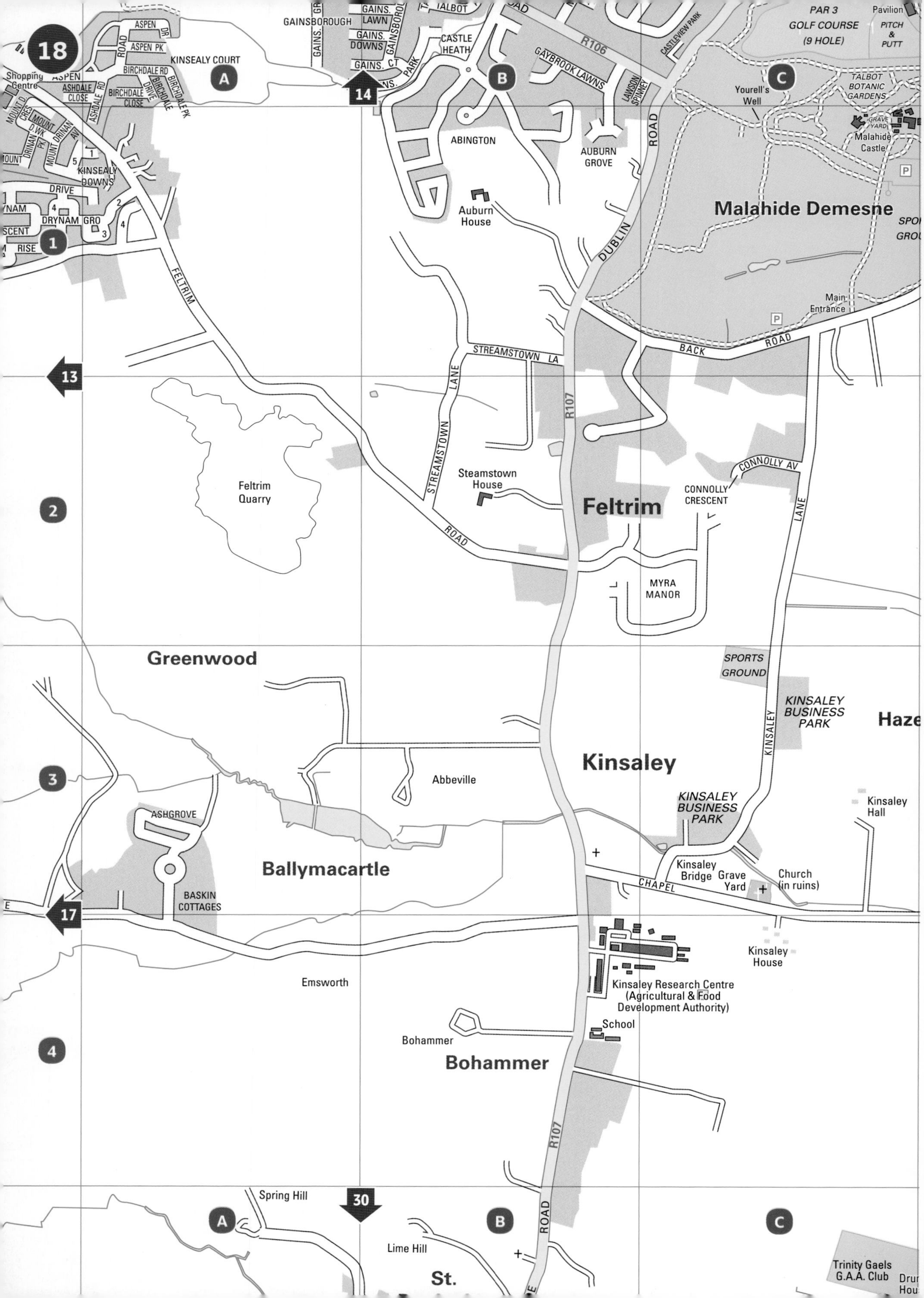
18
Feltrim
Kinsaley
Malahide Demesne
Greenwood
Ballymacartle
Bohammer
ABINGTON
AUBURN GROVE
Auburn House
Steamstown House
Feltrim Quarry
CONNOLLY CRESCENT
MYRA MANOR
SPORTS GROUND
KINSALEY BUSINESS PARK
Kinsaley Hall
Kinsaley Bridge
Grave Yard
Church (in ruins)
Kinsaley House
Kinsaley Research Centre (Agricultural & Food Development Authority)
School
Abbeville
ASHGROVE
BASKIN COTTAGES
Emsworth
Spring Hill
Lime Hill
Trinity Gaels G.A.A. Club
PAR 3 GOLF COURSE (9 HOLE)
PITCH & PUTT
Pavilion
TALBOT BOTANIC GARDENS
Yourell's Well
Malahide Castle
Main Entrance
KINSEALY COURT
KINSEALY DOWNS
GAINSBOROUGH
CASTLE HEATH
GAYBROOK LAWNS
LAWSON SPINNEY
CASTLEVIEW PARK
FELTRIM ROAD
STREAMSTOWN LANE
STREAMSTOWN LA
DUBLIN ROAD
BACK ROAD
CONNOLLY AV
KINSALEY LANE
CHAPEL
R106
R107
13
14
17
30

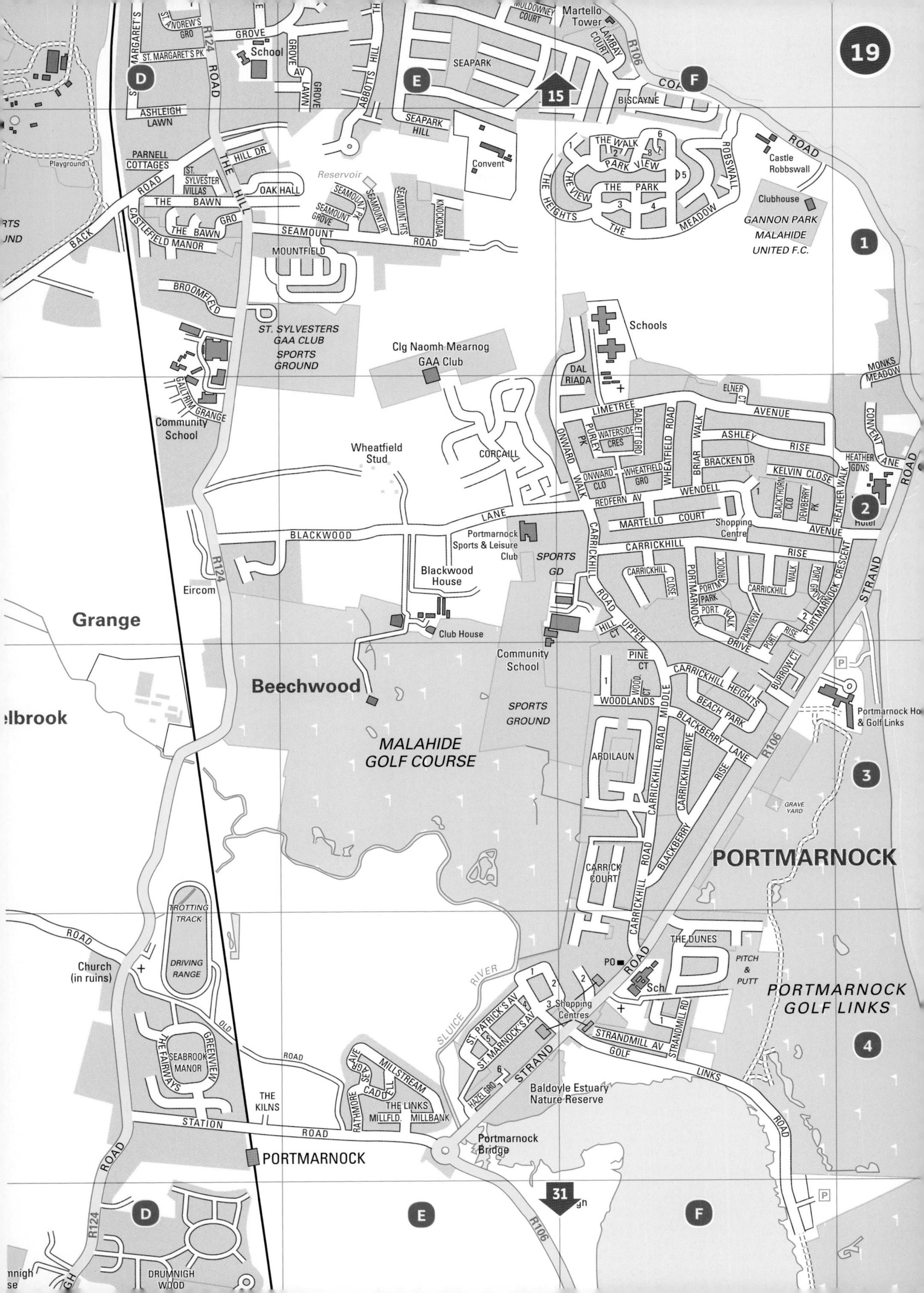

Martello Tower
MULDOWNEY COURT
LAMBAY COURT
SEAPARK
SEAPARK HILL
15
BISCAYNE
COAST ROAD
R106
ST. ANDREW'S GRO
ST. MARGARET'S
ST. MARGARET'S PK
GROVE
School
R124 ROAD
ASHLEIGH LAWN
GROVE AV
GROVE LAWN
ABBOTTS HILL
Convent
Reservoir
PARNELL COTTAGES
Playground
HILL DR
THE HILL
ST. SYLVESTER VILLAS
OAK HALL
BACK ROAD
THE BAWN
THE BAWN GRO
CASTLEFIELD MANOR
SEAMOUNT GROVE
SEAMOUNT PK
SEAMOUNT DR
SEAMOUNT HTS
KNOCKDARA
SEAMOUNT ROAD
MOUNTFIELD
THE WALK
PARK VIEW
THE VIEW
THE PARK
THE HEIGHTS
THE MEADOW
ROBSWALL
Castle Robbswall
Clubhouse
GANNON PARK MALAHIDE UNITED F.C.
BROOMFIELD
ST. SYLVESTERS GAA CLUB SPORTS GROUND
Clg Naomh Mearnog GAA Club
Schools
DAL RIADA
MONKS MEADOW
GAILTRIM GRANGE
Community School
ELNER CT
LIMETREE AVENUE
PURLEY PK
WATERSIDE CRES
RADLETT GRO
WHEATFIELD ROAD
BRIAR WALK
ASHLEY RISE
BRACKEN DR
CONVENT LANE
HEATHER GDNS
KELVIN CLOSE
ONWARD WALK
ONWARD CLO
WHEATFIELD GRO
WENDELL AVENUE
BLACKTHORN CLO
DEWBERRY PK
HEATHER WALK
Hotel
CORCAILL
Wheatfield Stud
REDFERN AV
MARTELLO COURT
Shopping Centre
BLACKWOOD LANE
Portmarnock Sports & Leisure Club
SPORTS GD
CARRICKHILL RISE
CARRICKHILL CLOSE
PORTMARNOCK PARK
PORTMARNOCK CRESCENT
PORT GROVE
CARRICKHILL WALK
PORTMARNOCK DRIVE
PORT. WALK
PARKVIEW
PORT. RISE
Blackwood House
Eircom
Grange
Club House
HILL CT
UPPER
CARRICKHILL ROAD
STRAND ROAD
Community School
PINE CT
WOOD. CT
BURROW CT
CARRICKHILL HEIGHTS
BEACH PARK
Portmarnock House & Golf Links
Beechwood
elbrook
WOODLANDS
SPORTS GROUND
MIDDLE
BLACKBERRY LANE
CARRICKHILL DRIVE
RISE
MALAHIDE GOLF COURSE
ARDILAUN
GRAVE YARD
PORTMARNOCK
CARRICK COURT
BLACKBERRY
TROTTING TRACK
DRIVING RANGE
ROAD
Church (in ruins)
THE DUNES
PO
PITCH & PUTT
Sch
SLUICE RIVER
ST. PATRICK'S AV
ST. MARNOCK'S AV
Shopping Centres
PORTMARNOCK GOLF LINKS
OLD
GREENVIEW
SEABROOK MANOR
THE FAIRWAYS
STRANDMILL AV
STRANDMILL RD
GOLF LINKS ROAD
STRAND
HAZEL GRO
RATHMORE
SEAGRAVE
CADDELL
MILLSTREAM
THE LINKS
MILLFLD.
MILLBANK
Baldoyle Estuary Nature Reserve
THE KILNS
STATION ROAD
PORTMARNOCK
Portmarnock Bridge
31
R106
R124
DRUMNIGH WOOD
D
E
F
1
2
3
4

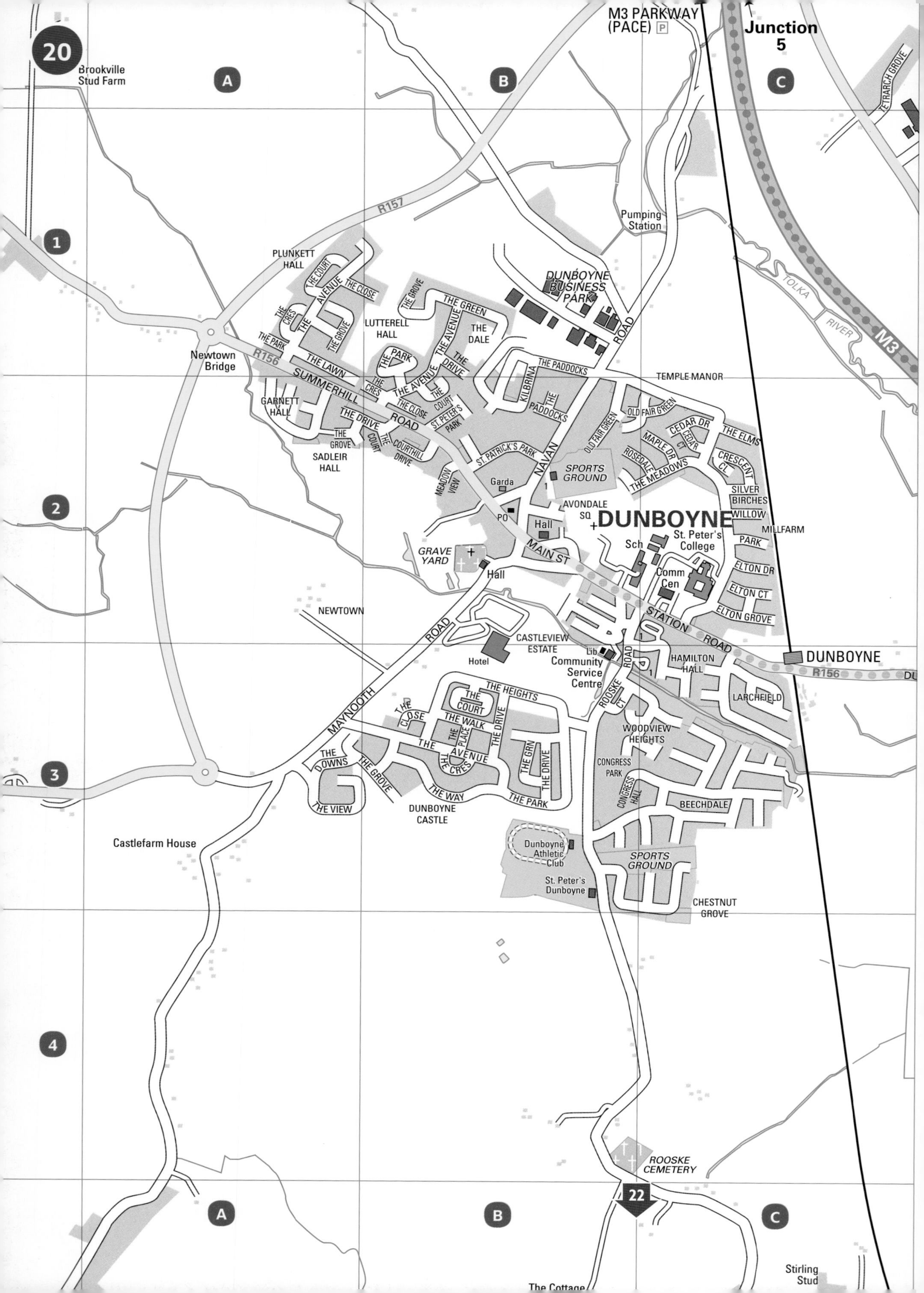
Brookville Stud Farm
A
B
C
M3 PARKWAY (PACE) P
Junction 5
TETRARCH GROVE
R157
1
2
3
4
Pumping Station
TOLKA RIVER
M3
PLUNKETT HALL
THE COURT
THE AVENUE
THE CLOSE
THE CRES
THE GROVE
THE PARK
THE LAWN
LUTTERELL HALL
THE GROVE
THE GREEN
THE DALE
THE AVENUE
THE PARK
THE DRIVE
THE CRES
THE AVENUE
THE COURT
THE CLOSE
ST. PETER'S PARK
DUNBOYNE BUSINESS PARK
ROAD
NAVAN
THE PADDOCKS
KILBRINA
THE PADDOCKS
TEMPLE MANOR
Newtown Bridge
R156
SUMMERHILL ROAD
GARNETT HALL
THE DRIVE
THE GROVE
COURT
THE COURTHILL DRIVE
SADLEIR HALL
ST. PATRICK'S PARK
MEADOW VIEW
Garda
OLD FAIR GREEN
SPORTS GROUND
CEDAR DR
CEDAR CT
THE ELMS
MAPLE DR
ROSEDALE
THE MEADOWS
CRESCENT CL
SILVER BIRCHES
WILLOW PARK
MILLFARM
AVONDALE SQ
DUNBOYNE
PO
Hall
Sch
St. Peter's College
MAIN ST
GRAVE YARD
Hall
Comm Cen
ELTON DR
ELTON CT
ELTON GROVE
NEWTOWN
STATION ROAD
ROAD
CASTLEVIEW ESTATE
Hotel
Lib
Community Service Centre
ROAD
ROOSKE CT
HAMILTON HALL
DUNBOYNE
R156
LARCHFIELD
MAYNOOTH ROAD
THE HEIGHTS
THE COURT
THE CLOSE
THE WALK
THE PLACE
THE DRIVE
THE AVENUE
THE CRES
THE GRN
THE DRIVE
THE DOWNS
THE GROVE
THE WAY
THE PARK
THE VIEW
DUNBOYNE CASTLE
WOODVIEW HEIGHTS
CONGRESS PARK
CONGRESS HALL
BEECHDALE
Castlefarm House
Dunboyne Athletic Club
SPORTS GROUND
St. Peter's Dunboyne
CHESTNUT GROVE
ROOSKE CEMETERY
22
Stirling Stud
The Cottage

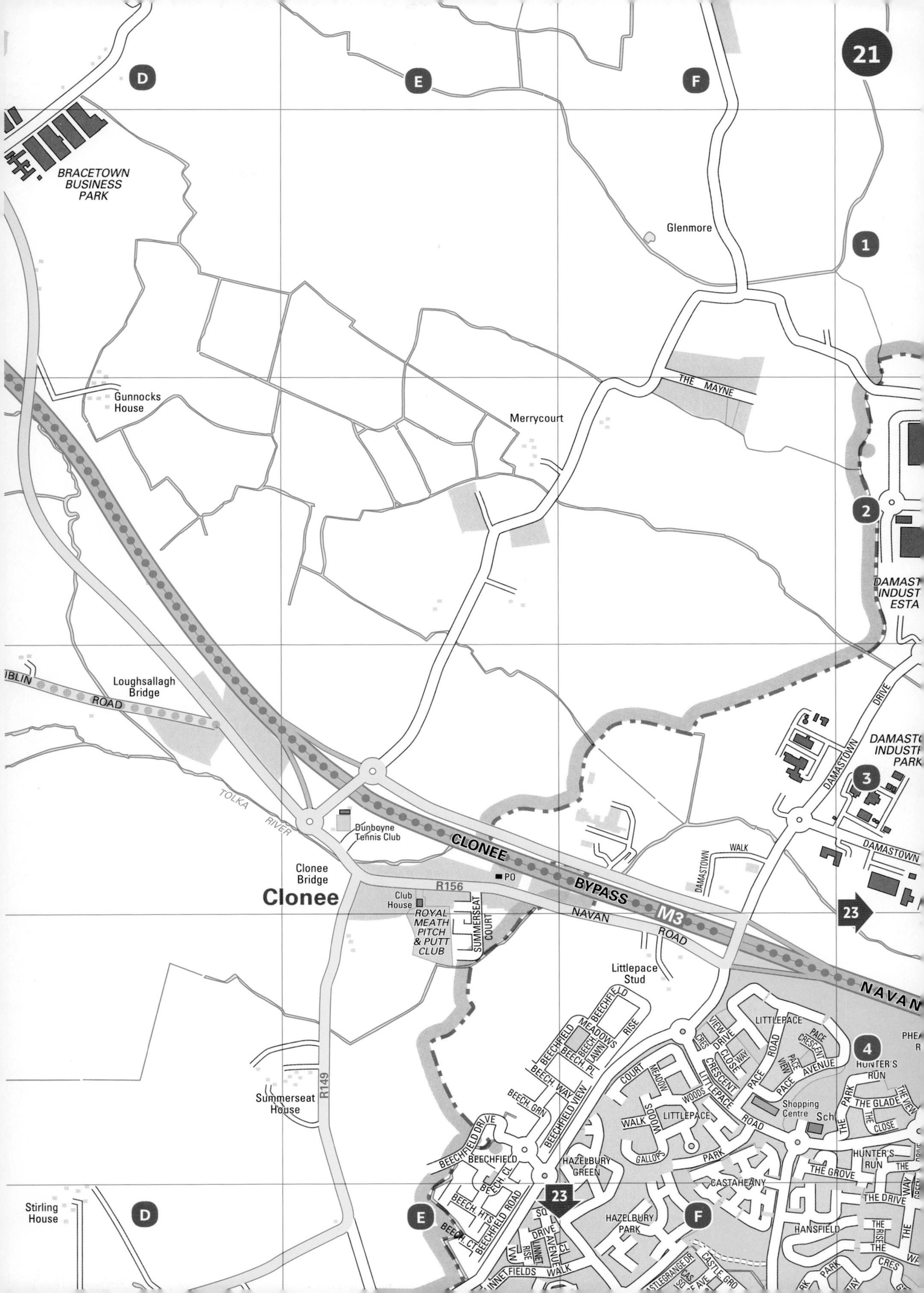
D
E
F
BRACETOWN BUSINESS PARK
Glenmore
1
THE MAYNE
Gunnocks House
Merrycourt
2
DAMAST INDUST ESTA
Loughsallagh Bridge
BLIN ROAD
DAMASTOWN DRIVE
DAMAST INDUST PARK
3
TOLKA RIVER
Dunboyne Tennis Club
CLONEE BYPASS M3
PO
Clonee Bridge
Clonee
R156
Club House
ROYAL MEATH PITCH & PUTT CLUB
SUMMERSEAT COURT
NAVAN ROAD
DAMASTOWN WALK
DAMASTOWN
23
Littlepace Stud
NAVAN
BEECHFIELD MEADOWS
BEECHFIELD RISE
BEECH. LAWN
BEECH. PL
BEECH. WAY
BEECH. GRN
BEECHFIELD VIEW
BEECHFIELD DRIVE
BEECHFIELD
BEECH. CL
BEECH. HTS
BEECHFIELD ROAD
BEECH. CT
LITTLEPACE
VIEW
DRIVE
CRES
CLOSE
WAY
PACE ROAD
PACE CRESCENT
PACE VIEW
PACE AVENUE
COURT
MEADOW
WOODS
CRESCENT
LITTLEPACE ROAD
WALK
GALLOPS
PARK
Shopping Centre
Sch
4
HUNTER'S RUN
PHEA
THE PARK
THE GLADE
THE VIEW
THE CLOSE
THE GROVE
THE DRIVE
THE WAY
HANSFIELD
THE RISE
HAZELBURY GREEN
CASTAHEANY
HAZELBURY PARK
Summerseat House
R149
Stirling House
23
SQ
DRIVE
AVENUE
LINNET RISE
CL
LINNET FIELDS WALK
CASTLEGRANGE DR
CASTLE GRO
CRES

22
DUNBOYNE CASTLE
Dunboyne Athletic Club
SPORTS GROUND
St. Peter's Dunboyne
20
CHESTNUT GROVE
A
B
C
1
2
3
4
ROOSKE CEMETERY
Stirling House
Stirling Stud
The Cottage
Athdara
Hilltown House
R149
Barnhill
Westmanstown Park
40
CONFEY PARK

Dunboyne Tennis Club
Clonee Bridge
Clonee
D
R156
PO
Club House
ROYAL MEATH PITCH & PUTT CLUB
SUMMERSEAT COURT
CLONEE BYPASS
M3
NAVAN ROAD
E
21
DAMASTOWN
DAMASTOWN GRN
F
ROAD
WESTPOINT BUSINESS PARK
R149
Littlepace Stud
BEECHFIELD MEADOWS
BEECHFIELD RISE
BEECH. WAY
BEECHFIELD VIEW
BEECH. GRN
BEECHFIELD DRIVE
BEECHFIELD
BEECH. HTS
BEECHFIELD ROAD
BEECH. CT
LITTLEPACE
PACE ROAD
PACE CRESCENT
PACE AVENUE
LITTLEPACE CRESCENT
LITTLEPACE ROAD
LITTLEPACE
GALLOPS
WALK
WOODS
MEADOW
Shopping Centre
Sch
PHEASANT RUN
HUNTER'S RUN
THE GLADE
THE CLOSE
SWALLOWBROOK
1
BRAMBLEFIELD
ARCHERS WOOD
THORNBURY APTS
School
Community Centre
HAZELBURY GREEN
HAZELBURY PARK
CASTAHEANY
HUNTER'S RUN
THE GROVE
THE DRIVE
DEERHAVEN
HUNTSTOWN WOOD
HUNTSTOWN GREEN
HUNTSTOWN DRIVE
HUNTSTOWN COURT
HUNTSTOWN AVENUE
HANSFIELD
WESTHAVEN
CARNE
FERNDALE
GLENEALY DOWNS
LINNETFIELDS
LINNET FIELDS WALK
ROSEDALE
CASTLEGRANGE
CASTLE GRO
MANORFIELDS
MANOR CRES
RUSHEENEY
CASTLEWOOD
HUNTSTOWN
2
PINEBROOK GLEN
PINEBROOK HEIGHTS
BLACKWOOD
BLACKWOOD LAWN
HANSFIELD
LILLYS WAY
THE CRES
NORTH ST
THE AVENUE
LATCHFORD GREEN
LATCHFORD CL
LATCHFORD PK
BEECHWOOD DOWNS
MEADOW COPSE
MEADOW DRIVE
MEADOW WAY
Sch
BLAKESFIELD
24
HARTSTOWN PARK
ONGAR VILLAGE
BARRY LANE
RAVENSWOOD
CHERRYFIELD
ONGAR PARK
WILLANS WAY
WILLANS DRIVE
ONGAR GREEN
HAYWORTH DRIVE
DELHURST AVENUE
STRALEM TERRACE
Hartstown
ALLENDALE
Sch
Hall
PO
Shopping Centre
OAKVIEW AVENUE
OAKVIEW WAY
HAZELWOOD AVE
3
ANNALY TER
ANNALY GROVE
CHERRYFIELD LAWN
ELMWOOD CL
STONEBRIDGE
ALLENDALE COPSE
STONEBRIDGE RD
WILLOW WOOD PK
WILLOW WOOD GROVE
HARTSTOWN ROAD
INGLEWOOD
ONGAR ROAD
ALLENDALE SQUARE
WINDERMERE
MOUNT SYMON
LOHUNDA PARK
Clonsilla
ALDEMERE
St. Joseph's Hospital
CHARNWOOD
HANSFIELD (under construction)
PORTERS GATE
4
CASTLEFIELD COURT
CASTLEFIELD PARK
CASTLEFIELD WOODS
Pakenham Bridge
LC
Barberstown House
Beech Park House
CLONSILLA
CLONSILLA ROAD
LAMBOURNE AVE
LAMBOURNE PARK
WEAVER'S ROW
PO
Hall
THE VILLAGE
Callaghan Bridge
Green Mount
ROYAL CANAL
41
E
F
R121
TENNIS COURTS
SPORTS PITCHES
Westmanstown Sports Centre

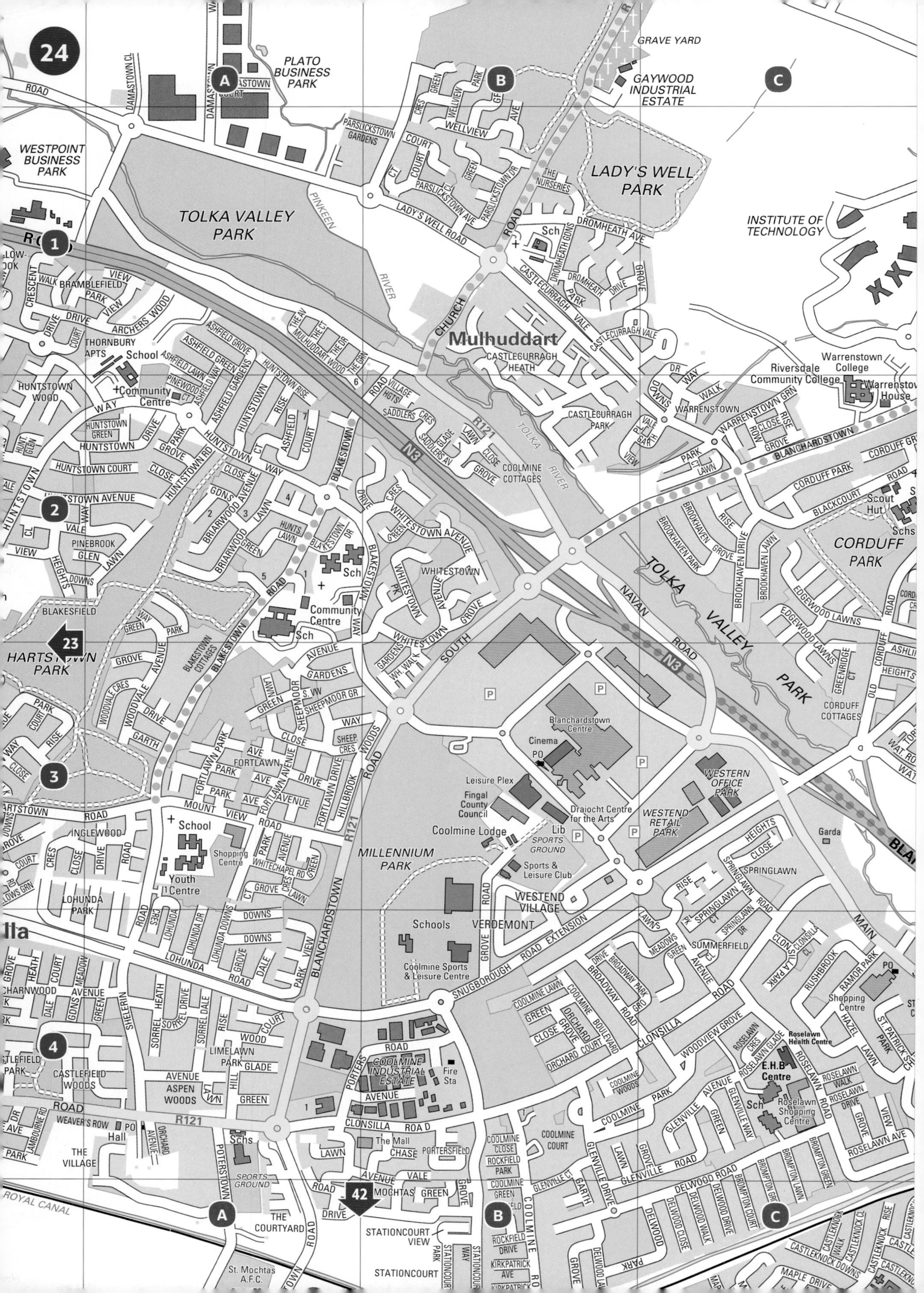

A
B
C
1
2
3
4
PLATO BUSINESS PARK
GRAVE YARD
GAYWOOD INDUSTRIAL ESTATE
WESTPOINT BUSINESS PARK
DAMASTOWN CL
DAMASTOWN COURT
ROAD
PARSLICKSTOWN GARDENS
WELLVIEW
WELLVIEW PARK
LADY'S WELL PARK
TOLKA VALLEY PARK
PINKEEN RIVER
PARSLICKSTOWN AVE
PARSLICKSTOWN DR
LADY'S WELL ROAD
THE NURSERIES
INSTITUTE OF TECHNOLOGY
DROMHEATH AVE
DROMHEATH GDNS
DROMHEATH PARK
DROMHEATH DRIVE
CASTLECURRAGH VALE
CHURCH ROAD
Sch
Mulhuddart
CASTLECURRAGH HEATH
CASTLECURRAGH PARK
BRAMBLEFIELD PARK
BRAMBLEFIELD VIEW
ARCHERS WOOD
THORNBURY APTS
School
Community Centre
HUNTSTOWN WOOD
ASHFIELD GROVE
ASHFIELD GREEN
ASHFIELD LAWN
ASHFIELD WAY
ASHFIELD GARDENS
PINEWOOD
HUNTSTOWN RISE
MULHUDDART WOOD
VILLAGE HGTS
SADDLERS CRES
SADDLERS AV
SADDLERS GLADE
R121
TOLKA RIVER
COOLMINE COTTAGES
Riversdale Community College
Warrenstown College
Warrenstown House
WARRENSTOWN
WARRENSTOWN GRN
BLANCHARDSTOWN
CORDUFF PARK
BLACKCOURT
Scout Hut
Schs
CORDUFF PARK
HUNTSTOWN GREEN
HUNTSTOWN DRIVE
HUNTSTOWN COURT
HUNTSTOWN AVENUE
HUNTSTOWN RD
HUNTSTOWN WAY
N3
BLAKESTOWN
WHITESTOWN AVENUE
WHITESTOWN
BROOKHAVEN PARK
BROOKHAVEN GROVE
BROOKHAVEN DRIVE
BROOKHAVEN LAWN
TOLKA VALLEY PARK
EDGEWOOD LAWNS
PINEBROOK GLEN
BRIARWOOD AVENUE
BRIARWOOD GREEN
BLAKESFIELD
23
HARTSTOWN PARK
Sch
Community Centre
BLAKESTOWN COTTAGES
WHITESTOWN GROVE
WHITESTOWN GARDENS
NAVAN ROAD
SOUTH
GREENRIDGE CT
CORDUFF COTTAGES
SHEEPMOOR GR
SHEEPMOOR WAY
WOODVALE CRES
WOODVALE DRIVE
GARTH
FORTLAWN PARK
FORTLAWN AVENUE
FORTLAWN DRIVE
HILLBROOK WOODS
Blanchardstown Centre
Cinema
PO
Leisure Plex
Fingal County Council
Draiocht Centre for the Arts
Lib
Coolmine Lodge
SPORTS GROUND
Sports & Leisure Club
WESTERN OFFICE PARK
WESTEND RETAIL PARK
Garda
MILLENNIUM PARK
MOUNT VIEW ROAD
School
INGLEWOOD
Shopping Centre
Youth Centre
WHITECHAPEL RD
LOHUNDA PARK
LOHUNDA DOWNS
LOHUNDA ROAD
BLANCHARDSTOWN ROAD
WESTEND VILLAGE
VERDEMONT
Schools
SPRINGLAWN
SPRINGLAWN CT
SPRINGLAWN DR
SUMMERFIELD
Coolmine Sports & Leisure Centre
SNUGBOROUGH ROAD EXTENSION
BROADWAY PARK
ORCHARD GROVE
ORCHARD COURT
COOLMINE BOULEVARD
CLONSILLA ROAD
CLONSILLA PARK
RUSHBROOK
RAMOR PARK
Shopping Centre
Roselawn Health Centre
E.H.B Centre
Roselawn Shopping Centre
COOLMINE INDUSTRIAL ESTATE
Fire Sta
PORTERSTOWN ROAD
CASTLEFIELD WOODS
ASPEN WOODS
LIMELAWN PARK
WEAVER'S ROW
Hall
THE VILLAGE
Schs
SPORTS GROUND
CLONSILLA ROAD
The Mall
PORTERSFIELD
COOLMINE COURT
GLENVILLE ROAD
DELWOOD ROAD
BROMPTON GREEN
ROSELAWN AVE
ROYAL CANAL
42
THE COURTYARD
STATIONCOURT VIEW
STATIONCOURT
St. Mochtas A.F.C.
ROCKFIELD DRIVE
KIRKPATRICK AVE
CASTLEKNOCK DOWNS
MAPLE DRIVE

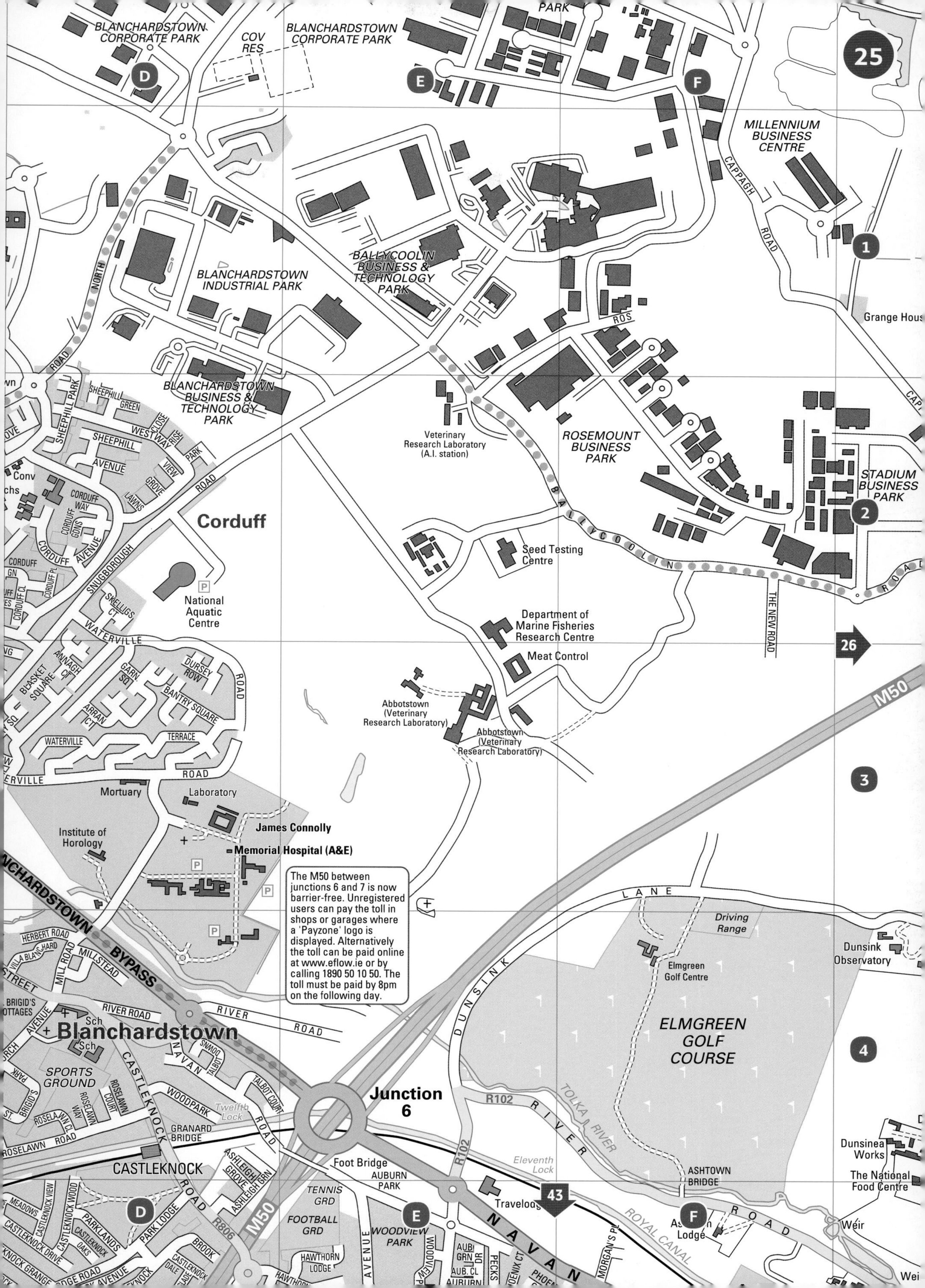

BLANCHARDSTOWN CORPORATE PARK
COV RES
BLANCHARDSTOWN CORPORATE PARK
PARK
D
E
F
MILLENNIUM BUSINESS CENTRE
CAPPAGH ROAD
1
BALLYCOOLIN BUSINESS & TECHNOLOGY PARK
BLANCHARDSTOWN INDUSTRIAL PARK
NORTH ROAD
Grange House
ROS
BLANCHARDSTOWN BUSINESS & TECHNOLOGY PARK
SHEEPHILL
SHEEPHILL PARK
GREEN
WESTWAY
CLOSE
RISE
SHEEPHILL AVENUE
PARK
VIEW
GROVE
LAWNS
AVENUE
ROAD
Veterinary Research Laboratory (A.I. station)
ROSEMOUNT BUSINESS PARK
STADIUM BUSINESS PARK
2
Conv
chs
CORDUFF WAY
CORDUFF GDNS
Corduff
CORDUFF AVENUE
CORDUFF
SNUGBOROUGH
BALLYCOOLIN ROAD
Seed Testing Centre
National Aquatic Centre
SKELLIGS CT
Department of Marine Fisheries Research Centre
THE NEW ROAD
26
WATERVILLE
Meat Control
ANNAGH CT
DURSEY ROW
BLASKET SQUARE
GARN. SQ.
BANTRY SQUARE
ROAD
Abbotstown (Veterinary Research Laboratory)
Abbotstown (Veterinary Research Laboratory)
M50
ARRAN CT
WATERVILLE
TERRACE
ERVILLE
ROAD
3
Mortuary
Laboratory
Institute of Horology
James Connolly Memorial Hospital (A&E)
The M50 between junctions 6 and 7 is now barrier-free. Unregistered users can pay the toll in shops or garages where a 'Payzone' logo is displayed. Alternatively the toll can be paid online at www.eflow.ie or by calling 1890 50 10 50. The toll must be paid by 8pm on the following day.
LANE
Driving Range
HERBERT ROAD
VILLA BLANCHARD
MILL ROAD
MILLSTEAD
BLANCHARDSTOWN BYPASS
STREET
Dunsink Observatory
Elmgreen Golf Centre
DUNSINK
BRIGID'S COTTAGES
RIVER ROAD
RIVER ROAD
Sch
Blanchardstown
Sch
ELMGREEN GOLF COURSE
4
NAVAN
TALBOT
SPORTS GROUND
CASTLEKNOCK
ROSELAWN COURT
ROSELAWN WAY
WOODPARK
TALBOT COURT
Junction 6
R102
Twelfth Lock
TOLKA RIVER
RIVER
ROSELAWN ROAD
GRANARD BRIDGE
ROAD
Dunsinea Works
CASTLEKNOCK
ASHLEIGH GROVE
ASHLEIGH GRN
Foot Bridge
AUBURN PARK
Eleventh Lock
ASHTOWN BRIDGE
The National Food Centre
R102
43
TENNIS GRD
Travelodge
ROYAL CANAL
D
FOOTBALL GRD
E
F
Ashtown Lodge
ROAD
Weir
PARK LODGE
R806
M50
WOODVIEW PARK
NAVAN
MEADOWS
CASTLEKNOCK VIEW
CASTLEKNOCK WOOD
PARKLANDS
CASTLEKNOCK OAKS
CASTLEKNOCK DRIVE
BROOK
AVENUE
HAWTHORN LODGE
AUB. GRN
AUB. CL
AUBURN
PECKS
MORGAN'S PL
Weir

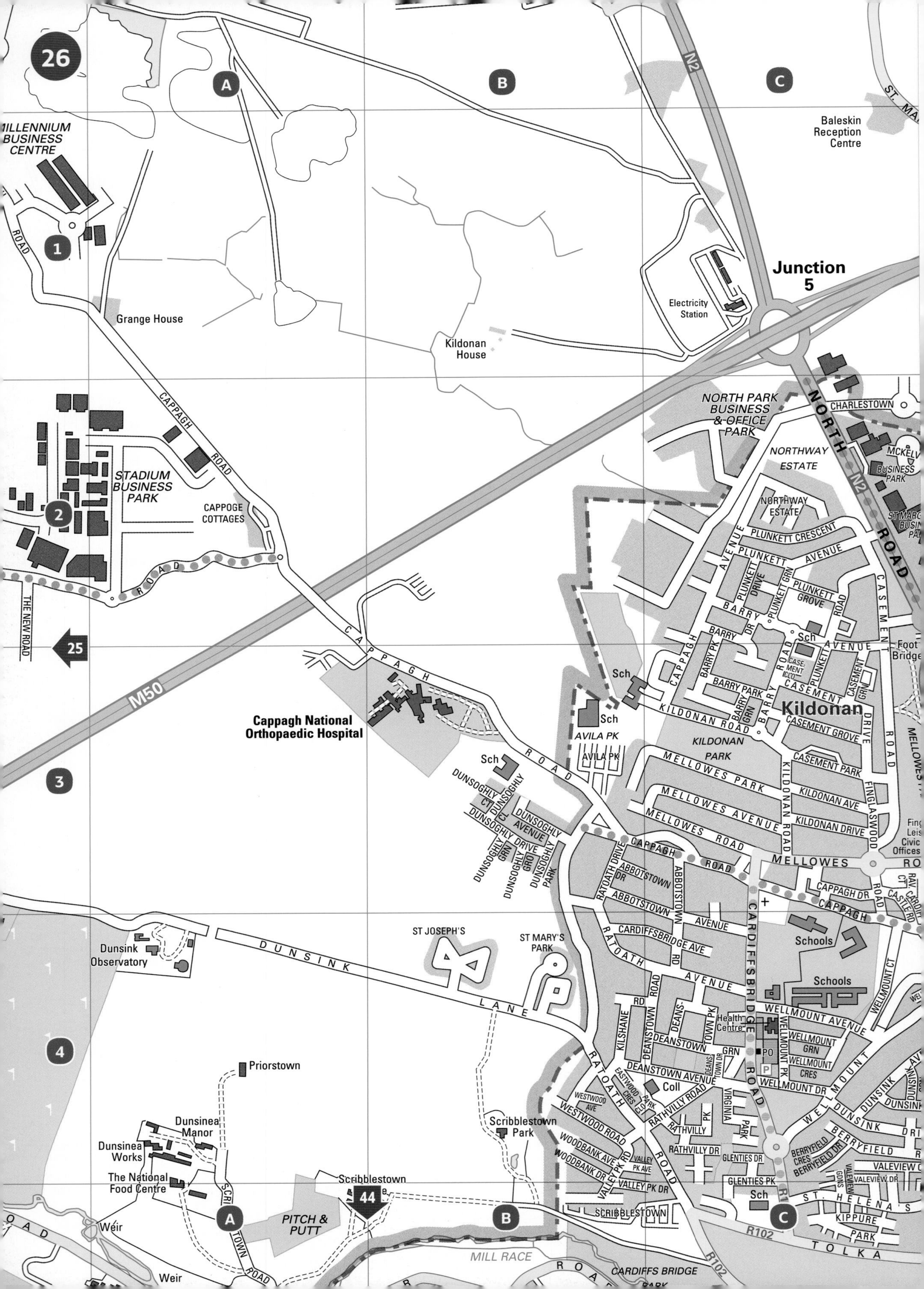

A
B
C
MILLENNIUM BUSINESS CENTRE
Baleskin Reception Centre
Junction 5
Electricity Station
Grange House
Kildonan House
N2
NORTH ROAD
NORTH PARK BUSINESS & OFFICE PARK
CHARLESTOWN
NORTHWAY ESTATE
STADIUM BUSINESS PARK
CAPPOGE COTTAGES
CAPPAGH ROAD
THE NEW ROAD
25
M50
Cappagh National Orthopaedic Hospital
PLUNKETT CRESCENT
PLUNKETT AVENUE
PLUNKETT DRIVE
PLUNKETT GRN
PLUNKETT GROVE
BARRY AVENUE
BARRY PK
BARRY DR
BARRY PARK
BARRY GRN
BARRY ROAD
CASEMENT ROAD
CASEMENT AVENUE
CASEMENT GROVE
CASEMENT PARK
CASEMENT DRIVE
Foot Bridge
Sch
Kildonan
KILDONAN ROAD
KILDONAN PARK
KILDONAN AVE
KILDONAN DRIVE
AVILA PK
MELLOWES PARK
MELLOWES AVENUE
MELLOWES ROAD
FINGLASWOOD ROAD
DUNSOGHLY CT
DUNSOGHLY CL
DUNSOGHLY AVENUE
DUNSOGHLY DRIVE
DUNSOGHLY GRN
DUNSOGHLY GRO
DUNSOGHLY PARK
RATOATH DRIVE
ABBOTSTOWN DR
ABBOTSTOWN AVENUE
CARDIFFSBRIDGE AVE
CARDIFFSBRIDGE ROAD
RATOATH AVENUE
RATOATH ROAD
CAPPAGH DR
Schools
ST JOSEPH'S
ST MARY'S PARK
DUNSINK LANE
Dunsink Observatory
1
2
3
4
Priorstown
Dunsinea Manor
Dunsinea Works
The National Food Centre
Scribblestown Park
PITCH & PUTT
44
Weir
MILL RACE
CARDIFFS BRIDGE
KILSHANE RD
DEANSTOWN ROAD
DEANSTOWN PK
DEANSTOWN GRN
DEANSTOWN AVENUE
DEANSTOWN DR
Health Centre
PO
WELLMOUNT AVENUE
WELLMOUNT GRN
WELLMOUNT CRES
WELLMOUNT PK
WELLMOUNT DR
WELLMOUNT CT
Coll
WESTWOOD AVE
WESTWOOD ROAD
EASTWOOD CRES
RATHVILLY ROAD
RATHVILLY PK
RATHVILLY DR
VIRGINIA PARK
GLENTIES DR
GLENTIES PK
WOODBANK AVE
WOODBANK DR
VALLEY PK RD
VALLEY PK AVE
VALLEY PK DR
SCRIBBLESTOWN
SCRIBBLESTOWN ROAD
BERRYFIELD CRES
BERRYFIELD DR
BERRYFIELD
VALEVIEW DR
DUNSINK
ST. HELENA'S
KIPPURE PARK
R102
R1
TOLKA
Fingal Leisure Civic Offices

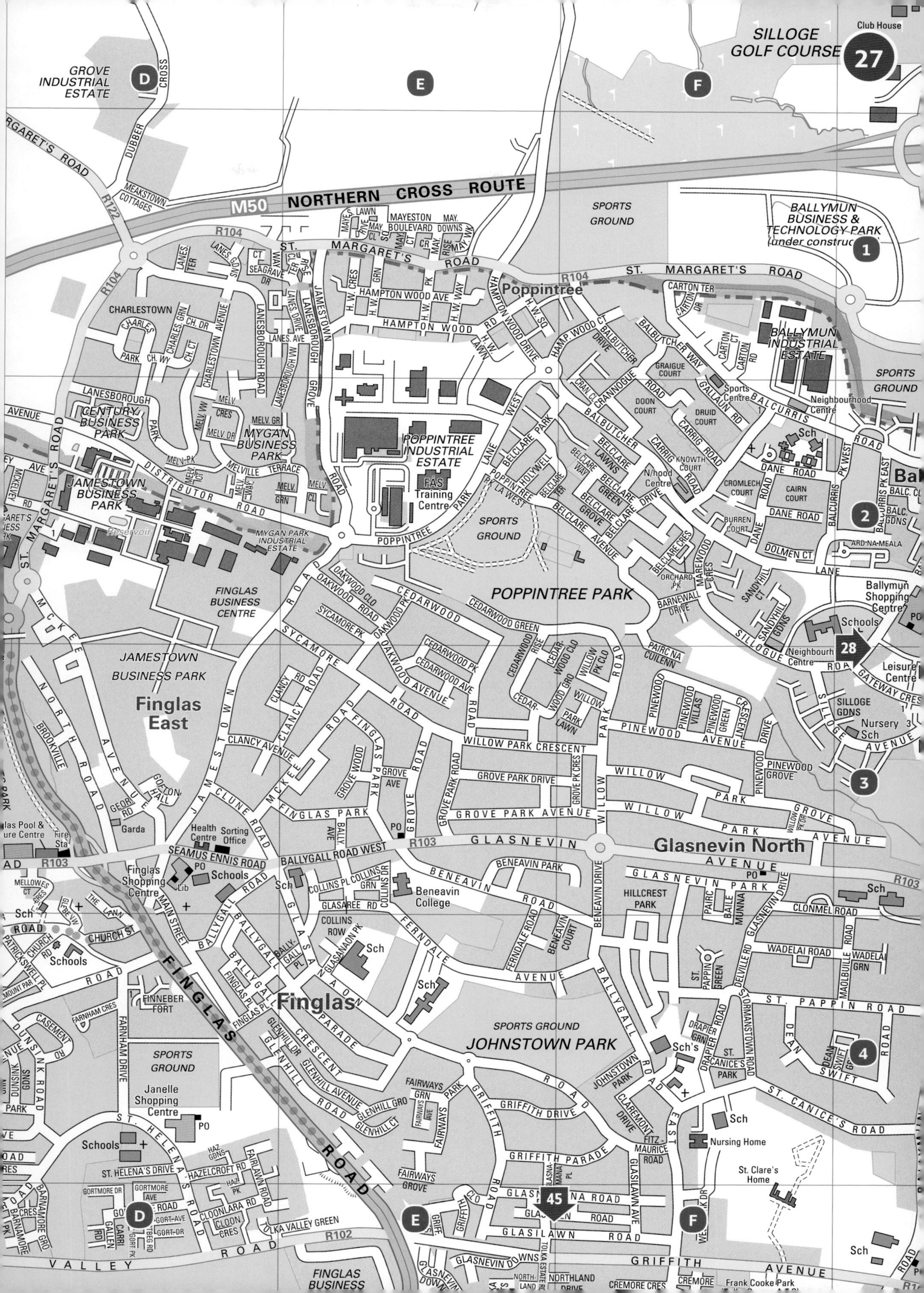
27
SILLOGE
GOLF COURSE
Club House
GROVE
INDUSTRIAL
ESTATE
CROSS
DUBBER
ST. MARGARET'S ROAD
MEAKSTOWN
COTTAGES
R122
M50
NORTHERN CROSS ROUTE
SPORTS
GROUND
BALLYMUN
BUSINESS &
TECHNOLOGY PARK
(under construc
R104
MAYES. LAWN
MAYESTON
BOULEVARD
MAY. DOWNS
ST. MARGARET'S ROAD
CHARLESTOWN
CHARLESTOWN AVENUE
LANESBOROUGH ROAD
JAMESTOWN
HAMPTON WOOD AVE
HAMPTON WOOD
Poppintree
HAMPTON WOOD DRIVE
CARTON TER
CARTON DR
BALBUTCHER DRIVE
BALBUTCHER WAY
BALLYMUN
INDUSTRIAL
ESTATE
SPORTS
GROUND
Neighbourhood
Centre
CENTURY
BUSINESS
PARK
LANESBOROUGH
PARK
MYGAN
BUSINESS
PARK
POPPINTREE
INDUSTRIAL
ESTATE
FÁS
Training
Centre
WEST
LANE
BELCLARE PARK
GRAIGUE
COURT
DOON
COURT
DRUID
COURT
CARRIG ROAD
Sports
Centre
BALCURRIS
Sch
JAMESTOWN
BUSINESS
PARK
MELVILLE TERRACE
DISTRIBUTOR ROAD
ST. MARGARET'S ROAD
MYGAN PARK
INDUSTRIAL
ESTATE
Reservoir
POPPINTREE PARK
SPORTS
GROUND
N/hood
Centre
KNOWTH
COURT
CROMLECH
COURT
CAIRN
COURT
DANE ROAD
BALCURRIS PK EAST
DOLMEN CT
ARD-NA-MEALA
LANE
FINGLAS
BUSINESS
CENTRE
POPPINTREE PARK
OAKWOOD ROAD
CEDARWOOD
CEDARWOOD GREEN
BARNEWALL
DRIVE
ORCHARD
PK
SANDYHILL
GDNS
Ballymun
Shopping
Centre
Schools
28
SILLOGUE ROAD
Neighbourh
Centre
Leisure
Centre
GATEWAY CRES
JAMESTOWN
BUSINESS PARK
Finglas
East
SYCAMORE ROAD
CLANCY AVENUE
PAIRC NA
CUILENN
PINEWOOD AVENUE
PINEWOOD DRIVE
SILLOGE
GDNS
Nursery
Sch
SILLOGE AVENUE
NORTH ROAD
BROOKVILLE
WILLOW PARK CRESCENT
GROVE PARK DRIVE
GROVE PARK AVENUE
WILLOW PARK
WILLOW PARK GROVE
WILLOW PARK AVENUE
PINEWOOD
GROVE
CLUNE ROAD
FINGLAS PARK
GROVE ROAD
Garda
Health
Centre
Sorting
Office
Fire
Sta
R103
GLASNEVIN
Glasnevin North
AVENUE
SEAMUS ENNIS ROAD
BALLYGALL ROAD WEST
Finglas
Shopping
Centre
Lib
Schools
Beneavin
College
BENEAVIN ROAD
BENEAVIN PARK
BENEAVIN DRIVE
HILLCREST
PARK
GLASNEVIN PARK
CLONMEL ROAD
R103
Sch
CHURCH ST
Schools
MAIN STREET
FINGLAS ROAD
Sch
COLLINS
ROW
GLASANAON PK
FERNDALE AVENUE
FERNDALE ROAD
BENEAVIN
COURT
WADELAI ROAD
WADELAI
GRN
ST. PAPPIN ROAD
FINNEBER
FORT
Finglas
PARADE
SPORTS GROUND
JOHNSTOWN PARK
STORMANSTOWN ROAD
DEAN SWIFT
4
SPORTS
GROUND
Janelle
Shopping
Centre
FARNHAM DRIVE
GLENHILL AVENUE
GLENHILL ROAD
FAIRWAYS
GRIFFITH DRIVE
JOHNSTOWN
PARK
Sch's
ST.
CANICE'S
PARK
ST. CANICE'S ROAD
Sch
Nursing Home
ST. HELENA'S DRIVE
Schools
PO
HAZELCROFT RD
FAIRLAWN ROAD
GRIFFITH PARADE
FITZ-
MAURICE
ROAD
St. Clare's
Home
45
GLASNAMANA ROAD
GLASILAWN ROAD
TOLKA VALLEY GREEN
R102
VALLEY ROAD
GRIFFITH AVENUE
FINGLAS
BUSINESS
NORTHLAND
DRIVE
CREMORE CRES
CREMORE
Frank Cooke Park
Sch
D
E
F
1
2
3

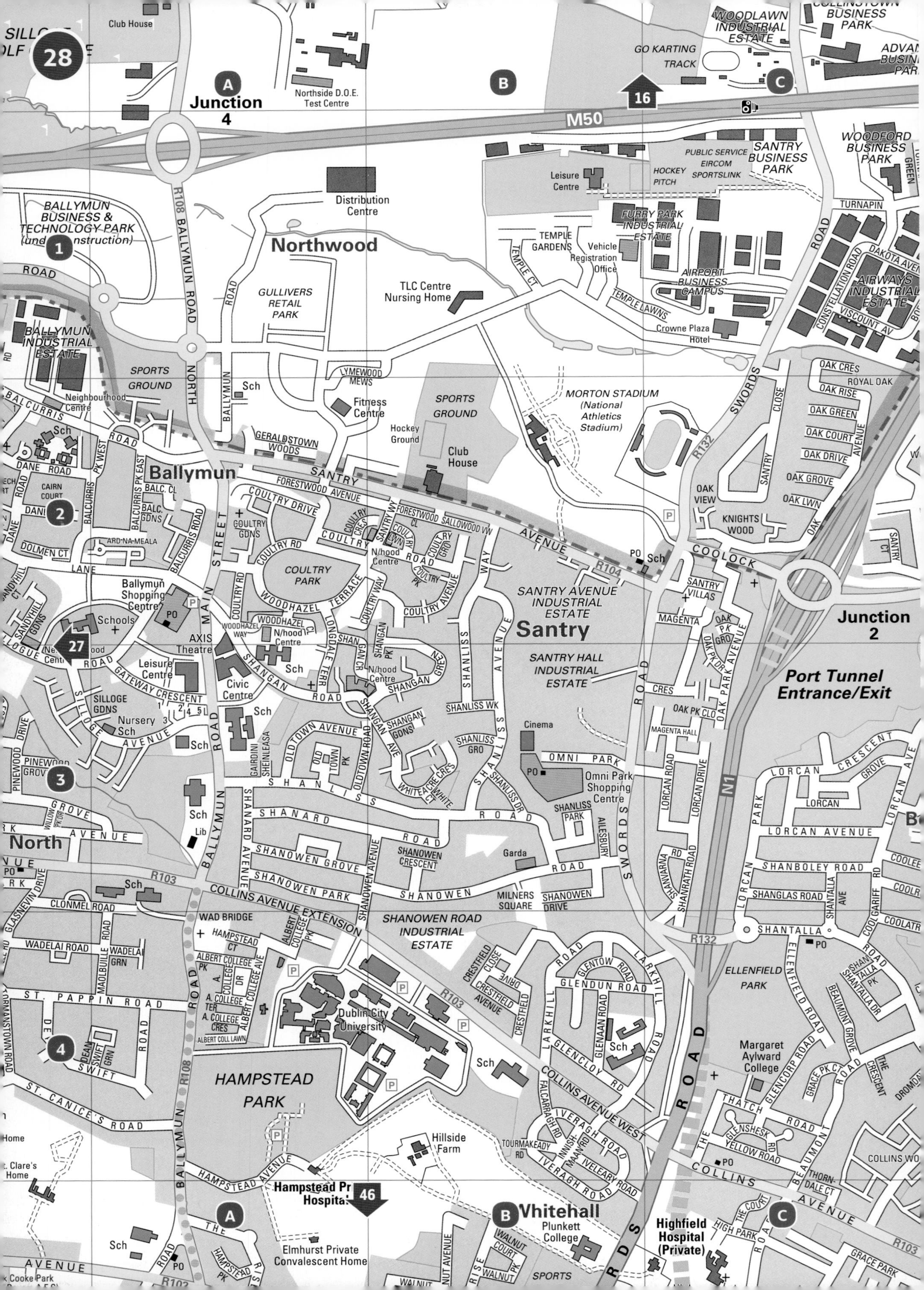
28
Club House
A
B
C
Junction 4
Northside D.O.E. Test Centre
WOODLAWN INDUSTRIAL ESTATE
COLLINSTOWN BUSINESS PARK
GO KARTING TRACK
16
M50
WOODFORD BUSINESS PARK
SANTRY BUSINESS PARK
PUBLIC SERVICE EIRCOM SPORTSLINK
HOCKEY PITCH
Leisure Centre
Distribution Centre
R108 BALLYMUN ROAD
BALLYMUN BUSINESS & TECHNOLOGY PARK (under construction)
1
Northwood
GULLIVERS RETAIL PARK
TLC Centre Nursing Home
TEMPLE GARDENS
TEMPLE CT
Vehicle Registration Office
FURRY PARK INDUSTRIAL ESTATE
AIRPORT BUSINESS CAMPUS
TEMPLE LAWNS
Crowne Plaza Hotel
TURNAPIN
DAKOTA AVE
CONSTELLATION ROAD
AIRWAYS INDUSTRIAL ESTATE
VISCOUNT AV
BALLYMUN INDUSTRIAL ESTATE
SPORTS GROUND
NORTH
BALLYMUN
Sch
LYMEWOOD MEWS
Fitness Centre
SPORTS GROUND
Hockey Ground
Club House
MORTON STADIUM (National Athletics Stadium)
SWORDS
R132
OAK CRES
ROYAL OAK
OAK RISE
OAK GREEN
OAK COURT
OAK DRIVE
OAK GROVE
OAK LWN
OAK VIEW
KNIGHTS WOOD
SANTRY CLOSE
Neighbourhood Centre
BALCURRIS
ROAD
DANE ROAD
CAIRN COURT
2
Ballymun
GERALDSTOWN WOODS
SANTRY
FORESTWOOD AVENUE
BALC. CL
BALC. GDNS
BALCURRIS ROAD
COULTRY DRIVE
COULTRY GDNS
FORESTWOOD CL
SALLOWOOD VW
AVENUE
COULTRY CRES
SANTRY WY
COULTRY RD
COULTRY PARK
N/hood Centre
COULTRY GRO
COULTRY PK
COULTRY AVENUE
COULTRY WAY
WOODHAZEL TERRACE
WOODHAZEL WAY
N/hood Centre
LONGDALE TERR
SHANGAN PK
SHANGAN GREEN
SHANGAN ROAD
ARD-NA-MEALA
DOLMEN CT
LANE
SANDYHILL CT
SANDYHILL GDNS
Ballymun Shopping Centre
PO
Schools
27
AXIS Theatre
Civic Centre
Leisure Centre
GATEWAY CRESCENT
SILLOGE GDNS
Nursery Sch
SILLOGE AVENUE
MAIN STREET
PO
Sch
R104
COOLOCK
SANTRY VILLAS
MAGENTA
OAK PK GRO
OAK PK DR
OAK PARK AVE
Junction 2
Santry
SANTRY AVENUE INDUSTRIAL ESTATE
SANTRY HALL INDUSTRIAL ESTATE
Port Tunnel Entrance/Exit
SHANLISS WK
SHANLISS GRO
SHANLISS AVENUE
SHANLISS DR
Cinema
OMNI PARK
Omni Park Shopping Centre
MAGENTA HALL
OAK PK CLO
CRES
LORCAN ROAD
LORCAN DRIVE
N1
LORCAN CRESCENT
LORCAN GROVE
LORCAN AVE
LORCAN PARK
LORCAN AVENUE
OLDTOWN AVENUE
OLD TOWN PK
OLDTOWN ROAD
SHANGAN GDNS
SHANGAN AVE
WHITEACRE CRES
WHITEACRE CT
GAIRDINI SHEINLEASA
PINEWOOD DRIVE
PINEWOOD GROV
3
WILLOW PK DR
GROVE
North
AVENUE
Lib
SHANLISS ROAD
SHANARD ROAD
SHANARD AVENUE
SHANOWEN GROVE
SHANOWEN AVENUE
SHANOWEN CRESCENT
SHANOWEN PARK
SHANOWEN ROAD
Garda
SHANLISS PARK
AILESBURY
MILNERS SQUARE
SHANOWEN DRIVE
SHANOWEN ROAD INDUSTRIAL ESTATE
SHANVARNA RD
SHANRATH ROAD
SHANBOLEY ROAD
SHANGLAS ROAD
SHANTALLA AVE
COOLGARIFF RD
COOLEE
COOLRI
COOLATR
R103
COLLINS AVENUE EXTENSION
CLONMEL ROAD
GLASNEVIN DRIVE
WAD BRIDGE
HAMPSTEAD CT
ALBERT COLLEGE PK
WADELAI ROAD
WADELAI GRN
MADLBUILLE ROAD
ALBERT COLLEGE PK
A. COLLEGE DR
ALBERT COLLEGE AVE
A. COLLEGE TER
A. COLLEGE CRES
ALBERT COLL LAWN
Dublin City University
CRESTFIELD CLOSE
CRESTFIELD DRIVE
CRESTFIELD AVENUE
LARKHILL ROAD
GLENTOW ROAD
GLENDUN ROAD
GLENAAN ROAD
GLENCLOY RD
SHANTALLA
R132
PO
ELLENFIELD PARK
ELLENFIELD ROAD
SHANTALLA PK
SHANTALLA DR
BEAUMONT GROVE
ST. PAPPIN ROAD
4
DEAN SWIFT GRN
DEAN SWIFT
ST. CANICE'S ROAD
HAMPSTEAD PARK
Sch
COLLINS AVENUE WEST
FALCARRAGH RD
IVERAGH ROAD
INNISHMAAN RD
IVELEARY ROAD
TOURMAKEADY RD
SWORDS ROAD
Margaret Aylward College
GLENCORP ROAD
GRACE PK CT
THE CRESCENT
DROMDA
THATCH ROAD
GLENSHESK RD
YELLOW ROAD
BEAUMONT
COLLINS AVENUE
THORNDALE CT
COLLINS WO
Home
St. Clare's Home
Hillside Farm
HAMPSTEAD AVENUE
Hampstead Private Hospital
46
Whitehall
Plunkett College
WALNUT COURT
WALNUT PK
WALNUT RISE
WALNUT AVENUE
Elmhurst Private Convalescent Home
THE RISE
HAMPSTEAD PK
SPORTS
Highfield Hospital (Private)
HIGH PARK
THE COURT
GRACE PARK
R103
R102
PO
Cooke Park

Clonshaugh
Junction 3
M50
M32
N32
17
30
48
47
BELCAMP PARK
SPORTS GROUND
TENNIS & BASKETBALL COURTS
St. Michaels House (Residential Care Home)
Bewley's Hotel
WILLSBOROUGH INDUSTRIAL ESTATE
CLONSHAUGH INDUSTRIAL ESTATE
I.D.A. SMALL INDUSTRIAL CENTRE
CLONSHAUGH BUSINESS & TECHNOLOGY PARK
RIVER SANTRY
SPORTS GROUND
PLAYING FIELD
Subway
Community Centre
Northside Shopping Centre
Subways
Lib
Health Centre
Kilmore
Astro Park
Oscar Traynor Coaching & Dev Cen
STARDUST MEMORIAL PARK
Sports Centre
Cooklock Dev Cen
Northside Civic Cen
Retail Centre
Northside Arts & Cultural Centre
Convalescent Home
Beaumont
St. Paul's Hospital
Beaumont Hospital (A&E)
Coolock
Garda
Chanel College
BUTTERLY BUSINESS PARK
Shopping Centre
St. Brigids Shopping Mall
Mercy College
ROCKFIELD PARK
ST. DAVIDS PARK AND WOOD
Convent
OSCAR TRAYNOR ROAD
MALAHIDE ROAD
R104
R107
GREENCASTLE ROAD
CLONSHAUGH AVENUE
CLONSHAUGH ROAD
MOATVIEW AVENUE
PRIORSWOOD AVENUE
CROMCASTLE ROAD
KILBARRON ROAD
CASTLETIMON ROAD
BALLYSHANNON ROAD
KILMORE ROAD
KILMORE AVENUE
KILMORE CLOSE
KILMORE DRIVE
ARDMORE DRIVE
MONTROSE DRIVE
SKELLY'S LANE
COOLOCK DRIVE
CHANEL ROAD
GRACEFIELD ROAD
BROOKWOOD ROAD
RIVERSIDE ROAD
FERRYCARRIG ROAD
BUNRATTY ROAD
ADARE ROAD
ELM MOUNT ROAD
COLLINS AVENUE
CELTIC PARK AVENUE
COOLGREENA ROAD
CASTLEKEVIN ROAD
MASK ROAD
MASK AVENUE
DANIELI ROAD
ST. BRENDAN'S AVENUE
COOLOCK VILLAGE
OLD MALAHIDE ROAD

A
B
C
18
1
2
3
4
29
48
Spring Hill
Lime Hill
St. Doolagh's
St. Doolagh's Park
Saintdoolaghs
Trinity Gaels G.A.A. Club
Burgage
PITCH & PUTT
CEMETERY
SPORTS GROUND
Balgriffin
MALAHIDE ROAD
R107
FINGAL BURIAL GROUND
BALGRIFFIN ROAD
Belcamp Hutchinson
Wellfield Bridge
ST. SAMSON CT
ST. SAMSON SQ
CASTLEMOYNE
BALGRIFFIN COTTAGES
Balgriffin Park
Belcamp College
SPORTS GROUND
THE HOLE IN THE WALL ROAD
N32
CITY JUNCTION BUSINESS PARK
MAYNE RIV. AVE
Hilton Dublin Airport
DARNDALE PARK
Darndale
BELCAMP GARDENS
BELCAMP CRESCENT
TULIP COURT
Sch
Community Centre
PRIMROSE GROVE
SNOWDROP WALK
BELCAMP LANE
MOATVIEW GDNS
BELCAMP GRN
BELCAMP AVENUE
BELCAMP GROVE
PRIORSWOOD ROAD
FERRYCARRIG PARK
FERRYCARRIG ROAD
FERRYCARRIG AVENUE
MARIGOLD AVE
R841
CLARE HALL AVENUE
Leisure Centre
TEMPLEVIEW
Clare Hall Shopping Centre
CLARE VILLAGE
GROVE LANE
GROVE PK
TEMPLEVIEW GREEN
TEMPLEVIEW PARK
TEMP. SQ
TEMP. COPSE
TEMPLE VW AVE
ELMFIELD WAY
ELM RISE
ELMFIELD WALK
ELMFIELD GROVE
ELMFIELD GREEN
ELMFIELD
ELM. LAWN
GRATTAN LODGE
GRATTAN HALL
St. Colombuns
Clare Hall
GREENWOOD AVENUE
GREENWOOD DR
GREENWOOD WAY
NURNEY LAWN
WHYTELEAF GROVE
MANOR DR
ARDARA AVENUE
GRANGEMORE CRESCENT
GRANGEMORE DR
GRANGEMORE LAWN
GRANGEMORE ROAD
GRANGEMORE AVENUE
ROSAPENNA DRIVE
Donaghmede Shopping Centre
SPORTS GROUND
Ayrfield Community Sports & Leisure Centre
BLUNDEN DRIVE
NEWTOWN ROAD
NEWTOWN AVENUE
NEWTOWN INDUSTRIAL ESTATE
SLADEMORE AVENUE
SLADEMORE CT
GLENTWORTH PARK
ELTON PK
ELTON DR
CLONROSSE DRIVE
FOXHILL AVE
FOXHILL DRIVE
FOXHILL CRES
FOXHILL PARK
FOXHILL WAY
FOXHILL CT
FOXHILL GRN
MILLBROOK ROAD
MILLBROOK AVENUE
MILLBROOK GRO
STREAMVILLE ROAD
CEDAR PARK
LENTISK LAWN
KILFENORA DRIVE
CARRAROE AVENUE
TARA LAWN
WOODVIEW PK
HOWTH VW PK
HOLYWELL AVE
HOLYWELL CRESCENT
HOLYWELL RD
THE BEECHES
ST. DONAGH'S
R809
GRANGE
COOLOCK INDUSTRIAL ESTATE
GREENCASTLE AVENUE
GREENCASTLE PARADE
GREENCASTLE CRES
CASTLE ELMS
NEWTOWN COTTS
NEWTOWN DRIVE
AYREFIELD PLACE
AYREFIELD DRIVE
AYREFIELD AVE
AYREFIELD GRO
RATHVALE AVE
RATHVALE
RATHVALE PARK
LIMEWOOD AVE
LIMEWOOD RD
LIMEWOOD PK
Leisureplex
UCI Cinema
R104
KILBARRACK ROAD
Fire Sta
Subway
Tennis Court
St. Monica's Youth Centre
MILLWOOD VILLAS
MILLWOOD PARK
TONLEGEE ROAD
TONLEGEE DRIVE
TONLEGEE AVENUE
GLENAYLE RD
WOODBINE ROAD
WOODBINE CLO
WOODBINE DRIVE
WOODBINE PARK
MOUNT OLIVE ROAD
OLIVE PARK
MOUNT OLIVE GROVE
SWANS NEST ROAD
Kilbarrack Shopping Centre
Schs
KILBARRACK
OLD MALAHIDE ROAD
Garda
BROOKVILLE CRESCENT
BEECHPARK CT
VILLAGE
DUNREE PARK
GLENFARNE RD
SPRINGDALE ROAD
GLENWOOD ROAD
MOATFIELD ROAD
MOATFIELD AVENUE
MOATFIELD PK
ST. BRENDAN'S AVE
ST. BRENDAN'S PARK
ENNEL PARK
Convent
Mercy
Health Centre
PO
EDENMORE PARK
EDENMORE AVE
EDENMORE
Hilltop Shopping Centre
GRANGE PARK
GRANGE PARK PARADE
GRANGE PARK RISE
GRANGE PK GRN
GRANGE ROAD
GRANGE PARK DRIVE

Baldoyle Estuary Nature Reserve
THE KILNS
STATION ROAD
PORTMARNOCK
Portmarnock Bridge
19
Murragh
R124
ROAD
DRUMNIGH WOOD
Drumnigh
DRUMNIGH
Maynetown
R123
MAYNE ROAD
Moyne Lodge
MOYNE PARK
Mayne Bridge
Snugborough
MAYNE RIVER
R106
COAST ROAD
Portmarnock Golf Club Club House
FATHER COLLINS PARK
SPORTS GROUNDS
Clongriffin
Stapolin
MAIN STREET
BEAU PARK ST
Trinity Sports & Leisure Centre
Grange Community College
NEW GROVE ESTATE
GRANGE LODGE AVE
BEAU PARK ROW
BEAU PARK SQUARE
STATION WAY
RAILWAY ROAD
RAILWAY MEWS
GRANGE ABBEY ROAD
GRANGE ABBEY DRIVE
R809
GRANGE ROAD
GRANGE ABBEY CRESCENT
GRANGE ABBEY GROVE
School
DONAGHMEDE PARK
LONGFIELD ROAD
RED ARCHES DR
RED ARCHES AVENUE
STAPOLIN AVENUE
MYRTLE AVE
STAPOLIN LAWNS
CASTLEROSSE CRESCENT
CASTLE ROSSE DRIVE
CASTLE ROSSE VIEW
GRANGE PARK
Health Centre
Community Hall
St Mary's Hospital
ADMIRAL PARK
WILLIE NOLAN RD
COLLEGE STREET
MAIN ST
STRAND
Baldoyle
GEORGIAN HAMLET
BROOKSTONE RD
DUBLIN STREET
Grave Yard
Nursing Home
PO
Lib
32
GRANGE AVENUE
GRANGE PARADE
GRANGE CLOSE
GRANGE DRIVE
BALDOYLE INDUSTRIAL ESTATE
GRANGE WAY
Racecourse Shopping Centre
SEAGRANGE AV
SEAGRANGE DR
SEAGRANGE ROAD
ABBEY PARK
MARIAN PARK
SEAGRANGE PARK
TUSCANY PARK
MEADOWBROOK AVENUE
PARKVALE
TURNBERRY
WARREN GREEN
MOYCLARE DRIVE
MOYCLARE ROAD
MOYCLARE CLO
BURROWFIELD
SEACLIFF RD
SEACLIFF DR
SEACLIFF AVENUE
NEWBROOK ROAD
NEWBROOK AVE
CARNDONAGH PARK
CARNDONAGH DRIVE
CARNDONAGH ROAD
DONAGHMEDE ROAD
CARNDONAGH LWN
Garda
BAYSIDE
HOWTH JUNCTION
ST. DONAGH'S PK
KILBARRACK WAY
KILBARRACK PARADE
KILBARRACK INDUSTRIAL ESTATE
SPORTS GROUND
VERBENA LAWNS
VERBENA PK
VERBENA GRO
BAYSIDE BOULEVARD NORTH
BAYSIDE WALK
BAYSIDE PARK
SARTO LAWN
SARTO PARK
ALDEN ROAD
ALDEN PARK
ALDEN DRIVE
VERBENA AVENUE
BAYSIDE SQ. NORTH
BAYSIDE SQ. EAST
BAYSIDE SQ. WEST
SUTTON GROVE
SUTTON PARK
SUTTON COURT
SUTTON DOWNS
SEAFIELD CT
LAWNS
RAILWAY AVENUE
BALDOYLE ROAD
49
Kilbarrack
KILBARRACK CEMETERY
R105
R104
SUTTO
KILBARRACK ROAD
BRIARFIELD GROVE
BRIARFIELD VILLAS
THORNVILLE ROAD
THORNVILLE PARK
THORNVILLE DRIVE
KILBARRACK GARDENS
KILBARRACK GROVE
KILBARRACK AVENUE
Greendale Shopping Centre
SARTO ROAD
SARTO RISE
RONCALLI ROAD
BEACH VIEW
JAMES JOYCE CT
DUBLIN ROAD
Sch
D
E
F
1
2
3
4

A
B
C
Community Hall
St. Mary's Hospital
Baldoyle
Portmarnock Point
Cush Point
Sutton G.C. Clubhouse
MAIN ST
STRAND
COLLEGE STREET
DUBLIN STREET
Grave Yard
PO
Lib
Sch
31
TURNBERRY
WARRENHOUSE ROAD
WARREN GREEN
MOYCLARE DRIVE
MOYCLARE PARK
MOYCLARE AVE
MOYCLARE ROAD
MOYCLARE GDNS
BURROWFIELD ROAD
JAMES McCORMACK GARDENS
STATION ROAD
R809
LC
1
2
3
4
SUTTON GOLF COURSE
Suncroft
BURROW ROAD
CLAREMONT ROAD
SUTTON
LAUDERS LA
GOLF LINKS
SUTTON PARK
SUTTON PARK LAWNS
SEAFIELD CT
BALDOYLE ROAD
RAILWAY AVENUE
THE CRES
BINN EADAIR VIEW
THE COURT
RUGBY GROUND
Sutton Cross Shopping Centre
P
Sutton
R105
DUBLIN ROAD
SPORTS GROUND
CHURCH ROAD
GLENCARRIG
Convent
Schools
Marine Hotel
GREENFIELD ROAD
Sutton Strand
Sutton Creek
SANTA SABINA MNR
OFFINGTON PARK
OFFINGTON DRIVE
OFFINGTON AVENUE
OFFINGTON LAWN
OFFINGTON COURT
OLD CASTLE AVENUE
STRAND ROAD
CARRICKBRACK HEATH
DUNCARRIG
CARRICKBRACK HILL
CARRICKBRACK PARK
CARRICKBRACK LAWN
CARRICKBRACK ROAD
CEMETERY
LA VISTA AVE
ST. FINTAN'S ROAD
ST. FINTAN'S PK
ST. FINTAN'S CRES
ST. FINTAN'S GROVE
Bayview House
Old Quay
SHIELMARTIN DRIVE
SHIELMARTIN ROAD
SHIELMARTIN RD
SHIELMARTIN PK
SOUTH HILL
Sea Lawn
Sutton Castle
49
34

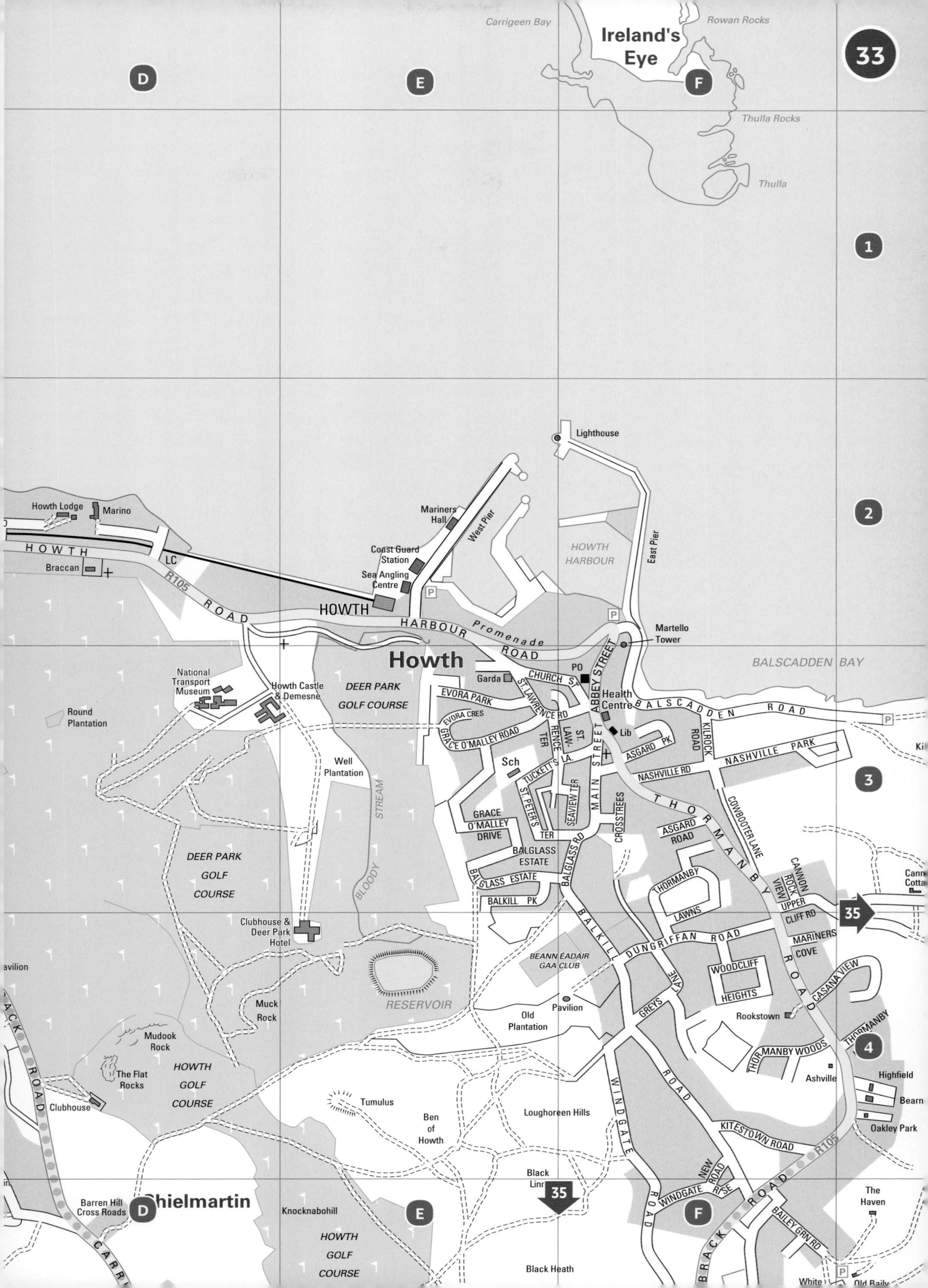
33
Ireland's Eye
Carrigeen Bay
Rowan Rocks
Thulla Rocks
Thulla
D
E
F
1
2
3
4
Lighthouse
Howth Lodge
Marino
Mariners Hall
West Pier
East Pier
HOWTH HARBOUR
Coast Guard Station
Sea Angling Centre
HOWTH ROAD
R105
LC
Braccan
HOWTH
HARBOUR ROAD
Promenade
Martello Tower
BALSCADDEN BAY
Howth
National Transport Museum
Howth Castle & Demesne
DEER PARK GOLF COURSE
Round Plantation
Garda
PO
CHURCH ST
ABBEY STREET
Health Centre
BALSCADDEN ROAD
EVORA PARK
EVORA CRES
GRACE O'MALLEY ROAD
ST. LAWRENCE RD
ST. LAWRENCE TER
Lib
ASGARD PK
KILROCK ROAD
NASHVILLE PARK
NASHVILLE RD
Well Plantation
Sch
TUCKETT'S LA.
ST. PETER'S TER
SEAVIEW TER
MAIN STREET
CROSSTREES
THORMANBY ROAD
COWBOOTER LANE
ASGARD ROAD
GRACE O'MALLEY DRIVE
BALGLASS ESTATE
BALGLASS RD
BALKILL PK
BALKILL ROAD
STREAM
BLOODY STREAM
DEER PARK GOLF COURSE
THORMANBY LAWNS
CANNON ROCK VIEW
UPPER CLIFF RD
MARINERS COVE
35
Clubhouse & Deer Park Hotel
BEANN EADAIR GAA CLUB
DUNGRIFFAN ROAD
WOODCLIFF HEIGHTS
CASANA VIEW
Muck Rock
RESERVOIR
Pavilion
Old Plantation
GREYS LANE
Rookstown
Mudook Rock
THORMANBY WOODS
THORMANBY
Ashville
Highfield
Bearn
Oakley Park
The Flat Rocks
HOWTH GOLF COURSE
Clubhouse
Tumulus
Ben of Howth
Loughoreen Hills
WINDGATE ROAD
KITESTOWN ROAD
Black Linn
NEW ROAD
WINDGATE RISE
BAILEY GRN RD
The Haven
Barren Hill Cross Roads
Shielmartin
Knocknabohill
HOWTH GOLF COURSE
Black Heath
White
Old Baily
avilion
Ki
Cann Cotta

Sutton Cross Shopping Centre
PO
DUBLIN ROAD
HOWTH ROAD
Braccan
LC
R105
ROAD
SPORTS GROUND
CHURCH ROAD
32
GLENCARRIG
Marine Hotel
GREENFIELD ROAD
Convent
Schools
Sutton Strand
Sutton Creek
SANTA SABINA MNR
OFFINGTON PARK
OFFINGTON DRIVE
OFFINGTON AVENUE
OFFINGTON LAWN
OFFINGTON
OFFINGTON COURT
National Transport Museum
Round Plantation
DEER PARK GOLF COURSE
Clubhouse
Muck Rock
Mudook Rock
The Flat Rocks
HOWTH GOLF COURSE
STRAND ROAD
CARRICKBRACK HEATH
DUNCARRIG
OLD CASTLE AVENUE
SPORTS GROUND
Sch
CARRICKBRACK ROAD
Pavilion
CARRICKBRACK HILL
CARRICK-BRACK PARK
LA VISTA AVE
CEMETERY
CARRICK-BRACK LAWN
ST. FINTAN'S PK
ST. FINTAN'S CRES
SPORTS GROUND
Old Quay
Bayview House
ST. FINTAN'S GROVE
ST. FINTAN'S ROAD
Sch
SOUTH HILL
Clubhouse
SHIELMARTIN DRIVE
SHIELMARTIN ROAD
Sea Lawn
Shielmartin House
SHIELMARTIN RD
Barren Hill Cross Roads
Shielmartin
SHIEL-MARTIN PK
Sutton Castle
Martello Tower
Somali
BALSAGGART STREAM
Pumping House
Shearwater
CLIFF WALK
The Cliffs
Sheep Hole
A
B
C
1
2
3
4

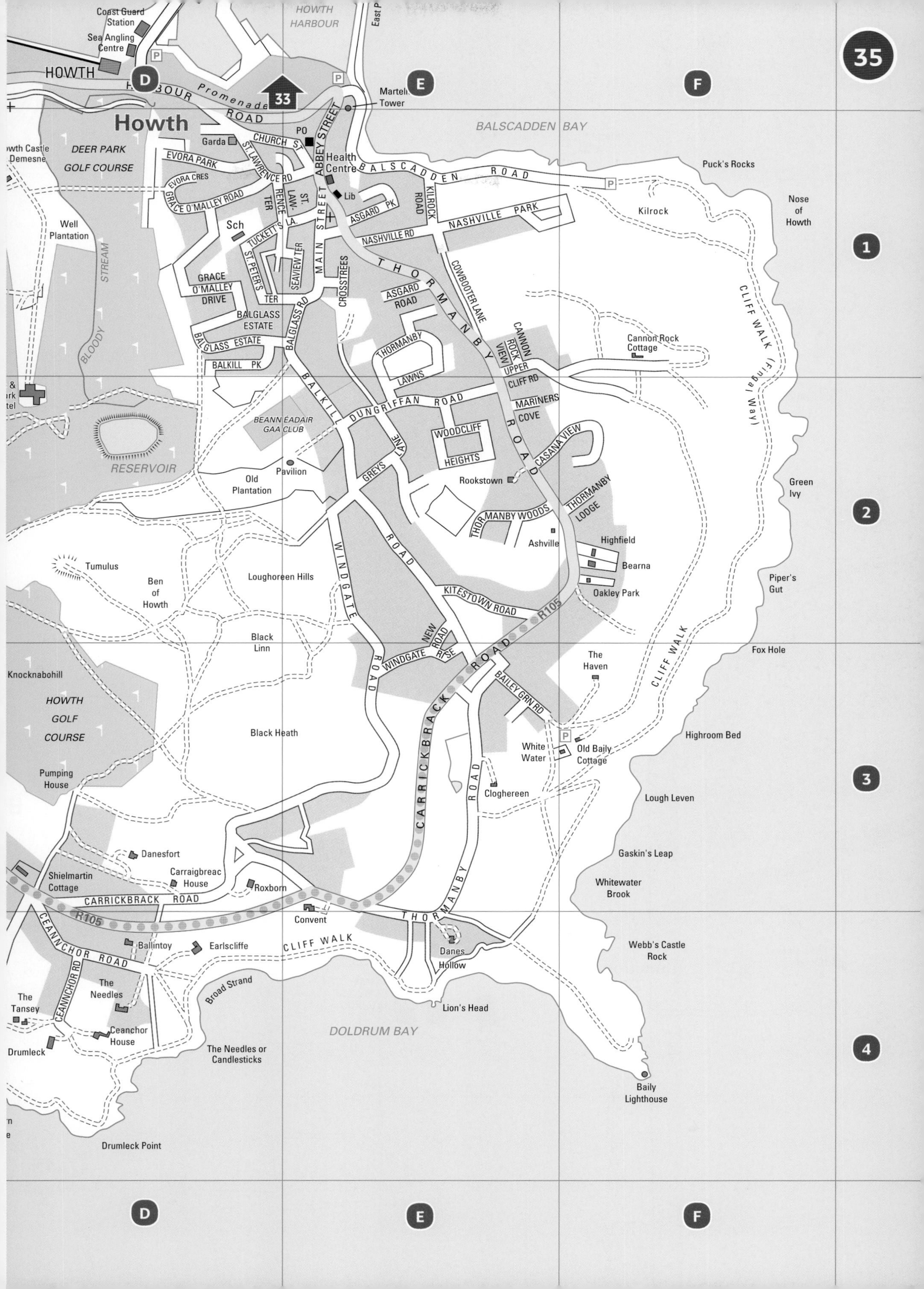
HOWTH HARBOUR
Coast Guard Station
Sea Angling Centre
HOWTH
HARBOUR ROAD
Promenade
33
Martello Tower
Howth
Garda
PO
CHURCH ST
ABBEY STREET
Health Centre
BALSCADDEN BAY
BALSCADDEN ROAD
Puck's Rocks
Howth Castle Demesne
DEER PARK GOLF COURSE
EVORA PARK
EVORA CRES
GRACE O'MALLEY ROAD
ST LAWRENCE RD
TER
RENCE
ST. LAW-
Lib
KILROCK ROAD
Kilrock
Nose of Howth
Well Plantation
Sch
TUCKETT'S LA.
ASGARD PK
NASHVILLE PARK
NASHVILLE RD
MAIN STREET
ST. PETERS TER
SEAVIEW TER
STREAM
GRACE O'MALLEY DRIVE
CROSSTREES
THORMANBY ROAD
COWBOOTER LANE
ASGARD ROAD
CLIFF WALK (Fingal Way)
BALGLASS ESTATE
BALGLASS RD
BALKILL PK
BLOODY
THORMANBY LAWNS
CANNON ROCK VIEW
UPPER CLIFF RD
Cannon Rock Cottage
BALKILL
DUNGRIFFAN ROAD
MARINERS COVE
BEANN EADAIR GAA CLUB
WOODCLIFF HEIGHTS
CASANA VIEW
RESERVOIR
Pavilion
Old Plantation
GREYS LANE
Rookstown
THORMANBY LODGE
Green Ivy
THORMANBY WOODS
Ashville
Highfield
Bearna
Oakley Park
Tumulus
Ben of Howth
Loughoreen Hills
WINDGATE ROAD
KITESTOWN ROAD
R105
Piper's Gut
Black Linn
NEW ROAD
RISE
WINDGATE
Fox Hole
The Haven
CLIFF WALK
Knocknabohill
HOWTH GOLF COURSE
CARRICKBRACK ROAD
BAILEY GRN RD
Black Heath
Highroom Bed
White Water
Old Baily Cottage
Pumping House
ROAD
Cloghereen
Lough Leven
Danesfort
Gaskin's Leap
Shielmartin Cottage
Carraigbreac House
Roxborn
Whitewater Brook
CARRICKBRACK ROAD
R105
Convent
THORMANBY
CEANNCHOR ROAD
Ballintoy
Earlscliffe
CLIFF WALK
Danes Hollow
Webb's Castle Rock
The Needles
The Tansey
CEANNCHOR RD
Broad Strand
Lion's Head
Ceanchor House
DOLDRUM BAY
Drumleck
The Needles or Candlesticks
Baily Lighthouse
Drumleck Point
D
E
F
1
2
3
4

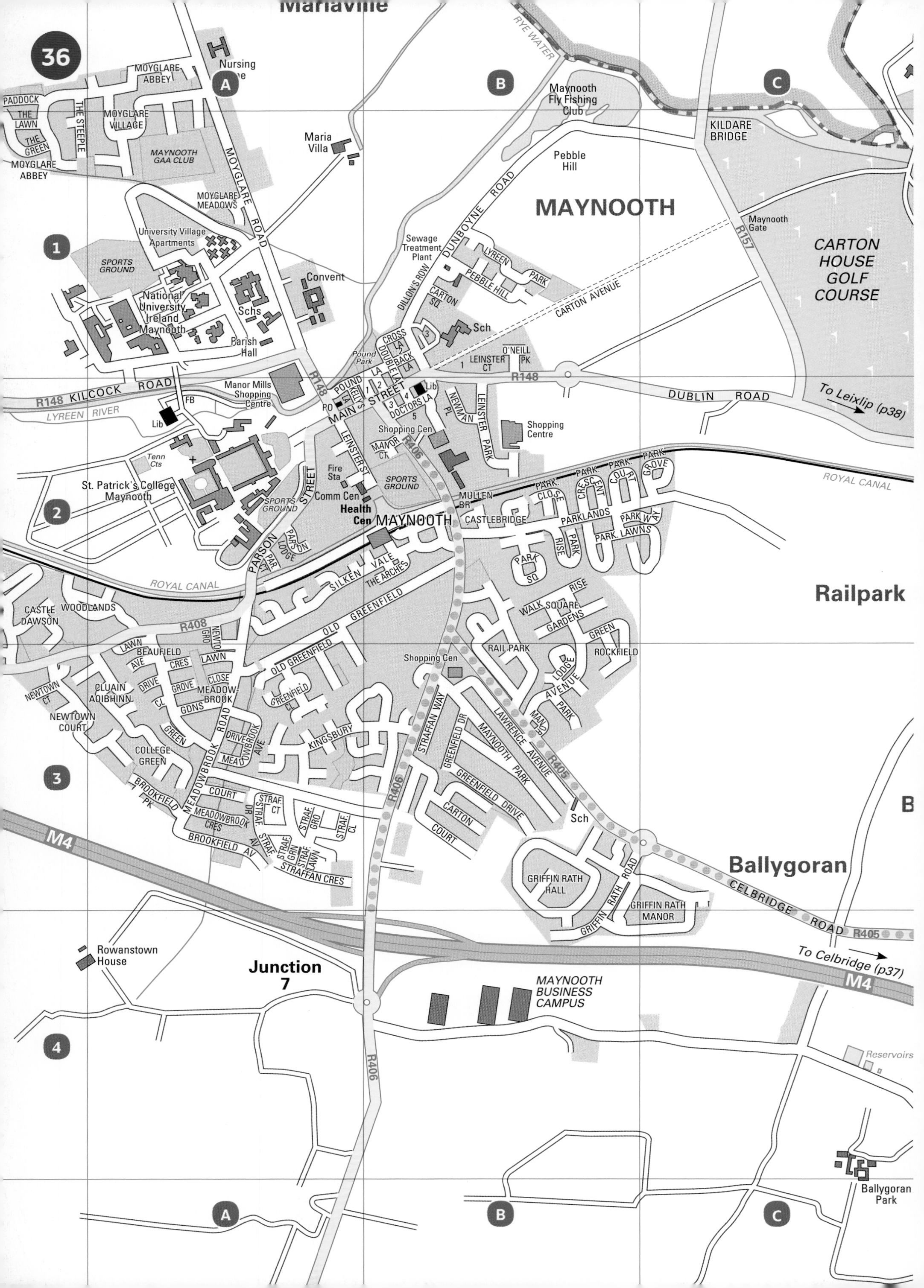
Mariaville
Nursing Home
MOYGLARE ABBEY
PADDOCK
THE LAWN
THE GREEN
THE STEEPLE
MOYGLARE VILLAGE
MAYNOOTH GAA CLUB
MOYGLARE ABBEY
MOYGLARE ROAD
RYE WATER
Maynooth Fly Fishing Club
KILDARE BRIDGE
Maria Villa
Pebble Hill
MAYNOOTH
MOYGLARE MEADOWS
University Village Apartments
SPORTS GROUND
National University Ireland Maynooth
Schs
Convent
Parish Hall
Sewage Treatment Plant
DUNBOYNE ROAD
DILLON'S ROW
LYREEN PARK
PEBBLE HILL
CARTON SQ
CARTON AVENUE
Sch
Maynooth Gate
R157
CARTON HOUSE GOLF COURSE
R148 KILCOCK ROAD
LYREEN RIVER
FB
Lib
Manor Mills Shopping Centre
R148
POUND LA
Pound Park
CROSS LA
DOUBLE LA
BACK LA
NEILL'S
MAIN STREET
DOCTORS LA
PO
Lib
LEINSTER CT
O'NEILL PK
NEWMAN PL
LEINSTER PARK
DUBLIN ROAD
To Leixlip (p38)
Shopping Cen
Shopping Centre
MANOR CT
R406
LEINSTER ST
SPORTS GROUND
Tenn Cts
St. Patrick's College Maynooth
SPORTS GROUND
PARSON STREET
Fire Sta
Comm Cen
Health Cen
MAYNOOTH
MULLEN BR
CASTLEBRIDGE
PARK CLOSE
PARK CRESCENT
PARK COURT
PARK GROVE
PARKLANDS
PARK WAY
PARK LAWNS
PARK RISE
PARK SQ
ROYAL CANAL
PARSON LODGE
PAR CT
SILKEN VALE
THE ARCHES
ROYAL CANAL
Railpark
CASTLE DAWSON
WOODLANDS
R408
NEWTOWN GRO
OLD GREENFIELD
RISE
WALK
SQUARE
GARDENS
GREEN
RAIL PARK
ROCKFIELD
LODGE
AVENUE
PARK
MANOR
LAWN
BEAUFIELD AVE
CRES
LAWN
CLOSE
OLD GREENFIELD
Shopping Cen
NEWTOWN CT
CLUAIN AOIBHINN
DRIVE
GROVE
MEADOWBROOK
CL
GDNS
GREENFIELD CL
NEWTOWN COURT
ROAD
DRIVE
MEADOWBROOK AVE
KINGSBURY
STRAFFAN WAY
GREENFIELD DR
MAYNOOTH PARK
LAWRENCE AVENUE
R405
COLLEGE GREEN
GREEN
MEAD
MEADOWBROOK
COURT
STRAF. CT
STRAF. DR
STRAF. GRO
STRAF. CL
GREENFIELD DRIVE
BROOKFIELD PK
MEADOWBROOK CRES
CARTON COURT
Sch
M4
BROOKFIELD AV
STRAF. GRN
STRAF. LAWN
STRAFFAN CRES
Ballygoran
GRIFFIN RATH HALL
GRIFFIN RATH ROAD
GRIFFIN RATH MANOR
CELBRIDGE ROAD
R405
Rowanstown House
Junction 7
MAYNOOTH BUSINESS CAMPUS
To Celbridge (p37)
M4
R406
Reservoirs
Ballygoran Park
A
B
C
1
2
3
4

To Maynooth (p36)
M4
Junction 6
38
R449
LEIXLIP
D
E
F
1
2
3
4
SPORTS GROUND
College
R405
MAYNOOTH ROAD
CRODAUN FOREST PARK
FB
CRO. CT
KILWOGAN MANOR
LAWNS
WOODS
CRES
DRIVE
AVENUE
WAY
CASTLE VILLAGE
RISE
WALK
THORNHILL MEADOWS
PARK
COURT
CL
BALLYORAN VIEW
HAWTHORN VIEW
ASHGROVE
THORNHILL GARDENS
Sch
THE PADDOCK
THORNHILL HEIGHTS
BEATTY GROVE
BEATTY GRO
BEATTY PARK
WILLOWBROOK PK
WILLOW LODGE
THE WALLED GARDENS
THE CROFT
THE ELMS
WOODVIEW
CHERRYWOOD
THE LAWN
CASTLE GRO
CEDARWOOD
THE AVENUE
THE WOODLANDS
THE DRIVE
THE COPPINS
THE WILLOWS
THE OAKS
ROWAN CLOSE
THE COURT
Castletown House
P
Barnhall Rugby Football Club
THE MEADOWS
THE GLADE
THE WALK
THE CRESCENT
THE COURT
MILL
W.B.GRO
WILLOW LAWNS
THE DRIVE
OLDTOWN MILL
THE CLOSE
OLDTOWN ROAD
Health Cen
TEMPLE GRO
Garda
THE PARK
WOLSTAN HAVEN ROAD
CELBRIDGE IND EST
Shopping Centre
R405
BIG LANE
CHEST. GRO
LARK MEWS
DARA COURT
DARA CT
CILLDARA CL
Veterinary Hospital
ELM PK
DARA CRES
RIVER LIFFEY
St. Wolstan's Abbey
Riding School
Shinkeen Bridge
BALLYOULSTER PARK
THE LAWN
THE VIEW
R403
THE DALE
WOLSTAN HAVEN AVE
THE GREEN
VANESSA LAWNS
VANESSA CL
THE CLOSE
OLDTOWN COTTS
CHURCH ROAD
ST. PATRICK'S PARK
PATRICK'S PARK
Sch
MAIN STREET
CELBRIDGE
CEM
DUBLIN ROAD
PRIORY WAY
PRIORY CL
PRIORY CHASE
PRIORY VIEW
PRIORY GRO
ST RAPHAEL'S AVENUE
St. Raphael's
PRIORY GREEN
RAPHAEL'S AVENUE
PRIORY CRES
PRIORY CT
PRIORY DR
THE COURTYARD
PRIORY WALK
PRIORY LODGE
OAKLEIGH
ENGLISH ROW
Community Centre
Celbridge Abbey
CLANE ROAD
FB
Rock Bridge
ST. WOLSTAN'S ABBEY
THE CRESCENT
THE VIEW
THE GLADE
THE DOWNS
THE AVENUE
THE PARK
PRIMROSE HILL
THE LITTLE GROVE
Sch
Grove House
PRIMROSE HILL
TEMPLE LAWNS
THE GROVE
SIMMONSTOWN PARK
NEWTOWN ROAD
SIMMONSTOWN MANOR
WILLOW SQUARE
WILLOW CR
WILLOW GREEN
WILLOW LAWN
WILLOW CL
WILLOW VIEW
WILLOW BROOK
WILLOW DR
WILLOW RISE
WILLOW PARK
WILLOW WAY
WILLOW AVENUE
PRIMROSE GATE
Sch
SPRINGFIELD CL
CELBRIDGE ABBEY
THE LAWNS
THE GROVE
ABBEYFARM
THE CRES
ABBEY PARK
RIVERVIEW
THE PARK
THE DRIVE
Simmonstown House
TEMPLE MANOR
CALENDARS MILL
The Cottage
CELBRIDGE G.A.A.
Elm Hall
ABBEY GRN
RIVER LAWNS
ABBEY CT
THE DRIVE
THE LAWNS
THE COURT
THE CLOSE
THE CRES

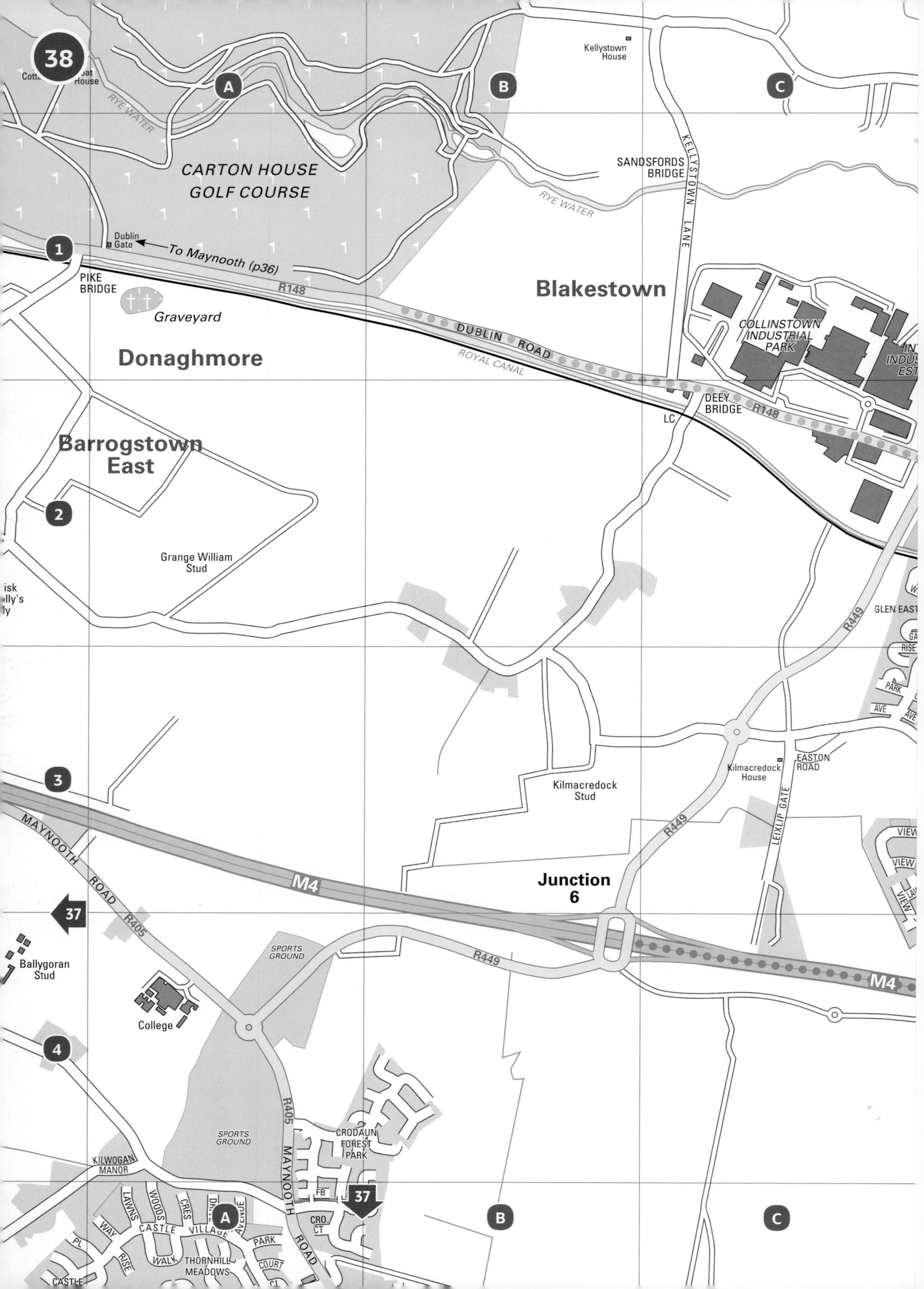

Kellystown House
CARTON HOUSE GOLF COURSE
RYE WATER
SANDSFORDS BRIDGE
KELLYSTOWN LANE
Dublin Gate
To Maynooth (p36)
PIKE BRIDGE
Graveyard
R148
Blakestown
COLLINSTOWN INDUSTRIAL PARK
DUBLIN ROAD
ROYAL CANAL
Donaghmore
DEEY BRIDGE
LC
Barrogstown East
Grange William Stud
R449
GLEN EASTON
RISE
PARK
AVE
Kilmacredock House
EASTON ROAD
Kilmacredock Stud
LEIXLIP GATE
VIEW
MAYNOOTH ROAD
M4
Junction 6
R405
SPORTS GROUND
Ballygoran Stud
College
CRODAUN FOREST PARK
KILWOGAN MANOR
LAWNS
WOODS
CRES
AVENUE
WAY
CASTLE VILLAGE
PARK
PL
RISE
WALK
THORNHILL MEADOWS
COURT
CASTLE
FB
CRO. CT

37
37

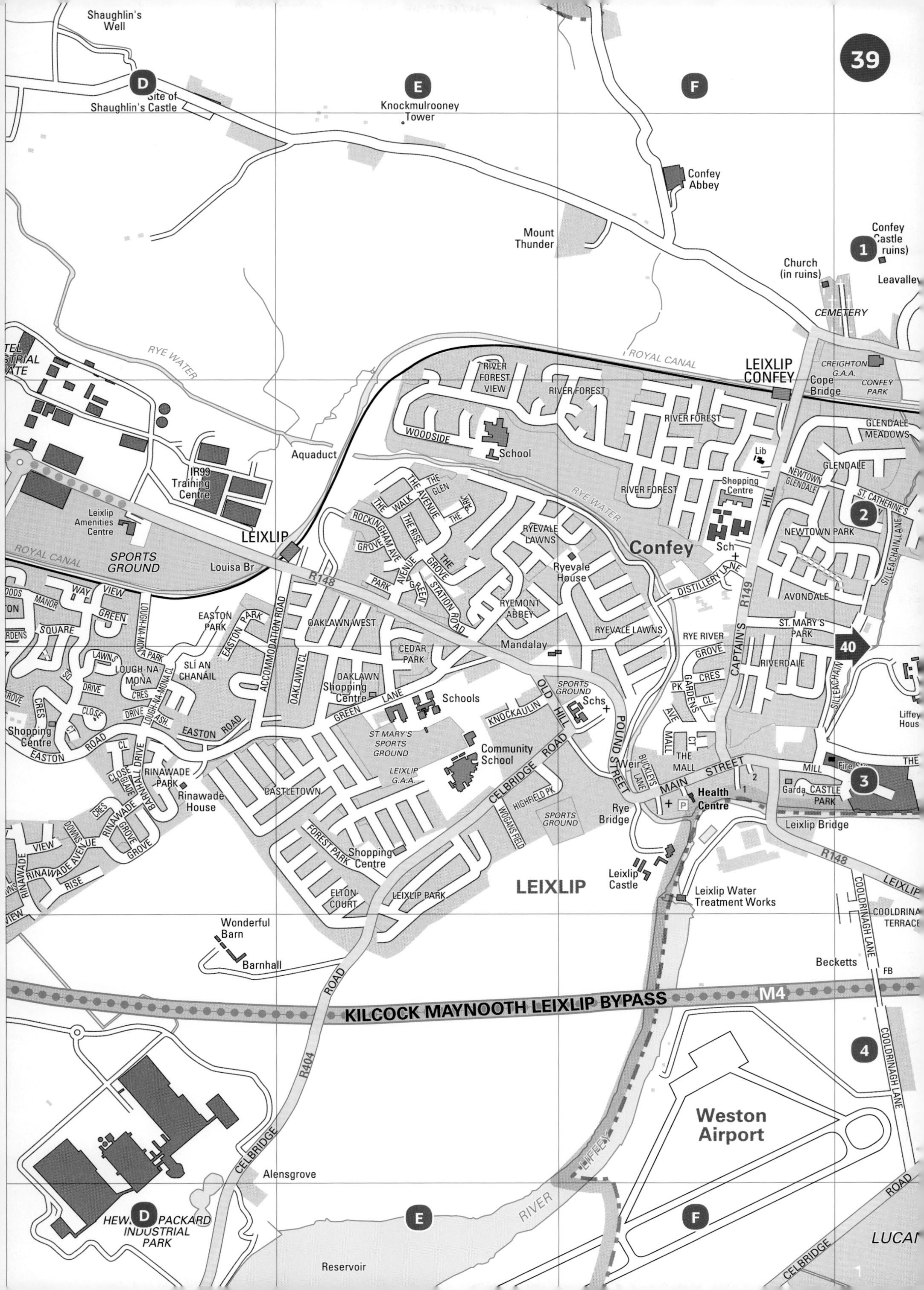
Shaughlin's Well
Site of Shaughlin's Castle
Knockmulrooney Tower
Confey Abbey
Mount Thunder
Confey Castle (ruins)
Church (in ruins)
Leavalley
CEMETERY
RYE WATER
ROYAL CANAL
LEIXLIP CONFEY
CREIGHTON G.A.A.
CONFEY PARK
Cope Bridge
RIVER FOREST VIEW
RIVER FOREST
WOODSIDE
School
GLENDALE MEADOWS
GLENDALE
NEWTOWN GLENDALE
ST. CATHERINE'S
Aquaduct
IR99 Training Centre
Leixlip Amenities Centre
LEIXLIP
SPORTS GROUND
Louisa Br
R148
Shopping Centre
Lib
RIVER FOREST
NEWTOWN PARK
Confey
Sch
RYEVALE LAWNS
Ryevale House
DISTILLERY LANE
HILL
R149
CAPTAIN'S
AVONDALE
ST. MARY'S PARK
40
THE GLEN
THE AVENUE
THE WALK
THE PARK
ROCKINGHAM AVE
THE RISE
GROVE
THE GROVE
AVENUE
GREEN
STATION ROAD
PARK
RYEMONT ABBEY
RYEVALE LAWNS
RYE RIVER GROVE
RIVERDALE
SILLEACHAIN LANE
SILLEACHAIN
Liffey House
MANOR
WAY
VIEW
GREEN
SQUARE
LOUGH-NA-MONA PARK
EASTON PARK
EASTON PARK
ACCOMMODATION ROAD
OAKLAWN WEST
CEDAR PARK
Mandalay
LAWNS
LOUGH-NA-MONA
SLÍ AN CHANÁIL
OAKLAWN CL
OAKLAWN Shopping Centre
GREEN LANE
Schools
OLD HILL
SPORTS GROUND
Schs
POUND STREET
KNOCKAULIN
PK GARDENS
CRES
CL
AVE
MALL
CT
THE MALL
MAIN STREET
Weir
BUCKLEYS LANE
Health Centre
MILL
Fire Sta
THE
3
Garda
CASTLE PARK
Leixlip Bridge
SQ
DRIVE
CRES
CLOSE
DRIVE
ASH
LOUGH-NA-MONA CL
EASTON ROAD
Shopping Centre
EASTON
ROAD
CT
CL
CLOSE
GLADE
RINAWADE PARK
BAWNOGUE DRIVE
Rinawade House
ST MARY'S SPORTS GROUND
Community School
LEIXLIP G.A.A.
CASTLETOWN
CELBRIDGE ROAD
HIGHFIELD PK
WOGANSFIELD
SPORTS GROUND
Rye Bridge
R148
LEIXLIP
CRES
RINAWADE
GROVE
DOWNS
VIEW
AVENUE
RINAWADE
GROVE
RISE
VIEW
FOREST PARK
Shopping Centre
ELTON COURT
LEIXLIP PARK
LEIXLIP
Leixlip Castle
Leixlip Water Treatment Works
COOLDRINAGH TERRACE
COOLDRINAGH LANE
Wonderful Barn
Barnhall
ROAD
Becketts
FB
M4
KILCOCK MAYNOOTH LEIXLIP BYPASS
R404
COOLDRINAGH LANE
Weston Airport
CELBRIDGE
Alensgrove
RIVER LIFFEY
HEWLETT PACKARD INDUSTRIAL PARK
Reservoir
ROAD
CELBRIDGE
LUCAN
D
E
F
1
2
4

A
B
C
22
CONFEY PARK
Westmanstown Park
Confey Castle (in ruins)
Church (in ruins)
Leavalley
SPORTS GROUND
CEMETERY
Confey House
Allenswood House
LEIXLIP CONFEY
CREIGHTON G.A.A.
CONFEY PARK
Cope Bridge
Royal Canal Amenity Group
R149
GLENDALE MEADOWS
GLENDALE
NEWTOWN GLENDALE
ST. CATHERINE'S VIEW
Collins Bridge
ROYAL CANAL
NEWTOWN PARK
SILLEACHAIN LANE
AVONDALE
ST. MARY'S PARK
39
RIVERDALE
St. Catherines Park Hotel
St. Catherines
Liffey Valley House Hotel
Leixlip Wastewater Treatment Works
THE BLACK AVENUE
Fire Sta
MILL LANE BUSINESS PARK
LEIXLIP
CASTLE PARK
Leixlip Bridge
LARAGHCON
R148
LEIXLIP ROAD
COOLDRINAGH LANE
COOLDRINAGH TERRACE
Club House
LIFFEY VALLEY GOLF COURSE
LIFFEY VALLEY PARK
WEIRVIEW
BARNHILL CROSS RD
Weir
Becketts
FB
M4
Weir
Dunavarra
MAIN ST
Junction 5
N4 LEIXLIP ROAD
WESTON CRESCENT
WESTON DR
WESTON PARK
WESTFIELD AVE
WESTON WAY
WESTON
WESTON HEIGHTS
KEW PARK CRES
KEW PARK
KEW PARK AVE
MEADOW COURT
THE CRESCENT
RIVER LIFFEY
Lucan House
GRAVE YARD
SARSFIELD CT
Garda
PRIMROSE LANE
ADAMSTOWN ROAD
R121
R835
CELBRIDGE ROAD
CNOC AOIBHEAN
R403
MILLSTREAM ROAD
OLD CORNMILL RD
WOODVIEW
ARDEEVIN DRIVE
ARDEEVIN AVENUE
ARDEEVIN CT
Shopping Centre
LUCAN
Mount Zion
VESEY PARK
50
A
B
C
Club House
LUCAN GOLF COURSE
WOODVIEW HEIGHTS
DODSBORO ROAD
CHERRY LAWNS
GREEN
HILLCREST DRIVE
HILLCREST CLOSE
PO
Sch
AIRLIE HEIGHTS
N4
HILLCREST

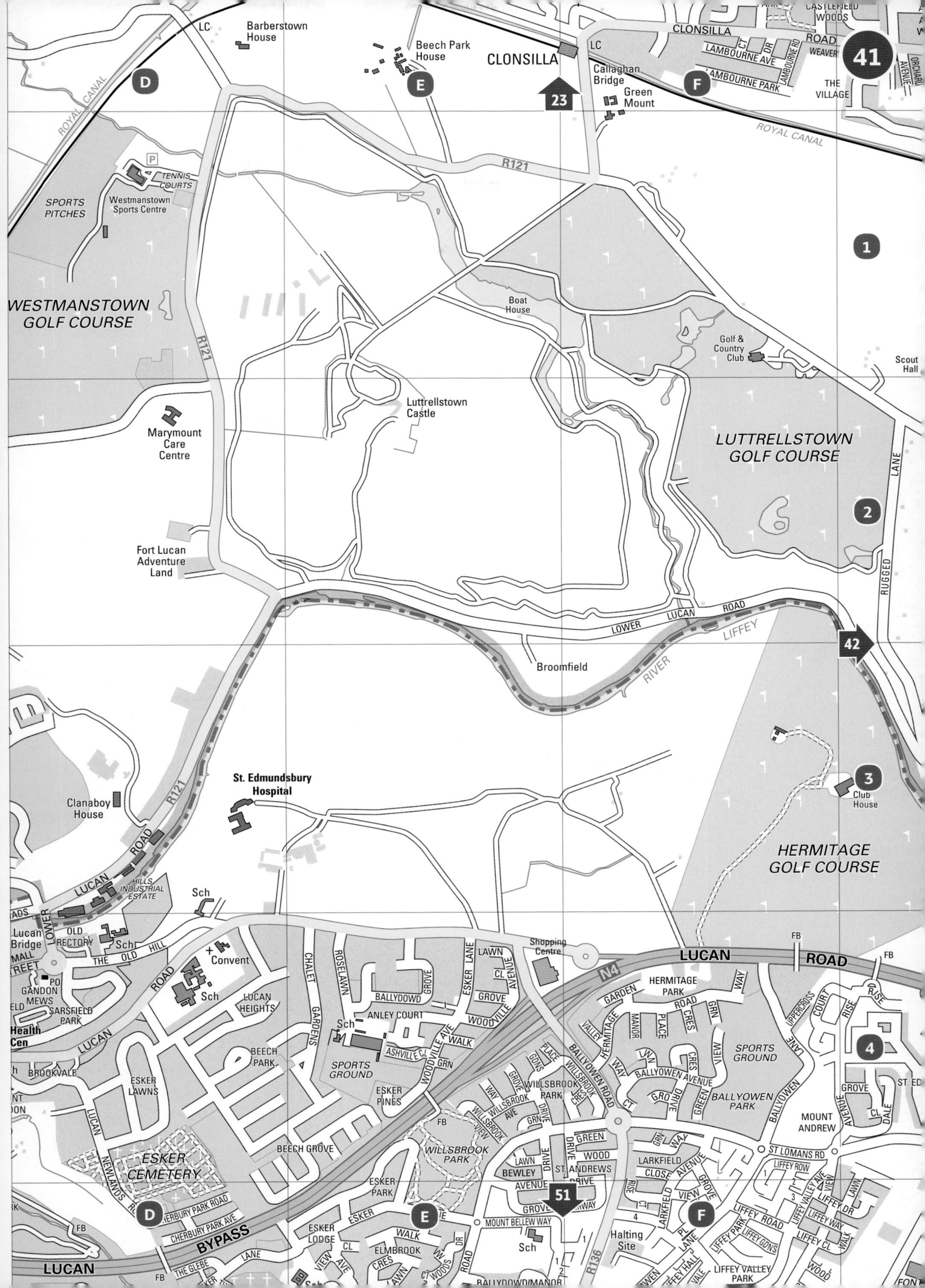
LC
Barberstown House
Beech Park House
CLONSILLA
LC
Callaghan Bridge
Green Mount
CLONSILLA
ROAD
LAMBOURNE AVE
CT
DR
LAMBOURNE RD
LAMBOURNE PARK
WEAVER'S
CASTLEFIELD WOODS
THE VILLAGE
ORCHARD AVENUE
ROYAL CANAL
ROYAL CANAL
D
E
F
23
R121
P
TENNIS COURTS
SPORTS PITCHES
Westmanstown Sports Centre
WESTMANSTOWN GOLF COURSE
R121
1
Boat House
Golf & Country Club
Scout Hall
Luttrellstown Castle
Marymount Care Centre
LUTTRELLSTOWN GOLF COURSE
LANE
RUGGED
2
Fort Lucan Adventure Land
LOWER LUCAN ROAD
RIVER LIFFEY
Broomfield
42
3
Club House
St. Edmundsbury Hospital
Clanaboy House
R121
LUCAN ROAD
HILLS INDUSTRIAL ESTATE
HERMITAGE GOLF COURSE
Sch
Lucan Bridge
LOWER
OLD RECTORY
Sch
THE OLD HILL
MAIN STREET
PO
GANDON MEWS
SARSFIELD PARK
Health Cen
Convent
Sch
ROAD
LUCAN HEIGHTS
LUCAN
BROOKVALE
CHALET GARDENS
ROSELAWN
BALLYDOWD GROVE
ESKER LANE
LAWN CL
GROVE
AVENUE
WOODVILLE
ANLEY COURT
Sch
ASHVILLE CL
WALK
WOODVILLE AVE
GRN
SPORTS GROUND
BEECH PARK
ESKER LAWNS
ESKER PINES
Shopping Centre
FB
LUCAN ROAD
N4
FB
HERMITAGE PARK
GARDEN
ROAD
WAY
VALLEY
HERMITAGE
MANOR
PLACE
CRES
GRN
UPPERCROSS
COURT
RISE
RISE
RD
SPORTS GROUND
LANE
VIEW
CRES
BALLYOWEN AVENUE
BALLYOWEN PARK
BALLYOWEN
4
GROVE
AVENUE
CL
DALE
ST. ED
MOUNT ANDREW
WAY
LWN
CT
GRO
DRIVE
GREEN
BALLYOWEN ROAD
WILLSBROOK CRES
WILLSBROOK PARK
PLACE
GDNS
GROVE
WAY
WILLSBROOK AVE
DRIVE
GRN
WILLSBROOK VIEW
WILLSBROOK PARK
FB
LUCAN
ESKER CEMETERY
NEWLANDS RD
BEECH GROVE
CHERBURY PARK ROAD
CHERBURY PARK AVE
D
FB
BYPASS
LUCAN
THE GLEBE
LANE
FB
ESKER PARK
ESKER
E
ESKER LODGE
VIEW
AVE
CL
WALK
ELMBROOK CRES
LAWN
CT WOODS
ROAD
DR
MOUNT BELLEW WAY
Sch
BALLYDOWD MANOR
LAWN
BEWLEY
DRIVE
ST. ANDREWS
AVENUE
DRIVE
GREEN
WOOD
GROVE
51
WAY
R136
Halting Site
LARKFIELD
CLOSE
AVENUE
RISE
CT
LARKFIELD
VIEW
GROVE
GRN
WAY
F
PL
LANE
LIFFEY HALL
VALE
LIFFEY VALLEY PARK
LIFFEY PARK
LIFFEY GDNS
LIFFEY ROAD
ST LOMANS RD
LIFFEY ROW
LIFFEY VALLEY AVE
VIEW
LIFFEY WAY
LIFFEY DR
LAWN
LIFFEY CL
WALK
WOOD
FONT

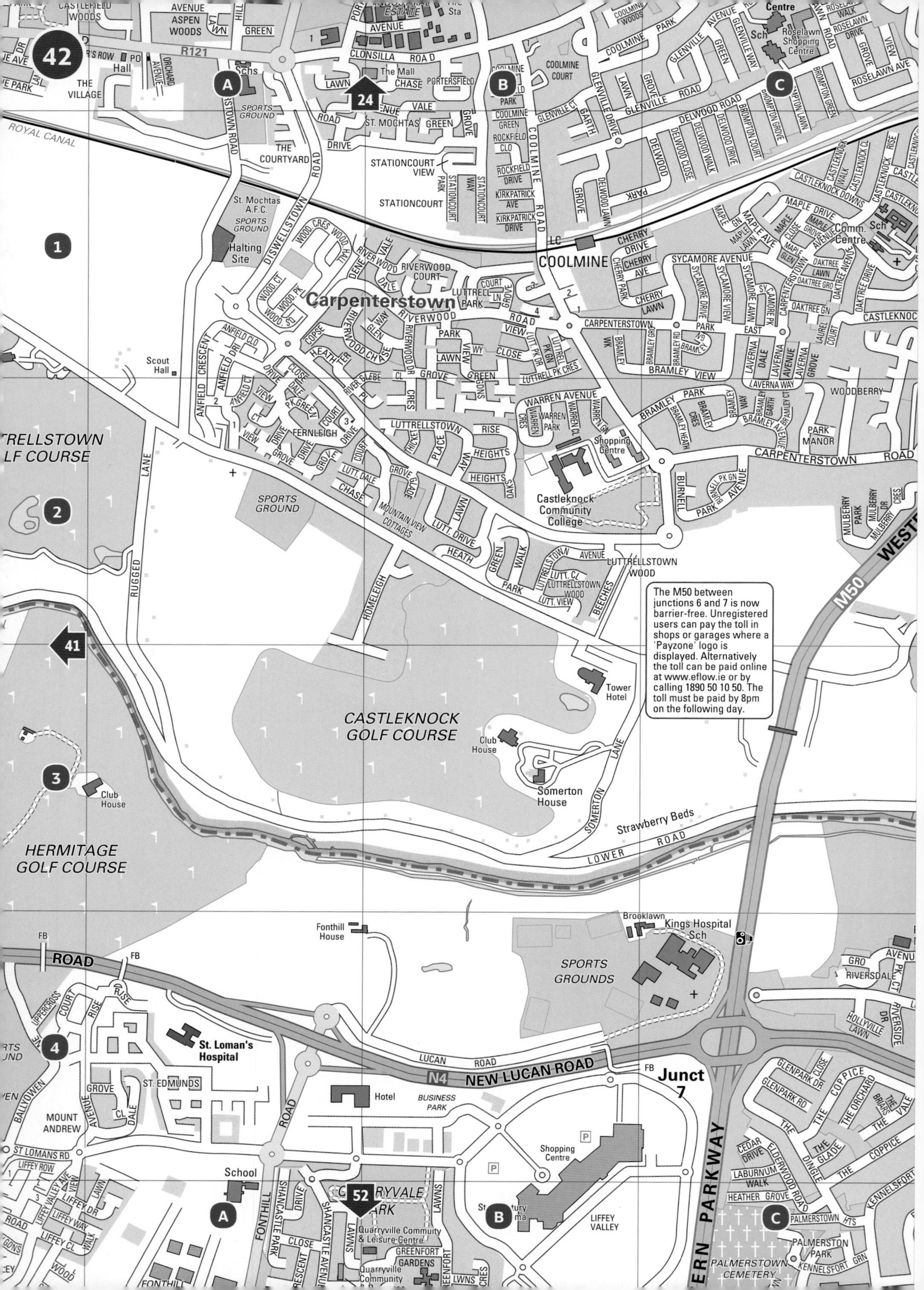
CASTLEFIELD WOODS
AVENUE
ASPEN WOODS
LAWN
HILL
GREEN
R121
CLONSILLA ROAD
THE VILLAGE
Hall
PO
ORCHARD AVENUE
Schs
A
B
C
The Mall
PORTERSFIELD
CHASE
LAWN
24
VALE
ST. MOCHTAS
GREEN
DRIVE
ROAD
GROVE
SPORTS GROUND
ROYAL CANAL
THE COURTYARD
STATIONCOURT VIEW
STATIONCOURT
STATIONCOURT PARK
STATIONCOURT WAY
COOLMINE PARK
COOLMINE GREEN
COOLMINE COURT
COOLMINE WOODS
COOLMINE
ROCKFIELD CLO
ROCKFIELD DRIVE
KIRKPATRICK AVE
KIRKPATRICK DRIVE
COOLMINE ROAD
GLENVILLE CT
GLENVILLE GARTH
GLENVILLE DRIVE
GLENVILLE ROAD
GLENVILLE AVENUE
GLENVILLE WAY
GLENVILLE GREEN
GROVE
LAWN
PARK
DELWOOD ROAD
DELWOOD
DELWOOD CLOSE
DELWOOD WALK
DELWOOD DRIVE
DELWOOD PARK
DELWOOD LAWN
DELWOOD GROVE
BROMPTON GROVE
BROMPTON COURT
BROMPTON LAWN
BROMPTON GREEN
ROSELAWN ROAD
ROSELAWN WALK
ROSELAWN DRIVE
ROSELAWN GROVE
ROSELAWN AVE
ROSELAWN VIEW
Roselawn Shopping Centre
Sch
Centre
CASTLEKNOCK DOWNS
CASTLEKNOCK WALK
CASTLEKNOCK CL
CASTLEKNOCK RISE
St. Mochtas A.F.C.
SPORTS GROUND
Halting Site
DISWELLSTOWN ROAD
1
LC
COOLMINE
CHERRY DRIVE
CHERRY AVE
CHERRY PARK
CHERRY LAWN
MAPLE DRIVE
MAPLE GN
MAPLE AVE
MAPLE LAWN
MAPLE CLOSE
MAPLE GROVE
MAPLE GLEN
MAPLE AVENUE
Comm. Centre
Sch
OAKTREE LAWN
OAKTREE GRO
OAKTREE AVENUE
OAKTREE DRIVE
OAKTREE GN
SYCAMORE AVENUE
SYCAMORE DRIVE
SYCAMORE VIEW
SYCAMORE LAWN
SYCAMORE PK
CARPENTERSTOWN PARK EAST
CARPENTERSTOWN AVENUE
LAUREL COURT
CASTLEKNOCK
WOOD CRES
WOOD HALL
WOOD CT
WOOD PK
WOOD SQ
DENE
VALE
RIVERWOOD
RIVERWOOD COURT
DALE
LUTTRELL PARK
COURT
LN
GROVE
Carpenterstown
RIVERWOOD ROAD
RIVERWOOD GLEN
RIVERWOOD WAY
RIVERWOOD CHASE
RIVERWOOD DR
COPSE
HEATH
TER
ANFIELD CLO
ANFIELD DRI
ANFIELD CRESCENT
ANFIELD CT
ANFIELD VIEW
Scout Hall
PARK
VIEW
LAWN
WY
CLOSE
LUTT. PK DR
LUTTRELL PK GN
LUTTRELL PK CRES
GROVE
GREEN
GDNS
CL
CRES
GLEBE
RIVER
PL
BRAMLEY WK
BRAMLEY GRO
BRAMLEY RD
BRAMLEY GN
BRAMLEY VIEW
BRAMLEY PARK
BRAMLEY HEATH
BRAMLEY CRES
BRAMLEY WAY
BRAMLEY GARTH
BRAMLEY CT
BRAMLEY AVENUE
LAVERNA DALE
LAVERNA AVENUE
LAVERNA GROVE
LAVERNA WAY
WOODBERRY
PARK MANOR
CARPENTERSTOWN ROAD
DRIVE
CLOSE
DALE
VIEW
PK GREEN
COURT
DRIVE
CT
GROVE
FERNLEIGH
WARREN AVENUE
WARREN CRES
WARREN PARK
WARREN CL
WARREN GN
LUTTRELLSTOWN
THICKET
PLACE
WAY
RISE
HEIGHTS
OAKS
Shopping Centre
Castleknock Community College
BURNELL
BURNELL PK GN
BURNELL PARK AVENUE
MULBERRY PARK
MULBERRY DR
MULBERRY CRES
LUTTRELLSTOWN GOLF COURSE
LANE
RUGGED
2
SPORTS GROUND
LUTT. DALE
CHASE
GROVE
GLADE
LAWN
LUTT. DRIVE
HEATH
MOUNTAIN VIEW COTTAGES
GREEN
WALK
PARK
LUTTRELLSTOWN AVENUE
LUTT. CL
LUTTRELLSTOWN WOOD
LUTT. VIEW
BEECHES
LUTTRELLSTOWN WOOD
HOMELEIGH
M50
WESTERN PARKWAY
The M50 between junctions 6 and 7 is now barrier-free. Unregistered users can pay the toll in shops or garages where a 'Payzone' logo is displayed. Alternatively the toll can be paid online at www.eflow.ie or by calling 1890 50 10 50. The toll must be paid by 8pm on the following day.
41
Tower Hotel
CASTLEKNOCK GOLF COURSE
Club House
Somerton House
SOMERTON LANE
3
Club House
HERMITAGE GOLF COURSE
Strawberry Beds
LOWER ROAD
Fonthill House
Brooklawn
Kings Hospital Sch
SPORTS GROUNDS
FB
ROAD
FB
GRO
AVENUE
PK CT
RIVERSDALE
HOLLYVILLE LAWN
DR
RIVERSIDE
UPPERCROSS
COURT
RISE
RISE
4
SPORTS GROUND
St. Loman's Hospital
LUCAN ROAD
N4 NEW LUCAN ROAD
FB
Junct 7
GLENPARK DR
GLENPARK CLOSE
GLENPARK RD
THE COPPICE
THE ORCHARD
THE BRIARS
THE VALE
THE DINGLE
THE GLADE
THE COPPICE
BALLYOWEN
MOUNT ANDREW
GROVE
CL
DALE
AVENUE
ST. EDMUNDS
Hotel
BUSINESS PARK
ROAD
Shopping Centre
P
P
ST LOMANS RD
LIFFEY ROW
LIFFEY VALLEY AVE
LIFFEY VIEW
LIFFEY DR
LIFFEY WAY
LIFFEY LAWN
LIFFEY CL
LIFFEY WALK
LIFFEY WOOD
LIFFEY ROAD
School
A
FONTHILL
SHANCASTLE DRIVE
SHANCASTLE PARK
SHANCASTLE AVENUE
CLOSE
52
QUARRYVALE PARK
Quarryville Community & Leisure Centre
GREENFORT GARDENS
GREENFORT
LAWNS
CRES
LWNS
Quarryville Community
B
LIFFEY VALLEY
CEDAR DRIVE
ELDERWOOD ROAD
LABURNUM WALK
HEATHER GROVE
C
PALMERSTOWN HTS
PALMERSTOWN PARK
KENNELSFORT GRN
KENNELSFORT
PALMERSTOWN CEMETERY

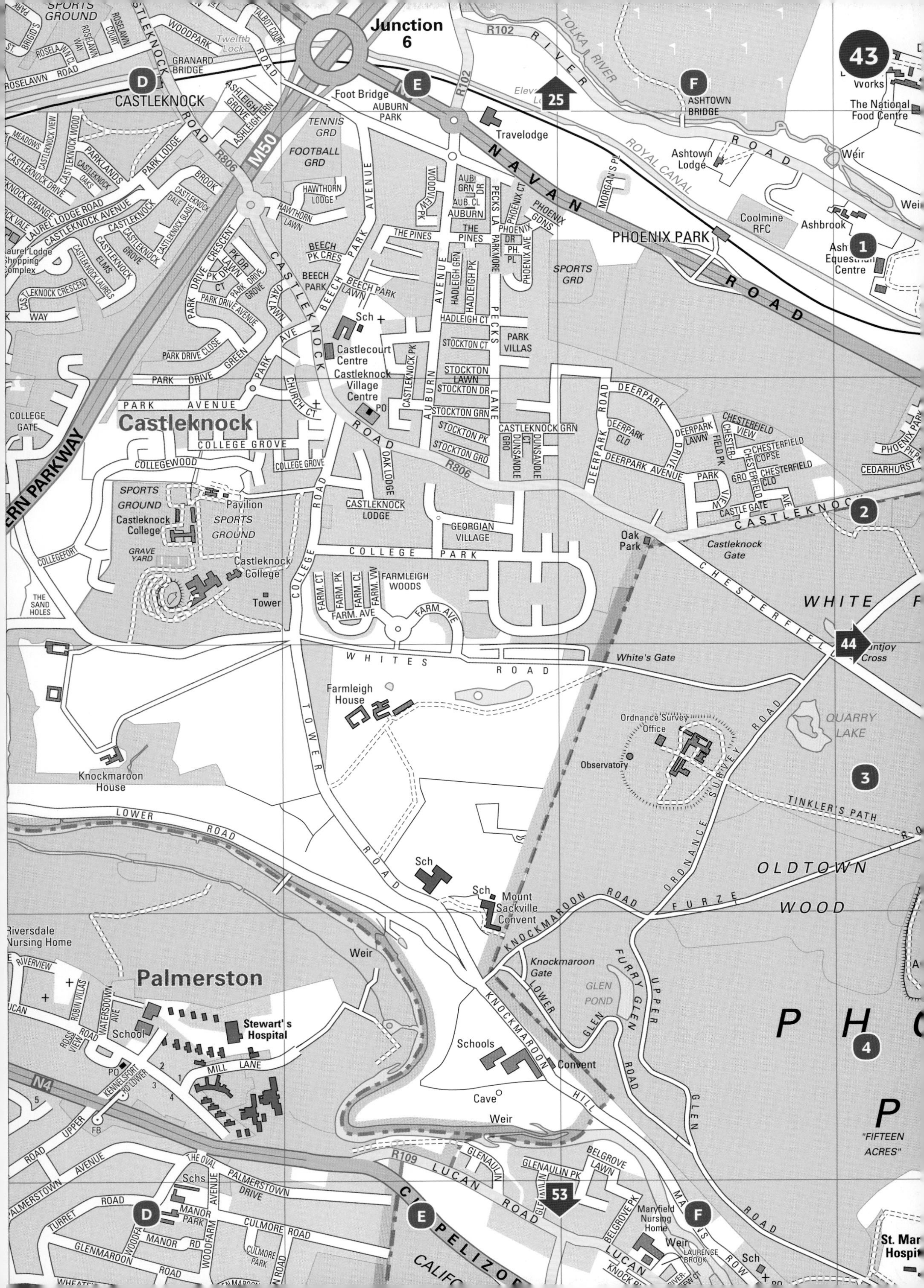
43
Junction 6
SPORTS GROUND
ST. BRIGID'S
ROSELAWN COURT
ROSELAWN WAY
ROSELAWN CL.
ROSELAWN ROAD
WOODPARK
Twelfth Lock
GRANARD BRIDGE
TALBOT COURT
ROAD
D
CASTLEKNOCK
CASTLEKNOCK ROAD
ASHLEIGH GROVE
ASHLEIGH GRN
ASHLEIGH GRO
E
Foot Bridge
AUBURN PARK
R102
RIVER
TOLKA RIVER
25
F
ASHTOWN BRIDGE
Works
The National Food Centre
Travelodge
TENNIS GRD
FOOTBALL GRD
M50
R806
MEADOWS
CASTLEKNOCK VIEW
CASTLEKNOCK WOOD
PARKLANDS
CASTLEKNOCK OAKS
CASTLEKNOCK DRIVE
PARK LODGE
BROOK
KNOCK GRANGE
LAUREL LODGE ROAD
CASTLEKNOCK AVENUE
CASTLEKNOCK DALE
CASTLEKNOCK GLADE
HAWTHORN LODGE
HAWTHORN LAWN
AVENUE
WOODVIEW PK
AUB. GRN
AUB. DR
AUB. CL
AUBURN
PECKS LA
PHOENIX CT
PHOENIX GDNS
NAVAN
MORGAN'S PL
ROYAL CANAL
ROAD
Ashtown Lodge
Weir
Coolmine RFC
Ashbrook
PHOENIX PARK
1
Ashtown Equestrian Centre
ROAD
CK VALE
Laurel Lodge Shopping Complex
CASTLEKNOCK GROVE
CASTLEKNOCK ELMS
CASTLEKNOCK LAURELS
CASTLEKNOCK CRESCENT
WAY
PARK DRIVE CRESCENT
PK DR LAWN
PK DR CT
PARK DRIVE GROVE
PARK DRIVE AVENUE
OAKLAWN
CASTLEKNOCK
BEECH PK CRES
BEECH PARK
BEECH PARK LAWN
THE PINES
PARKMORE
DR
PH. PL
PHOENIX AVE
HADLEIGH GRN
HADLEIGH PK
HADLEIGH CT
SPORTS GRD
Sch
PECKS LANE
PARK VILLAS
PARK DRIVE CLOSE
GREEN
PARK DRIVE
AVE
PARK
CHURCH CT
Castlecourt Centre
Castleknock Village Centre
PO
CASTLEKNOCK PK
AUBURN
STOCKTON CT
STOCKTON LAWN
STOCKTON DR
STOCKTON GRN
STOCKTON PK
STOCKTON GRO
CASTLEKNOCK GRN
DUNSANDLE GRO
DUNSANDLE CT
DEERPARK ROAD
DEERPARK
DEERPARK CLO
DEERPARK LAWN
DRIVE
CHESTERFIELD VIEW
CHESTER. FIELD PK
CHESTERFIELD COPSE
CHESTERFIELD GRO
CHESTERFIELD CLO
DEERPARK AVENUE
PARK VIEW
CASTLE GATE
AVE
PHOENIX PARK
CEDARHURST
PARK AVENUE
Castleknock
COLLEGE GATE
COLLEGE GROVE
COLLEGEWOOD
COLLEGE GROVE
OAK LODGE
ROAD
R806
ERN PARKWAY
SPORTS GROUND
Pavilion
Castleknock College
SPORTS GROUND
CASTLEKNOCK LODGE
GEORGIAN VILLAGE
CASTLEKNOCK
2
Oak Park
Castleknock Gate
GRAVE YARD
Castleknock College
COLLEGEFORT
COLLEGE PARK
COLLEGE
FARM. CT
FARM. PK
FARM. CL
FARM. VW
FARMLEIGH WOODS
FARM. AVE
FARM. AVE
Tower
THE SAND HOLES
CHESTERFIELD
WHITE
44
Mountjoy Cross
WHITES ROAD
White's Gate
Farmleigh House
TOWER
Ordnance Survey Office
Observatory
SURVEY ROAD
QUARRY LAKE
3
Knockmaroon House
TINKLER'S PATH
LOWER ROAD
ROAD
ORDNANCE
OLDTOWN
WOOD
Sch
Sch
Mount Sackville Convent
KNOCKMAROON ROAD
FURZE
Riversdale Nursing Home
Weir
RIVERVIEW
Palmerston
ROBIN VILLAS
WATERSDOWN AVE
ROSS VIEW
ROAD
UCAN
School
Stewart's Hospital
MILL LANE
Knockmaroon Gate
LOWER GLEN
GLEN POND
FURRY GLEN
UPPER GLEN ROAD
KNOCKMAROON HILL
Schools
Convent
P H
4
N4
PO
KENNELSPORT RD LOWER
FB
UPPER
Cave
Weir
P
"FIFTEEN ACRES"
R109
GLENAULIN
GLENAULIN PK
BELGROVE LAWN
LUCAN ROAD
53
ROAD
AVENUE
PALMERSTOWN AVENUE
THE OVAL
Schs
AVENUE
PALMERSTOWN DRIVE
D
MANOR PARK
TURRET ROAD
CULMORE ROAD
E
CHAPELIZOD
F
Maryfield Nursing Home
BELGROVE PK
Weir
LAURENCE BROOK
ROW
Sch
PO
St. Mar Hospit
GLENMAROON
MANOR RD
WOODFARM AVENUE
CULMORE PARK
LUCAN
KNOCK
CALIFO
ROAD

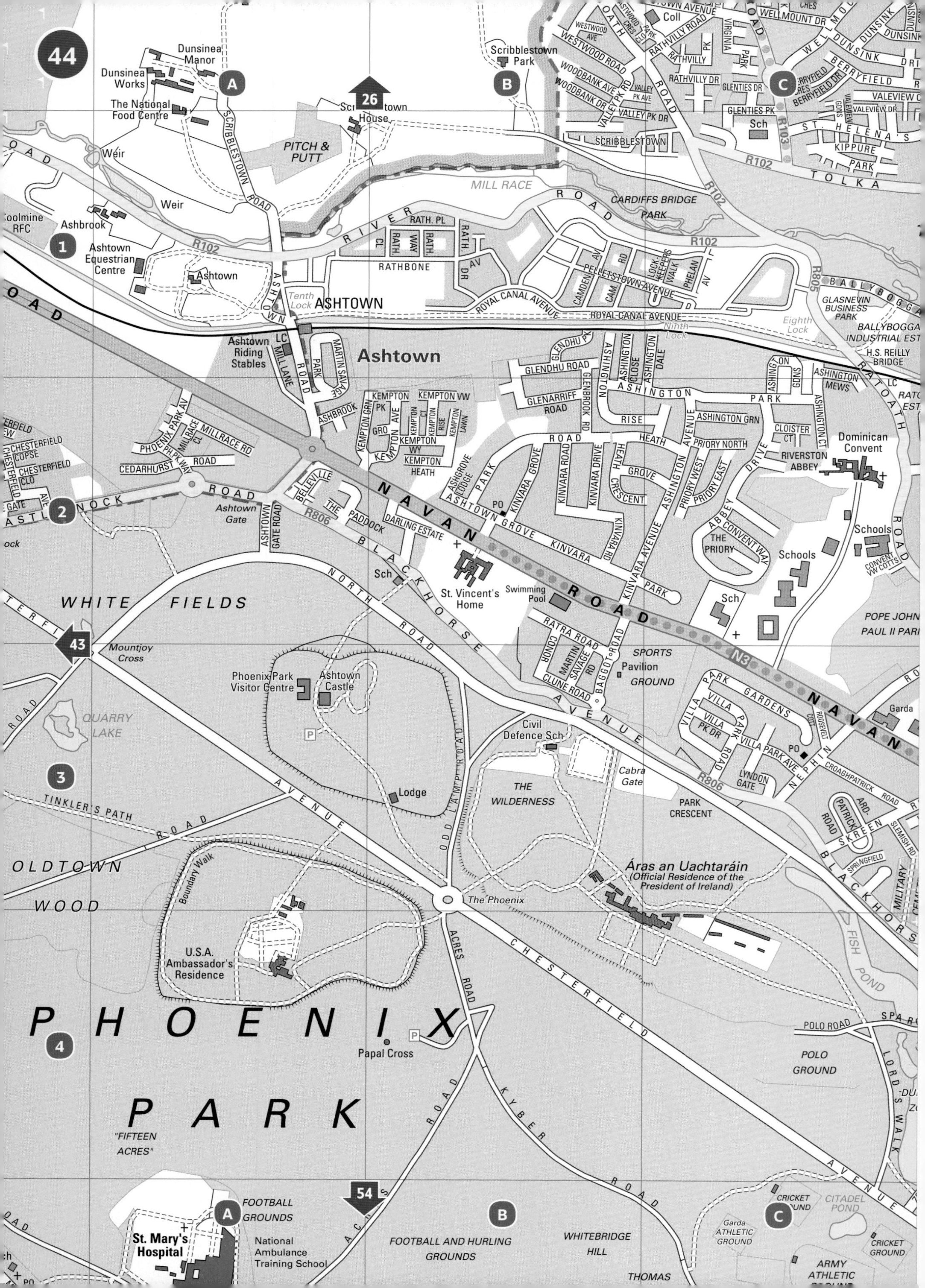
Dunsinea Manor
Dunsinea Works
The National Food Centre
Scribblestown House
Scribblestown Park
SCRIBBLESTOWN ROAD
PITCH & PUTT
26
MILL RACE
Weir
Coolmine RFC
Ashbrook
Ashtown Equestrian Centre
Ashtown
R102
RIVER ROAD
RATH. PL
RATHBONE
CARDIFFS BRIDGE PARK
PELLETSTOWN AVENUE
ROYAL CANAL AVENUE
Tenth Lock
ASHTOWN
Ninth Lock
Eighth Lock
GLASNEVIN BUSINESS PARK
BALLYBOGGAN INDUSTRIAL EST
H.S. REILLY BRIDGE
WESTWOOD ROAD
WOODBANK AVE
WOODBANK DR
VALLEY PK DR
RATHVILLY ROAD
RATHVILLY DR
GLENTIES DR
GLENTIES PK
SCRIBBLESTOWN
WELLMOUNT DR
DUNSINK
BERRYFIELD DR
VALEVIEW DR
ST. HELENA'S
KIPPURE PARK
TOLKA
R103
R805
Ashtown Riding Stables
MILL LANE
Ashtown
MARTIN SAVAGE PARK
GLENDHU ROAD
GLENARRIFF ROAD
ASHINGTON PARK
ASHINGTON GRN
ASHINGTON MEWS
RATOATH ROAD
KEMPTON GRN
KEMPTON AVE
KEMPTON HEATH
HEATH ROAD
PRIORY NORTH
PRIORY WEST
PRIORY EAST
CLOISTER CT
RIVERSTON ABBEY
Dominican Convent
PHOENIX PARK AVE
MILLRACE RD
CHESTERFIELD
CEDARHURST ROAD
CASTLEKNOCK ROAD
Ashtown Gate
ASHTOWN GATE ROAD
R806
THE PADDOCK
DARLING ESTATE
NAVAN ROAD
ASHTOWN GROVE
KINVARA PARK
KINVARA AVENUE
KINVARA GROVE
KINVARA ROAD
KINVARA DRIVE
HEATH CRESCENT
ABBEY CONVENT WAY
THE PRIORY
Schools
St. Vincent's Home
Swimming Pool
Sch
PO
WHITE FIELDS
43
Mountjoy Cross
NORTH ROAD
BLACKHORSE AVENUE
RATRA ROAD
CONOR
MARTIN SAVAGE RD
BAGGOT ROAD
CLUNE ROAD
SPORTS GROUND
Pavilion
POPE JOHN PAUL II PARK
N3
VILLA PARK GARDENS
VILLA PARK ROAD
VILLA PARK AVE
LYNDON GATE
NEPHIN
CROAGHPATRICK ROAD
SKREEN
Garda
Phoenix Park Visitor Centre
Ashtown Castle
QUARRY LAKE
Civil Defence Sch
Cabra Gate
THE WILDERNESS
PARK CRESCENT
Lodge
ODD LAMP ROAD
TINKLER'S PATH
OLDTOWN WOOD
Boundary Walk
The Phoenix
Áras an Uachtaráin
(Official Residence of the President of Ireland)
U.S.A. Ambassador's Residence
CHESTERFIELD AVENUE
ACRES ROAD
FISH POND
MILITARY
PHOENIX PARK
Papal Cross
"FIFTEEN ACRES"
POLO ROAD
POLO GROUND
LORD'S WALK
KYBER ROAD
54
FOOTBALL GROUNDS
St. Mary's Hospital
National Ambulance Training School
FOOTBALL AND HURLING GROUNDS
WHITEBRIDGE HILL
THOMAS
Garda ATHLETIC GROUND
CRICKET GROUND
CITADEL POND
ARMY ATHLETIC
1
2
3
4
A
B
C

45
27
46
55
84
D
E
F
1
2
3
4
Janelle Shopping Centre
PO
Schools
ST. HELENA'S DRIVE
HAZELCROFT RD
FAIRLAWN ROAD
GORTMORE DR
GORTMORE AVE
GORTMORE ROAD
CLOONLARA RD
CLOON CRES
TOLKA VALLEY GREEN
BARNAMORE CRES
BARNAMORE GRO
VALLEY ROAD
R102
FINGLAS BUSINESS PARK
TOLKA VALLEY PARK
TOLKA RIVER
FINGLASWOOD BRIDGE
BALLYBOGGAN ROAD
GLASNEVIN COURT
GLASNEVIN WOODS
TOLKA VALLEY BUSINESS PARK
TOLKA VALLEY INDUSTRIAL ESTATE
DUBLIN INDUSTRIAL ESTATE
LAGAN ROAD
BOYNE RD
BANN RD
NORE ROAD
BARROW ROAD
SLANEY ROAD
SLANEY CLOSE
BLACKWATER ROAD
MOYLE ROAD
LEE ROAD
BROOMBRIDGE INDUSTRIAL ESTATE
BROOMBRIDGE
WM ROWAN HAMILTON BRIDGE
Seventh Lock
ROYAL CANAL
CLAREMONT COURT
THE WILLOWS
N2 FINGLAS ROAD
PROSPECT CEMETERY
The O'Connell Circle
O'Connells Monument
BOTANIC GARDENS
Weir
GLASNEVIN BRIDGE
FAIRWAYS PARK
FAIRWAYS GROVE
GLENHILL AVENUE
GLENHILL GRO
GLENHILL CT
GRIFFITH DRIVE
GRIFFITH PARADE
GLASNAMANA ROAD
GLASMEEN ROAD
GLASILAWN ROAD
GLASILAWN AVE
GRIFFITH AVENUE
GLASNEVIN DOWNS
NORTHLAND DRIVE
CREMORE CRES
CREMORE DR
Frank Cooke Park (Tolka Rovers A.F.C)
CREMORE ROAD
FINGLAS ROAD OLD
CREMORE LAWN
VIOLET HILL RD
VIOLET HILL PARK
VIOLET HILL DRIVE
RIVERBANK HALL
CLAREMONT DRIVE
FITZ-MAURICE ROAD
Nursing Home
St. Clare's Home
WEST PARK DR
ST. CANICE'S
Sch
Convent
Bon Secours Hospital
Glasnevin
ST. MOBHI BOITHRIN
ST. MOBHI DRIVE
CHURCH AVE
ST. DAVID'S
VINCENT TER
GLASNEVIN HILL
RIVER GDNS
BOTANIC ROAD
ADDISON PL
ADDISON TER
DANESWELL
FAIRFIELD RD
CLIFTONVILLE RD
MARGUERITE ROAD
PROSPECT SQ
ST. TERESA'S RD
DE COURCY SQ
PROSPECT AVE
BOTANIC MEWS
PROSPECT WY
PROSPECT BOTANIC RD
IONA ROAD
IONA PARK
LINDSAY RD
CLAREVILLE GRO
CLAREVILLE PARK
CLAREVILLE CT
TOWER VW COTTS
BENGAL TER
ST. PHILOMENA'S ROAD
DALCASSIAN DOWNS
SHANDON GARDENS
SHANDON PARK
SHANDON CRESCENT
SHANDON DRIVE
Sixth Lock
CROSS GUNS BR
DAVID PK
DAVID RD
WIGAN RD
WHITWORTH RD
LEINSTER ST NORTH
MUNSTER ST
ULSTER ST
CONNAUGHT STREET
TRAMWAY COTTS
NORFOLK ROAD
CABRA PARK
ST. PETER'S RD
DALYMOUNT PARK
ROYSE ROAD
ENNISKERRY RD
DEVERY'S LANE
ROYAL CANAL BANK
Mountjoy Prison
ARRAN AVE
COWLEY PL
Phibsborough
N3
N2 ROAD
NORTH CIRCULAR ROAD
Ice Rink
Garda
Mater Misericordiae Hospital
BERKELEY RD
BERKELEY ST
ECCLES ST
GOLDSMITH STREET
ST. VINCENT CENT
SARSFIELD ST
O'CONNELL AVE
GERALDINE ST
CITY BASIN
BLESSINGTON ST
PRIM. AVE
PRIMROSE ST
AUBURN ST
ST. JOSEPH'S
WELLINGTON ST
FONTENOY ST
Youth Hostel
WESTERN WAY
DORSET
PALMERSTON PL
MOUNTJOY ST
DOMINICK ST UPPER
ST MARY'S TER
GRANBY
HENRIETTA LANE
HENRIETTA ST
Library
LINENHALL PAR
KINGS INNS ST
BOLTON ST
Inst. of Tech.
Parnell Centre
PARNELL
Cabra
CARNLOUGH ROAD
BANNOW ROAD
VENTRY PARK
VENTRY DR
VENTRY ROAD
BROOMBRIDGE ROAD
KILLALA ROAD
KILKIERAN ROAD
KILKIERAN CT
ST. FINBAR'S ROAD
Coll
LISCANNOR RD
MULROY RD
FAUSSAGH ROAD
FAUSSAGH AVENUE
R805
RATOATH ROAD
St. Edmund's School
DINGLE ROAD
DUNMANUS ROAD
INVER ROAD
DRUMCLIFFE DR
DRUMCLIFFE ROAD
PINEHURST
SWILLY ROAD
ATTRACTA ROAD
ST. FINTAN RD
ST. FINTAN TER
ST. EITHNE RD
ST. JARLATH ROAD
Health Centre
DELVIN RD
ANNALY RD
GALMOY RD
BREGIA RD
QUARRY ROAD
FERRIS ROAD
ULLAGH RD
FERTULLAGH RD
OFFALY ROAD
IMAAL RD
CUALA RD
LEIX ROAD
DOWTH AVENUE
NEW GRANGE ROAD
CABRA ROAD
Lib
Shopping Centre
DUNARD CT
DUNARD DRIVE
DUNARD AVENUE
DUNARD WK
DUNARD PK
DUNARD ROAD
EARLS CT
CARAGH ROAD
PARKVW
GLENBEIGH PK
GLENBEIGH RD
MCKEE PK
MCKEE DR
GLENMORE RD
GLENCAR RD
OLD CABRA ROAD
Cabra Ho
CABRA DRIVE
CABRA GRO
ANNAMOE TER
ANNAMOE ROAD
ANNAMOE RD
ANNAMOE PK
ANNAMOE DRIVE
ANNAMOE PARADE
ABERCORN TERRACE
CHARLEVILLE ROAD
MOUNT PK
CHERRY AVE
ST PETERS AVE
ROSEMOUNT ROAD
RATHDOWN ROAD
GRANGEGORMAN UPPER
BLACKHORSE INDUSTRIAL ESTATE
BLACKHORSE GRO
ELLESMERE AVE
DOON AVE
GLENARD AVE
ARDMORE AVE
EVERTON AVE
R101
Park Shopping Centre
McKee Barracks
AVENUE ROAD
PHOENIX MNR
MARLBOROUGH RD
MARLBOROUGH MEWS
Garda H.Q.
ATHLONE RD
NORTH CIRCULAR ROAD
DRUMALEE RD
DRUMALEE PK
PRUSSIA ST
DOWN SQ
ST. JOSEPH'S CT
I.D.A. INDUSTRIAL CENTRE
AUBURN WK
ST. JOSEPH'S RD
AUGHRIM STREET
AUGHRIM LA
Grangegorman Project-under development (formerly St. Brendan's Hospital)
PLAYING FIELD
Pavilion
FINGAL PL
R806
MARNE VILLAS
Bus Depot & DOE Vehicle Test Centre
ROYAL CANAL TER
PHIBSBOROUGH ROAD
PHIBSBOROUGH PLACE
WHITES LANE NORTH
Fire Sta
GREAT WESTERN SQUARE
GRT WESTERN VILLAS
AVONDALE RD
AVONDALE AVE
LESLIES BDGS
MONCK PL
CONSTITUTION HILL
BROADSTONE
TEMPLE COTTS
King's Inns
PREBEND ST
CHURCH ST UPP
COLERAINE ST
Stanhope Centre
STANHOPE GRN
GRANGEGORMAN
KIRWAN ST
MANOR ST
MANOR PLACE
STONEYBATTER
District Court
FOUNTAIN PL
BRUNSWICK STREET NORTH
KING ST NORTH
Arbour Hill Prison
ARBOUR HILL
CAVALRY ROW
SLADE RW
MONTPELIER GDNS
St. Bricins Military Hosp
TEMPLE CT
OXMANTOWN RD
CARNEW ST
COWPER ST
ARKLOW ST
BEN EDAR ROAD
NIALL ST
FINN ST
HALLIDAY RD
O'DEVANEY GDNS
ROSS RD
Band Stand
The Hollow
PEOPLE'S GARDEN
Department of Defence
INFIRMARY ROAD
FOUNTAIN
Gough

46
HAMPSTEAD PARK
Hillside Farm
28
Hampstead Private Hospital
Elmhurst Private Convalescent Home
Whitehall
Plunkett College
Highfield Hospital (Private)
Highpark Convent
SPORTS GROUND
HOMEFARM FOOTBALL GROUND
Whitehill College of Further Education
Broomhill
Maryfield College
Cross & Passion C
M50 PORT TUNNEL
N1 SWORDS ROAD
R102
R103
COLLINS AVENUE
COLLINS AVENUE WEST
GRIFFITH AVENUE
HOME FARM ROAD
GRIFFITH DOWNS
Bon Secours Hospital
Glasnevin
Convent
Weir
GLASNEVIN BRIDGE
Dept of Defence
ST. MOBHIS BRIDGE
Dominican College
All Hallows College
Hampton Hermitage & Theresian Trust
GRIFFITH WALK
St. Patrick's National School
Drumcondra
GRIFFITH PARK
DRUMCONDRA ROAD UPPER
DRUMCONDRA ROAD LOWER
St. Joseph's Sch
TOLKA PK
St. Vincent's Hospital
Marino
Monastery
Convent
Archbishop's Ho
Holy Cross College
TOLKA RIVER
DRUMCONDRA
45
Mountjoy Prison
Royal Canal Bank
CROKE PARK
G.A.A. Mus
CLONLIFFE ROAD
FAIRVIEW STRAND
Fire Sta
ANNESLEY BRIDGE
PLAYGROUND
Foot Bridge
NORTH CIRCULAR ROAD
Mater Misericordiae Hospital (A&E)
Mater Private Hosp
Children's University Hospital
Crossacre Comm Training Cen
S.F.X. City Theatre
CROKE PARK INDUSTRIAL ESTATE
Schools
Institute of Technology
Belvedere College
James Joyce Cen
Dublin Writers Mus
Municipal Art Gallery
Rotunda Hosp
PARNELL STREET
Marino Coll
85
56
CONNOLLY
INNER DOCK
Dublin Institute of Technology
Larkin Comm College
ILAC Centre
Parnell Centre
MARINER'S PORT
R101
Medical Cen
N2 ROAD
DORSET ST UPPER
DORSET STREET LOWER
O'CONNELL ST. UPPER
WESTERN WAY
King's Inns
Library
Inst. of Tech.
A
B
C
1
2
3
4

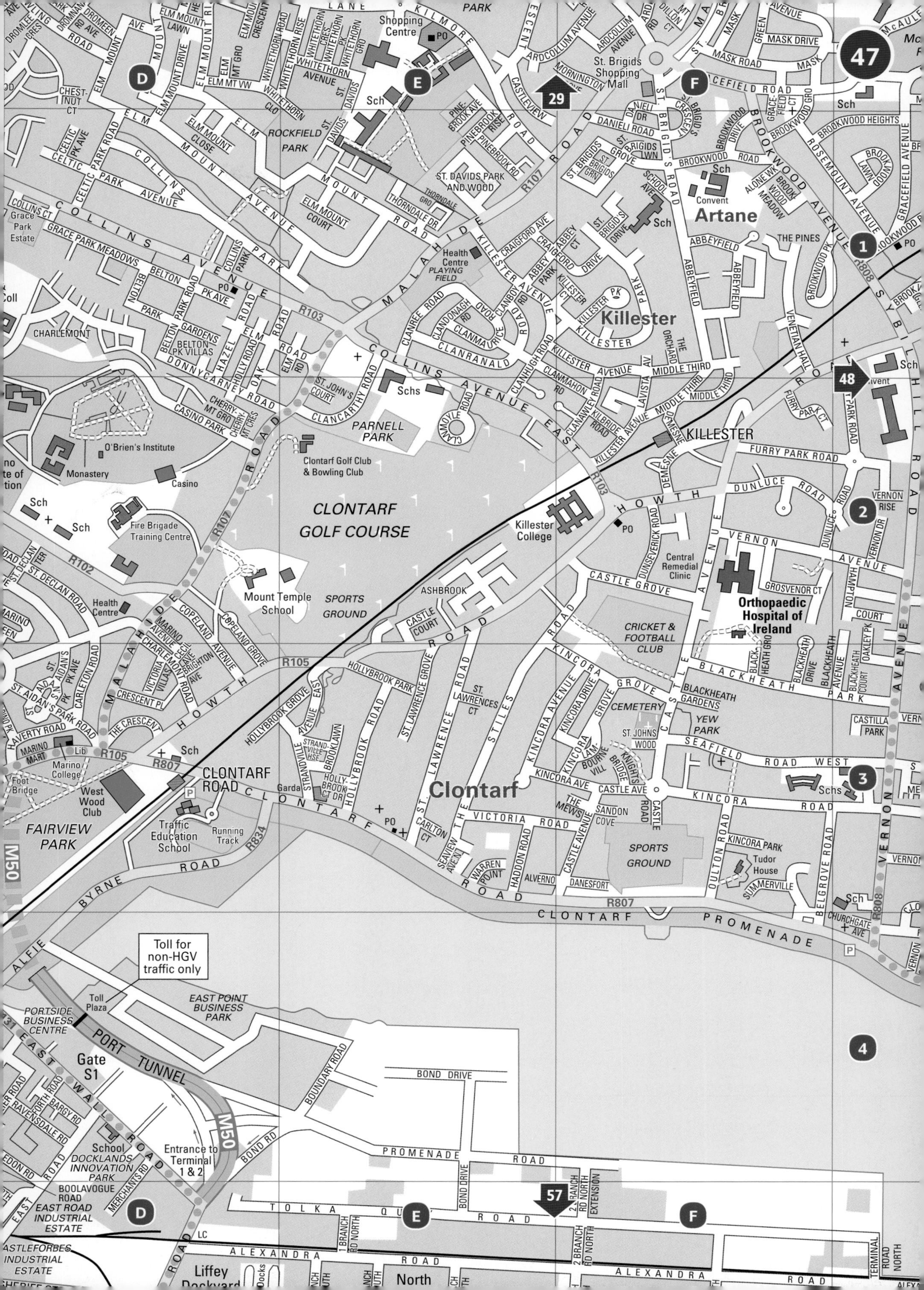
Artane
Killester
Clontarf
CLONTARF GOLF COURSE
FAIRVIEW PARK
EAST POINT BUSINESS PARK
PORTSIDE BUSINESS CENTRE
DOCKLANDS INNOVATION PARK
EAST ROAD INDUSTRIAL ESTATE
CASTLEFORBES INDUSTRIAL ESTATE
Toll for non-HGV traffic only
Toll Plaza
PORT TUNNEL
M50
Entrance to Terminal 1 & 2
Gate S1
School
St. Brigids Shopping Mall
Shopping Centre
ROCKFIELD PARK
ST. DAVIDS PARK AND WOOD
PARNELL PARK
Clontarf Golf Club & Bowling Club
Mount Temple School
SPORTS GROUND
O'Brien's Institute
Monastery
Casino
Fire Brigade Training Centre
Health Centre
Killester College
Central Remedial Clinic
Orthopaedic Hospital of Ireland
CRICKET & FOOTBALL CLUB
CEMETERY
YEW PARK
Tudor House
Marino College
West Wood Club
Traffic Education School
Running Track
Garda
Convent
THE PINES
KILLESTER
CLONTARF ROAD
MALAHIDE ROAD
COLLINS AVENUE
COLLINS AVENUE EAST
HOWTH ROAD
CLONTARF ROAD
CLONTARF PROMENADE
ALFIE BYRNE ROAD
EAST WALL ROAD
PROMENADE ROAD
TOLKA QUAY ROAD
ALEXANDRA ROAD
BOND DRIVE
BOUNDARY ROAD
KILLESTER AVENUE
KINCORA ROAD
SEAFIELD ROAD WEST
VERNON AVENUE
SYBIL HILL ROAD
BROOKWOOD AVENUE
FURRY PARK ROAD
DUNLUCE ROAD
CASTLE AVENUE
STILES ROAD
ST. LAWRENCE ROAD
HOLLYBROOK ROAD
R103
R105
R107
R102
R807
R808
R834
29
48
57
D
E
F
1
2
3
4

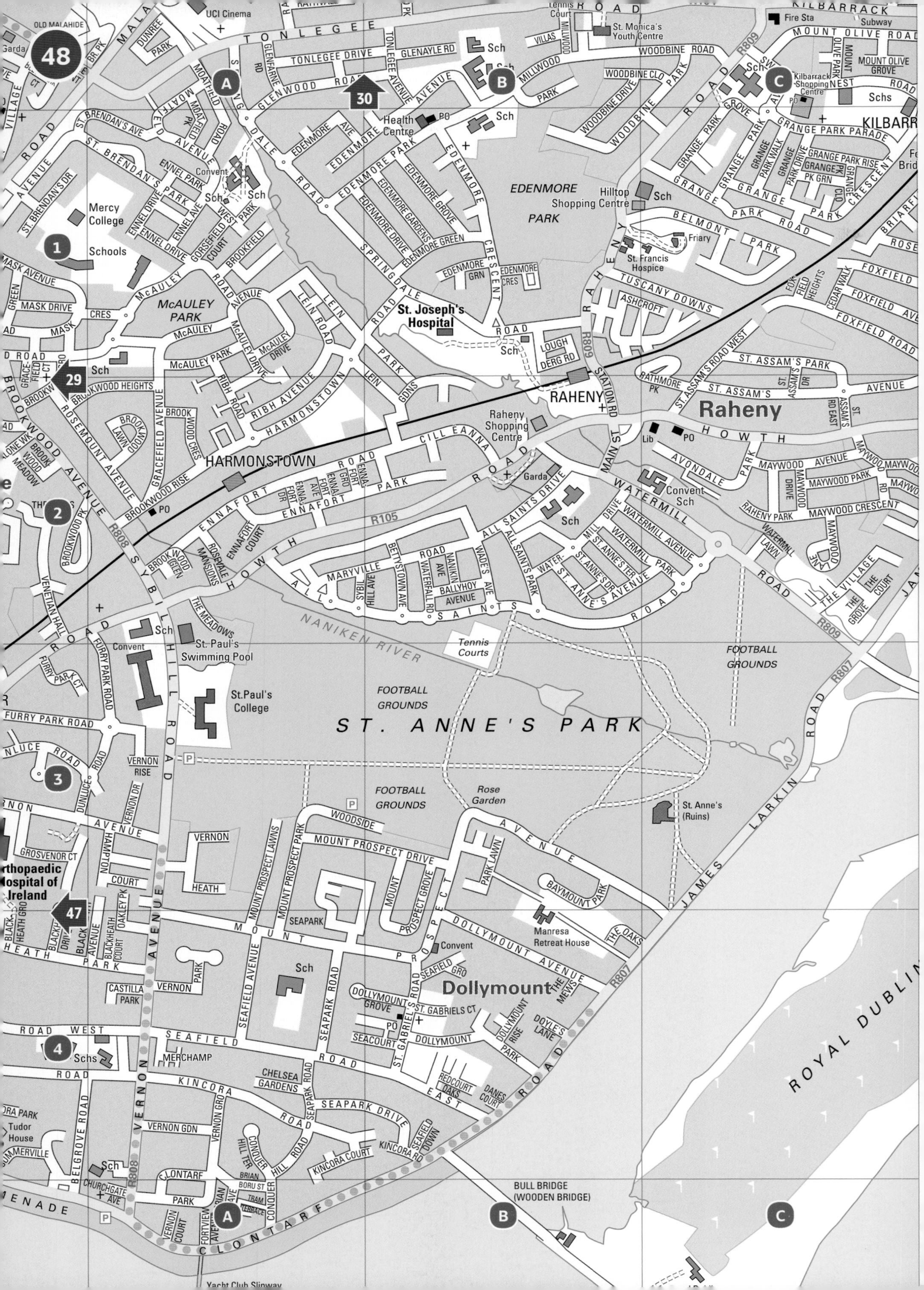
OLD MALAHIDE
UCI Cinema
TONLEGEE ROAD
Tennis Court
St. Monica's Youth Centre
KILBARRACK
Fire Sta
Subway
MOUNT OLIVE ROAD
TONLEGEE DRIVE
GLENAYLE RD
Sch
VILLAS
MILLWOOD
WOODBINE ROAD
R809
OLIVE PARK
MOUNT OLIVE GROVE
MOUNT OLIVE GROVE
DUNREE PARK
GLENFARNE RD
TONLEGEE AVENUE
MILLWOOD PARK
WOODBINE CLO
Kilbarrack Shopping Centre
NEST ROAD
Schs
PO
MOATFIELD
MOATFIELD PK
GLENWOOD ROAD
30
Health Centre
PO
Sch
WOODBINE DRIVE
WOODBINE PARK
GRANGE PARK GROVE
GRANGE PARK PARADE
KILBARR
ST. BRENDAN'S AVE
ST. BRENDAN'S PARK
ENNEL PARK
Convent
Sch
EDENMORE AVE
EDENMORE PARK
EDENMORE
EDENMORE GARDENS
EDENMORE GROVE
EDENMORE DRIVE
EDENMORE GREEN
EDENMORE CRESCENT
EDENMORE PARK
Hilltop Shopping Centre
GRANGE PARK WALK
GRANGE PARK DRIVE
GRANGE PARK RISE
GRANGE PK GRN
GRANGE CLO
GRANGE PARK CRESCENT
GRANGE PARK ROAD
ST. BRENDAN'S DR
AVENUE ROAD
Mercy College
ENNEL DRIVE
ENNEL AVE
WEST PARK
GORSEFIELD COURT
BROOKFIELD
SPRINGDALE ROAD
BELMONT PARK
Friary
St. Francis Hospice
TUSCANY DOWNS
ASHCROFT
BRIARFIELD
ROSE
FOXFIELD
FOXFIELD HEIGHTS
CEDAR WALK
FOXFIELD AVE
FOXFIELD ROAD
1
Schools
MASK AVENUE
MASK DRIVE
MASK CRES
McAULEY PARK
McAULEY AVENUE
McAULEY DRIVE
McAULEY PARK
LEIN ROAD
LEIN PARK
LEIN GDNS
St. Joseph's Hospital
EDENMORE GRN
EDENMORE CRES
ROAD
Sch
LOUGH DERG RD
ST. ASSAM'S ROAD WEST
ST. ASSAM'S PARK
RATHMORE PK
ST. ASSAM'S DR
ST. ASSAM'S AVENUE
ST. ASSAM'S RD EAST
GRACEFIELD CT
29
Sch
BROOKWOOD
BROOKWOOD HEIGHTS
ROSEMOUNT AVENUE
BROOKLAWN
BROOKWOOD
GRACEFIELD AVENUE
RIBH ROAD
RIBH AVENUE
HARMONSTOWN ROAD
BROOKWOOD CRES
RAHENY
STATION RD
Raheny
Raheny Shopping Centre
CILL EANNA
Lib
PO
HOWTH ROAD
MAIN ST
BROOKWOOD AVENUE
BROOKWOOD MEADOW
HARMONSTOWN
BROOKWOOD RISE
ENNAFORT ROAD
ENNAFORT PARK
ENNAFORT DR
ENNAFORT AVE
ENNAFORT GRO
ENNAFORT CT
Garda
AVONDALE PARK
MAYWOOD AVENUE
MAYWOOD DRIVE
MAYWOOD PARK
MAYWOOD CRESCENT
MAYWOOD LANE
RAHENY PARK
Convent
Sch
2
BROOKWOOD PK
PO
R808
R105
ENNAFORT COURT
ALL SAINTS DRIVE
ALL SAINTS PARK
Sch
WATERMILL ROAD
WATERMILL DRIVE
WATERMILL AVENUE
WATERMILL PARK
WATERMILL LAWN
ST. ANNE'S TER
ST. ANNE'S DR
ST. ANNE'S AVENUE
THE VILLAGE
THE COURT
THE GROVE
SYBIL HILL ROAD
BROOKWOOD GLEN
ROSEVALE MANSIONS
MARYVILLE ROAD
SYBIL HILL AVE
BETTYSTOWN AVE
WATERFALL RD
NANIKIN AVE
BALLYHOY AVENUE
WADE'S AVE
ALL SAINTS ROAD
R809
VENETIAN HALL
THE MEADOWS
Sch
Convent
St. Paul's Swimming Pool
NANIKEN RIVER
Tennis Courts
FOOTBALL GROUNDS
FURRY PARK CT
FURRY PARK ROAD
St.Paul's College
FOOTBALL GROUNDS
ST. ANNE'S PARK
R807
DUNLUCE ROAD
3
VERNON RISE
P
FOOTBALL GROUNDS
Rose Garden
St. Anne's (Ruins)
JAMES LARKIN ROAD
VERNON DR
VERNON AVENUE
WOODSIDE
P
GROSVENOR CT
HAMPTON COURT
VERNON HEATH
MOUNT PROSPECT LAWNS
MOUNT PROSPECT PARK
MOUNT PROSPECT DRIVE
MOUNT PROSPECT GROVE
PARK LAWN
BAYMOUNT PARK
Orthopaedic Hospital of Ireland
47
OAKLEY PK
SEAPARK
MOUNT PROSPECT AVENUE
DOLLYMOUNT AVENUE
Manresa Retreat House
THE OAKS
BLACKHEATH GRO
BLACKHEATH DRIVE
BLACKHEATH AVENUE
BLACKHEATH COURT
BLACKHEATH PARK
VERNON PARK
Sch
SEAFIELD AVENUE
SEAPARK ROAD
Convent
SEAFIELD GRO
SEAFIELD ROAD
Dollymount
THE MEWS
CASTILLA PARK
DOLLYMOUNT GROVE
ST. GABRIELS CT
PO
SEACOURT
ST. GABRIEL'S RD
DOLLYMOUNT RISE
DOLLYMOUNT PARK
DOYLE'S LANE
ROAD WEST
SEAFIELD ROAD
4
Schs
MERCHAMP
KINCORA ROAD
CHELSEA GARDENS
REDCOURT OAKS
DANES COURT
SEAFIELD ROAD EAST
ROYAL DUBLIN
BELGROVE ROAD
VERNON GRO
SEAPARK DRIVE
SEAFIELD DOWN
Tudor House
VERNON GDN
SUMMERVILLE
CONQUER HILL TER
CONQUER HILL ROAD
KINCORA COURT
KINCORA RD
Sch
CLONTARF PARK
BRIAN
BORU ST
TRAM
TERRACE
CHURCHGATE AVE
R808
BULL BRIDGE (WOODEN BRIDGE)
PROMENADE
P
A
B
C
VERNON COURT
FORTVIEW AVENUE
BRIAN AVE
CLONTARF ROAD
Yacht Club Slipway

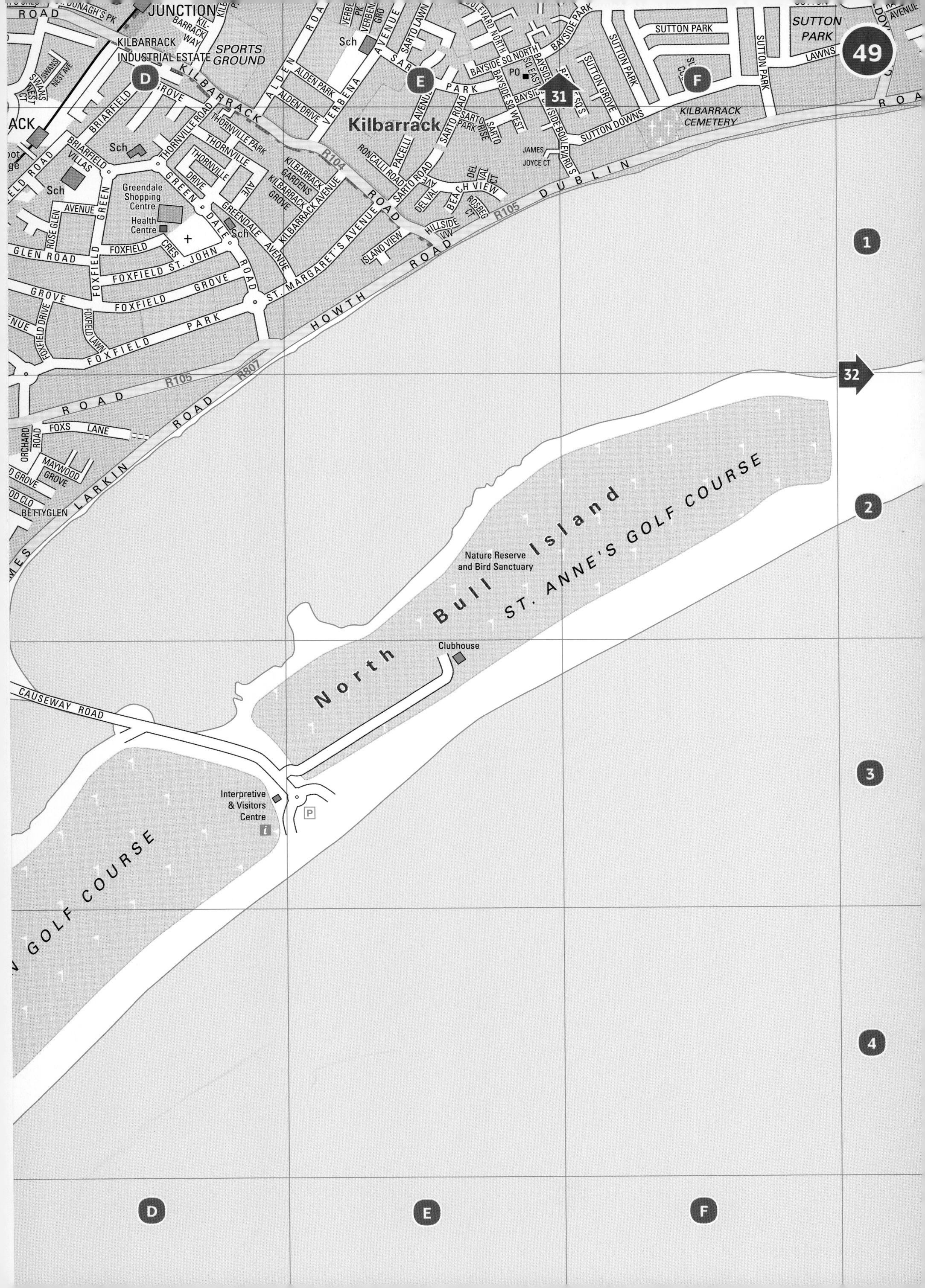
JUNCTION
KILBARRACK INDUSTRIAL ESTATE
SPORTS GROUND
Kilbarrack
SUTTON PARK
KILBARRACK CEMETERY
Greendale Shopping Centre
Health Centre
Sch
PO
JAMES JOYCE CT
HOWTH ROAD
DUBLIN ROAD
R105
R104
R807
JAMES LARKIN ROAD
CAUSEWAY ROAD
FOXS LANE
BETTYGLEN
North Bull Island
Nature Reserve and Bird Sanctuary
ST. ANNE'S GOLF COURSE
Clubhouse
Interpretive & Visitors Centre
GOLF COURSE
D
E
F
1
2
3
4
31
32

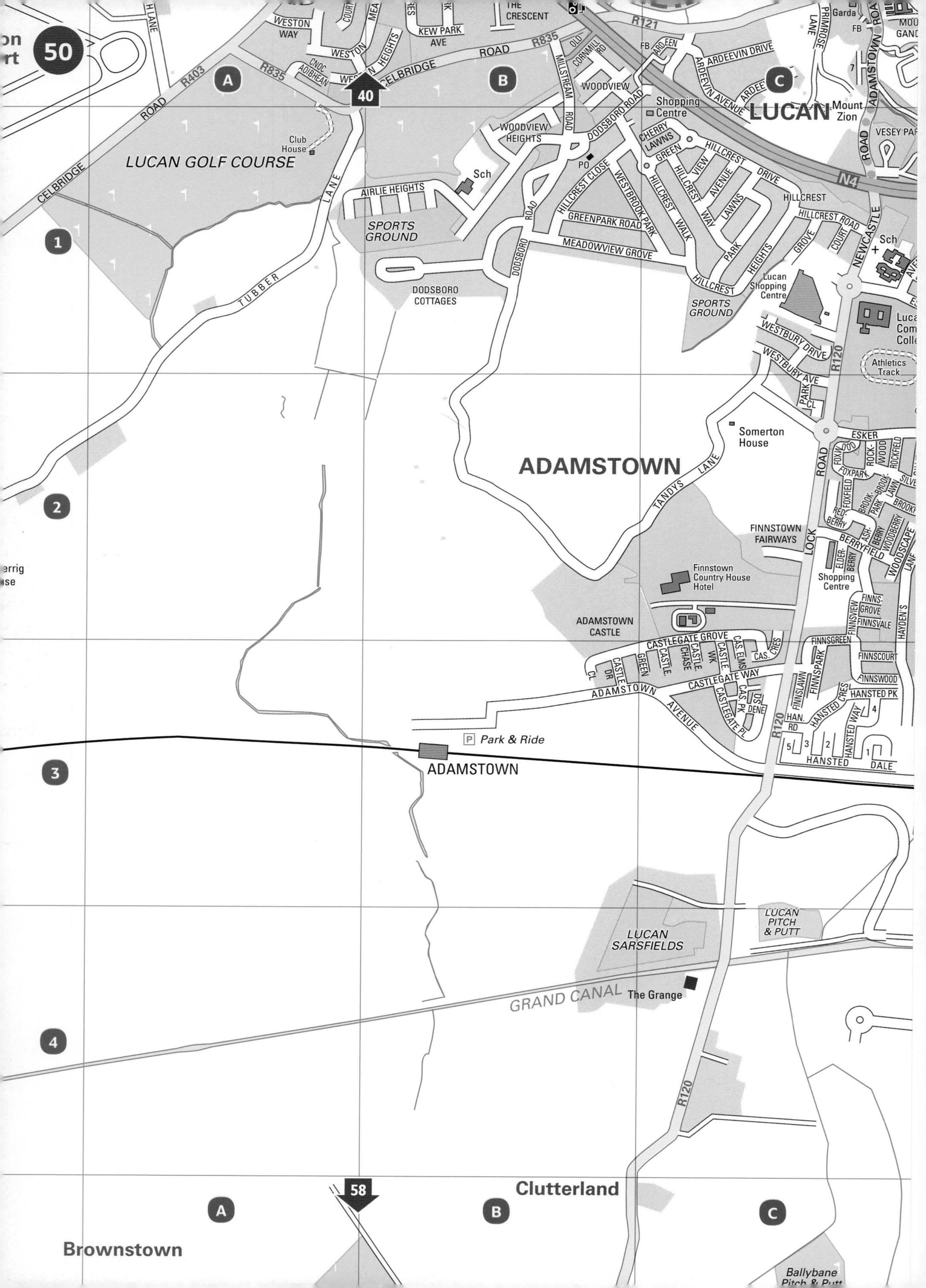
A
B
C
1
2
3
4
40
58
LUCAN
ADAMSTOWN
LUCAN GOLF COURSE
Club House
CELBRIDGE ROAD
R403
R835
CELBRIDGE ROAD
WESTON WAY
WESTON HEIGHTS
CNOC AOIBHEAN
KEW PARK AVE
THE CRESCENT
R121
MILLSTREAM ROAD
OLD CORNMILL RD
WOODVIEW
WOODVIEW HEIGHTS
DODSBORO ROAD
Shopping Centre
CHERRY LAWNS
GREEN
HILLCREST DRIVE
HILLCREST VIEW
HILLCREST AVENUE
HILLCREST LAWNS
HILLCREST WAY
HILLCREST WALK
HILLCREST PARK
HILLCREST HEIGHTS
HILLCREST GROVE
HILLCREST COURT
HILLCREST ROAD
HILLCREST CLOSE
WESTBROOK PARK
GREENPARK ROAD
MEADOWVIEW GROVE
PO
Sch
AIRLIE HEIGHTS
SPORTS GROUND
DODSBORO COTTAGES
TUBBER LANE
ARDEEVIN DRIVE
ARDEEVIN AVENUE
PRIMROSE LANE
Garda
FB
Mount Zion
ADAMSTOWN ROAD
VESEY PARK
N4
NEWCASTLE
Sch
Lucan Shopping Centre
SPORTS GROUND
WESTBURY DRIVE
WESTBURY AVE
PARK CL
Athletics Track
R120
Somerton House
TANDYS LANE
ESKER
LOCK ROAD
FOXPARK
ROCKWOOD
ROCKFIELD
BROOKPARK
BROOKLAWN
REDBERRY
ASHBERRY
WOODBERRY
WOODSCAPE
BERRYFIELD
ELDERBERRY
FINNSTOWN FAIRWAYS
Finnstown Country House Hotel
Shopping Centre
FINNSGROVE
FINNSVALE
FINNSVIEW
HAYDEN'S LANE
ADAMSTOWN CASTLE
CASTLEGATE GROVE
CASTLEGATE WAY
CAS. ELMS
CAS. CRES
CASTLE GREEN
CASTLE DR
CASTLE CHASE
CASTLE WK
FINNSGREEN
FINNSCOURT
FINNSPARK
FINNSLAWN
FINNSWOOD
HANSTED PK
HANSTED CRES
HANSTED WAY
HAN. RD
HANSTED DALE
ADAMSTOWN AVENUE
CASTLEGATE PL
CAS. PK
CAS. DENE
Park & Ride
ADAMSTOWN
LUCAN PITCH & PUTT
LUCAN SARSFIELDS
GRAND CANAL
The Grange
Clutterland
Brownstown
Ballybane Pitch & Putt

51
41
52
59
D
E
F
1
2
3
4
LUCAN
BYPASS
ESKER LAWNS
ESKER PINES
ESKER CEMETERY
NEWLANDS ROAD
CHERBURY PARK ROAD
CHERBURY PARK AVE
BEECH GROVE
WILLSBROOK PARK
ESKER PARK
ESKER LODGE
ESKER LANE
ELMBROOK
MOUNT BELLEW WAY
Sch
Halting Site
BALLYOWEN PARK
MOUNT ANDREW
ST LOMANS RD
LARKFIELD
LIFFEY VALLEY PARK
LIFFEY ROAD
FONTH RETAI PARK
THE GLEBE
BURIAL GROUND
Coláiste Cois Life
ESKER MANOR
CANNONBROOK
ST FINIAN'S
ESKER DRIVE
ARTHUR GRIFFITH PARK
SPORTS GROUND
ESKER SOUTH
Lucan Sports & Leisure Centre
GRIFFEEN VALLEY PARK
ESKER MEADOW
BALLYDOWD MANOR
FFORESTER
CASTLE RIADA
Ballyowen Castle Shopping & Medical Centre
CLUAIN RÍ
COLTHURST
COLTHURST CRESCENT
ROCHFORT DOWNS
EARLSFORT
ABBEYWOOD
ABBEYDALE
NEWLANDS ROAD
GLENVALE
FOXBOROUGH
FOXBOROUGH DOWNES
FOXBOROUGH DRIVE
MOY GLAS VIEW
MOY GLAS CHASE
GRIFFEEN GLEN BOULEVARD
JOHNSBRIDGE
GRANGE MANOR
THE OLD FORGE
GRIFFEEN RIVER
HAYDENS PARK
ROSBERRY
OLDBRIDGE
TULLYHALL
Training & Education Centre
Ballyowen Resource Centre
BALGADDY
Halting Site
BALLYOWEN PARK
R136
Rona
KILCRONAN AVENUE
DEANSRATH AVE
DEANSRATH ROAD
MELROSE GROVE
MELROSE PARK
LINDISFARNE AVENUE
LINDISFARNE GROVE
ASHWOOD
SPORTS GROUND
GRANGE CASTLE INTERNATIONAL BUSINESS PARK
GRANGE VIEW ROAD
KILMAHUDDRICK ROAD
Health Centre
School
Community Centre
PO
WESTBOURNE
LEALAND
ALPINE HEIGH
THE GABLES
R134

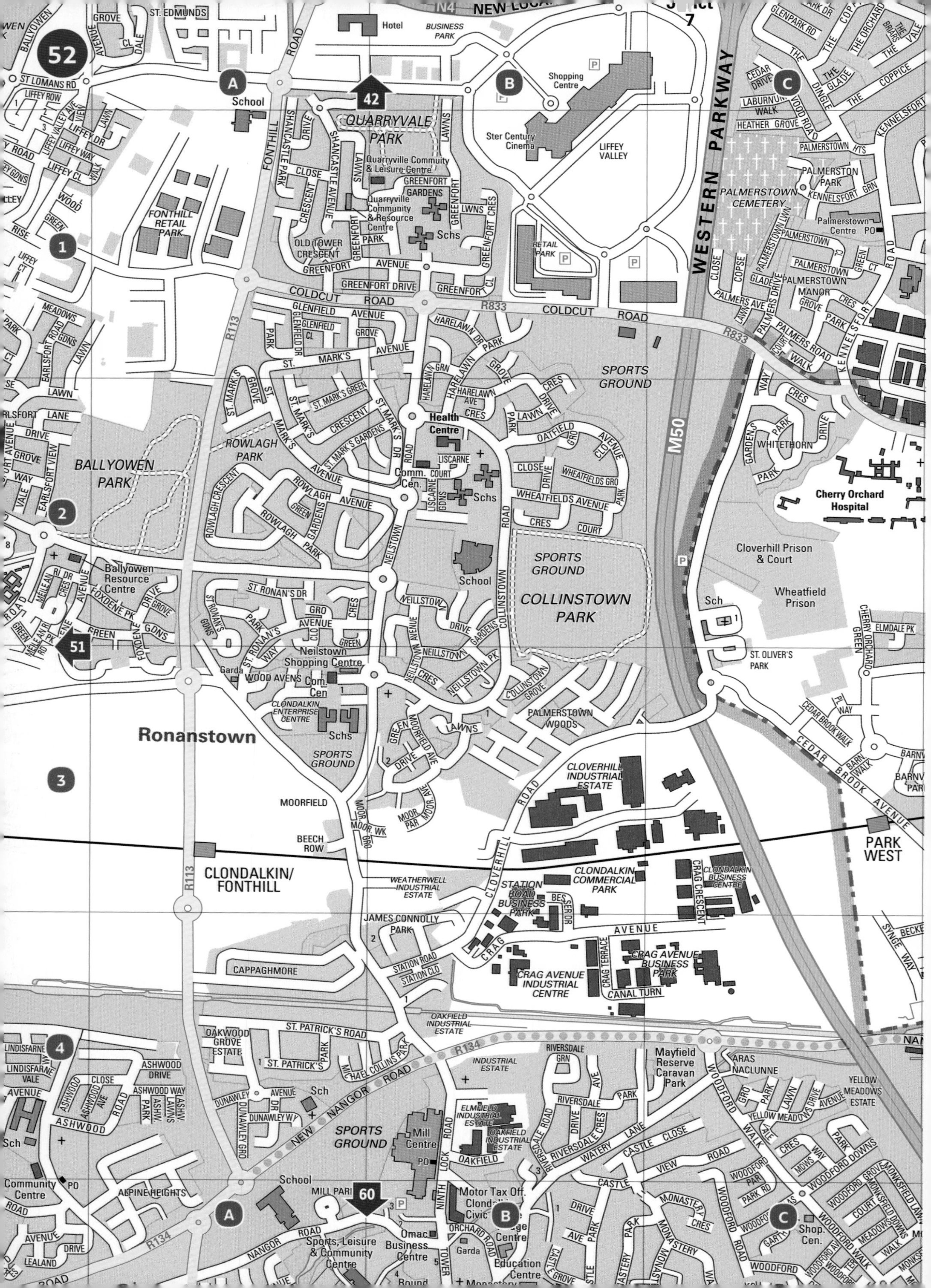
52
42
51
60
N4
NEW LUCAN
Junction 7
Hotel
BUSINESS PARK
Shopping Centre
Ster Century Cinema
LIFFEY VALLEY
RETAIL PARK
WESTERN PARKWAY
M50
ST. EDMUNDS
GROVE
AVENUE
CL
DALE
BALLYOWEN
ST LOMANS RD
LIFFEY ROW
LIFFEY VALLEY AVE
LIFFEY DR
LIFFEY WAY
LIFFEY CL
LIFFEY CT
LAWN
WALK
VIEW
WOOD
GREEN
RISE
School
FONTHILL ROAD
FONTHILL RETAIL PARK
QUARRYVALE PARK
SHANCASTLE DRIVE
SHANCASTLE PARK
SHANCASTLE AVENUE
SHANCASTLE LAWNS
CLOSE
CRESCENT
Quarryville Community & Leisure Centre
Quarryville Community & Resource Centre
GREENFORT GARDENS
GREENFORT LWNS
GREENFORT CRES
GREENFORT LAWNS
OLD TOWER CRESCENT
GREENFORT PARK
GREENFORT AVENUE
GREENFORT DRIVE
GREENFORT CL
Schs
COLDCUT ROAD
R833
R113
GLENFIELD AVENUE
GLENFIELD DR
GLENFIELD CL
GLENFIELD GROVE
PARK
HARELAWN DR
HARELAWN GRN
HARELAWN PARK
HARELAWN GROVE
HARELAWN AVE
HARELAWN CRES
ST. MARK'S AVENUE
ST. MARK'S GROVE
ST. MARK'S GREEN
ST. MARK'S CRESCENT
ST. MARK'S GARDENS
ST. MARK'S DR
ROWLAGH PARK
ROWLAGH CRESCENT
ROWLAGH AVENUE
ROWLAGH GREEN
ROWLAGH GARDENS
ROWLAGH PARK
Health Centre
LISCARNE COURT
LISCARNE GDNS
Comm. Cen.
Schs
SPORTS GROUND
OATFIELD DRIVE
OATFIELD LAWN
OATFIELD PARK
OATFIELD CRES
OATFIELD AVENUE
OATFIELD GRO
OATFIELD CLO
WHEATFIELDS CLOSE
WHEATFIELDS DRIVE
WHEATFIELDS GRO
WHEATFIELDS AVENUE
WHEATFIELDS PARK
WHEATFIELDS CRES
WHEATFIELDS COURT
BALLYOWEN PARK
MEADOWS
EARLSFORT ROAD
EARLSFORT GDNS
EARLSFORT LAWN
EARLSFORT LANE
EARLSFORT DRIVE
EARLSFORT GROVE
EARLSFORT WAY
EARLSFORT VALE
EARLSFORT VIEW
Ballyowen Resource Centre
FOXDENE AVENUE
FOXDENE PK
FOXDENE DRIVE
FOXDENE GROVE
FOXDENE GDNS
FOXDENE GREEN
MEILEAN RD
NEILSTOWN ROAD
School
COLLINSTOWN ROAD
COLLINSTOWN PARK
SPORTS GROUND
ST. RONAN'S DR
ST. RONAN'S GDNS
ST. RONAN'S PARK
ST. RONAN'S AVENUE
ST. RONAN'S CLO
ST. RONAN'S GRO
ST. RONAN'S CRES
ST. RONAN'S GREEN
ST. RONAN'S WAY
NEILLSTOWN DRIVE
NEILLSTOWN AVENUE
NEILLSTOWN GARDENS
NEILLSTOWN CRES
NEILLSTOWN PK
COLLINSTOWN GROVE
Neilstown Shopping Centre
Garda
WOOD AVENS
Com. Cen
CLONDALKIN ENTERPRISE CENTRE
Schs
SPORTS GROUND
Ronanstown
MOORFIELD
MOORFIELD GREEN
MOORFIELD DRIVE
MOORFIELD AVE
MOORFIELD LAWNS
MOOR. WK
MOOR. GRO
MOOR. PAR
MOOR. AVE
PALMERSTOWN WOODS
BEECH ROW
CLOVERHILL INDUSTRIAL ESTATE
CLOVERHILL ROAD
CLONDALKIN/ FONTHILL
WEATHERWELL INDUSTRIAL ESTATE
STATION ROAD BUSINESS PARK
BESSER DR
CLONDALKIN COMMERCIAL PARK
CLONDALKIN BUSINESS CENTRE
CRAG CRESCENT
JAMES CONNOLLY PARK
CRAG AVENUE
CRAG TERRACE
CRAG AVENUE BUSINESS PARK
CRAG AVENUE INDUSTRIAL CENTRE
CANAL TURN
STATION ROAD
STATION CLO
CAPPAGHMORE
OAKFIELD INDUSTRIAL ESTATE
OAKWOOD GROVE ESTATE
ST. PATRICK'S ROAD
ST. PATRICK'S PARK
ST. PATRICK'S
MICHAEL COLLINS PARK
R134
NEW NANGOR ROAD
INDUSTRIAL ESTATE
RIVERSDALE GRN
RIVERSDALE AVE
RIVERSDALE PARK
RIVERSDALE DRIVE
RIVERSDALE CRES
RIVERSDALE ROAD
Mayfield Reserve Caravan Park
ARAS NACLUNNE
YELLOW MEADOWS ESTATE
YELLOW MEADOWS DRIVE
YELLOW MEADOWS AVENUE
LINDISFARNE
LINDISFARNE VALE
AVENUE
ASHWOOD CLOSE
ASHWOOD AVE
ASHWOOD ROAD
ASHWOOD DRIVE
ASHWOOD WAY
ASHW. LAWNS
ASHWOOD
DUNAWLEY AVENUE
DUNAWLEY DR
DUNAWLEY WAY
DUNAWLEY GRO
Sch
SPORTS GROUND
Mill Centre
ELMFIELD INDUSTRIAL ESTATE
OAKFIELD INDUSTRIAL ESTATE
OAKFIELD
NINTH LOCK ROAD
WATERY LANE
CASTLE CLOSE
CASTLE VIEW ROAD
CASTLE DRIVE
CASTLE AVE
CASTLE PARK
MONASTERY CRES
MONASTERY PARK
WOODFORD WALK
WOODFORD PARK
WOODFORD PARK RD
WOODFORD ROAD
WOODFORD DOWNS
WOODFORD GROVE
WOODFORD COURT
WOODFORD MEADOWS
WOODFORD
Shop. Cen.
MONKSFIELD
Community Centre
PO
ALPINE HEIGHTS
LEALAND
NANGOR ROAD
School
MILL PARK
Motor Tax Off.
Sports, Leisure & Community Centre
Omac Business Centre
ORCHARD ROAD
Garda
Education Centre
TOWER
GLENPARK RD
CEDAR DRIVE
LABURNUM WALK
HEATHER GROVE
THE DINGLE
THE GLADE
THE COPPICE
THE ORCHARD
THE BRIARS
THE VALE
KENNELSFORT
PALMERSTOWN HTS
PALMERSTON PARK
KENNELSFORT GRN
PALMERSTOWN CEMETERY
Palmerstown Centre
PALMERSTOWN LWN
PALMERSTOWN GREEN
PALMERSTOWN CT
PALMERSTOWN MANOR
PALMERSTOWN CLOSE
PALMERSTOWN COPSE
GLADE
PALMERS AVE
PALMERS DRIVE
PALMERS CRES
PALMERS PARK
PALMERS GROVE
PALMERS ROAD
PALMERS COURT
PALMERS WALK
PALMERS LAWN
WHITETHORN
Cherry Orchard Hospital
Cloverhill Prison & Court
Wheatfield Prison
Sch
ST. OLIVER'S PARK
CHERRY ORCHARD GREEN
ELMDALE PK
CEDAR BROOK WALK
CEDAR BROOK AVENUE
CEDAR BROOK WAY
BARN WALK
PARK WEST
SYNGE WAY
A
B
C
1
2
3
4

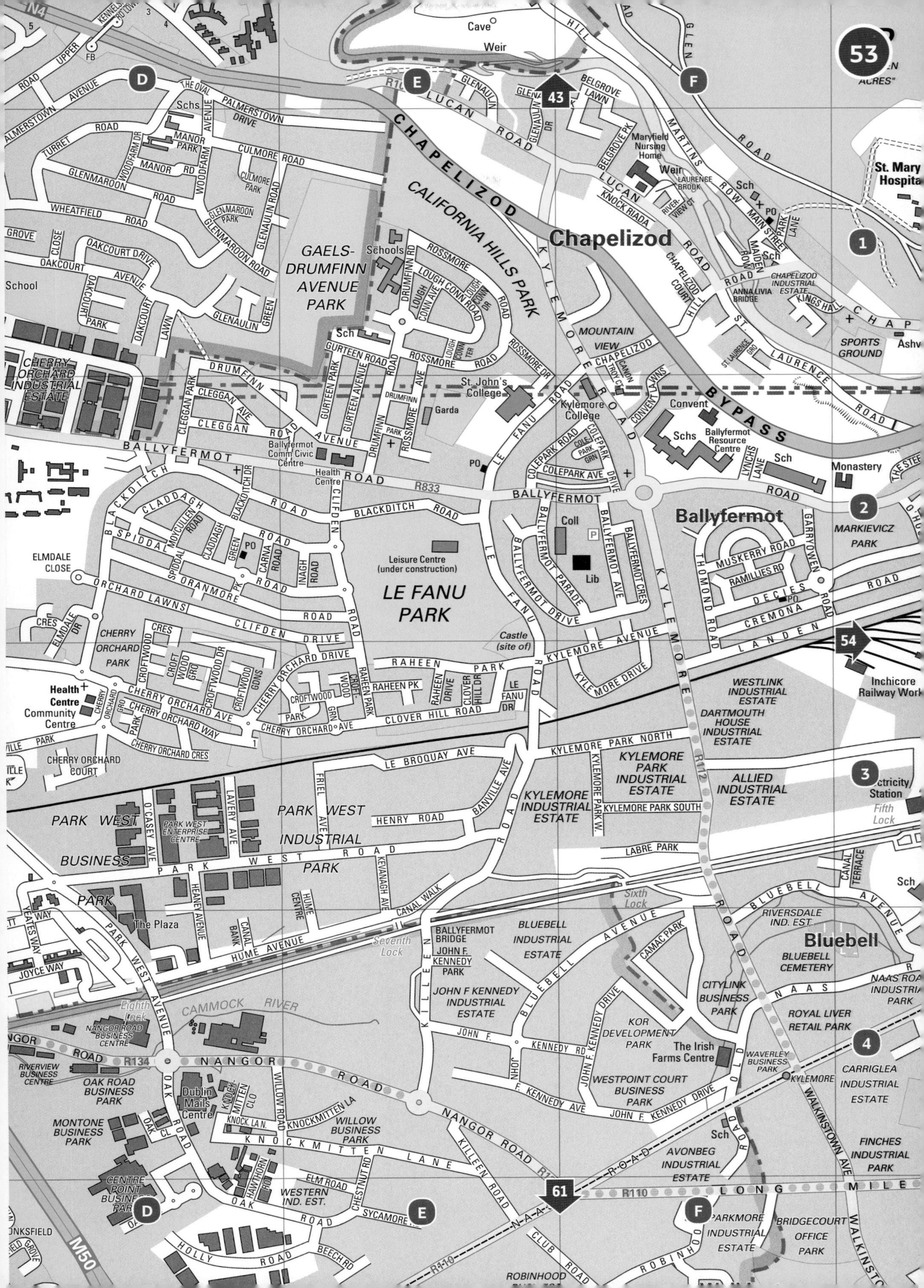
Chapelizod
Ballyfermot
Bluebell
CHAPELIZOD BYPASS
CALIFORNIA HILLS PARK
GAELS-DRUMFINN AVENUE PARK
LE FANU PARK
CHERRY ORCHARD INDUSTRIAL ESTATE
CHERRY ORCHARD PARK
PARK WEST BUSINESS PARK
PARK WEST INDUSTRIAL PARK
PARK WEST ENTERPRISE CENTRE
KYLEMORE PARK INDUSTRIAL ESTATE
KYLEMORE INDUSTRIAL ESTATE
ALLIED INDUSTRIAL ESTATE
WESTLINK INDUSTRIAL ESTATE
DARTMOUTH HOUSE INDUSTRIAL ESTATE
BLUEBELL INDUSTRIAL ESTATE
JOHN F. KENNEDY PARK
JOHN F KENNEDY INDUSTRIAL ESTATE
KOR DEVELOPMENT PARK
WESTPOINT COURT BUSINESS PARK
CITYLINK BUSINESS PARK
ROYAL LIVER RETAIL PARK
NAAS ROAD INDUSTRIAL PARK
CARRIGLEA INDUSTRIAL ESTATE
FINCHES INDUSTRIAL PARK
AVONBEG INDUSTRIAL ESTATE
PARKMORE INDUSTRIAL ESTATE
BRIDGECOURT OFFICE PARK
RIVERSDALE IND. EST.
BLUEBELL CEMETERY
WAVERLEY BUSINESS PARK
The Irish Farms Centre
NANGOR ROAD BUSINESS CENTRE
RIVERVIEW BUSINESS CENTRE
OAK ROAD BUSINESS PARK
MONTONE BUSINESS PARK
CENTRE POINT BUSINESS PARK
WILLOW BUSINESS PARK
WESTERN IND. EST.
Dublin Mails Centre
The Plaza
MOUNTAIN VIEW
SPORTS GROUND
MARKIEVICZ PARK
St. Mary's Hospital
Inchicore Railway Works
Electricity Station
Maryfield Nursing Home
St. John's College
Kylemore College
Ballyfermot Comm Civic Centre
Ballyfermot Resource Centre
Health Centre
Community Centre
Leisure Centre (under construction)
Castle (site of)
Convent
Monastery
Coll
Lib
Garda
Schools
Schs
Sch
School
PO
Cave
Weir
CHAPELIZOD INDUSTRIAL ESTATE
ANNA LIVIA BRIDGE
BALLYFERMOT BRIDGE
JOHN F. KENNEDY PARK
Fifth Lock
Sixth Lock
Seventh Lock
Eighth Lock
CAMMOCK RIVER
BALLYFERMOT ROAD
R833
LUCAN ROAD
KYLEMORE ROAD
R112
NANGOR ROAD
R134
NAAS ROAD
LONG MILE ROAD
R110
PARK WEST AVENUE
PARK WEST ROAD
KILLEEN ROAD
KNOCKMITTEN LANE
OAK ROAD
HOLLY ROAD
CLUB ROAD
ROBINHOOD ROAD
WALKINSTOWN AVE
BLUEBELL AVENUE
LANDEN ROAD
CREMONA ROAD
DECIES ROAD
GARRYOWEN ROAD
THOMOND ROAD
MUSKERRY ROAD
RAMILLIES RD
LE FANU ROAD
LE FANU DR
KYLEMORE AVENUE
KYLEMORE DRIVE
KYLEMORE PARK NORTH
KYLEMORE PARK SOUTH
KYLEMORE PARK W.
LABRE PARK
HENRY ROAD
BANVILLE AVE
LE BROQUAY AVE
FRIEL AVE
KEVANAGH AVE
CANAL WALK
HUME AVENUE
HUME CENTRE
CANAL BANK
HEANEY AVENUE
O'CASEY AVE
LAVERY AVE
JOYCE WAY
YEATES WAY
CHERRY ORCHARD AVE
CHERRY ORCHARD WAY
CHERRY ORCHARD CRES
CHERRY ORCHARD DRIVE
CHERRY ORCHARD COURT
CLOVER HILL ROAD
CLOVER HILL DR
RAHEEN PARK
RAHEEN PK
RAHEEN DRIVE
CROFTWOOD PARK
CROFTWOOD DR
CROFTWOOD GDNS
CROFTWOOD CRES
CLIFDEN DRIVE
CLIFDEN ROAD
ORCHARD LAWNS
ORANMORE ROAD
SPIDDAL ROAD
CLADDAGH ROAD
BLACKDITCH ROAD
BLACKDITCH DR
MOYCULLEN ROAD
CARNA ROAD
INAGH ROAD
ELMDALE CLOSE
ELMDALE DR
CLEGGAN ROAD
CLEGGAN AVE
CLEGGAN PARK
DRUMFINN AVENUE
DRUMFINN PARK
DRUMFINN ROAD
GURTEEN ROAD
GURTEEN PARK
GURTEEN AVENUE
ROSSMORE ROAD
ROSSMORE AVE
ROSSMORE DR
LOUGH CONN ROAD
LOUGH CONN AVE
COLEPARK ROAD
COLEPARK AVE
COLEPARK DRIVE
BALLYFERMOT PARADE
BALLYFERMOT DRIVE
BALLYFERMOT AVE
BALLYFERMOT CRES
CONVENT LAWNS
CHAPELIZOD HILL ROAD
CHAPELIZOD COURT
KNOCK RIADA
RIVERVIEW CT
MARTINS ROW
MAIN STREET
MAIDEN ROW
PARK LANE
ST. LAURENCE ROAD
ST. LAURENCE GRO
KINGS HALL
LYNCHS LANE
BELGROVE LAWN
BELGROVE PK
GLENAULIN
GLENAULIN DR
GLENAULIN ROAD
GLENAULIN GREEN
GLENMAROON ROAD
GLENMAROON PARK
WHEATFIELD ROAD
OAKCOURT AVENUE
OAKCOURT DRIVE
OAKCOURT PARK
OAKCOURT LAWN
CULMORE ROAD
CULMORE PARK
MANOR RD
MANOR PARK
WOODFARM AVENUE
WOODFARM DR
PALMERSTOWN DRIVE
PALMERSTOWN AVENUE
TURRET ROAD
THE OVAL
UPPER ROAD
KENNELSFORT ROAD
N4
M50
CANAL TERRACE
KNOCKMITTEN CLO
KNOCKMITTEN LA
WILLOW ROAD
CHESTNUT RD
SYCAMORE RD
ELM ROAD
HAWTHORN
BEECH RD
KYLEMORE
43
54
61
1
2
3
4
D
E
F

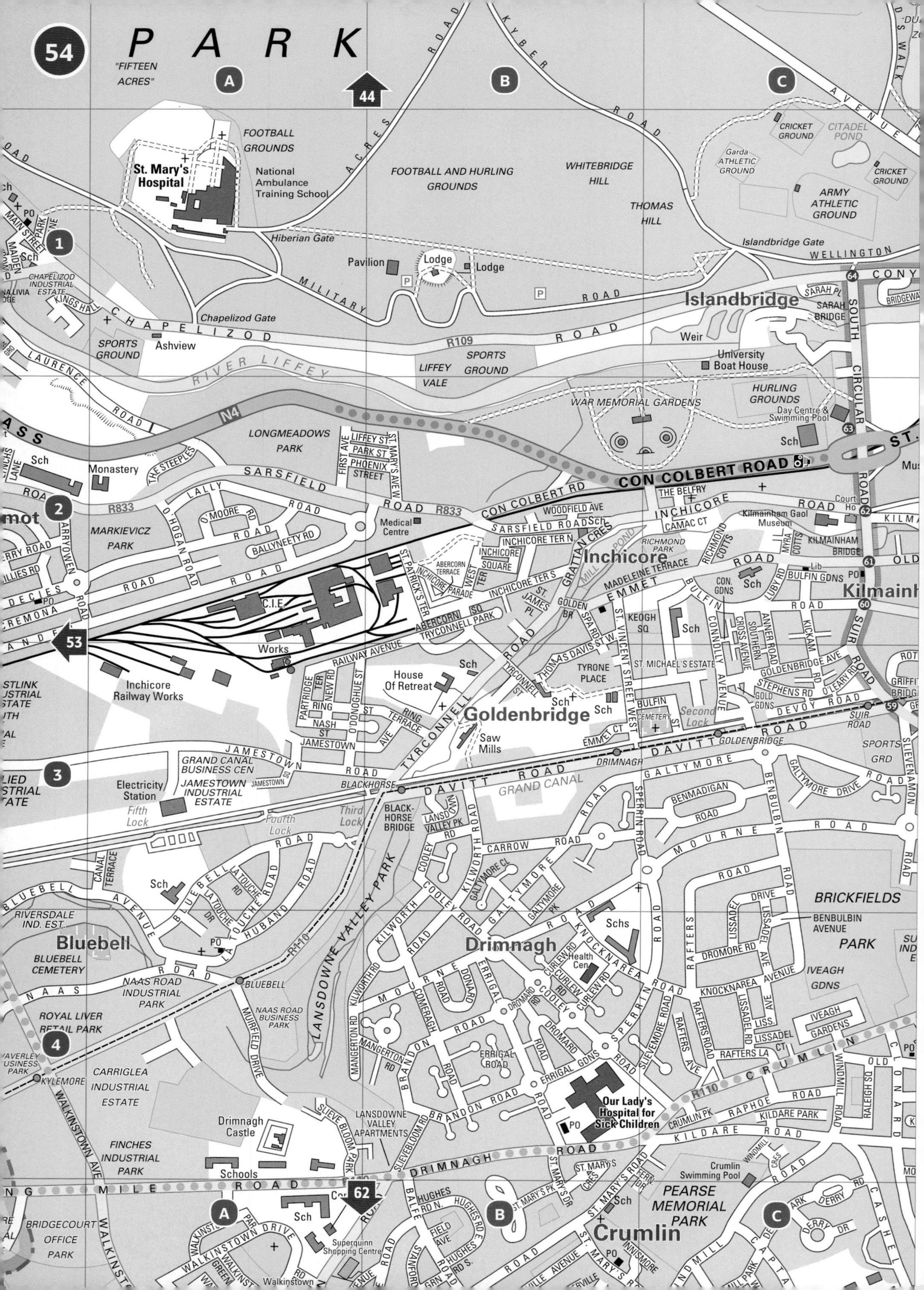
PARK
"FIFTEEN ACRES"
A
B
C
44
St. Mary's Hospital
FOOTBALL GROUNDS
National Ambulance Training School
FOOTBALL AND HURLING GROUNDS
WHITEBRIDGE HILL
THOMAS HILL
KYBER ROAD
ACRES ROAD
CRICKET GROUND
CITADEL POND
Garda ATHLETIC GROUND
ARMY ATHLETIC GROUND
Hiberian Gate
Islandbridge Gate
WELLINGTON
Pavilion
Lodge
MILITARY ROAD
Chapelizod Gate
CHAPELIZOD ROAD
CHAPELIZOD INDUSTRIAL ESTATE
KINGS HALL
MAIN STREET
MAIDEN
PARK
PO
Sch
1
Islandbridge
SARAH PL
SARAH BRIDGE
CONYNGHAM
BRIDGEWATER
SOUTH CIRCULAR ROAD
Ashview
SPORTS GROUND
R109
Weir
University Boat House
RIVER LIFFEY
LIFFEY VALE
SPORTS GROUND
LAURENCE ROAD
WAR MEMORIAL GARDENS
HURLING GROUNDS
Day Centre & Swimming Pool
N4
LONGMEADOWS PARK
LIFFEY ST
PARK ST
PHOENIX STREET
FIRST AVE
ST. MARY'S AVE W
CON COLBERT ROAD
THE BELFRY
Monastery
THE STEEPLES
SARSFIELD ROAD
R833
2
MARKIEVICZ PARK
LALLY ROAD
O'MOORE RD
O'HOGAN ROAD
BALLYNEETY RD
Medical Centre
CON COLBERT RD
WOODFIELD AVE
SARSFIELD ROAD
INCHICORE ROAD
Court Ho
Kilmainham Gaol Museum
CAMAC CT
INCHICORE TER N
INCHICORE SQUARE
RICHMOND PARK
RICHMOND COTTS
KILMAINHAM BRIDGE
Inchicore
GRATTAN CRES
MILL POND
ABERCORN TERRACE
INCHICORE PARADE
WEST TER
ST. PATRICK'S TER
INCHICORE TER S
ST. JAMES PL
MADELEINE TERRACE
EMMET ROAD
GOLDEN BR
C.I.E.
Works
53
CREMONA
DECIES
KYLEMORE
ABERCORN SQ
TYRCONNELL PARK
Inchicore Railway Works
RAILWAY AVENUE
CON. GDNS
Sch
Lib
PO
BULFIN GDNS
BULFIN ROAD
LUBY RD
Kilmainham
KEOGH SQ
SPA RD
ST. VINCENT STREET W
THOMAS DAVIS ST W
TYRONE PLACE
ST. MICHAEL'S ESTATE
CONNOLLY AVENUE
CROSS AVENUE
SOUTHERN
ANNER ROAD
KICKHAM
GOLDENBRIDGE AVE
STEPHENS RD
O'LEARY RD
SUIR ROAD
House Of Retreat
PARTRIDGE TER
NEW RD
RING ST
NASH ST
O'DONOGHUE ST
RING TERRACE
JAMESTOWN AVE
TYRCONNELL ROAD
Goldenbridge
Saw Mills
BULFIN
CEMETERY
Second Lock
EMMET CT
DEVOY ROAD
SUIR ROAD
GOLDENBRIDGE
DAVITT ROAD
DRIMNAGH
SPORTS GRD
SLIEVENAMON
3
JAMESTOWN ROAD
GRAND CANAL BUSINESS CEN
JAMESTOWN INDUSTRIAL ESTATE
Electricity Station
Fifth Lock
Fourth Lock
Third Lock
BLACKHORSE
BLACKHORSE BRIDGE
GRAND CANAL
GALTYMORE ROAD
GALTYMORE DRIVE
BENMADIGAN ROAD
BENBULBIN ROAD
MOURNE ROAD
LANSDOWNE VALLEY PK
KILWORTH ROAD
CARROW ROAD
SPERRIN ROAD
CANAL TERRACE
BLUEBELL AVENUE
LATOUCHE RD
HUBAND ROAD
RIVERSDALE IND. EST.
Bluebell
BLUEBELL CEMETERY
COOLEY ROAD
GALTYMORE CL
GALTYMORE PK
Schs
KNOCKNAREA ROAD
Drimnagh
Health Cen
CURLEW RD
BRICKFIELDS PARK
BENBULBIN AVENUE
LISSADEL DRIVE
LISSADEL AVE
DROMORE RD
IVEAGH GDNS
KNOCKNAREA AVENUE
IVEAGH GARDENS
RAFTERS ROAD
RAFTERS LA
NAAS ROAD
NAAS ROAD INDUSTRIAL PARK
NAAS ROAD BUSINESS PARK
R110
ROYAL LIVER RETAIL PARK
4
LANSDOWNE VALLEY PARK
MUIRFIELD DRIVE
KILWORTH RD
MANGERTON RD
COMERAGH ROAD
DONARD
ERRIGAL ROAD
DROMARD
ERRIGAL GDNS
BRANDON ROAD
SLIEVEMORE ROAD
CRUMLIN ROAD
WINDMILL ROAD
RALEIGH SQ
OLD COUNTY RD
CLONARD
Our Lady's Hospital for Sick Children
CRUMLIN PK
RAPHOE ROAD
KILDARE PARK
KILDARE ROAD
KYLEMORE
WALKINSTOWN AVE
CARRIGLEA INDUSTRIAL ESTATE
Drimnagh Castle
FINCHES INDUSTRIAL PARK
Schools
SLIEVE BLOOM PARK
LANSDOWNE VALLEY APARTMENTS
DRIMNAGH ROAD
ST. MARY'S CRES
ST. MARY'S RD
FERN DR
Crumlin Swimming Pool
WINDMILL CRES
LONG MILE ROAD
62
BRIDGECOURT OFFICE PARK
WALKINSTOWN DRIVE
Sch
Superquinn Shopping Centre
HUGHES RD N.
HUGHES RD E.
HUGHES RD S.
FIELD AVE
BALFE
STANNFORD
PEARSE MEMORIAL PARK
Crumlin
ST. MARY'S PK
DERRY RD
DERRY DR
CASHEL
Walkinstown

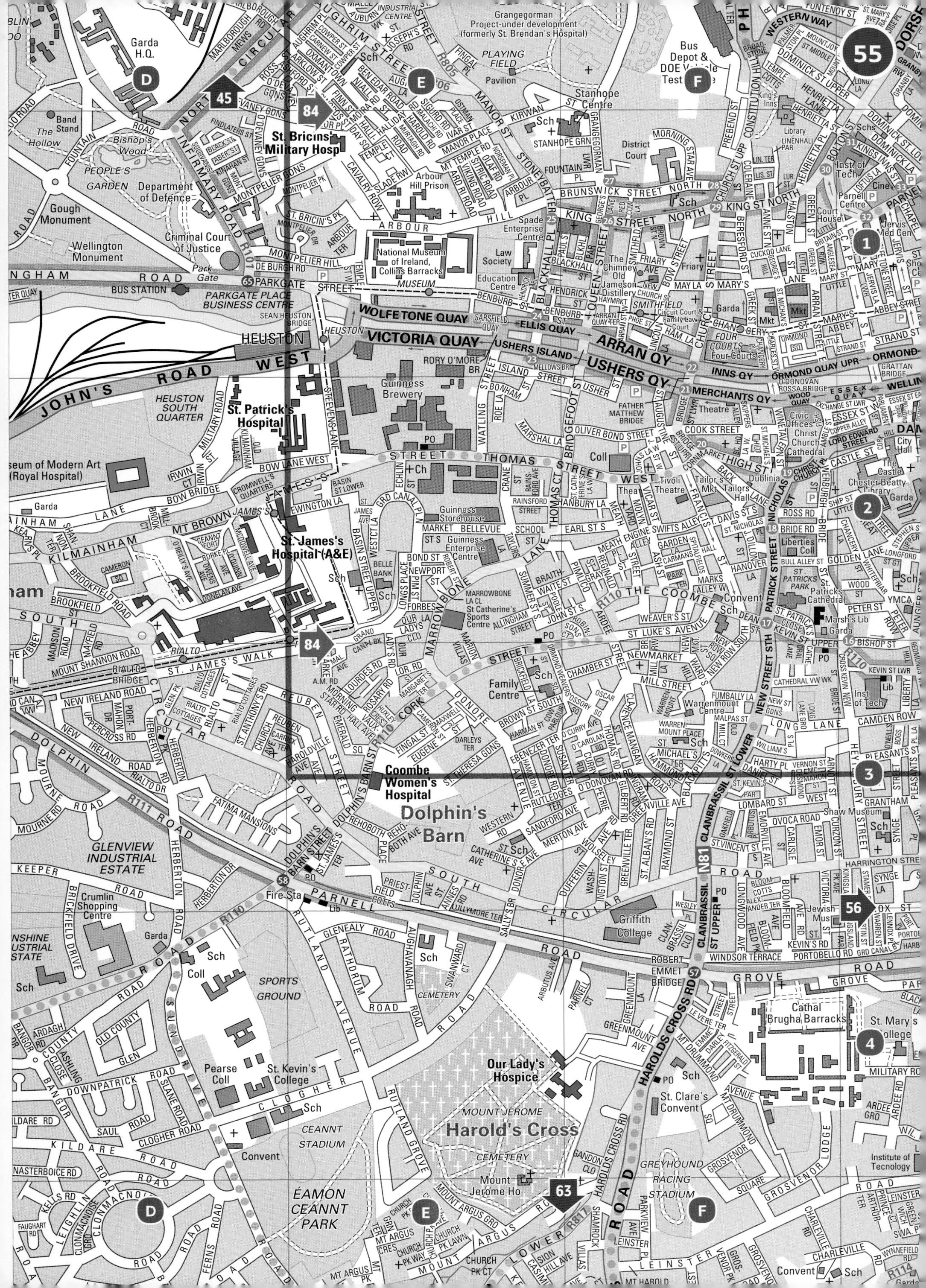
Garda H.Q.
D
E
F
45
84
56
63
Grangegorman Project-under development (formerly St. Brendan's Hospital)
PLAYING FIELD
Pavilion
Bus Depot & DOE Vehicle Test
Stanhope Centre
District Court
St. Bricins' Military Hosp
Arbour Hill Prison
Band Stand
The Hollow
Bishop's Wood
PEOPLE'S GARDEN
Department of Defence
Gough Monument
Wellington Monument
Criminal Court of Justice
Park Gate
BUS STATION
PARKGATE PLACE BUSINESS CENTRE
National Museum of Ireland, Collins Barracks
MUSEUM
Law Society
Education Centre
Spade Enterprise Centre
The Chimney
Old Jameson Distillery
King's Inns
Library
Inst of Tech
Parnell Centre
Court House
Jervis Med Cen
HEUSTON
HEUSTON SOUTH QUARTER
St. Patrick's Hospital
Guinness Brewery
WOLFETONE QUAY
VICTORIA QUAY
ARRAN QY
USHERS QY
USHERS ISLAND
ELLIS QUAY
INNS QY
ORMOND QUAY UPR
MERCHANTS QY
WOOD QUAY
ESSEX QUAY
FOUR COURTS
Four Courts
Garda
Mkt
Theatre
Civic Offices
Christ Church Cathedral
City Hall
The Castle
Chester Beatty Library
Dublinia
Tivoli Theatre
Tailor's Mkt
Tailors Hall
Museum of Modern Art (Royal Hospital)
Guinness Storehouse
Guinness Enterprise Centre
St. James's Hospital (A&E)
MARROWBONE LA CL
St Catherine's Sports Centre
THOMAS STREET WEST
JOHN'S ROAD WEST
ST. JAMES'S WALK
Liberties Coll
St. Patricks Park
St. Patricks Cathedral
Marsh's Lib
YMCA
Convent
Inst of Tech
Family Centre
Warrenmount Centre
Coombe Women's Hospital
Dolphin's Barn
GLENVIEW INDUSTRIAL ESTATE
Crumlin Shopping Centre
Fire Sta
Lib
Griffith College
Shaw Museum
Jewish Mus
SOUTH CIRCULAR ROAD
GRAND CANAL
PARNELL ROAD
HAROLDS CROSS RD
Cathal Brugha Barracks
St. Mary's College
SPORTS GROUND
CEMETERY
Pearse Coll
St. Kevin's College
CEANNT STADIUM
ÉAMON CEANNT PARK
Our Lady's Hospice
MOUNT JEROME CEMETERY
Harold's Cross
Mount Jerome Ho
GREYHOUND RACING STADIUM
St. Clare's Convent
Institute of Tecnology
R805
R101
R110
R111
R817
N81
R114

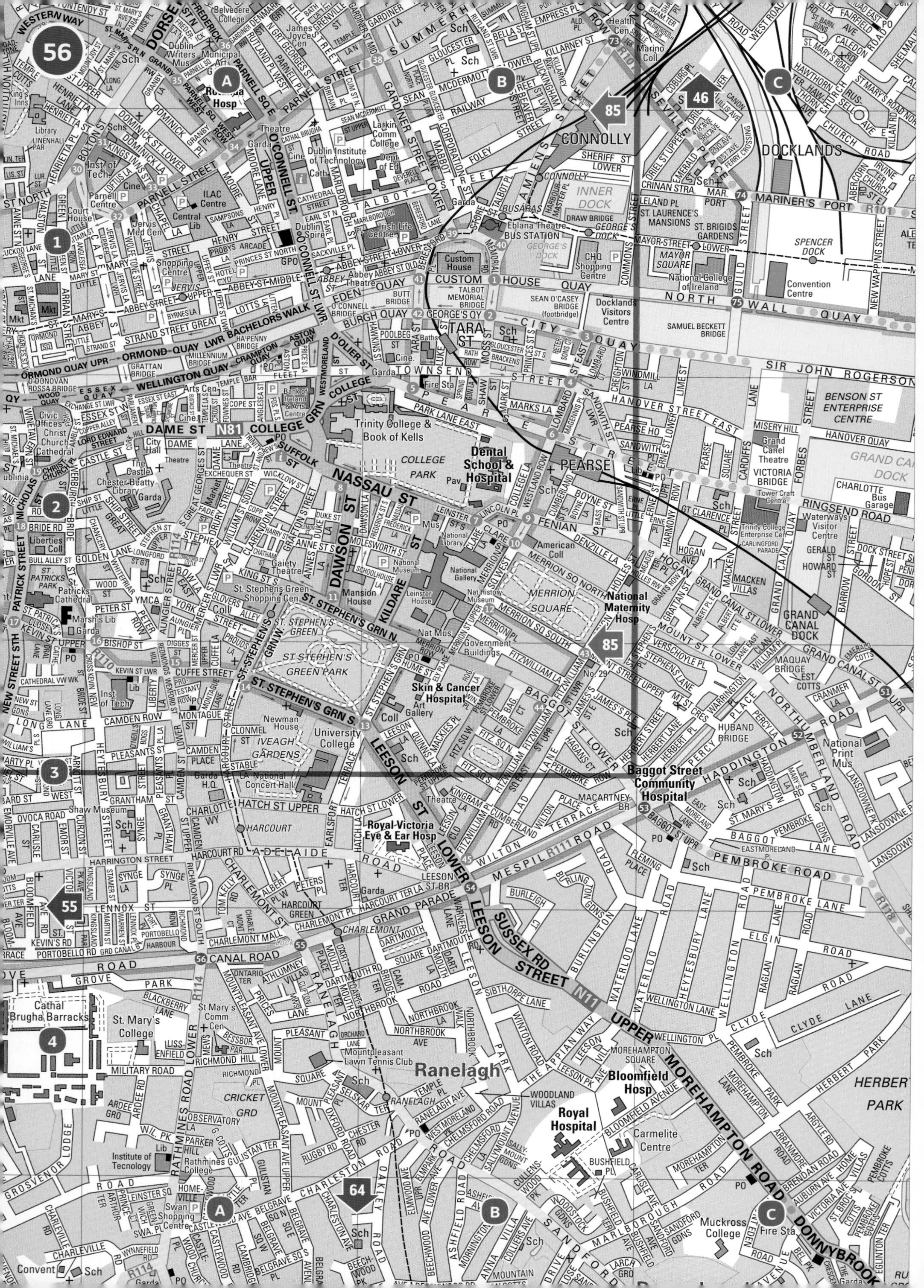
56
A
B
C
1
2
3
4
46
85
55
64
CONNOLLY
DOCKLANDS
INNER DOCK
SPENCER DOCK
GRAND CANAL DOCK
Convention Centre
National College of Ireland
CHQ Shopping Centre
Custom House
BUSARAS
MAYOR SQUARE
CUSTOM HOUSE QUAY
NORTH WALL QUAY
CITY QUAY
SIR JOHN ROGERSON'S QUAY
Samuel Beckett Bridge
Sean O'Casey Bridge (footbridge)
Talbot Memorial Bridge
Butt Bridge
O'Connell Bridge
Ha'penny Bridge
Millennium Bridge
Grattan Bridge
O'Donovan Rossa Bridge
BACHELORS WALK
ORMOND QUAY UPR
ORMOND QUAY LWR
WELLINGTON QUAY
ESSEX QUAY
BURGH QUAY
GEORGE'S QY
EDEN QUAY
O'CONNELL ST
UPPER O'CONNELL ST
PARNELL STREET
PARNELL SQ. E
Rotunda Hosp
Dublin Writers Mus
Belvedere College
James Joyce Cen
Dublin Spire
GPO
ABBEY STREET LOWER
Abbey Theatre
ILAC Centre
Central Lib
Jervis Shopping Centre
Mkt
Library
King's Inns
Inst. of Tech.
Dublin Institute of Technology
Larkin Comm College
Irish Life Centre
Bank of Ireland & Arts Centre
Arts Cen
Civic Offices
Christ Church Cathedral
DAME ST
N81
COLLEGE GRN
City Hall
The Castle
Chester Beatty Library
Trinity College & Book of Kells
COLLEGE PARK
Dental School & Hospital
PEARSE
PEARSE ST
TOWNSEND ST
NASSAU ST
DAWSON ST
KILDARE ST
National Library
National Museum
National Gallery
Leinster House
Nat History Museum
Government Buildings
MERRION SQUARE
MERRION SQ NORTH
MERRION SQ SOUTH
National Maternity Hosp
American Coll
Gaiety Theatre
St. Stephens Green Shopping Cen
Mansion House
ST. STEPHEN'S GRN N.
ST. STEPHEN'S GRN S.
ST. STEPHEN'S GREEN PARK
Newman House
University College
IVEAGH GARDENS
National Concert Hall
Skin & Cancer Hospital
Royal Victoria Eye & Ear Hosp
HARCOURT
CHARLEMONT
RANELAGH
Ranelagh
Liberties Coll
ST. PATRICKS PARK
St. Patricks Cathedral
Marsh's Lib
PATRICK STREET
NEW STREET STH
CAMDEN ROW
Shaw Museum
Garda H.Q.
ADELAIDE ROAD
LEESON STREET LOWER
Baggot Street Community Hospital
HADDINGTON ROAD
NORTHUMBERLAND ROAD
National Print Mus
GRAND CANAL ST LOWER
Waterways Visitor Centre
Grand Canal Theatre
BENSON ST ENTERPRISE CENTRE
HANOVER QUAY
RINGSEND ROAD
Charlotte Bus Garage
Tower Craft Centre
Trinity College Enterprise Cen
Hogan Ave
Huband Bridge
Maquay Bridge
Victoria Bridge
GRAND CANAL
Cathal Brugha Barracks
St. Mary's College
CANAL ROAD
GROVE PARK
RATHMINES ROAD LOWER
Institute of Tecnology
Rathmines College
Swan Shopping Centre
CRICKET GRD
Mountpleasant Lawn Tennis Club
N11
SUSSEX RD
UPPER LEESON STREET
MOREHAMPTON ROAD
Bloomfield Hosp
Royal Hospital
Carmelite Centre
Muckross College
HERBERT PARK
DONNYBROOK
R101
R110
R111
R114
R118
Convent
Fire Sta
Sch
PO
Garda

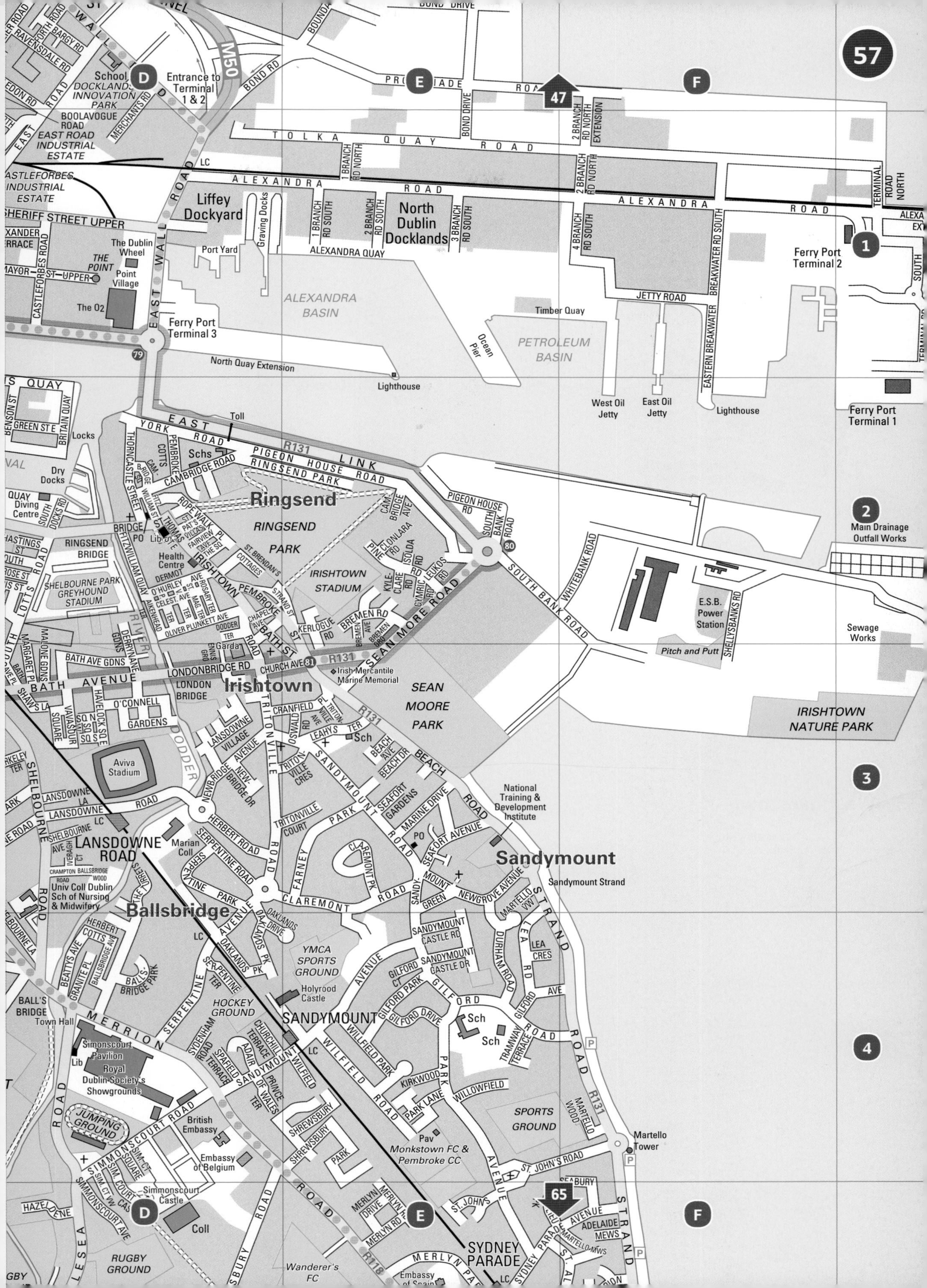

D
E
F
47
65
1
2
3
4
M50
Entrance to Terminal 1 & 2
School
DOCKLANDS INNOVATION PARK
BOOLAVOGUE ROAD
EAST ROAD INDUSTRIAL ESTATE
CASTLEFORBES INDUSTRIAL ESTATE
SHERIFF STREET UPPER
BOND RD
BOND DRIVE
PROMENADE ROAD
TOLKA QUAY ROAD
ALEXANDRA ROAD
1 BRANCH RD NORTH
2 BRANCH RD NORTH
2 BRANCH RD NORTH EXTENSION
1 BRANCH RD SOUTH
2 BRANCH RD SOUTH
3 BRANCH RD SOUTH
4 BRANCH RD SOUTH
TERMINAL ROAD NORTH
TERMINAL ROAD SOUTH
Liffey Dockyard
Graving Docks
North Dublin Docklands
Port Yard
ALEXANDRA QUAY
ALEXANDRA BASIN
The Dublin Wheel
THE POINT
Point Village
The O2
EAST WALL ROAD
CASTLEFORBES RD
MAYOR ST UPPER
Ferry Port Terminal 3
North Quay Extension
Lighthouse
Ocean Pier
Timber Quay
PETROLEUM BASIN
JETTY ROAD
EASTERN BREAKWATER
BREAKWATER RD SOUTH
West Oil Jetty
East Oil Jetty
Ferry Port Terminal 2
Ferry Port Terminal 1
Toll
EAST LINK
YORK ROAD
R131
PIGEON HOUSE ROAD
RINGSEND PARK ROAD
CAMBRIDGE ROAD
Schs
Ringsend
RINGSEND PARK
IRISHTOWN STADIUM
PIGEON HOUSE RD
SOUTH BANK ROAD
SOUTH BANK ROAD
WHITEBANK ROAD
E.S.B. Power Station
SHELLYSBANKS RD
Pitch and Putt
Main Drainage Outfall Works
Sewage Works
IRISHTOWN NATURE PARK
SEAN MORE ROAD
SEAN MOORE PARK
Irish Mercantile Marine Memorial
Dry Docks
Diving Centre
RINGSEND BRIDGE
SHELBOURNE PARK GREYHOUND STADIUM
Health Centre
IRISHTOWN
PEMBROKE
BATH ST
CHURCH AVE
LONDONBRIDGE RD
BATH AVENUE
LONDON BRIDGE
Irishtown
O'CONNELL GARDENS
Garda
RIVER DODDER
Aviva Stadium
LANSDOWNE ROAD
LANSDOWNE VILLAGE
TRITONVILLE ROAD
SANDYMOUNT ROAD
BEACH ROAD
National Training & Development Institute
Sandymount
Sandymount Strand
STRAND ROAD
Marian Coll
HERBERT ROAD
SERPENTINE AVENUE
CLAREMONT ROAD
Univ Coll Dublin Sch of Nursing & Midwifery
Ballsbridge
YMCA SPORTS GROUND
Holyrood Castle
HOCKEY GROUND
SANDYMOUNT
GILFORD ROAD
Sch
MERRION ROAD
Town Hall
BALL'S BRIDGE
Simmonscourt Pavilion
Royal Dublin Society's Showgrounds
JUMPING GROUND
British Embassy
Embassy of Belgium
Simmonscourt Castle
Coll
RUGBY GROUND
WILFIELD ROAD
Pav
Monkstown FC & Pembroke CC
SPORTS GROUND
Martello Tower
ST. JOHN'S ROAD
SYDNEY PARADE
MERLYN PARK
R118
Wanderer's FC
Embassy of Spain

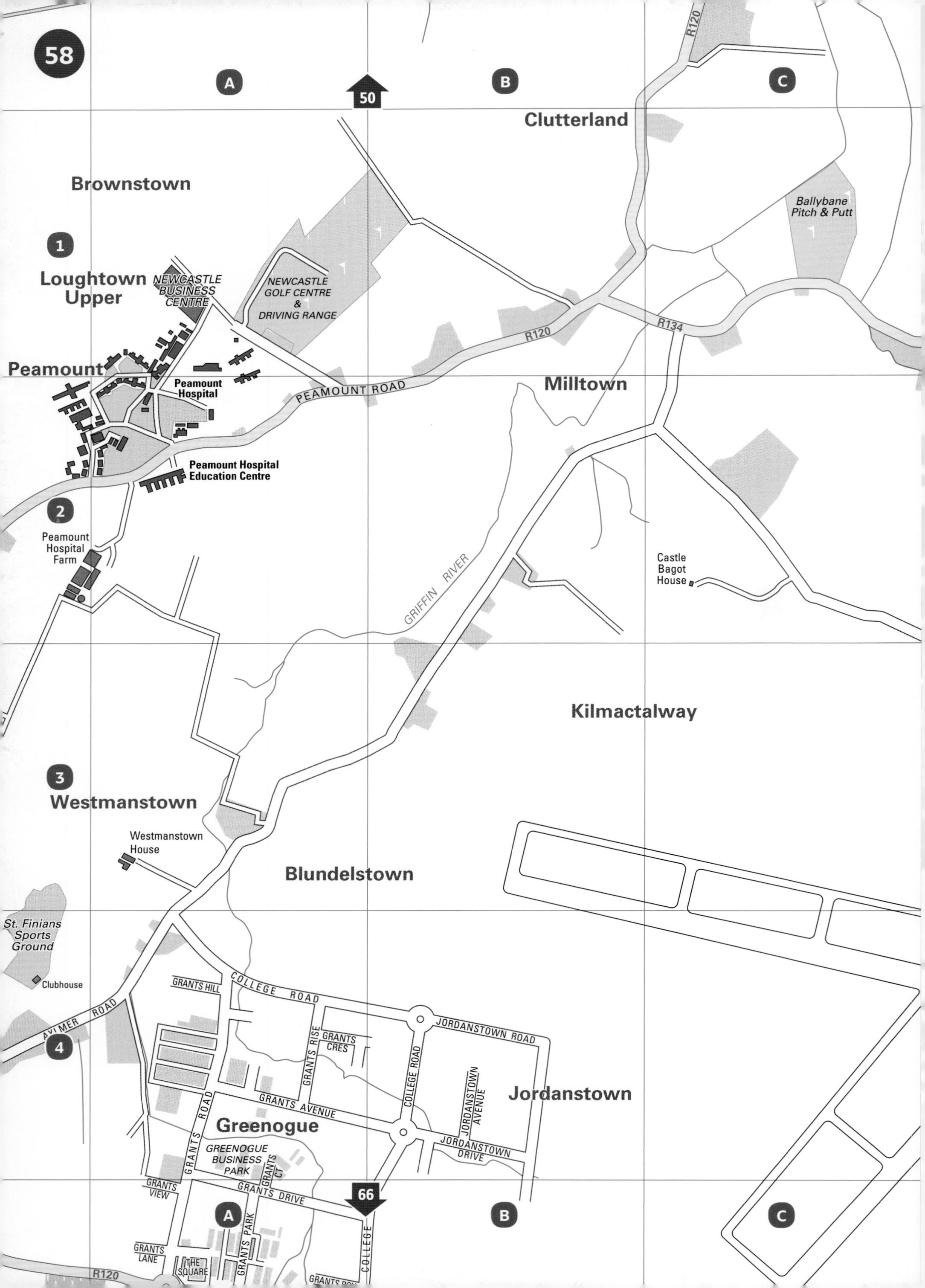
A
B
C
50
Clutterland
Brownstown
Ballybane
Pitch & Putt
1
Loughtown
Upper
NEWCASTLE
BUSINESS
CENTRE
NEWCASTLE
GOLF CENTRE
&
DRIVING RANGE
R120
R134
Peamount
Peamount
Hospital
PEAMOUNT ROAD
Milltown
Peamount Hospital
Education Centre
2
Peamount
Hospital
Farm
Castle
Bagot
House
GRIFFIN RIVER
Kilmactalway
3
Westmanstown
Westmanstown
House
Blundelstown
St. Finians
Sports
Ground
Clubhouse
GRANTS HILL
COLLEGE ROAD
AYLMER ROAD
4
JORDANSTOWN ROAD
GRANTS RISE
GRANTS
CRES
COLLEGE ROAD
JORDANSTOWN
AVENUE
Jordanstown
GRANTS AVENUE
GRANTS ROAD
Greenogue
JORDANSTOWN
DRIVE
GREENOGUE
BUSINESS
PARK
GRANTS
CT
GRANTS
VIEW
GRANTS DRIVE
66
A
B
C
GRANTS
LANE
THE
SQUARE
GRANTS PARK
COLLEGE
R120

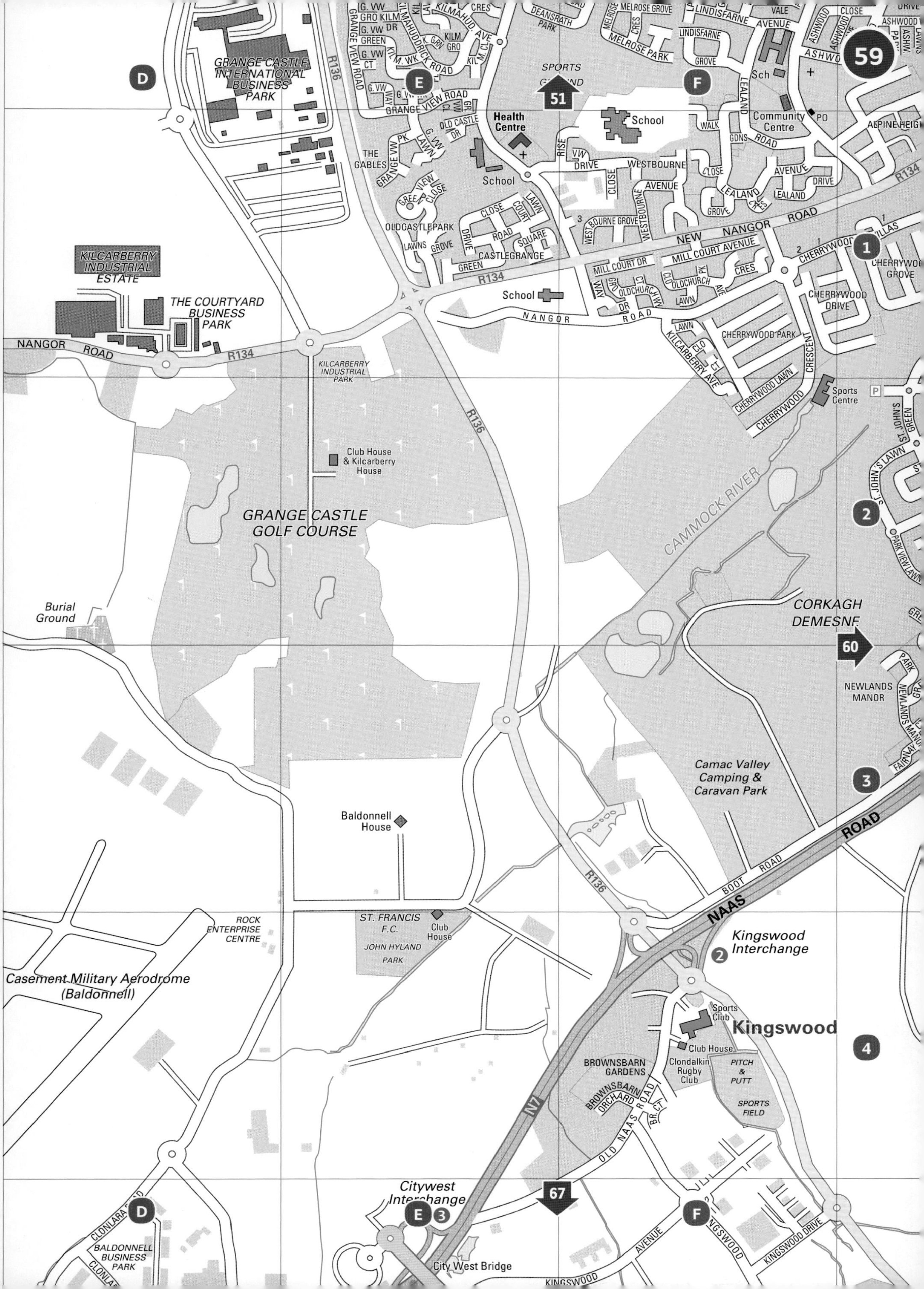
GRANGE CASTLE INTERNATIONAL BUSINESS PARK
KILCARBERRY INDUSTRIAL ESTATE
THE COURTYARD BUSINESS PARK
NANGOR ROAD
R134
R136
KILCARBERRY INDUSTRIAL PARK
Club House & Kilcarberry House
GRANGE CASTLE GOLF COURSE
Burial Ground
Baldonnell House
ST. FRANCIS F.C.
Club House
JOHN HYLAND PARK
ROCK ENTERPRISE CENTRE
Casement Military Aerodrome (Baldonnell)
BALDONNELL BUSINESS PARK
CLONLARA ROAD
Citywest Interchange
City West Bridge
67
51
60
SPORTS GROUND
Health Centre
School
Sch
Community Centre
PO
THE GABLES
OLDCASTLEPARK
CASTLEGRANGE
NEW NANGOR ROAD
MILL COURT AVENUE
MILL COURT DR
OLDCHURCH
WESTBOURNE
LEALAND
LINDISFARNE
MELROSE PARK
MELROSE GROVE
DEANSRATH PARK
GRANGE VIEW ROAD
KILMAHUDDRICK ROAD
ALPINE HEIGHTS
CHERRYWOOD VILLAS
CHERRYWOOD GROVE
CHERRYWOOD DRIVE
CHERRYWOOD PARK
CHERRYWOOD LAWN
CHERRYWOOD CRESCENT
KILCARBERRY AVE
Sports Centre
CAMMOCK RIVER
ST. JOHN'S LAWN
ST. JOHN'S GREEN
PARK VIEW LAWN
CORKAGH DEMESNE
NEWLANDS MANOR
Camac Valley Camping & Caravan Park
BOOT ROAD
NAAS ROAD
N7
Kingswood Interchange
Kingswood
Sports Club
Club House
Clondalkin Rugby Club
PITCH & PUTT
SPORTS FIELD
BROWNSBARN GARDENS
BROWNSBARN ORCHARD
OLD NAAS ROAD
KINGSWOOD AVENUE
KINGSWOOD DRIVE
D
E
F
1
2
3
4

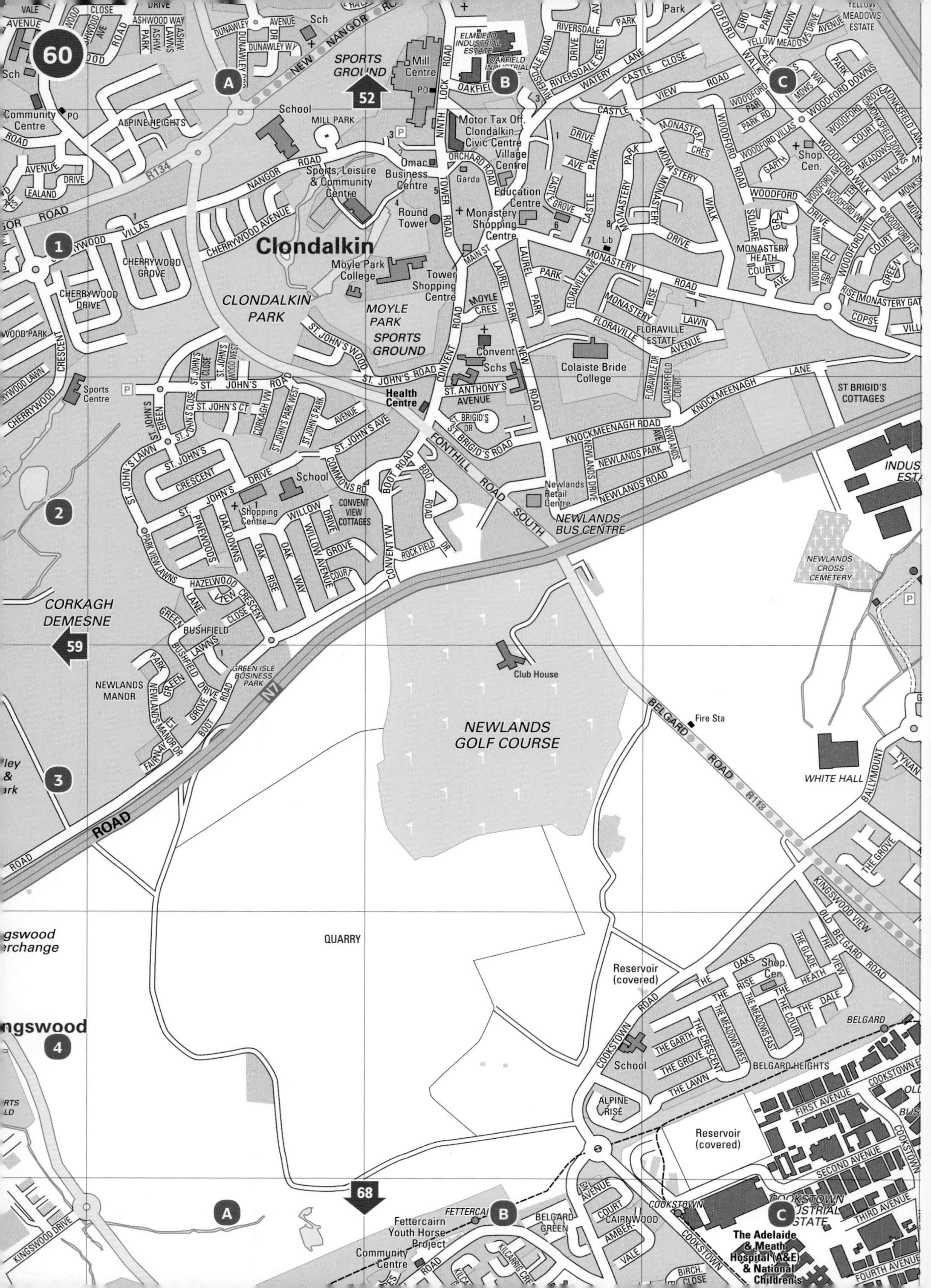
Clondalkin
CLONDALKIN PARK
MOYLE PARK SPORTS GROUND
SPORTS GROUND
52
59
68
NEWLANDS GOLF COURSE
Club House
QUARRY
CORKAGH DEMESNE
NEWLANDS BUS CENTRE
NEWLANDS CROSS CEMETERY
WHITE HALL
ST BRIGID'S COTTAGES
Reservoir (covered)
Reservoir (covered)
COOKSTOWN INDUSTRIAL ESTATE
The Adelaide & Meath Hospital (A&E) & National Children's
Fettercairn Youth Horse Project
Community Centre
Community Centre
Sports Centre
Sports, Leisure & Community Centre
Omac Business Centre
Mill Centre
Motor Tax Off.
Clondalkin Civic Centre
Village Centre
Garda
Education Centre
Round Tower
Monastery Shopping Centre
Tower Shopping Centre
Moyle Park College
Convent Schs
Colaiste Bride College
Health Centre
Newlands Retail Centre
Shopping Centre
Shop. Cen.
Shop. Cen.
School
School
School
Lib
PO
Fire Sta
ELMFIELD INDUSTRIAL ESTATE
OAKFIELD INDUSTRIAL
GREEN ISLE BUSINESS PARK
NEWLANDS MANOR
FLORAVILLE ESTATE
BELGARD HEIGHTS
BELGARD
COOKSTOWN
FETTERCAIRN
YELLOW MEADOWS ESTATE
MILL PARK
ALPINE HEIGHTS
NEW NANGOR ROAD
NANGOR ROAD
R134
N7
ROAD
BELGARD ROAD
R113
FONTHILL ROAD SOUTH
NINTH LOCK ROAD
TOWER ROAD
CONVENT ROAD
NEW ROAD
MAIN ST
ORCHARD ROAD
MONASTERY ROAD
KNOCKMEENAGH ROAD
KNOCKMEENAGH LANE
NEWLANDS ROAD
NEWLANDS PARK
NEWLANDS DRIVE
LAUREL PARK
FLORAVILLE AVE
FLORAVILLE AVENUE
ST. JOHN'S ROAD
ST. JOHN'S WOOD
ST. JOHN'S DRIVE
ST. JOHN'S CRESCENT
ST. JOHN'S LAWN
ST. JOHN'S AVE
ST. JOHN'S PARK WEST
ST. ANTHONY'S AVENUE
ST. BRIGID'S ROAD
CHERRYWOOD AVENUE
CHERRYWOOD VILLAS
CHERRYWOOD GROVE
CHERRYWOOD DRIVE
CRESCENT
BOOT ROAD
COMMONS RD
CONVENT VIEW COTTAGES
ROCK FIELD DR.
WILLOW DRIVE
WILLOW AVENUE
OAK DOWNS
OAK RISE
OAK WAY
PINEWOODS
PARK VIEW LAWNS
HAZELWOOD VIEW
HAZELWOOD CRESCENT
BUSHFIELD LAWNS
BUSHFIELD DRIVE
FAIRWAY
MONASTERY PARK
MONASTERY DRIVE
MONASTERY WALK
MONASTERY CRES
MONASTERY RISE
MONASTERY HEATH COURT
CASTLE CLOSE
CASTLE VIEW ROAD
CASTLE PARK
WATERY LANE
RIVERSDALE ROAD
RIVERSDALE CRES
WOODFORD ROAD
WOODFORD WALK
WOODFORD DOWNS
WOODFORD VILLAS
WOODFORD HILL
WOODFORD DRIVE
MONKSFIELD DOWNS
MONKSFIELD LAWN
BALLYMOUNT
THE GROVE
KINGSWOOD VIEW
OLD BELGARD ROAD
THE OAKS
THE GLADE
THE HEATH
THE DALE
THE COURT
THE RISE
THE GARTH
THE CRESCENT
THE GROVE
THE LAWN
THE MEADOWS WEST
THE MEADOWS EAST
COOKSTOWN ROAD
ALPINE RISE
BELGARD GREEN
CAIRNWOOD
AMBER VALE
FIRST AVENUE
SECOND AVENUE
THIRD AVENUE
FOURTH AVENUE
KINGSWOOD DRIVE
Kingswood Interchange
Kingswood
A
B
C
1
2
3
4

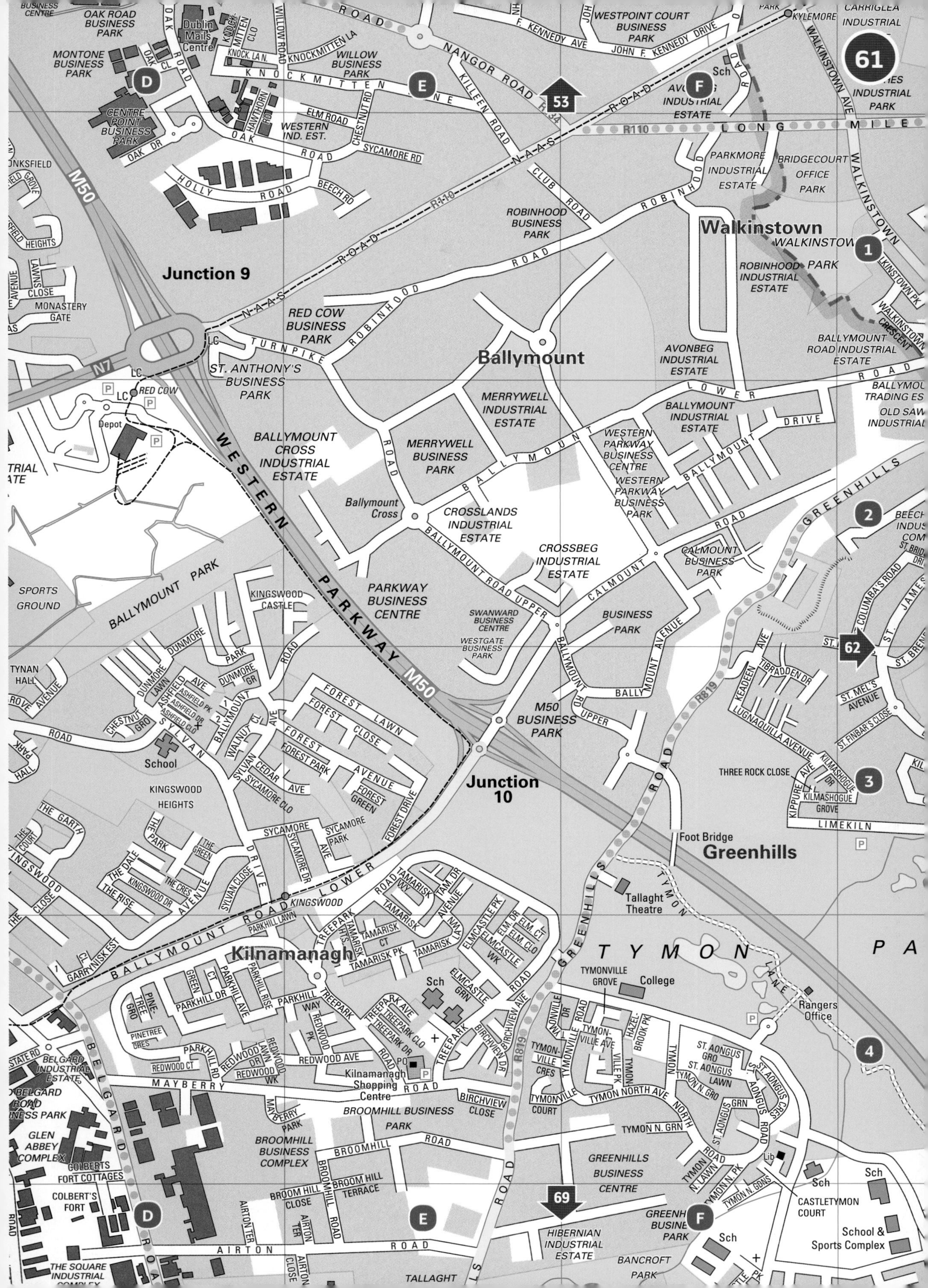
OAK ROAD BUSINESS PARK
MONTONE BUSINESS PARK
Dublin Mails Centre
KNOCKMITTEN CLO
KNOCKMITTEN LA
KNOCK. LA N.
WILLOW ROAD
WILLOW BUSINESS PARK
KNOCKMITTEN LANE
CENTRE POINT BUSINESS PARK
OAK DR
OAK CL
OAK ROAD
HAWTHORN RD
ELM ROAD
WESTERN IND. EST.
CHESTNUT RD
SYCAMORE RD
HOLLY ROAD
BEECH RD
NANGOR ROAD
KILLEEN ROAD
53
F. KENNEDY AVE
JOHN F. KENNEDY DRIVE
WESTPOINT COURT BUSINESS PARK
KYLEMORE
CARRIGLEA INDUSTRIAL
WALKINSTOWN AVE
INDUSTRIAL PARK
AVONBEG INDUSTRIAL ESTATE
Sch
R110
LONG MILE
NAAS ROAD
R34
CLUB ROAD
PARKMORE INDUSTRIAL ESTATE
BRIDGECOURT OFFICE PARK
WALKINSTOWN
ROBINHOOD BUSINESS PARK
ROBINHOOD ROAD
Walkinstown
WALKINSTOWN PARK
ROBINHOOD INDUSTRIAL ESTATE
Junction 9
M50
N7
LC
RED COW
Depot
RED COW BUSINESS PARK
ST. ANTHONY'S BUSINESS PARK
TURNPIKE
Ballymount
AVONBEG INDUSTRIAL ESTATE
BALLYMOUNT ROAD INDUSTRIAL ESTATE
WALKINSTOWN CRESCENT
LOWER BALLYMOUNT ROAD
BALLYMOUNT TRADING ESTATE
OLD SAW INDUSTRIAL
MERRYWELL INDUSTRIAL ESTATE
MERRYWELL BUSINESS PARK
BALLYMOUNT INDUSTRIAL ESTATE
BALLYMOUNT DRIVE
WESTERN PARKWAY BUSINESS CENTRE
WESTERN PARKWAY BUSINESS PARK
BALLYMOUNT CROSS INDUSTRIAL ESTATE
Ballymount Cross
CROSSLANDS INDUSTRIAL ESTATE
GREENHILLS ROAD
BEECH INDUSTRIAL COMPLEX
CROSSBEG INDUSTRIAL ESTATE
CALMOUNT BUSINESS PARK
CALMOUNT ROAD
BALLYMOUNT PARK
SPORTS GROUND
KINGSWOOD CASTLE
PARKWAY BUSINESS CENTRE
WESTERN PARKWAY
BALLYMOUNT ROAD UPPER
SWANWARD BUSINESS CENTRE
WESTGATE BUSINESS PARK
BUSINESS PARK
BALLYMOUNT AVENUE
ST. COLUMBA'S ROAD
ST. JAMES
ST. BRENDAN
62
TIBRADDEN DR
KEADEEN AVE
ST. MEL'S AVENUE
ST. FINBAR'S CLOSE
LUGNAQUILLA AVENUE
R819
M50 BUSINESS PARK
TYNAN HALL
DUNMORE PARK
DUNMORE GR
DUNMORE LAWN
ASHFIELD AVE
ASHFIELD PK
ASHFIELD DR
ASHFIELD CLO
CHESTNUT GRO
SYLVAN
School
WALNUT CL
FOREST LAWN
FOREST CLOSE
FOREST PARK
FOREST AVENUE
FOREST GREEN
FOREST DRIVE
SYLVAN CEDAR AVE
SYCAMORE CLO
KINGSWOOD HEIGHTS
Junction 10
THREE ROCK CLOSE
KILMASHOGUE DR
KILMASHOGUE GROVE
KIPPURE AVE
LIMEKILN
Foot Bridge
Greenhills
THE GARTH
THE COURT
THE PARK
THE GREEN
THE DALE
THE RISE
THE CRES
KINGSWOOD DR
KINGSWOOD AVENUE
SYCAMORE PARK
SYCAMORE DR
SYLVAN CLOSE
SYLVAN DRIVE
LOWER BALLYMOUNT ROAD
KINGSWOOD
Tallaght Theatre
TYMON LANE
TAMARISK WAY
TAMARISK HTS.
TAMARISK CT
TAMARISK PK
TAMARISK AVENUE
TREEPARK ROAD
ELMCASTLE PK
ELMCASTLE WK
ELM DR
ELM CT
ELM CLO
PARKHILL LAWN
GARRYNISK EST
Kilnamanagh
TYMON PARK
TYMONVILLE GROVE
College
Rangers Office
PINETREE GRO
PINETREE CRES
PARKHILL DR
PARKHILL AVE
PARKHILL RISE
PARKHILL WAY
PARKHILL RD
PARKHILL GREEN
REDWOOD CT
REDWOOD AVE
REDWOOD WK
REDWOOD DR
REDWOOD PK
TREEPARK AVE
TREEPARK CLO
TREEPARK DR
ELMCASTLE GRN
BIRCHVIEW DR
BIRCHVIEW AVE
TYMONVILLE DR
TYMONVILLE ROAD
TYMONVILLE AVE
TYMONVILLE CRES
TYMONVILLE COURT
HAZELBROOK PK
TYMON NORTH AVE
TYMON N. GRO
TYMON N. GRN
TYMON N. LAWN
TYMON N. PK
TYMON N. GDNS
ST. AONGUS GRO
ST. AONGUS LAWN
ST. AONGUS GRN
ST. AONGUS CRES
ST. AONGUS ROAD
Lib
BELGARD INDUSTRIAL ESTATE
BELGARD ROAD
BELGARD ROAD BUSINESS PARK
GLEN ABBEY COMPLEX
COLBERTS FORT COTTAGES
COLBERT'S FORT
MAYBERRY ROAD
MAYBERRY PARK
Kilnamanagh Shopping Centre
PO
BROOMHILL BUSINESS PARK
BIRCHVIEW CLOSE
BROOMHILL BUSINESS COMPLEX
BROOMHILL ROAD
BROOM HILL CLOSE
BROOM HILL TERRACE
AIRTON TER
AIRTON ROAD
AIRTON CLOSE
69
HIBERNIAN INDUSTRIAL ESTATE
GREENHILLS BUSINESS CENTRE
GREENHILLS BUSINESS PARK
CASTLETYMON COURT
School & Sports Complex
BANCROFT PARK
THE SQUARE INDUSTRIAL COMPLEX
TALLAGHT

62
KYLEMORE
CARRIGLEA INDUSTRIAL ESTATE
FINCHES INDUSTRIAL PARK
Drimnagh Castle
Schools
LANSDOWNE VALLEY APARTMENTS
54
Our Lady's Hospital for Sick Children
PO
R110
RAPHOE ROAD
KILDARE PARK
KILDARE ROAD
CRUMLIN PK
BRANDON ROAD
DRIMNAGH ROAD
NAAS ROAD
LONG MILE ROAD
Convent
Sch
BRIDGECOURT OFFICE PARK
WALKINSTOWN AVENUE
WALKINSTOWN DRIVE
WALKINSTOWN PARADE
WALKINSTOWN GREEN
WALKINSTOWN ROAD
Walkinstown Mall
Superquinn Shopping Centre
HUGHES RD N.
HUGHES RD E.
HUGHES RD S.
FIELD AVE
STANFORD GRN
BALFE ROAD
ST. MARY'S PK
ST. MARY'S CRES
ST. MARY'S DR
ST. MARY'S ROAD
FERN DR
Crumlin Swimming Pool
PEARSE MEMORIAL PARK
Crumlin
INNISMORE
WINDMILL ROAD
DERRY PARK
DERRY DR
DERRY RD
CASHEL ROAD
CAPTAINS ROAD
WINDMILL PARK
WINDMILL AVE
Schools
ARMAGH ROAD
Sch
Convent
Walkinstown
WALKINSTOWN PARK
ROBINHOOD INDUSTRIAL ESTATE
WALKINSTOWN PK
WALKINSTOWN CRESCENT
WALKINSTOWN CROSS
KILNAMANAGH ROAD
THOMAS MOORE ROAD
HARDBECK AVENUE
HARTY AVE
HARTY CT
WALLACE RD
BUNTING RD
JOHN McCORMACK AVENUE
BIGGER ROAD
SOMERVILLE AVENUE
SOMERVILLE GRN
SOMERVILLE PARK
LISLE ROAD
BALFE AVENUE
BALFE ROAD EAST
ESPOSITO RD
PERCY FRENCH RD
CROTTY AVE
O'DWYER RD
Lib
MOERAN ROAD
DOWLAND ROAD
FATHER KITT CT
ST. AGNES ROAD
ST. AGNES PARK
Garda
STANNAWAY ROAD
CAPTAINS AVE
CAPTAINS DRIVE
STANNAWAY AVENUE
BALLYMOUNT ROAD INDUSTRIAL ESTATE
R112
R819
PO
CROMWELLS FORT ROAD
BALLYMOUNT TRADING ESTATE
Greenhills Centre
OLD SAWMILLS INDUSTRIAL ESTATE
BEECHFIELD AVE
BEECHFIELD ROAD
CHERRY GROVE
Health Centre
Ashleaf Shopping Centre
ST. TERESA'S RD
ST. TERESA'S LA
STANNAWAY PARK
KIMMAGE ROAD WEST
KIMMAGE ROAD
LORCAN O'TOOLE PARK
PARK CRES
ROYSTON
GREENHILLS ROAD
MULCAHY KEANE ESTATE
ST. PETER'S ROAD
CHERRYFIELD AVE
CHERRYFIELD ROAD
CHERRYFIELD DR
BEECHFIELD CLOSE
ROEBUCK DR
WEST ROAD
DANGAN AVE
DANGAN DRIVE
DANGAN PARK
WESTBROOK RD
SHELTON PARK
SHELTON GROVE
SHELTON DRIVE
SHELTON GDNS
GREENHILLS INDUSTRIAL ESTATE
BEECHLAWN INDUSTRIAL COMPLEX
ST. PETER'S DRIVE
ST. PETER'S CRESCENT
QUARRY DR
HILLSBROOK GROVE
AVONDALE TER
HILLSBROOK AVENUE
HILLSBROOK DR
HILLSBROOK CRES
MUCKROSS GREEN
MUCKROSS PARK
MUCKROSS CRES
MUCKROSS DR
MUCKROSS AVENUE
MUCKROSS GRO
ST BRIDGET'S DRIVE
ST. JAMES'S ROAD
ST. COLUMBA'S ROAD
ST. BRENDAN'S CRESCENT
ST. ANTHONY'S CRESCENT
ST. MALACHY'S DR
ST. JOSEPH'S ROAD
ST. CONLETH'S ROAD
ST. PATRICK'S ROAD
ST PAUL'S DRIVE
LIMEKILN GRO
LIMEKILN LANE
Comm Centre
SPORTS GROUND
WHITEHALL ROAD
EAST AVENUE
ROCKFIELD DRIVE
ROCKFIELD AVENUE
WHITEHALL GDNS
PRIORY WALK
61
KILLIAN'S AVE
TIBRADDEN DR
ST. GERARD'S RD
Community Centre, Sports & Leisure
GREENTREES ROAD
GREENTREES PARK
GREENTREES DRIVE
ROCKFIELD ROAD
Terenure Badminton Centre
KIMMAGE MANOR WAY
PRIORY HALL
PRIORY WAY
Holy Ghost College
ST. MEL'S AVENUE
Greenhills College
Convent
Schools
FERNHILL ROAD
FERNHILL AVE
FERNHILL PK
GLENDALE PARK
PODDLE RIVER
WAINSFORT MANOR CRES
ST. FINBAR'S CLOSE
TEMPLE MANOR CLO
TEMPLE MANOR DR
TEMPLE MANOR GRO
TEMPLE MANOR WY
TEMPLE MANOR AVE
TEMPLE MANOR CT
MILLGATE DR
PO
WHITEHALL PK
WHITEHALL CLO
LIMEKILN CLO
AQUILLA AVENUE
KILMASHOGUE DR
KILMASHOGUE GROVE
LIMEKILN AVE
KILOHAN GROVE
MOUNTDOWN ROAD
MOUNTDOWN DR
MOUNTDOWN PARK
MOUNTDOWN AVE
LIMEKILN DR
TEMPLEVILLE ROAD
WELLINGTON PK
GROSVENOR COURT
WAINSFORT MANOR GRN
SPORTS GROUND
WAINSFORT MANOR DRIVE
WAINSFORT MANOR GRO
COLLEGE SQUARE
WAINSFORT ROAD
Wainsfort
Sch
LIMEKILN PK
LIMEKILN ROAD
GLENDOWN GRO
GLENDOWN CRES
GLENDOWN PK
GLENDOWN CT
GLENDOWN AVENUE
GLENDOWN ROAD
WAINSFORT AVE
WAINSFORT CRES
College
COLLEGE CRES
R112
Greenhills
OSPREY LAWN
OSPREY DR
OSPREY AVE
OSPREY PK
OSPREY ROAD
WILLINGTON CT
WILLINGTON GRN
WILLINGTON AVE
WILLINGTON GRO
WILLINGTON DR
WILLINGTON CRES
WELLINGTON LANE
GLENDOWN LAWN
THE HEATH
St Mary's College R.F.C
THE COURT
R817
TEMPLEVILLE DRIVE
TEMPLEVILLE AVE
PARK
RUSH RD
RUSH CRES
RUSH VW
RUSH AVE
RUSH DR
RUSH PK
RUSH GRO
RUSH WY
RUSH CT
KENNINGTON ROAD
KENNINGTON CLOSE
KENNINGTON CRES
KENNINGTON LAWN
WILDERWOOD GRO
ORWELL PK GRO
ORWELL PK GLEN
ORWELL PK CLO
ORWELL PK AVE
ORWELL PK GLADE
ORWELL PK LAWNS
ORWELL PK CRES
ORWELL PK DR
ORWELL PK WY
ORWELL PK GRN
CYPRESS DRIVE
THE AVE
THE CLOSE
THE WALK
CYPRESS DOWNS
CYPRESS GRO N.
CYPRESS GROVE ROAD
CYPRESS PK
Rangers Office
Templeogue United FC
St. MacDara's College
Orwell Shopping Centre
ORWELL ROAD
ORWELL PK RISE
ORWELL PK VW
ORWELL PARK
ORWELL PK HEIGHTS
ORWELL WATERCOURSE
PK DALE
DOMVILLE RD
DOMVILLE DR
CYPRESS LAWN
Alberta
ASHFIELD
FORTROSE
CYPRESS GARTH
CYPRESS
ST. AONGUS CRES
ST. AONGUS ROAD
Faughs GAA Club
Rossmore
Sch
TEMPLEOGUE LODGE
TEMPLEOGUE WOOD
ROSSMORE DR
ROSSMORE AVE
ROSSMORE GRO
ROSSMORE CLO
ROSSMORE PK
ROSSMORE LAWNS
ROSSMORE CRESCENT
Templeogue
TEMPLEOGUE ROAD
TEMPLEOGUE BRIDGE
TYMON
M50
Lib
Sch
Sch
CASTLETYMON COURT
School & Sports Complex
70
Golf Range
A
Foot Bridge
National Basketball Arena
East Millennium Sculpture
B
Spawell Leisure Centre
CEMETERY
CORRYB
C
Riversdale
BUTTERFIELD
BALLYMACE GRN
HILLCREST
SPAWELL BRIDGE
Halting
Cheeverstown Centre
OLD BRIDGE RD
KNOCKLYON ROAD
1
2
3
4
A
B
C

Harold's Cross
Mount Jerome Cemetery
Hospice
Éamon Ceannt Park
Ceannt Stadium
Greyhound Racing Stadium
Kimmage
Terenure
Rathgar
Rathfarnham
Willbrook
Bushy Park
Castle Golf Course
Black Wood
Terenure Sports Ground
Lakelands Park
Terenure College R.F.C
Terenure College
Stratford College
St. Luke's Hospital
Mount Carmel Hospital
Rathfarnham Castle
Rathfarnham Shopping Centre
Sundrive Shopping Centre
Cashel Business Centre
KCR Industrial Estate
St. Joseph's Convent
Synagogue
Driving Test Centre
Lucena Clinic
Orchardstown Cottage
Clubhouse
River Dodder
Institute of Tecnology
St. Clare's Convent
Mount Jerome Ho
Templeogue Road
Terenure Road North
Harolds Cross Road
Terenure Road East
Terenure Road West
Kimmage Road Lower
Rathgar Road
Dodder Park Road
Dodder Valley Park
Butterfield Avenue
Grange Road
Nutgrove
Rathfarnham Road
Highfield Road
Orwell Road
Bushy Park Road
Mount Argus Road
Leinster Road
Grosvenor Road
R817
R114
R112
R821
N81
55
64
71

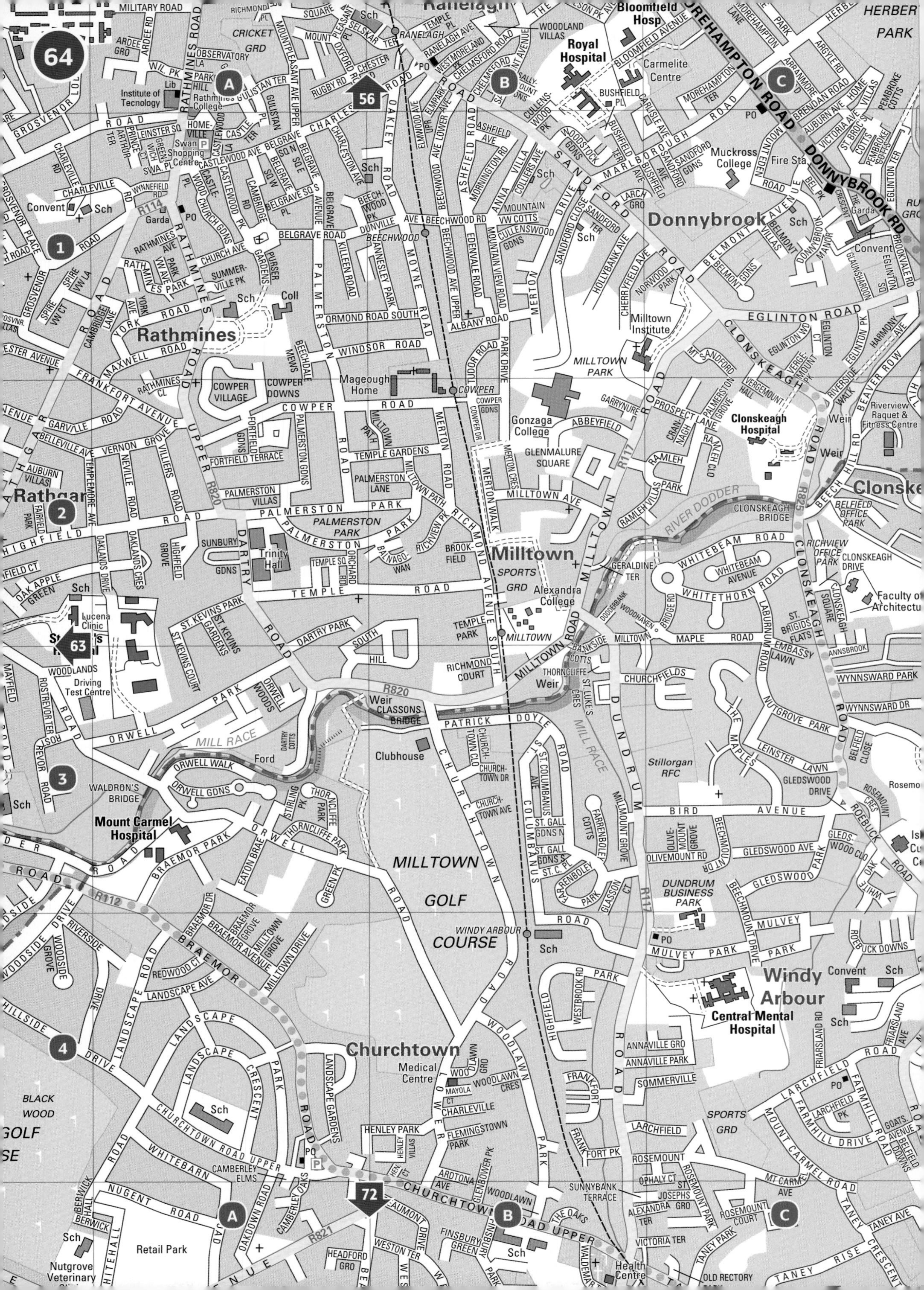
Ranelagh
Bloomfield Hosp
HERBERT PARK
Royal Hospital
Carmelite Centre
MILITARY ROAD
CRICKET GRD
Institute of Tecnology
Rathmines College
Swan Shopping Centre
Convent
Garda
Rathmines
Rathgar
Donnybrook
Muckross College
Fire Sta
Milltown Institute
MILLTOWN PARK
Gonzaga College
Clonskeagh Hospital
Riverview Raquet & Fitness Centre
Mageough Home
COWPER VILLAGE
COWPER DOWNS
PALMERSTON PARK
Trinity Hall
Milltown
SPORTS GRD
Alexandra College
RIVER DODDER
CLONSKEAGH BRIDGE
Faculty of Architecture
Lucena Clinic
Driving Test Centre
MILL RACE
CLASSONS BRIDGE
Clubhouse
Stillorgan RFC
WALDRON'S BRIDGE
Mount Carmel Hospital
MILLTOWN GOLF COURSE
WINDY ARBOUR
DUNDRUM BUSINESS PARK
Windy Arbour
Central Mental Hospital
Churchtown
Medical Centre
BLACK WOOD
GOLF
Retail Park
Nutgrove Veterinary
Health Centre
SPORTS GRD
RATHMINES ROAD UPPER
DARTRY ROAD
MILLTOWN ROAD
DUNDRUM ROAD
CLONSKEAGH ROAD
MOREHAMPTON ROAD
DONNYBROOK RD
EGLINTON ROAD
SANDFORD ROAD
PALMERSTON ROAD
CHURCHTOWN ROAD UPPER
BRAEMOR ROAD
ORWELL ROAD
TEMPLE ROAD
HIGHFIELD ROAD
COWPER ROAD
BEECHWOOD AVE
CHARLEVILLE ROAD
GROSVENOR ROAD
BIRD AVENUE
MAPLE ROAD
WHITEBEAM ROAD
WHITETHORN ROAD
LANDSCAPE ROAD
NUGENT ROAD
R114
R820
R117
R825
R112
R821
56
63
72
A
B
C
1
2
3
4

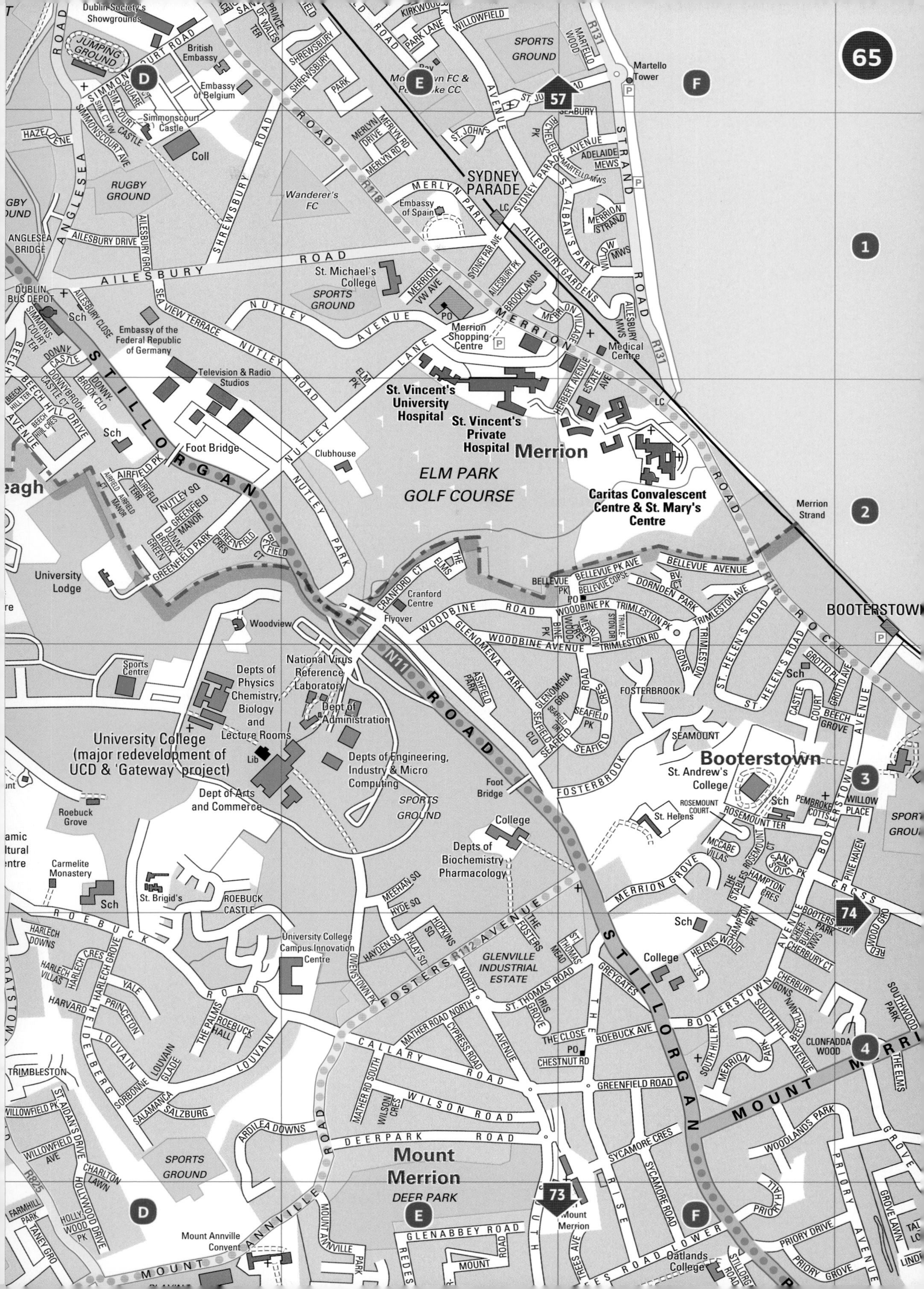
Dublin Society's Showgrounds
JUMPING GROUND
SIMMONSCOURT ROAD
British Embassy
Embassy of Belgium
Simmonscourt Castle
Coll
RUGBY GROUND
ANGLESEA ROAD
ANGLESEA BRIDGE
AILESBURY DRIVE
SHREWSBURY ROAD
Wanderer's FC
MERLYN PARK
Embassy of Spain
SYDNEY PARADE
SPORTS GROUND
Martello Tower
STRAND ROAD
AILESBURY ROAD
St. Michael's College
SPORTS GROUND
DUBLIN BUS DEPOT
Sch
Embassy of the Federal Republic of Germany
Television & Radio Studios
NUTLEY AVENUE
NUTLEY ROAD
Merrion Shopping Centre
MERRION ROAD
Medical Centre
St. Vincent's University Hospital
St. Vincent's Private Hospital
Merrion
Foot Bridge
STILLORGAN
Clubhouse
ELM PARK GOLF COURSE
Caritas Convalescent Centre & St. Mary's Centre
Merrion Strand
NUTLEY PARK
University Lodge
Cranford Centre
Flyover
BELLEVUE AVENUE
WOODBINE ROAD
WOODBINE AVENUE
BOOTERSTOWN
Woodview
Sports Centre
Depts of Physics Chemistry, Biology and Lecture Rooms
National Virus Reference Laboratory
Dept of Administration
N11
STILLORGAN ROAD
University College (major redevelopment of UCD & 'Gateway' project)
Lib
Depts of Engineering, Industry & Micro Computing
Dept of Arts and Commerce
SPORTS GROUND
Foot Bridge
FOSTERBROOK
SEAMOUNT
Booterstown
St. Andrew's College
St. Helens
Roebuck Grove
College
Depts of Biochemistry Pharmacology
MERRION GROVE
Carmelite Monastery
Sch
St. Brigid's
ROEBUCK CASTLE
ROEBUCK ROAD
University College Campus Innovation Centre
FOSTERS AVENUE
GLENVILLE INDUSTRIAL ESTATE
Sch
College
BOOTERSTOWN AVENUE
CLONFADDA WOOD
MOUNT MERRION AVENUE
CALLARY ROAD
WILSON ROAD
TRIMBLESTON
DEERPARK ROAD
GREENFIELD ROAD
SPORTS GROUND
Mount Merrion
DEER PARK
Mount Merrion
Mount Annville Convent
MOUNT ANNVILLE ROAD
Oatlands College
PRIORY AVENUE
PRIORY DRIVE
PRIORY GROVE
WOODLANDS PARK
D
E
F
1
2
3
4
57
73
74

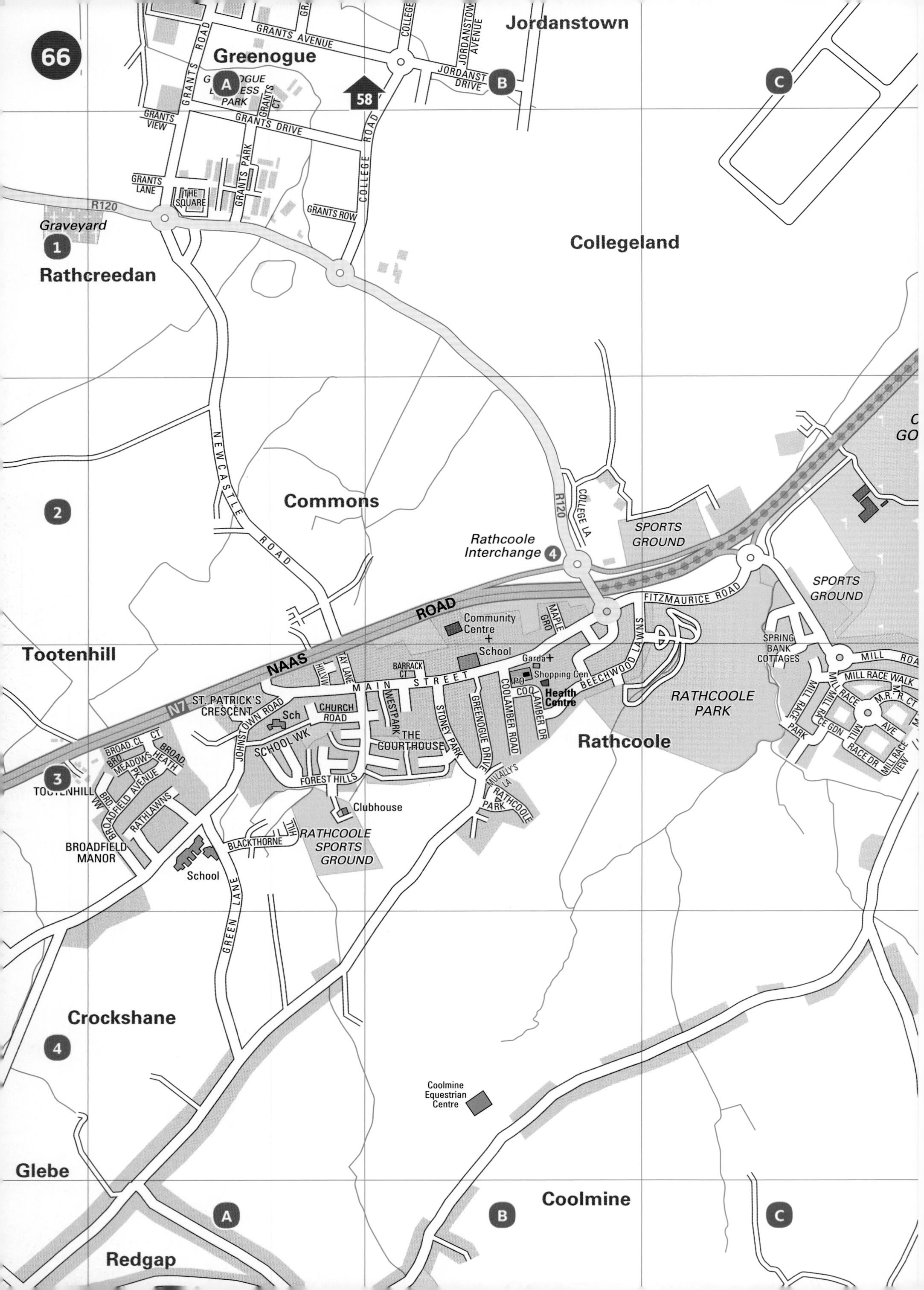
Jordanstown
Greenogue
GRANTS AVENUE
GRANTS ROAD
COLLEGE
JORDANSTOWN AVENUE
JORDANST DRIVE
GRANTS VIEW
GRANTS DRIVE
GRANTS CT
GRANTS PARK
GRANTS LANE
THE SQUARE
GRANTS ROW
COLLEGE ROAD
58
R120
Graveyard
Rathcreedan
Collegeland
NEWCASTLE ROAD
Commons
R120
COLLEGE LA
SPORTS GROUND
Rathcoole Interchange
FITZMAURICE ROAD
SPORTS GROUND
NAAS ROAD
N7
Community Centre
School
MAPLE GRO
Tootenhill
HILLVW
TAY LANE
BARRACK CT
MAIN STREET
Garda
Shopping Cen
PO
COO
Health Centre
BEECHWOOD LAWNS
SPRING BANK COTTAGES
MILL ROAD
MILL RACE WALK
ST. PATRICK'S CRESCENT
JOHNSTOWN ROAD
Sch
CHURCH ROAD
WESTPARK
THE COURTHOUSE
STONEY PARK
GREENOGUE DRIVE
COOLAMBER ROAD
LAMBER DR
RATHCOOLE PARK
Rathcoole
MILL RACE PARK
MILL RACE GDN
M.R. CT
AVE
MILL RACE DR
MILL RACE VIEW
BROAD. CL
CT
BROAD HEATH
BRO. MEADOWS
SCHOOL WK
FOREST HILLS
TOOTENHILL
BROADFIELD AVENUE
RATHLAWNS
Clubhouse
MULLALLY'S LA
RATHCOOLE PARK
BROADFIELD MANOR
BLACKTHORNE
HILL
RATHCOOLE SPORTS GROUND
School
GREEN LANE
Crockshane
Coolmine Equestrian Centre
Glebe
Coolmine
Redgap
A
B
C
1
2
3
4

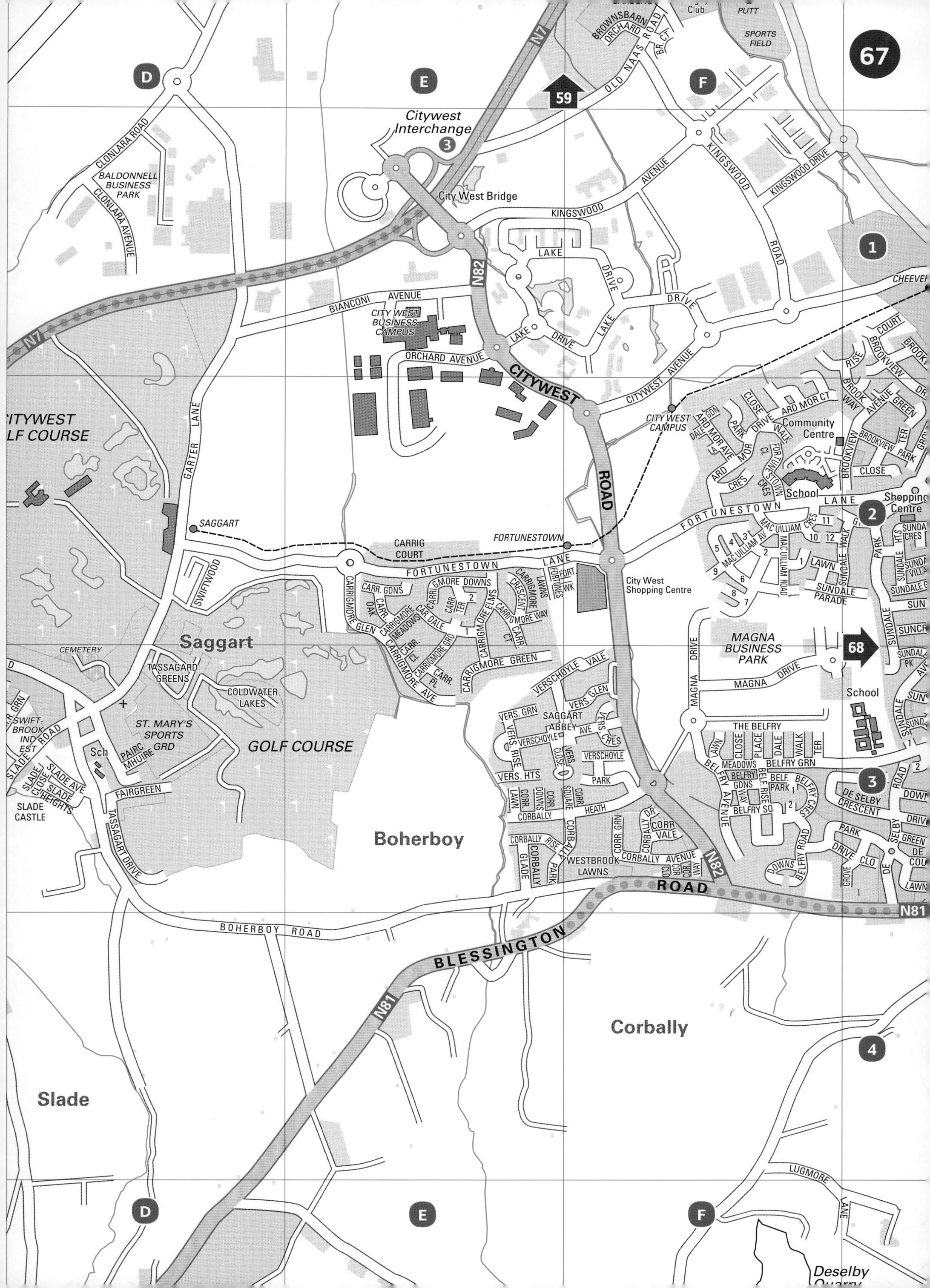

D
E
F
59
68
N7
N82
N81
Citywest Interchange
3
City West Bridge
BALDONNELL BUSINESS PARK
CLONLARA ROAD
CLONLARA AVENUE
BROWNSBARN ORCHARD
OLD NAAS ROAD
BR. CT.
Club
PUTT
SPORTS FIELD
KINGSWOOD AVENUE
KINGSWOOD ROAD
KINGSWOOD DRIVE
LAKE DRIVE
CHEEVER
1
BIANCONI AVENUE
CITY WEST BUSINESS CAMPUS
ORCHARD AVENUE
CITYWEST ROAD
CITYWEST AVENUE
CITY WEST CAMPUS
CITYWEST GOLF COURSE
GARTER LANE
SAGGART
FORTUNESTOWN
CARRIG COURT
FORTUNESTOWN LANE
SWIFTWOOD
City West Shopping Centre
Community Centre
School
Shopping Centre
2
ARD MOR CT
ARD MOR AVE
ARD MOR CRES
FORTUNESTOWN CL
FORTUNESTOWN CRES
BROOKVIEW
BROOKVIEW PARK
BROOKVIEW CLOSE
BROOK WAY
MAC UILLIAM CRES
MAC UILLIAM AVE
MAC UILLIAM ROAD
SUNDALE WALK
SUNDALE PARADE
SUNDALE ROAD
MAGNA BUSINESS PARK
MAGNA DRIVE
Saggart
CEMETERY
TASSAGARD GREENS
COLDWATER LAKES
ST. MARY'S SPORTS GRD
GOLF COURSE
CARRIGMORE GREEN
CARRIGMORE DOWNS
CARRIGMORE GLEN
CARRIGMORE AVE
VERSCHOYLE VALE
SAGGART ABBEY
VERSCHOYLE PARK
THE BELFRY
BELFRY GRN
BELFRY AVENUE
BELFRY SQ
BELFRY ROAD
DE SELBY CRESCENT
3
SWIFTBROOK IND EST
SLADE CASTLE
FAIRGREEN
PAIRC MHUIRE
Sch
TASSAGART DRIVE
Boherboy
CORBALLY HEATH
CORBALLY AVENUE
WESTBROOK LAWNS
BOHERBOY ROAD
BLESSINGTON ROAD
Corbally
4
Slade
LUGMORE LANE
Deselby Quarry

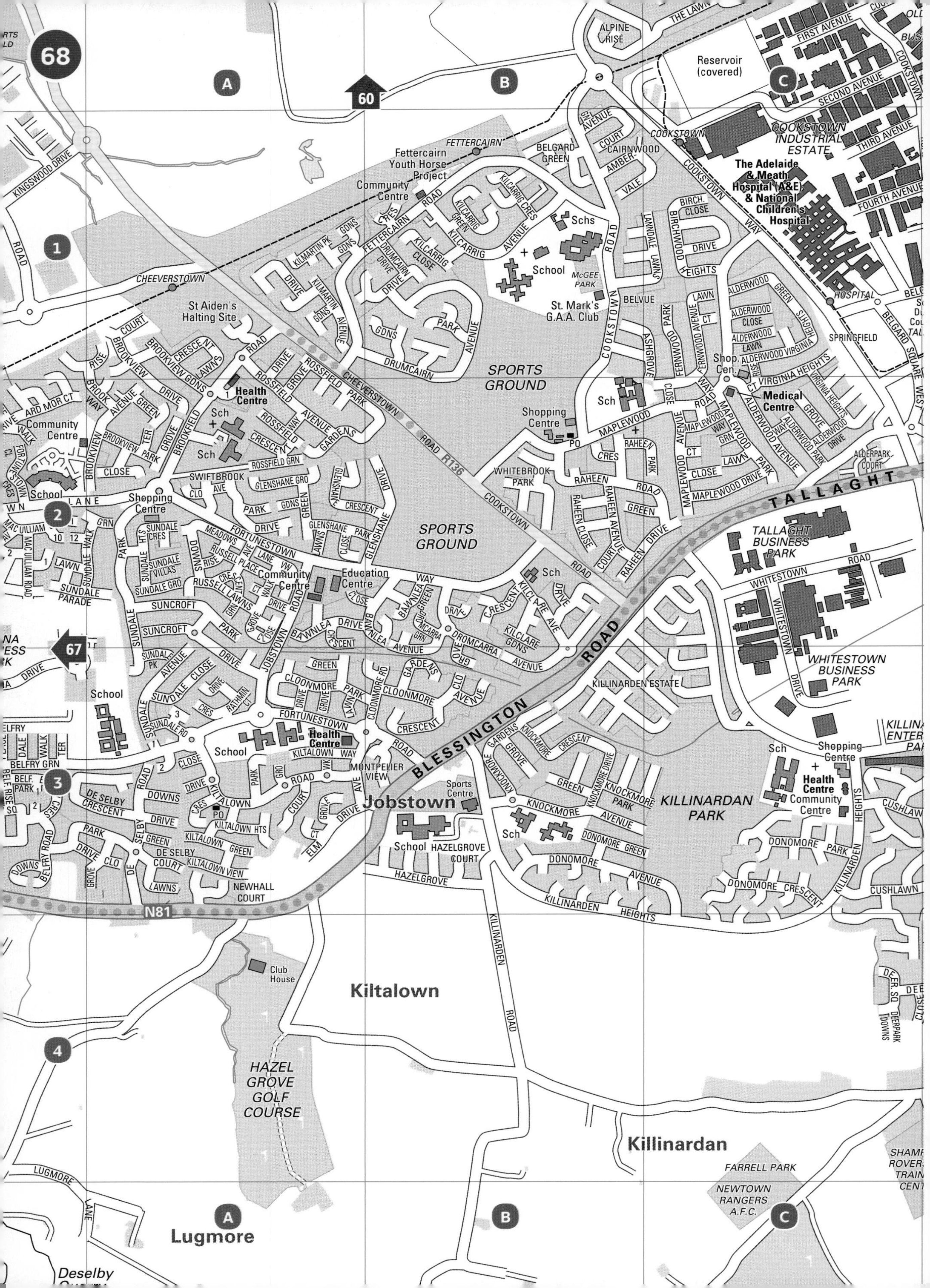
A
B
C
60
67
1
2
3
4
Reservoir (covered)
COOKSTOWN INDUSTRIAL ESTATE
The Adelaide & Meath Hospital (A&E) & National Children's Hospital
FIRST AVENUE
SECOND AVENUE
THIRD AVENUE
FOURTH AVENUE
THE LAWN
ALPINE RISE
COOKSTOWN
HOSPITAL
FETTERCAIRN
CHEEVERSTOWN
Fettercairn Youth Horse Project
Community Centre
BELGARD GREEN
CAIRNWOOD
AMBER-VALE
KILCARRIG CRES
KILCARRIG AVENUE
KILCARRIG CLOSE
KILMARTIN PK
KILMARTIN GDNS
DRUMCAIRN DRIVE
DRUMCAIRN PARK
DRUMCAIRN AVENUE
Schs
School
McGEE PARK
St. Mark's G.A.A. Club
BIRCH. CLOSE
BIRCHWOOD HEIGHTS
LANNDALE LAWNS
BELVUE
ASHGROVE
FERNWOOD PARK
FERNWOOD AVENUE
ALDERWOOD GREEN
ALDERWOOD CLOSE
ALDERWOOD LAWN
ALDERWOOD AVENUE
VIRGINIA HEIGHTS
SPRINGFIELD
BELGARD SQUARE WEST
Shop. Cen.
Medical Centre
St Aiden's Halting Site
KINGSWOOD DRIVE
BROOKVIEW
BROOKFIELD
ROSSFIELD
Health Centre
Sch
SPORTS GROUND
Shopping Centre
PO
MAPLEWOOD ROAD
MAPLEWOOD DRIVE
RAHEEN
WHITEBROOK PARK
ALDERPARK COURT
TALLAGHT
R136
COOKSTOWN ROAD
ARD MOR CT
Community Centre
FORTUNESTOWN
School
LANE
Shopping Centre
SWIFTBROOK
GLENSHANE
MAC UILLIAM
SUNDALE
FORTUNESTOWN WAY
RUSSELL
Education Centre
Community Centre
BAWNLEA
KILCLARE
DROMCARRA
TALLAGHT BUSINESS PARK
WHITESTOWN ROAD
WHITESTOWN BUSINESS PARK
WHITESTOWN DRIVE
SUNCROFT
JOBSTOWN
CLOONMORE
FORTUNESTOWN
KILLINARDEN ESTATE
BLESSINGTON ROAD
School
Health Centre
KILTALOWN
MONTPELIER VIEW
BELFRY
DE SELBY CRESCENT
Sports Centre
Jobstown
School
HAZELGROVE COURT
KNOCKMORE
DONOMORE
KILLINARDAN PARK
Sch
Shopping Centre
Health Centre
Community Centre
CUSHLAWN
KILLINARDEN HEIGHTS
HAZELGROVE
NEWHALL COURT
N81
Club House
Kiltalown
KILLINARDEN ROAD
HAZEL GROVE GOLF COURSE
Killinardan
FARRELL PARK
NEWTOWN RANGERS A.F.C.
LUGMORE LANE
Lugmore
Deselby

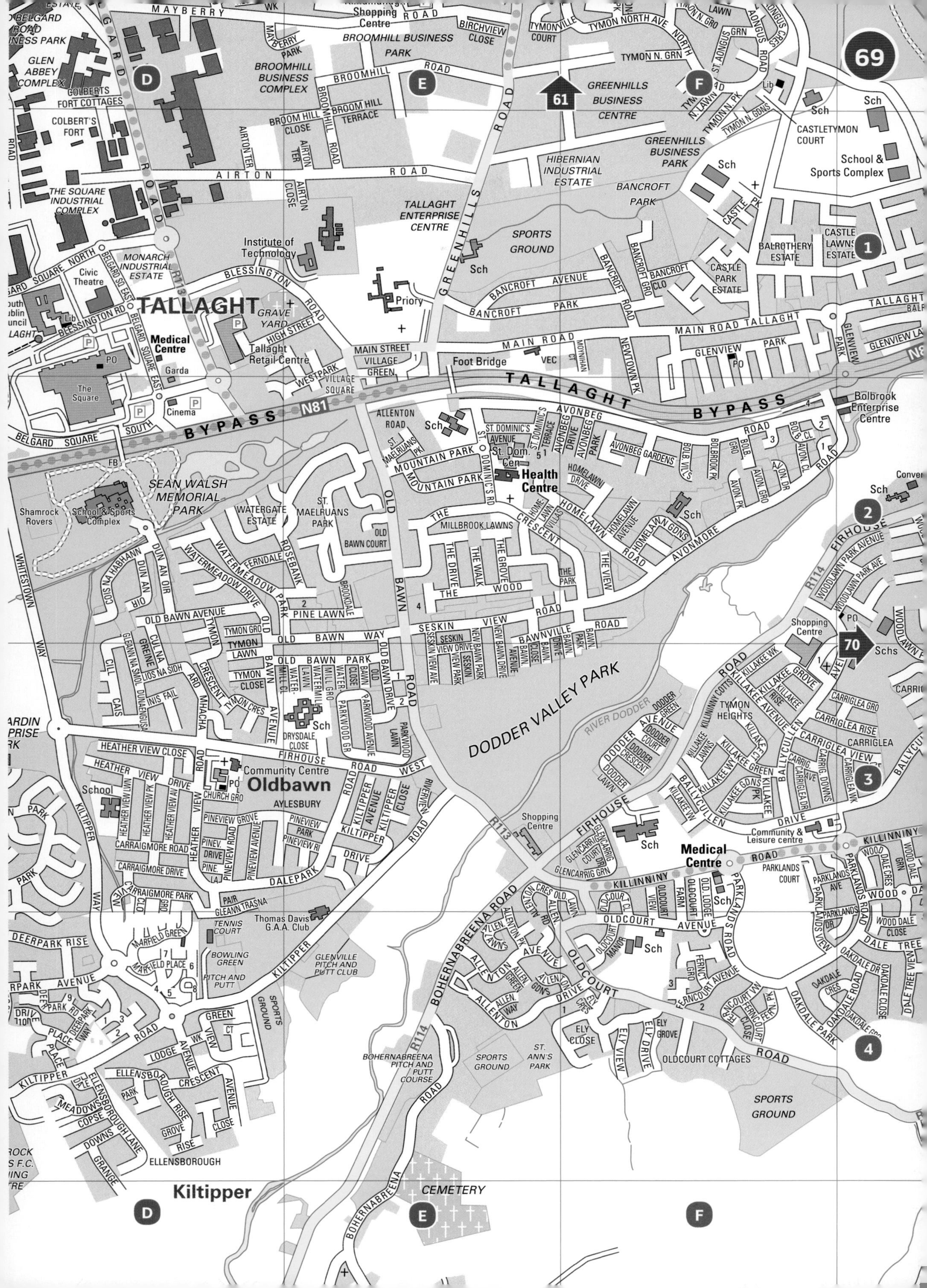
TALLAGHT
Oldbawn
Kiltipper
DODDER VALLEY PARK
RIVER DODDER
TALLAGHT BYPASS
N81
R113
R114
61
70
D
E
F
1
2
3
4
MAYBERRY
Shopping Centre
ROAD
BIRCHVIEW CLOSE
BROOMHILL BUSINESS PARK
MAYBERRY PARK
BROOMHILL BUSINESS COMPLEX
BROOMHILL ROAD
BROOMHILL ROAD
BROOM HILL TERRACE
BROOM HILL CLOSE
AIRTON TER
AIRTON ROAD
AIRTON CLOSE
GREENHILLS ROAD
GREENHILLS BUSINESS CENTRE
GREENHILLS BUSINESS PARK
HIBERNIAN INDUSTRIAL ESTATE
BANCROFT PARK
TYMONVILLE COURT
TYMON NORTH AVE
TYMON N. GRN
TYMON N. GRO
TYMON N. LAWN
TYMON N. PK
TYMON N. GDNS
ST. AONGUS GRN
AONGUS ROAD
AONGUS CRES
LAWN
Lib
Sch
CASTLETYMON COURT
School & Sports Complex
CASTLE PK
CASTLE LAWNS ESTATE
BALROTHERY ESTATE
CASTLE PARK ESTATE
BANCROFT AVENUE
BANCROFT PARK
BANCROFT ROAD
BANCROFT GRO
BANCROFT CLO
MAIN ROAD TALLAGHT
GLENVIEW PARK
GLENVIEW LAWN
TALLAGHT
PO
GLEN ABBEY COMPLEX
GOLBERTS FORT COTTAGES
COLBERT'S FORT
BELGARD ROAD
BELGARD BUSINESS PARK
THE SQUARE INDUSTRIAL COMPLEX
MONARCH INDUSTRIAL ESTATE
BELGARD SQUARE NORTH
BELGARD SQ. EAST
BELGARD SQUARE EAST
BELGARD SQUARE SOUTH
Civic Theatre
South Dublin County Council
BLESSINGTON RD
BLESSINGTON ROAD
Institute of Technology
TALLAGHT ENTERPRISE CENTRE
SPORTS GROUND
Priory
GRAVE YARD
HIGH STREET
Medical Centre
Tallaght Retail Centre
Garda
The Square
Cinema
MAIN STREET
VILLAGE GREEN
WESTPARK
VILLAGE SQUARE
MAIN ROAD
Foot Bridge
VEC
MOYNIHAN CT
NEWTOWN PK
Bolbrook Enterprise Centre
ALLENTON ROAD
ST. MAELRUANS PK
MOUNTAIN PARK
ST. DOMINIC'S AVENUE
ST. DOMINIC'S TERRACE
ST. DOMINIC'S RD
St. Dom. Cen.
AVONBEG DRIVE
AVONBEG PARK
AVONBEG ROAD
AVONBEG GARDENS
BOLB. VIL'S
BOLBROOK PK
BOLB. GRO
BOLB. AVON. CL
AVON. PK
AVON. GRO
AVON. DR
AVON. CL
Health Centre
HOMELAWN DRIVE
HOMELAWN VILLAS
HOMELAWN ROAD
HOMELAWN AVENUE
HOMELAWN GDNS
AVONMORE ROAD
SEAN WALSH MEMORIAL PARK
Shamrock Rovers
School & Sports Complex
FB
WATERGATE ESTATE
ST. MAELRUANS PARK
OLD BAWN COURT
OLD BAWN ROAD
THE MILLBROOK LAWNS
THE CRESCENT
THE DRIVE
THE WALK
THE GROVE
THE WOOD
THE PARK
THE VIEW
WATERMEADOW DRIVE
WATERMEADOW PARK
FERNDALE
ROSEBANK
BROOKDALE
PINE LAWN
COIS NA HABHANN
DUN AN OIR
OLD BAWN AVENUE
OLD BAWN WAY
OLD BAWN PARK
OLD BAWN DRIVE
SESKIN VIEW ROAD
SESKIN VIEW DRIVE
SESKIN VIEW AVE
SESKIN VIEW PARK
NEW BAWN PARK
NEW BAWN DRIVE
BAWNVILLE ROAD
BAWNVILLE AVENUE
TYMON GRO
TYMON LAWN
TYMON CLOSE
TYMON CRES
TYMON CRESCENT
GLEANN NA SMOL
CUL NA GREINE
LIOS NA SIDH
INIS FAIL
DUNAENGUSA
ARD MHACHA
CILL CAIS
WATERMILL
WATER MILL CL
MILL GRO
PARKWOOD DRIVE
PARKWOOD GR
PARKWOOD AVENUE
PARKWOOD LAWN
DRYSDALE CLOSE
WHITESTOWN WAY
FIRHOUSE ROAD
FIRHOUSE ROAD WEST
HEATHER VIEW CLOSE
HEATHER VIEW DRIVE
HEATHER VIEW LAWN
HEATHER VIEW PK
HEATHER VIEW AV
HEATHER VIEW ROAD
Community Centre
CHURCH GRO
AYLESBURY
School
PINEVIEW GROVE
PINEVIEW PARK
PINEVIEW RI
PINEVIEW ROAD
PINEVIEW AVENUE
PINEV. DRIVE
PINE. LA
CARRAIGMORE ROAD
CARRAIGMORE DRIVE
CARRAIGMORE PARK
CARRAIGMORE VIEW
KILTIPPER AVENUE
KILTIPPER CLOSE
KILTIPPER DRIVE
KILTIPPER ROAD
KILTIPPER WAY
RIVERVIEW
DALEPARK
GLEANN TRASNA
Thomas Davis G.A.A. Club
TENNIS COURT
BOWLING GREEN
PITCH AND PUTT
MARFIELD GREEN
MARFIELD PLACE
GLENVILLE PITCH AND PUTT CLUB
SPORTS GROUND
DEERPARK RISE
DEERPARK AVENUE
DEERPARK RD
DEERPARK WAY
DEERPARK PLACE
GREEN VIEW
LODGE AVENUE
ELLENSBOROUGH CRESCENT
ELLENSBOROUGH AVENUE
ELLENSBOROUGH PARK
ELLENSBOROUGH RISE
ELLENSBOROUGH GROVE
ELLENSBOROUGH CLOSE
ELLENSBOROUGH LANE
ELLENSBOROUGH
MEADOWS
COPSE
DOWNS
GRANGE
BOHERNABREENA ROAD
BOHERNABREENA PITCH AND PUTT COURSE
SPORTS GROUND
ST. ANN'S PARK
CEMETERY
Shopping Centre
Sch
FIRHOUSE ROAD
GLENCARRIG COURT
GLENCARRIG GRN
DODDER CRESCENT
DODDER COURT
DODDER AVENUE
DODDER GREEN
DODDER LAWN
KILLAKEE WK
KILLAKEE GROVE
KILLAKEE RISE
KILLAKEE AVENUE
KILLAKEE GREEN
KILLAKEE LAWNS
KILLAKEE CT
KILLAKEE GDNS
KILLAKEE PK
KILLAKEE VW
KILLININNY COTTS
TYMON HEIGHTS
BALLYCULLEN DRIVE
BALLYCULLEN AVE
CARRIGLEA GRO
CARRIGLEA RISE
CARRIGLEA VIEW
CARRIGLEA
CARRIGLEA DOWNS
CARRIGLEA DR
CARRIGLEA WK
CARRIG. AVE
Shopping Centre
Schs
WOODLAWN PARK AVENUE
WOODLAWN PARK AVE
WOODLAWN PARK
Community & Leisure centre
KILLININNY ROAD
Medical Centre
PARKLANDS COURT
PARKLANDS AVE
PARKLANDS ROAD
PARKLANDS VIEW
PARKLANDS DR
WOOD DALE GRN
WOOD DALE CRES
WOOD DALE CLOSE
DALE TREE
DALE TREE VIEW
OAKDALE DR
OAKDALE CRES
OAKDALE ROAD
OAKDALE PARK
OAKDALE CLOSE
OLDCOURT CL
OLDCOURT VIEW
OLDCOURT FARM
OLD. LODGE
OLDCOURT AVENUE
OLDCOURT MANOR
OLDCOURT ROAD
OLDCOURT COTTAGES
PARKLANDS ROAD
FERNCOURT AVENUE
FERNCOURT CLOSE
FERNCOURT VW
FERNCT. GRO
ALLENTON CRES
ALLENTON RD
ALLENTON LAWN
ALLENTON PK
ALLENTON LAWNS
ALLENTON AVENUE
ALLENTON GREEN
ALLENTON GDNS
ALLENTON DRIVE
ALLENTON WAY
ELY CLOSE
ELY VIEW
ELY DRIVE
ELY GROVE
ELY CRES
Sch
SPORTS GROUND

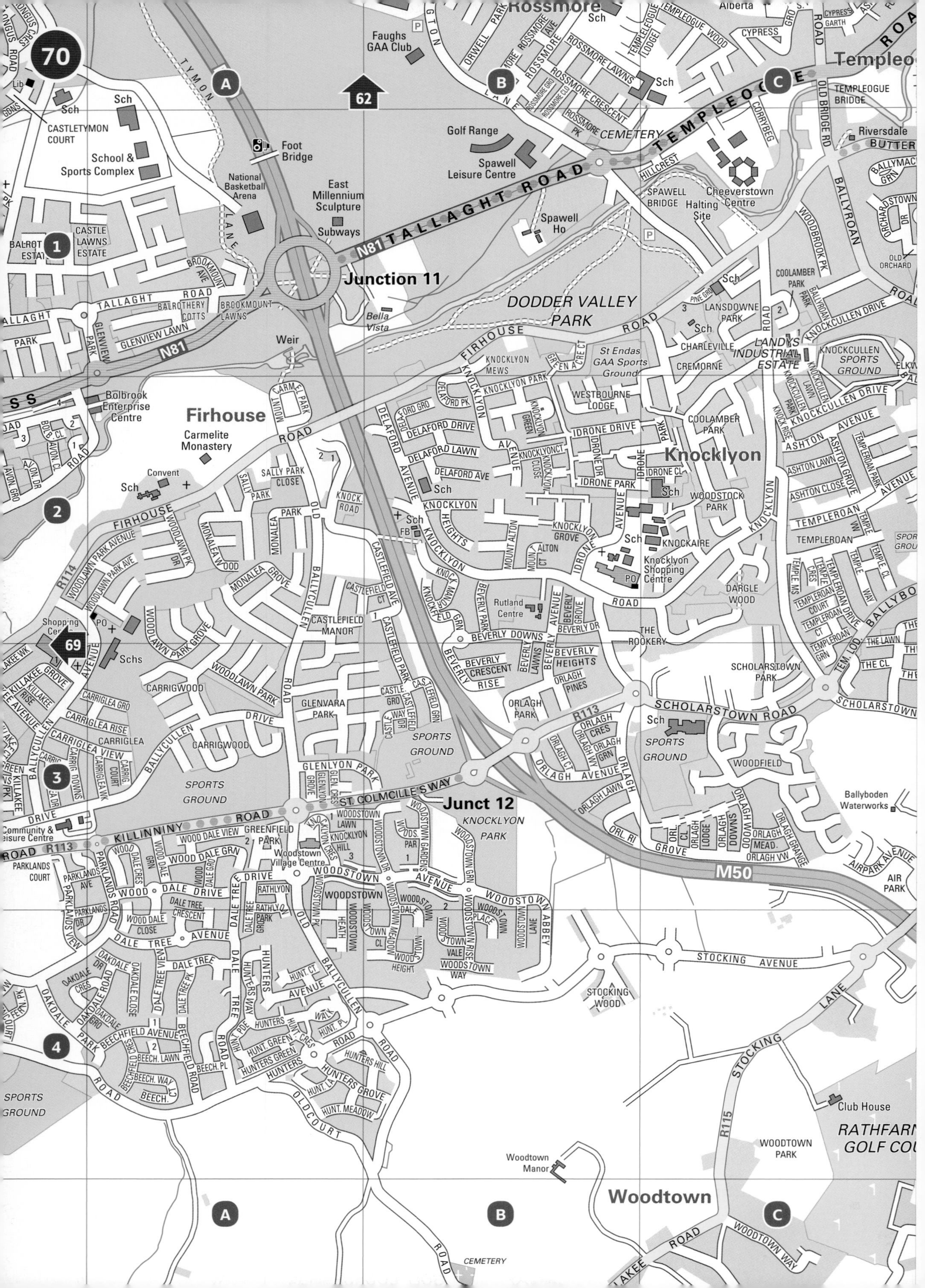
Rossmore
Faughs GAA Club
62
Sch
CASTLETYMON COURT
School & Sports Complex
TYMON LANE
Foot Bridge
National Basketball Arena
East Millennium Sculpture
Subways
Golf Range
Spawell Leisure Centre
CEMETERY
ROSSMORE LAWNS
ROSSMORE CRESCENT
TEMPLEOGUE WOOD
CYPRESS
Templeogue
TEMPLEOGUE BRIDGE
Riversdale
BUTTERFIELD
CORRYBEG
HILLCREST
SPAWELL BRIDGE
Halting Site
Cheeverstown Centre
Spawell Ho
TALLAGHT ROAD
TEMPLEOGUE ROAD
N81
CASTLE LAWNS ESTATE
BALROTHERY ESTATE
BROOKMOUNT AVE
BROOKMOUNT LAWNS
BALROTHERY COTTS
GLENVIEW LAWN
GLENVIEW PARK
Junction 11
Bella Vista
Weir
DODDER VALLEY PARK
FIRHOUSE ROAD
WOODBROOK PK
BALLYROAN
COOLAMBER PARK
LANSDOWNE PARK
CHARLEVILLE
CREMORNE
LANDYS INDUSTRIAL ESTATE
KNOCKCULLEN DRIVE
KNOCKCULLEN SPORTS GROUND
St Endas GAA Sports Ground
KNOCKLYON MEWS
KNOCKLYON PARK
GREEN ACRE CT
WESTBOURNE LODGE
Bolbrook Enterprise Centre
Firhouse
Carmelite Monastery
MOUNT CARMEL PARK
Convent
DELAFORD DRIVE
DELAFORD LAWN
DELAFORD AVE
DELAFORD AVENUE
IDRONE DRIVE
IDRONE PARK
IDRONE CL
Knocklyon
COOLAMBER PARK
ASHTON AVENUE
ASHTON LAWN
ASHTON CLOSE
ASHTON GROVE
TEMPLEROAN AVENUE
WOODSTOCK PARK
KNOCKLYON ROAD
KNOCKLYON HEIGHTS
KNOCKLYON GROVE
MOUNT ALTON
KNOCKAIRE
Knocklyon Shopping Centre
DARGLE WOOD
SALLY PARK
SALLY PARK CLOSE
MONALEA PARK
MONALEA WOOD
MONALEA GROVE
WOODLAWN PARK AVENUE
WOODLAWN PARK GROVE
WOODLAWN PARK
R114
CASTLEFIELD AVE
CASTLEFIELD MANOR
CASTLEFIELD PARK
Rutland Centre
BEVERLY DOWNS
BEVERLY CRESCENT
BEVERLY HEIGHTS
BEVERLY RISE
ORLAGH PINES
ORLAGH PARK
THE ROOKERY
SCHOLARSTOWN PARK
SCHOLARSTOWN ROAD
TEMPLEROAN
69
Schs
KILLAKEE GROVE
CARRIGLEA RISE
CARRIGLEA VIEW
CARRIGLEA
CARRIGWOOD
BALLYCULLEN DRIVE
BALLYCULLEN ROAD
GLENVARA PARK
SPORTS GROUND
GLENLYON PARK
ST. COLMCILLE'S WAY
Junct 12
KNOCKLYON PARK
R113
ORLAGH AVENUE
WOODFIELD
Ballyboden Waterworks
AIRPARK AVENUE
AIR PARK
M50
KILLININNY ROAD
Community & Leisure Centre
PARKLANDS COURT
WOOD DALE VIEW
GREENFIELD PARK
Woodstown Village Centre
WOODSTOWN AVENUE
WOODSTOWN ABBEY
WOOD DALE DRIVE
DALE TREE AVENUE
WOOD DALE CLOSE
STOCKING AVENUE
STOCKING WOOD
STOCKING LANE
OAKDALE ROAD
BEECHFIELD AVENUE
BEECHFIELD ROAD
HUNTERS AVENUE
HUNTERS ROAD
HUNTERS GREEN
HUNTERS GROVE
HUNT. MEADOW
OLDCOURT ROAD
R115
Club House
RATHFARNHAM GOLF COU
WOODTOWN PARK
Woodtown Manor
Woodtown
WOODTOWN WAY
CEMETERY
A
B
C
1
2
3
4

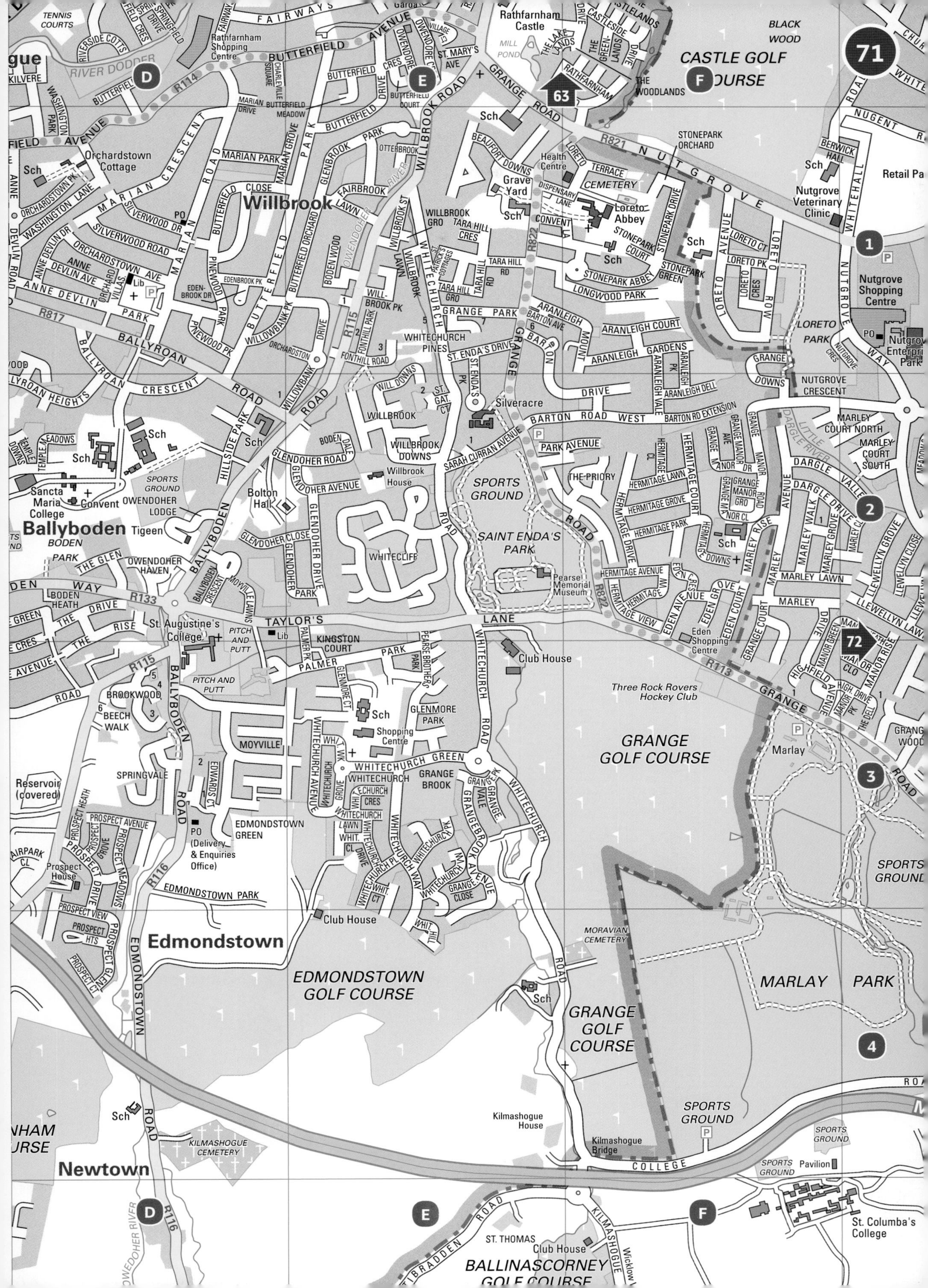
TENNIS COURTS
RIVERSIDE COTTS
SPRINGFIELD CRES
SPRINGFIELD DRIVE
SPRINGFIELD
FAIRWAYS
Rathfarnham Shopping Centre
RIVER DODDER
D
E
F
R114
BUTTERFIELD AVENUE
BUTTERFIELD
KILVERE
WASHINGTON PARK
FIELD AVENUE
Orchardstown Cottage
Sch
ORCHARDSTOWN PK
WASHINGTON LANE
ANNE DEVLIN DR
ANNE DEVLIN ROAD
ANNE DEVLIN AVE
ANNE DEVLIN
ORCHARDSTOWN AVE
ORCHARDSTOWN ROAD
ORCHARD VILLAS
MARIAN CRESCENT
MARIAN ROAD
MARIAN DRIVE
MARIAN PARK
MARIAN GROVE
CHARLEVILLE SQUARE
BUTTERFIELD MEADOW
BUTTERFIELD CRES
BUTTERFIELD COURT
BUTTERFIELD CLOSE
BUTTERFIELD PARK
BUTTERFIELD ORCHARD
BUTTERFIELD DRIVE
OWENDORE AVE
OWENDORE CRES
OWENDORE CT
VILLAGE CT
ST. MARY'S AVE
WILLBROOK ROAD
GRANGE ROAD
Rathfarnham Castle
MILL POND
THE LAKE LANDS
THE GREEN-LANDS
CASTLESIDE DRIVE
CASTLELANDS
RATHFARNHAM
THE WOODLANDS
63
BLACK WOOD
CASTLE GOLF COURSE
Willbrook
SILVERWOOD DR
SILVERWOOD ROAD
PO
Lib
P
EDENBROOK PK
EDEN-BROOK DR
PINEWOOD PARK
PINEWOOD PK
WILLOWBANK PK
WILLOWBANK DRIVE
ORCHARDSTON
GLENBROOK PARK
GLENBROOK ROAD
OTTERBROOK
FAIRBROOK LAWN
OWENDOHER RIVER
BODEN WOOD
WILLBROOK ST
WILLBROOK LAWN
WILLBROOK GRO
WILL-BROOK PK
R115
FONTHILL PARK
FONTHILL ROAD
WHITECHURCH PINES
WHITECHURCH ROAD
TARA HILL CRES
ST. PATRICK'S COTTAGES
TARA HILL RD
TARA HILL GRO
GRANGE PARK
ST. ENDA'S DRIVE
ST. ENDA'S PK
Sch
BEAUFORT DOWNS
Grave Yard
Health Centre
DISPENSARY LANE
CONVENT LA
LORETO TERRACE
CEMETERY
Loreto Abbey
STONEPARK COURT
STONEPARK DRIVE
STONEPARK ABBEY
STONEPARK GREEN
STONEPARK ORCHARD
R821 NUTGROVE
R822
LONGWOOD PARK
LORETO AVENUE
LORETO CT
LORETO PK
LORETO CRES
LORETO ROW
LORETO PARK
NUGENT ROAD
BERWICK HALL
Nutgrove Veterinary Clinic
WHITEHALL ROAD
Retail Pa
1
P
Nutgrove Shopping Centre
Nutgrove Enterprise Park
NUTGROVE WAY
NUTGROVE CRES
ARANLEIGH PARK
ARANLEIGH COURT
ARANLEIGH GARDENS
ARANLEIGH VALE
ARANLEIGH PK
ARANLEIGH DELL
ARANLEIGH MOUNT
ARANLEIGH DRIVE
BARTON AVE
BARTON DRIVE
GRANGE DOWNS
NUTGROVE CRESCENT
BALLYROAN ROAD
BALLYROAN CRESCENT
BALLYROAN HEIGHTS
R817
WILL DOWNS
ST. GAT. CT
WILLBROOK
WILLBROOK DOWNS
Silveracre
BARTON ROAD WEST
BARTON RD EXTENSION
P
PARK AVENUE
HERMITAGE CL
HERMITAGE LAWN
HERMITAGE COURT
HERMITAGE GROVE
HERMITAGE PARK
HERMITAGE DRIVE
HERMITAGE AVENUE
HERMITAGE VIEW
HERMITAGE
THE PRIORY
GRANGE MANOR AVE
GRANGE MANOR DR
GRANGE MANOR ROAD
GRANGE MANOR GRO
GRANGE MANOR CL
MARLEY COURT NORTH
MARLEY COURT SOUTH
LITTLE DARGLE RIVER
DARGLE VALLEY
DARGLE DRIVE
2
MARLEY AVENUE
MARLEY RISE
MARLEY WALK
MARLEY GROVE
MARLEY CL
MARLEY LAWN
MARLEY
LLEWELLYN GROVE
LLEWELLYN CLOSE
LLEWELLYN COURT
LLEWELLYN LAWN
TEMPLE MEADOWS
TEMPLE DOWNS
Sch
SPORTS GROUND
Sancta Maria College
Convent
OWENDOHER LODGE
HILLSIDE PARK
GLENDOHER ROAD
BODEN DALE
GLENDOHER AVENUE
Willbrook House
SARAH CURRAN AVENUE
SPORTS GROUND
SAINT ENDA'S PARK
Pearse Memorial Museum
Bolton Hall
Ballyboden
Tigeen
BODEN PARK
THE GLEN
OWENDOHER HAVEN
BALLYBODEN ROAD
BALLYBODEN CRESCENT
MOYVILLE LAWNS
GLENDOHER CLOSE
GLENDOHER DRIVE
GLENDOHER PARK
WHITECLIFF
EDEN AVENUE
EDEN CRES
EDEN GROVE
EDEN COURT
DOWNS
GRANGE COURT
BODEN WAY
R133
BODEN HEATH
THE DRIVE
THE RISE
THE GREEN
THE CRES
THE AVENUE
St. Augustine's College
PITCH AND PUTT
TAYLOR'S LANE
Lib
PALMER PK
KINGSTON COURT
PALMER PARK
PEARSE BROTHERS PARK
Club House
Eden Shopping Centre
72
MANOR GREEN
MANOR CLO
MANOR RISE
HIGHFIELD AVENUE
HIGH. DRIVE
MANOR PK
THE DELL
GRANGE WOOD
R113 GRANGE ROAD
Three Rock Rovers Hockey Club
R115
ROAD
BROOKWOOD
BEECH WALK
PITCH AND PUTT
GLENMORE CT
GLENMORE PARK
Sch
Shopping Centre
MOYVILLE
WHITECHURCH AVENUE
WHIT. WK
WHITECHURCH GREEN
WHITECHURCH GROVE
WHITECHURCH CRES
WHITECHURCH LAWN
WHIT. CL
WHITECHURCH DRIVE
WHITECHURCH PL
WHITECHURCH WAY
WHITECHURCH HILL
WHIT. CT
WHIT. HILL
GRANGE BROOK
GRANGEBROOK VALE
GRANGEBROOK AVENUE
GRANGEBROOK CLOSE
GRANGEBROOK PK
WHITECHURCH ROAD
GRANGE GOLF COURSE
Marlay
3
SPRINGVALE
Reservoir (covered)
EDWARDS CT
PO (Delivery & Enquiries Office)
EDMONDSTOWN GREEN
PROSPECT HEATH
PROSPECT AVENUE
PROSPECT GROVE
PROSPECT MEADOWS
PROSPECT DRIVE
Prospect House
FAIRPARK CL
PROSPECT VIEW
PROSPECT HTS
PROSPECT GLEN
PROSPECT CT
R116
EDMONDSTOWN PARK
Club House
Edmondstown
EDMONDSTOWN ROAD
SPORTS GROUND
MORAVIAN CEMETERY
EDMONDSTOWN GOLF COURSE
GRANGE GOLF COURSE
Sch
MARLAY PARK
4
Kilmashogue House
SPORTS GROUND
P
SPORTS GROUND
Kilmashogue Bridge
COLLEGE ROAD
SPORTS GROUND
Pavilion
Sch
KILMASHOGUE CEMETERY
Newtown
NHAM URSE
OWENDOHER RIVER
TIBRADDEN ROAD
ST. THOMAS
Club House
KILMASHOGUE
BALLINASCORNEY GOLF COURSE
St. Columba's College
Wicklow

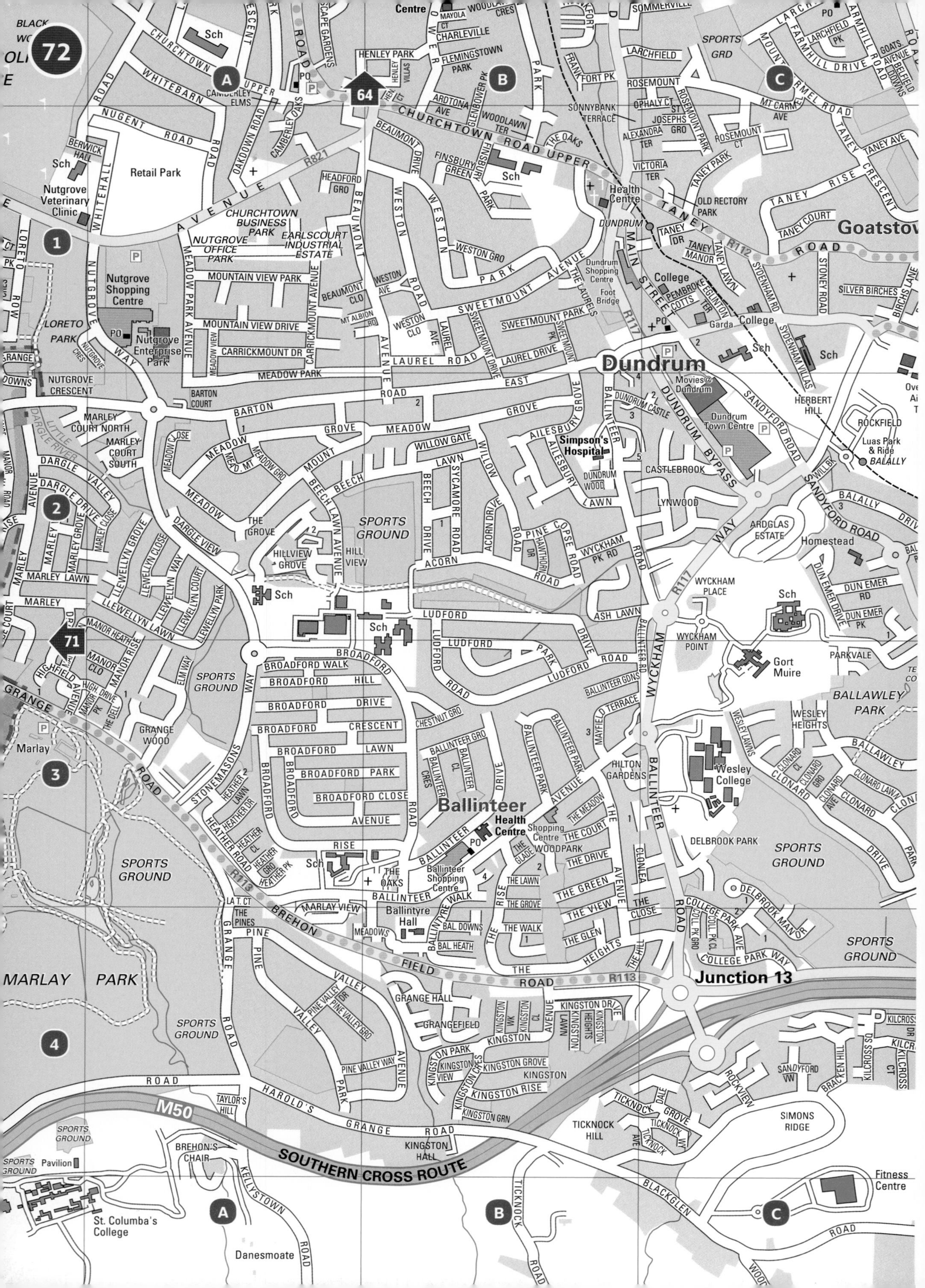
72
BLACK
Sch
CHURCHTOWN
WHITEBARN
ROAD
CAMBERLEY ELMS
UPPER
CAMBERLEY OAKS
OAKDOWN ROAD
ROAD
SCAPE GARDENS
Centre
MAYOLA CT
CHARLEVILLE
HENLEY PARK
HENLEY VILLAS
FLEMINGSTOWN PARK
ARDTONA AVE
GLENBOWER PK
WOODLAWN TER
CRES
PARK
64
A
B
C
PO
NUGENT ROAD
BERWICK HALL
Retail Park
R821
AVENUE
CHURCHTOWN ROAD UPPER
BEAUMONT DRIVE
FINSBURY GREEN
FINSBURY PARK
THE OAKS
HEADFORD GRO
BEAUMONT
WESTON
Nutgrove Veterinary Clinic
WHITEHALL
CHURCHTOWN BUSINESS PARK
NUTGROVE OFFICE PARK
EARLSCOURT INDUSTRIAL ESTATE
WESTON GRO
PARK
MOUNTAIN VIEW PARK
MOUNTAIN VIEW DRIVE
CARRICKMOUNT DR
CARRICKMOUNT AVENUE
MEADOW PARK AVENUE
MEADOW VIEW
BEAUMONT CLO
WESTON AVE
WESTON CLO
MT ALBION RD
LAUREL AVE
SWEETMOUNT AVENUE
SWEETMOUNT PARK
SWEETMOUNT DRIVE
SWEETMOUNT PK
LAUREL DRIVE
LAUREL ROAD
MEADOW PARK
AVENUE
THE LAURELS
1
LORETO
LORETO ROW
PK
NUTGROVE
Nutgrove Shopping Centre
Nutgrove Enterprise Park
LORETO PARK
NUTGROVE CRES
WAY
GRANGE
DOWNS
NUTGROVE CRESCENT
BARTON COURT
BARTON
ROAD
EAST
GROVE
MARLEY COURT NORTH
MARLEY COURT SOUTH
LITTLE DARGLE RIVER
MEADOW CLOSE
MEADOW
MEADOW MT
MEADOW GRO
MOUNT
GROVE
MEADOW
WILLOW GATE
LAWN
BEECH
BEECH LAWN AVENUE
BEECH DRIVE
SYCAMORE ROAD
WILLOW
ACORN DRIVE
ACORN
SPORTS GROUND
HILL VIEW
HILLVIEW GROVE
THE GROVE
DARGLE VIEW
DARGLE VALLEY
DARGLE DRIVE
DARGLE AVENUE
2
MARLEY GROVE
MARLEY CLOSE
MARLEY
MARLEY LAWN
MARLEY
MANOR
ROAD
COURT
LLEWELLYN GROVE
LLEWELLYN CLOSE
LLEWELLYN WAY
LLEWELLYN COURT
LLEWELLYN PARK
LLEWELLYN
LLEWELLYN LAWN
Sch
71
MANOR HEATH
MANOR CLO
MANOR RISE
HIGHFIELD AVENUE
HIGH. DRIVE
MANOR PK
THE DELL
ELM WAY
SPORTS GROUND
WAY
GRANGE WOOD
GRANGE
ROAD
Marlay
3
STONEMASONS
HEATHER LAWN
HEATHER DR
HEATHER CL
HEATHER GRO
HEATHER PK
HEATHER ROAD
R113
BROADFORD
BROADFORD WALK
BROADFORD HILL
BROADFORD DRIVE
BROADFORD CRESCENT
BROADFORD LAWN
BROADFORD PARK
BROADFORD CLOSE
BROADFORD AVENUE
BROADFORD RISE
LUDFORD
LUDFORD DRIVE
LUDFORD PARK
LUDFORD ROAD
Sch
CHESTNUT GRO
BALLINTEER GRO
BALLINTEER CL
BALLINTEER CRES
BALLINTEER DRIVE
BALLINTEER PARK
BALLINTEER AVENUE
Ballinteer
Health Centre
Shopping Centre
Ballinteer Shopping Centre
THE OAKS
Sch
MARLAY VIEW
Ballintyre Hall
BALLINTYRE WALK
BALLINTEER
BAL DOWNS
BAL HEATH
MEADOWS
LA T. CT
THE PINES
PINE
BREHON
FIELD
ROAD
THE RISE
THE LAWN
THE GROVE
THE WALK
THE GLADE
WOODPARK
THE MEADOW
THE COURT
THE DRIVE
THE GREEN
THE VIEW
THE GLEN
THE HEIGHTS
THE AVENUE
THE HILL
THE CLOSE
CLONLEA
MARLAY PARK
4
SPORTS GROUND
VALLEY
PINE VALLEY DR
PINE VALLEY GRO
PINE VALLEY WAY
VALLEY PARK
AVENUE
GRANGE HALL
GRANGEFIELD
KINGSTON
KINGSTON WK
KINGSTON CL
KINGSTON AVENUE
KINGSTON DRIVE
KINGSTON LAWN
KINGSTON HEIGHTS
KINGSTON PARK
KINGSTON VIEW
KINGSTON CRES
KINGSTON GROVE
KINGSTON RISE
KINGSTON GRN
ROAD
TAYLOR'S HILL
HAROLD'S GRANGE ROAD
KINGSTON HALL
M50
SOUTHERN CROSS ROUTE
SPORTS GROUND
Pavilion
BREHON'S CHAIR
KELLYSTOWN ROAD
St. Columba's College
Danesmoate
SOMMERVILLE
FRANK
FORT PK
LARCHFIELD
ROSEMOUNT
OPHALY CT
SUNNYBANK TERRACE
ST JOSEPHS GRO
ROSEMOUNT PARK
ROSEMOUNT CT
ALEXANDRA TER
VICTORIA TER
Health Centre
DUNDRUM
TANEY PARK
OLD RECTORY PARK
TANEY
TANEY DR
TANEY MANOR
TANEY LAWN
R112
Dundrum Shopping Centre
Foot Bridge
MAIN STREET
College
PEMBROKE COTTS
EGLINTON TER
R117
PO
Garda
College
Sch
Sch
Dundrum
Movies@Dundrum
Dundrum Town Centre
DUNDRUM BYPASS
DUNDRUM CASTLE
BALLINTEER ROAD
AILESBURY GROVE
AILESBURY
Simpson's Hospital
DUNDRUM WOOD
AILESBURY LAWN
CASTLEBROOK
LYNWOOD
PINE COPSE ROAD
HAWTHORN DR
WYCKHAM PK RD
ASH LAWN
WYCKHAM WAY
WYCKHAM PLACE
WYCKHAM POINT
BALLINTEER RD
BALLINTEER GDNS
MAYFIELD TERRACE
HILTON GARDENS
BALLINTEER
ROAD
Sch
Gort Muire
WESLEY LAWNS
Wesley College
DELBROOK PARK
SPORTS GROUND
DELBROOK MANOR
COLLEGE PARK AVE
COLL PK GRO
COLL PK CL
COLLEGE PARK WAY
SPORTS GROUND
Junction 13
ROCKVIEW
TICKNOCK DALE
TICKNOCK GROVE
TICKNOCK AVE
TICKNOCK WY
TICKNOCK HILL
SANDYFORD VW
SIMONS RIDGE
BRACKEN HILL
KILCROSS SQ
KILCROSS DR
KILCROSS CT
KILCROSS
TICKNOCK ROAD
BLACKGLEN ROAD
Fitness Centre
SPORTS GRD
MOUNT CARMEL
FARMHILL DRIVE
FARMHILL ROAD
LARCHFIELD PK
GOATS. AVENUE
BELFIELD DOWNS
CARMEL ROAD
MT CARMEL AVE
TANEY AVE
TANEY RISE
TANEY CRESCENT
TANEY COURT
Goatstow
ROAD
SYDENHAM ROAD
STONEY ROAD
SILVER BIRCHES
BIRCHES LANE
SYDENHAM VILLAS
Sch
HERBERT HILL
ROCKFIELD
Luas Park & Ride
BALALLY
SANDYFORD ROAD
WILL BK
BALALLY DRIVE
ARDGLAS ESTATE
Homestead
DUN EMER DRIVE
DUN EMER RD
DUN EMER PK
PARKVALE
BALLAWLEY PARK
WESLEY HEIGHTS
BALLAWLEY
CLONARD CL
CLONARD GRO
CLONARD AVE
CLONARD LAWN
CLONARD
DRIVE
CLONARD ROAD

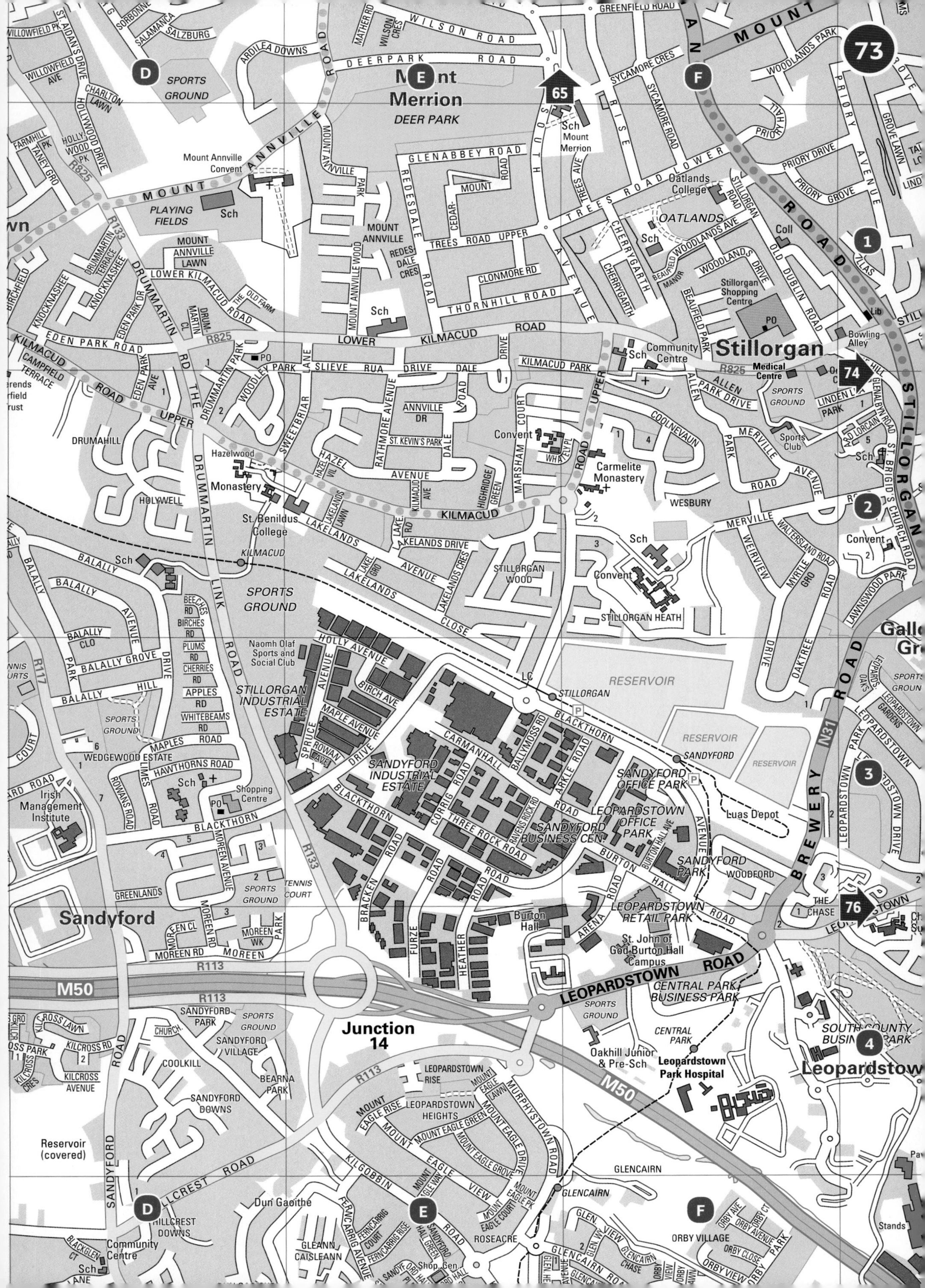
Mount Merrion
DEER PARK
Stillorgan
Sandyford
Junction 14
Leopardstown
SPORTS GROUND
Mount Annville Convent
PLAYING FIELDS
Sch
MOUNT ANNVILLE ROAD
WILSON ROAD
DEERPARK ROAD
GREENFIELD ROAD
MOUNT ANVILLE WOOD
GLENABBEY ROAD
REDESDALE ROAD
TREES ROAD UPPER
TREES ROAD LOWER
CLONMORE RD
THORNHILL ROAD
SOUTH AVENUE
SYCAMORE ROAD
SYCAMORE CRES
WOODLANDS PARK
PRIORY AVENUE
PRIORY DRIVE
PRIORY GROVE
Oatlands College
OATLANDS
CHERRYGARTH
WOODLANDS AVE
WOODLANDS DRIVE
OLD DUBLIN ROAD
Stillorgan Shopping Centre
PO
Lib
Bowling Alley
Coll
Community Centre
Medical Centre
LOWER KILMACUD ROAD
R825
EDEN PARK ROAD
KILMACUD ROAD UPPER
DRUMMARTIN ROAD
DRUMMARTIN LINK ROAD
R133
SLIEVE RUA DRIVE
KILMACUD PARK
ALLEN PARK DRIVE
COOLNEVAUN
MERVILLE ROAD
MERVILLE AVENUE
Sports Club
ST. BRIGID'S CHURCH ROAD
STILLORGAN ROAD
DRUMAHILL
HOLYWELL
Hazelwood Monastery
St. Benildus College
KILMACUD
Convent
Carmelite Monastery
WESBURY
STILLORGAN WOOD
STILLORGAN HEATH
LAKELANDS CLOSE
LAKELANDS AVENUE
LAKELANDS DRIVE
ANNVILLE DR
ST. KEVIN'S PARK
HAZEL AVENUE
RATHMORE AVENUE
SWEETBRIAR LANE
WEIRVIEW
WALTERSLAND ROAD
LAWNSWOOD PARK
MYRTLE GRO
OAKTREE ROAD
BALALLY AVENUE
BALALLY DRIVE
BALALLY GROVE
BALALLY HILL
BALALLY CLO
Naomh Olaf Sports and Social Club
STILLORGAN INDUSTRIAL ESTATE
HOLLY AVENUE
BIRCH AVE
MAPLE AVENUE
SPRUCE AVENUE
ROWAN LAVE
RESERVOIR
LC
STILLORGAN
SANDYFORD
BLACKTHORN ROAD
CARMANHALL ROAD
BALLYMOSS RD
ARKLE ROAD
SANDYFORD INDUSTRIAL ESTATE
SANDYFORD OFFICE PARK
LEOPARDSTOWN OFFICE PARK
SANDYFORD BUSINESS CEN.
SANDYFORD PARK
Luas Depot
BURTON HALL ROAD
THREE ROCK ROAD
CORRIG ROAD
BRACKEN ROAD
FURZE ROAD
HEATHER ROAD
Burton Hall
LEOPARDSTOWN RETAIL PARK
St. John of God Burton Hall Campus
LEOPARDSTOWN ROAD
CENTRAL PARK BUSINESS PARK
CENTRAL PARK
Oakhill Junior & Pre-Sch
Leopardstown Park Hospital
SOUTH COUNTY BUSINESS PARK
BREWERY ROAD
N31
LEOPARDSTOWN DRIVE
LEOPARDSTOWN GARDENS
WOODFORD
THE CHASE
WEDGEWOOD ESTATE
Irish Management Institute
MAPLES ROAD
HAWTHORNS ROAD
Shopping Centre
MOREEN AVENUE
MOREEN RD
GREENLANDS
TENNIS COURT
R117
R113
M50
SANDYFORD PARK
SANDYFORD VILLAGE
COOLKILL
BEARNA PARK
SANDYFORD DOWNS
KILCROSS AVENUE
Reservoir (covered)
SANDYFORD ROAD
HILLCREST ROAD
HILLCREST DOWNS
Community Centre
Dun Gaoithe
LEOPARDSTOWN RISE
LEOPARDSTOWN HEIGHTS
MOUNT EAGLE RISE
MOUNT EAGLE GREEN
MOUNT EAGLE DRIVE
MOUNT EAGLE VIEW
MURPHYSTOWN ROAD
KILGOBBIN ROAD
GLENCAIRN
GLENCAIRN VIEW
ROSEACRE
GLEANN CAISLEANN
ORBY VILLAGE
ORBY PARK
Stands
65
74
76
D
E
F
1
2
3
4

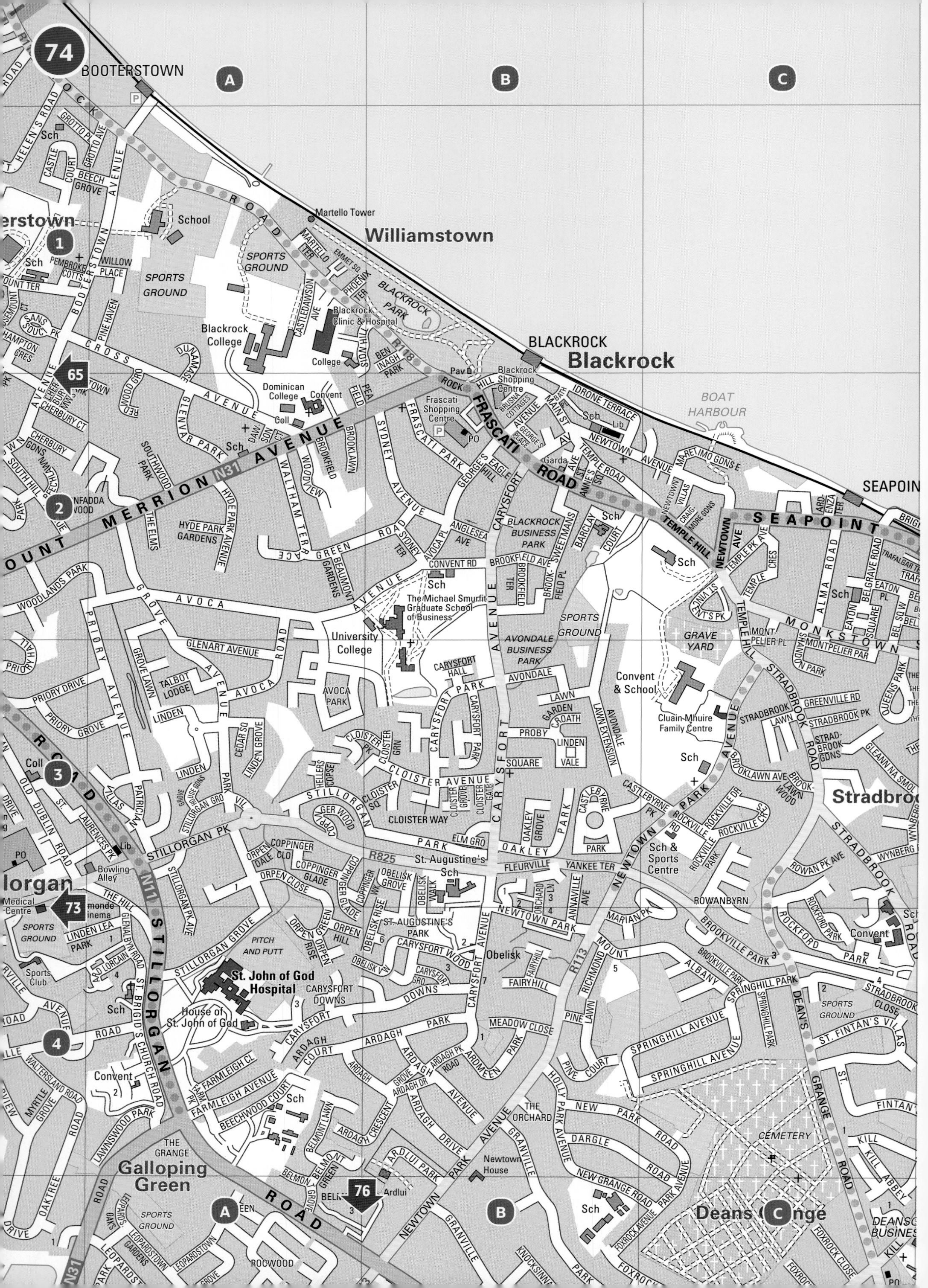
BOOTERSTOWN
A
B
C
Williamstown
Martello Tower
School
SPORTS GROUND
SPORTS GROUND
Blackrock College
Blackrock Clinic & Hospital
College
BLACKROCK PARK
BLACKROCK
Blackrock
BOAT HARBOUR
SEAPOINT
Blackrock Shopping Centre
Frascati Shopping Centre
Dominican College
Convent
Coll
Sch
PO
Lib
Garda
IDRONE TERRACE
NEWTOWN AVENUE
TEMPLE ROAD
TEMPLE HILL
SEAPOINT AVENUE
MONKSTOWN
FRASCATI ROAD
ROCK HILL
MAIN ST
MERRION AVENUE
N31
ROCK ROAD
R118
CROSS AVENUE
BOOTERSTOWN AVENUE
BLACKROCK BUSINESS PARK
AVONDALE BUSINESS PARK
SPORTS GROUND
GRAVE YARD
Convent & School
Cluain Mhuire Family Centre
The Michael Smurfit Graduate School of Business
University College
AVOCA PARK
AVOCA AVENUE
CARYSFORT AVENUE
CARYSFORT PARK
CLOISTER AVENUE
CLOISTER WAY
STILLORGAN PARK
R825
St. Augustine's Sch
ST. AUGUSTINE'S PARK
NEWTOWN PARK
NEWTOWN PARK AVENUE
YANKEE TER
FLEURVILLE
ROWANBYRN
STRADBROOK ROAD
Stradbrook
BROOKVILLE PARK
Sch & Sports Centre
Obelisk
FAIRYHILL
R113
SPRINGHILL PARK
SPRINGHILL AVENUE
DEAN'S GRANGE ROAD
SPORTS GROUND
CEMETERY
Deans Grange
PITCH AND PUTT
St. John of God Hospital
House of St. John of God
CARYSFORT DOWNS
ARDAGH PARK
STILLORGAN ROAD
N11
Bowling Alley
Medical Centre
Cinema
Sports Club
SPORTS GROUND
Convent
Galloping Green
THE GRANGE
SPORTS GROUND
Newtown House
Ardlui
THE ORCHARD
NEW PARK ROAD
DARGLE ROAD
NEWGRANGE ROAD
ROCWOOD
GRANVILLE
65
73
76
1
2
3
4

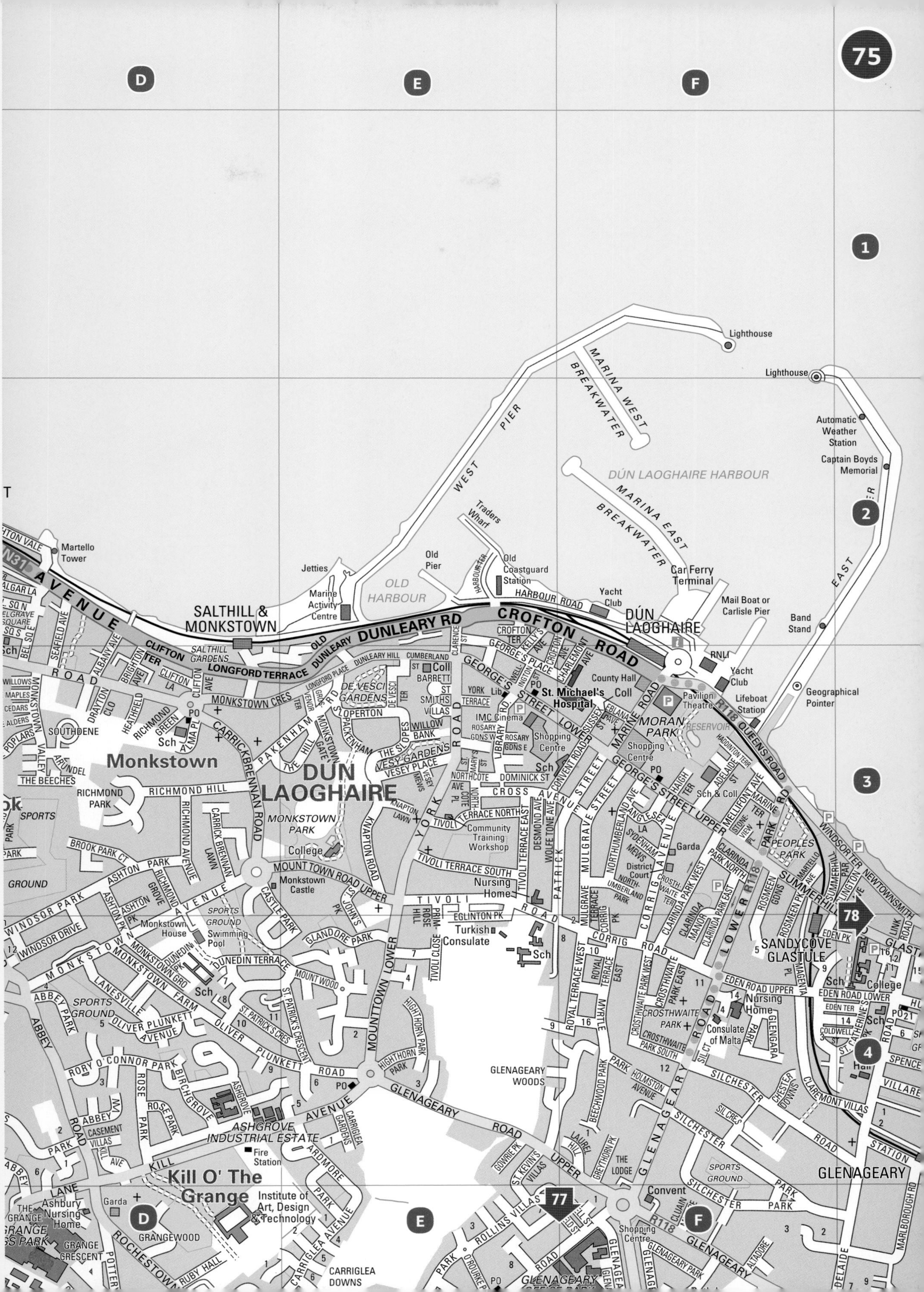
D
E
F
1
2
3
4
Lighthouse
Lighthouse
MARINA WEST BREAKWATER
WEST PIER
Automatic Weather Station
Captain Boyds Memorial
DÚN LAOGHAIRE HARBOUR
MARINA EAST BREAKWATER
Traders Wharf
EAST PIER
Martello Tower
Jetties
Old Pier
Old Coastguard Station
Car Ferry Terminal
OLD HARBOUR
Marine Activity Centre
Yacht Club
Mail Boat or Carlisle Pier
Band Stand
SALTHILL & MONKSTOWN
HARBOUR ROAD
DÚN LAOGHAIRE
CROFTON ROAD
DUNLEARY RD
OLD DUNLEARY
AVENUE
CLIFTON TER
SALTHILL GARDENS
LONGFORD TERRACE
RNLI
Yacht Club
County Hall
Coll
St. Michael's Hospital
Pavilion Theatre
Lifeboat Station
Geographical Pointer
MORAN PARK
RESERVOIR
R118 QUEENS ROAD
Shopping Centre
Monkstown
DUN LAOGHAIRE
DE VESCI GARDENS
MONKSTOWN CRES
CARRICKBRENNAN ROAD
RICHMOND HILL
RICHMOND PARK
THE BEECHES
SOUTHDENE
MONKSTOWN PARK
College
IMC Cinema
YORK ROAD
GEORGE'S STREET LOWER
GEORGE'S STREET UPPER
DOMINICK ST
CROSS AVENUE
PATRICK STREET
MULGRAVE STREET
Community Training Workshop
TIVOLI TERRACE SOUTH
TIVOLI ROAD
Nursing Home
Turkish Consulate
Sch
PEOPLES PARK
Garda
District Court
SANDYCOVE GLASTULE
78
MONKSTOWN ROAD UPPER
Monkstown Castle
Monkstown House
Swimming Pool
SPORTS GROUND
MONKSTOWN AVENUE
MOUNTTOWN LOWER
GLANDORE PARK
CORRIG ROAD
EDEN ROAD UPPER
EDEN ROAD LOWER
College
Nursing Home
Consulate of Malta
CROSTHWAITE PARK
SILCHESTER ROAD
GLENAGEARY ROAD LOWER
OLIVER PLUNKETT AVENUE
OLIVER PLUNKETT ROAD
RORY O'CONNOR PARK
GLENAGEARY WOODS
GLENAGEARY ROAD UPPER
ASHGROVE INDUSTRIAL ESTATE
Fire Station
Kill O' The Grange
Institute of Art, Design & Technology
Ashbury Nursing Home
Garda
GRANGEWOOD
ROCHESTOWN AVENUE
CARRIGLEA DOWNS
77
Convent
Shopping Centre
SPORTS GROUND
GLENAGEARY
CLAREMONT VILLAS
STATION ROAD
MARLBOROUGH RD

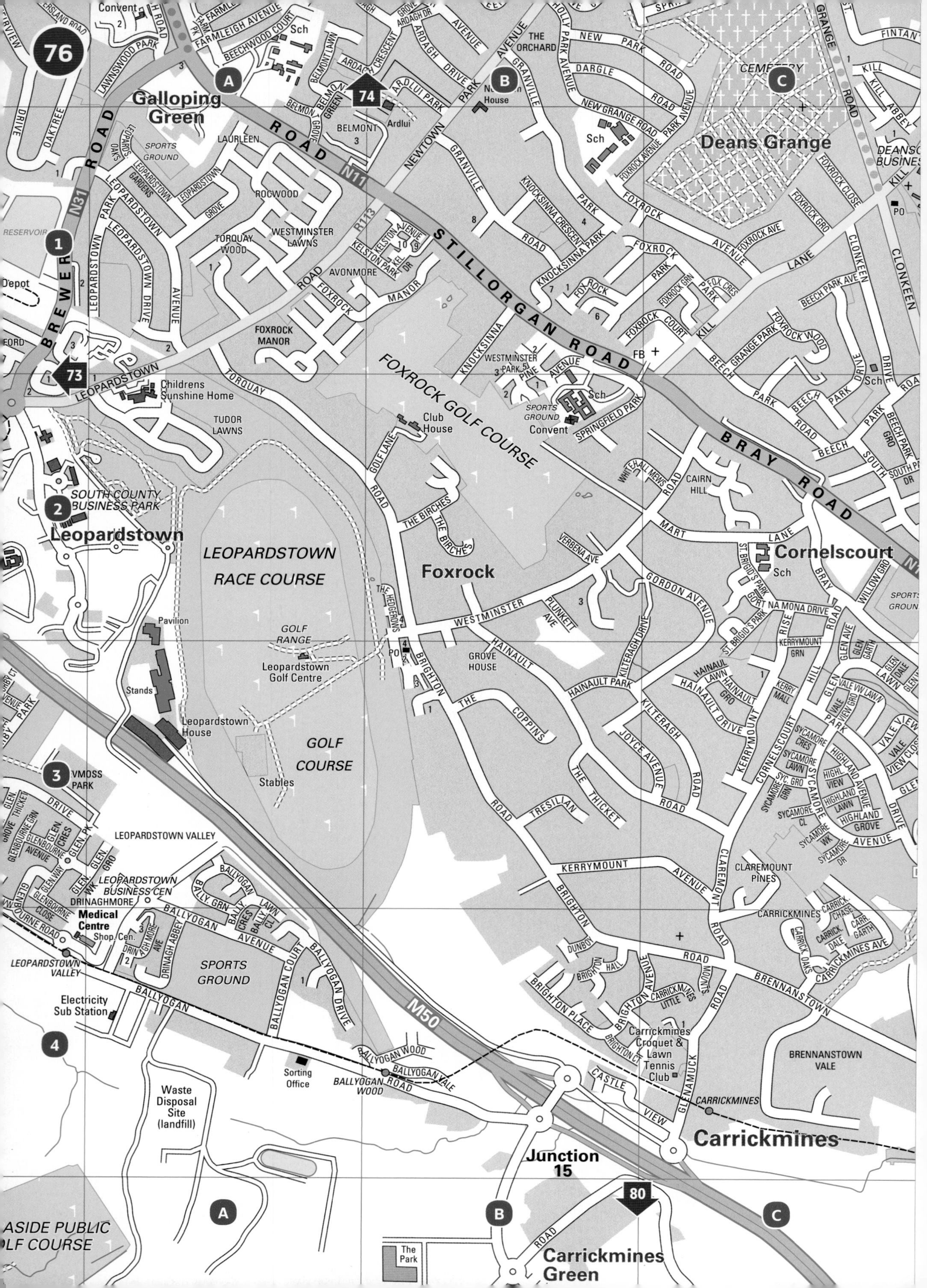
Galloping Green
Leopardstown
Foxrock
Deans Grange
Cornelscourt
Carrickmines
Carrickmines Green
Junction 15
74
73
80
A
B
C
1
2
3
4
STILLORGAN ROAD
N11
BRAY ROAD
BREWERY ROAD
N31
M50
LEOPARDSTOWN RACE COURSE
FOXROCK GOLF COURSE
GOLF COURSE
GOLF RANGE
Leopardstown Golf Centre
Pavilion
Stands
Leopardstown House
Stables
SOUTH COUNTY BUSINESS PARK
Childrens Sunshine Home
TUDOR LAWNS
FOXROCK MANOR
TORQUAY ROAD
LEOPARDSTOWN ROAD
WESTMINSTER ROAD
BRIGHTON ROAD
KERRYMOUNT AVENUE
CLAREMOUNT ROAD
BRENNANSTOWN ROAD
GLENAMUCK ROAD
BALLYOGAN ROAD
BALLYOGAN AVENUE
BALLYOGAN DRIVE
BALLYOGAN COURT
BALLYOGAN WOOD
BALLYOGAN VALE
LEOPARDSTOWN VALLEY
LEOPARDSTOWN BUSINESS CEN
DRINAGHMORE
Medical Centre
Shop. Cen.
SPORTS GROUND
Electricity Sub Station
Sorting Office
Waste Disposal Site (landfill)
Carrickmines Croquet & Lawn Tennis Club
CASTLE VIEW
BRENNANSTOWN VALE
CLAREMOUNT PINES
CARRICKMINES
CEMETERY
KILL LANE
FOXROCK AVENUE
FOXROCK PARK
KNOCKSINNA
GRANVILLE PARK
NEWTOWN PARK AVENUE
BEECH PARK ROAD
CLONKEEN DRIVE
MART LANE
GORDON AVENUE
KILTERAGH ROAD
HAINAULT ROAD
THE COPPINS
THE BIRCHES
THE THICKET
TRESILIAN
GROVE HOUSE
CAIRN HILL
Club House
Convent
Sch
PO
RESERVOIR
Depot
VMOSS PARK
The Park
ASIDE PUBLIC
LF COURSE

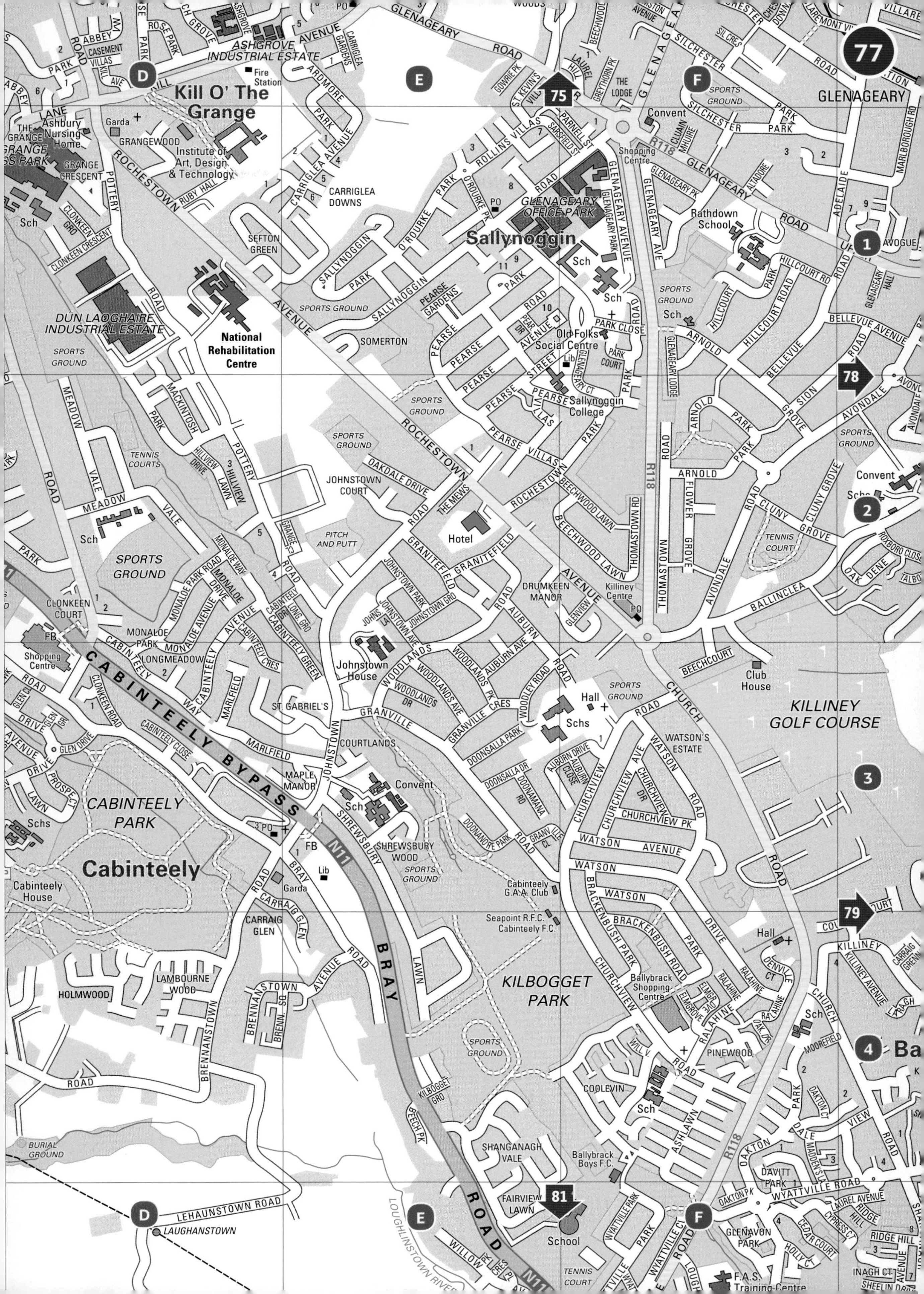
Kill O' The Grange
Ashgrove Industrial Estate
Glenageary
Sallynoggin
Glenageary Office Park
Institute of Art, Design & Technology
Dún Laoghaire Industrial Estate
National Rehabilitation Centre
Rochestown Avenue
Rochestown Road
Glenageary Road
Glenageary Avenue
Pottery Road
Meadow Vale
Clonkeen Road
Cabinteely Bypass
Cabinteely Park
Cabinteely
Cabinteely House
Johnstown House
Johnstown Road
Killiney Golf Course
Church Road
Kilbogget Park
Watson's Estate
Ballybrack Shopping Centre
Shanganagh Vale
Fairview Lawn
Bray Road
N11
Loughlinstown River
Lehaunstown Road
Laughanstown
Brennanstown Road
Lambourne Wood
Holmwood
Carraig Glen
Shrewsbury Wood
Drumkeen Manor
Killiney Centre
Thomastown Road
Avondale Road
Sion Road
Hillcourt Road
Rathdown School
Sallynoggin College
Old Folks Social Centre
Wyattville Road
F.A.S. Training Centre
Glenavon Park
Davitt Park
Oakton Park
Seapoint R.F.C.
Cabinteely F.C.
Cabinteely G.A.A. Club
Ballybrack Boys F.C.
Club House
Hotel
Convent
Sports Ground
Tennis Courts
Pitch and Putt
Burial Ground
75
78
79
81
D
E
F
1
2
3
4

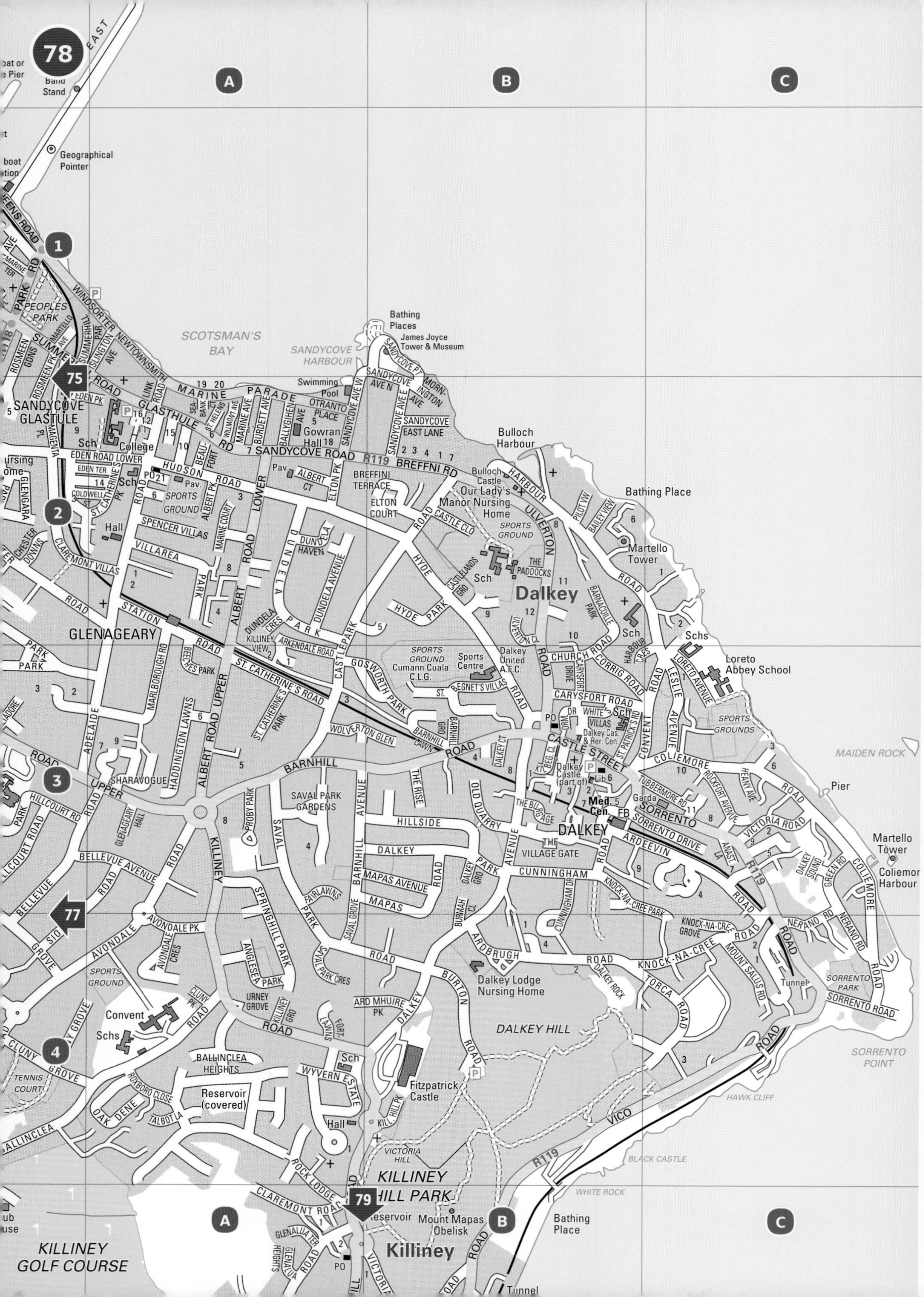
A
B
C
EAST
Band Stand
Geographical Pointer
SCOTSMAN'S BAY
SANDYCOVE HARBOUR
Bathing Places
James Joyce Tower & Museum
Swimming Pool
SANDYCOVE GLASTULE
QUEENS ROAD
WINDSORTER
PEOPLES PARK
NEWTOWNSMITH
MARINE PARADE
GLASTHULE RD
SANDYCOVE ROAD
R119
BREFFNI RD
SANDYCOVE AVE W
SANDYCOVE AVE N
SANDYCOVE AVE E
SANDYCOVE EAST LANE
SANDYCOVE PT
MORNINGTON AVE
OTRANTO PLACE
Gowran Hall
College
Sch
EDEN ROAD LOWER
EDEN TER
EDEN PK
HUDSON ROAD
SPORTS GROUND
SPENCER VILLAS
VILLAREA
CLAREMONT VILLAS
STATION ROAD
GLENAGEARY
ALBERT ROAD LOWER
ALBERT ROAD UPPER
MARINE COURT
ALBERT PK
ALBERT CT
ELTON PK
ELTON COURT
BREFFINI TERRACE
DUNDELA HAVEN
DUNDELA AVENUE
DUNDELA PARK
DUNDELA CRES
KILLINEY VIEW
ARKENDALE ROAD
CASTLEPARK ROAD
HYDE ROAD
HYDE PARK
CASTLE CLO
CASTLELANDS GRO
Bulloch Harbour
Bulloch Castle
Our Lady's Manor Nursing Home
HARBOUR ROAD
ULVERTON ROAD
ULVERTON CL
THE PADDOCKS
Dalkey
BARNACOILLE PARK
PILOT VW
BAILEY VIEW
Bathing Place
Martello Tower
Schs
Loreto Abbey School
LORETO AVENUE
LESLIE AVENUE
CONVENT ROAD
HARBOUR CRES
CORRIG ROAD
CHURCH ROAD
SPORTS GROUNDS
MAIDEN ROCK
Pier
SPORTS GROUND
Cumann Cuala C.L.G.
Sports Centre
Dalkey United A.F.C.
ST. BEGNET'S VILLAS
GOSWORTH PARK
ST. CATHERINE'S ROAD
ST. CATHERINE'S PARK
MARLBOROUGH RD
BEECHES PARK
HADDINGTON LAWNS
WOLVERTON GLEN
BARNHILL LAWN
BARNHILL GRO
BARNHILL ROAD
CARYSFORT ROAD
CARYSFORT DRIVE
WHITE'S VILLAS
ST. PATRICK'S RD
Dalkey Cas. & Her. Cen.
CASTLE STREET
Dalkey Castle (part of)
Lib
Med. Cen.
FB
Garda
COLIEMORE ROAD
TUBBERMORE RD
ROCKFORT AVENUE
HEANY AVE
VICTORIA ROAD
SORRENTO DRIVE
DALKEY
ARDEEVIN
ANASTASIA LA
DALKEY SOUND
GREEN RD
Martello Tower
Coliemore Harbour
ADELAIDE ROAD
SHARAVOGUE
UPPER GLENAGEARY ROAD
GLENAGEARY HALL
HILLCOURT RD
HILLCOURT ROAD
BELLEVUE AVENUE
BELLEVUE ROAD
PROBY PARK
KILLINEY ROAD
SAVAL PARK GARDENS
SAVAL PARK ROAD
BARNHILL AVENUE
THE RISE
OLD QUARRY
DALKEY CT
THE BULLOCK AGE
HILLSIDE
DALKEY PARK
DALKEY AVENUE
THE VILLAGE GATE
CUNNINGHAM ROAD
CUNNINGHAM DR
KNOCK-NA-CREE PARK
KNOCK-NA-CREE GROVE
KNOCK-NA-CREE ROAD
MAPAS AVENUE
MAPAS ROAD
FAIRLAWNS
SAVAL GROVE
DALKEY GRO
BURMAH CL
ARDBRUGH ROAD
Dalkey Lodge Nursing Home
DALKEY ROCK
TORCA ROAD
MOUNT SALUS RD
NERANO RD
SORRENTO PARK
SORRENTO ROAD
Tunnel
SORRENTO POINT
AVONDALE PK
AVONDALE CRES
AVONDALE GROVE
SPRINGHILL PARK
ANGLESEA PARK
URNEY GROVE
KILLINEY GRO
SAVAL PARK CRES
ARD MHUIRE PK
FORT-LAWNS
BURTON ROAD
DALKEY HILL
Convent
Schs
CLUNY PK
CLUNY GROVE
TENNIS COURT
BALLINCLEA HEIGHTS
WYVERN ESTATE
Fitzpatrick Castle
ROXBORO CLOSE
OAK DENE
TALBOT LA
Reservoir (covered)
BALLINCLEA
Hall
KILL HILL PK
VICTORIA HILL
HAWK CLIFF
VICO ROAD
BLACK CASTLE
WHITE ROCK
ROCK LODGE
CLAREMONT ROAD
KILLINEY HILL PARK
Reservoir
Mount Mapas Obelisk
Killiney
GLENALUA TER
GLENALUA HEIGHTS
VICTORIA
PO
KILLINEY GOLF COURSE
Bathing Place
Tunnel
75
77
79

Killiney
KILLINEY HILL PARK
KILLINEY GOLF COURSE
Ballybrack
Loughlinstown
SHANKILL
KILLINEY BAY
Fitzpatrick Castle
Reservoir (covered)
Killiney Centre
Club House
Mount Mapas Obelisk
Bathing Place
Tunnel
BLACK CASTLE
WHITE ROCK
VICO ROAD
R119
KILLINEY HILL ROAD
VICTORIA ROAD
CHURCH ROAD
R118
KENAH HILL
Canadian Ambassador's Residence
KILLINEY HEATH
Martello Tower
Australian Embassy
KILLINEY
STATION ROAD
STRAND ROAD
Kilmarnock
Psamtic Language Centre
Convent
MILITARY ROAD
WYATTVILLE ROAD
Ballybrack Shopping Centre
Ballybrack Boys F.C.
F.A.S. Training Centre
LOUGHLINSTOWN IND. ESTATE
Health Centre
European Foundation
Leisure Centre
SEAFIELD ROAD
Sewage Disposal Works
PITCH AND PUTT
SPORTS GROUND
COMMONS ROAD
St. Columcilles Hospital (A&E)
LOUGHLINSTOWN RIVER
White Gables
SHANGANAGH CLIFFS
RATHSALLAGH BRIDGE
M11
DUBLIN ROAD
R116
STONEBRIDGE ROAD
FALLS ROAD
SHANGANAGH ROAD
CLANMAWR
77
78
81
D
E
F
1
2
3
4

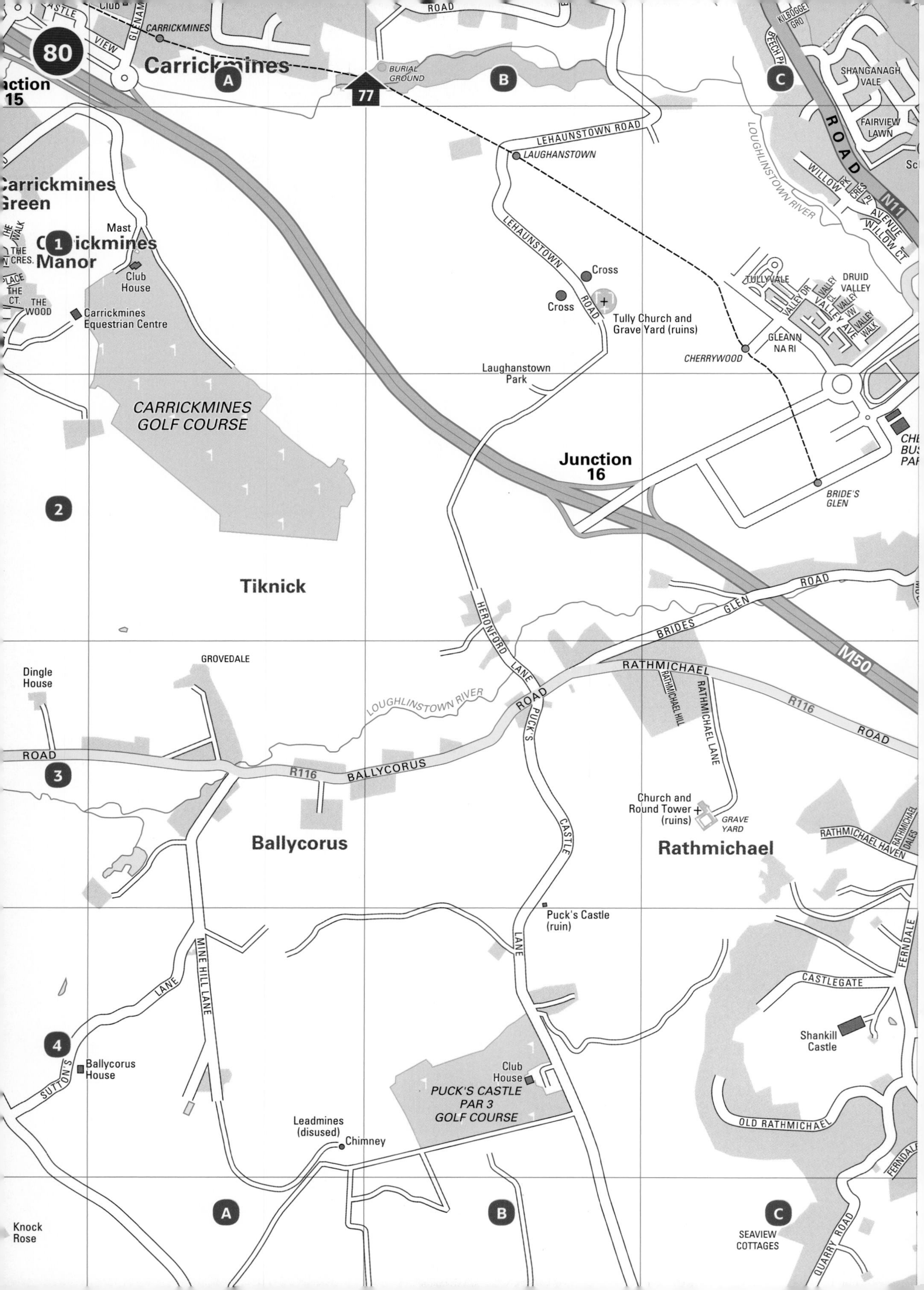

Carrickmines
CARRICKMINES
BURIAL GROUND
77
Junction 15
Carrickmines Green
Carrickmines Manor
Mast
Club House
Carrickmines Equestrian Centre
THE WALK
THE CRES.
PLACE
THE CT.
THE WOOD
GLENAMUCK
VIEW
CASTLE
ROAD
LEHAUNSTOWN ROAD
LAUGHANSTOWN
LEHAUNSTOWN ROAD
Cross
Cross
Tully Church and Grave Yard (ruins)
Laughanstown Park
CARRICKMINES GOLF COURSE
Junction 16
CHERRYWOOD
GLEANN NA RI
BRIDE'S GLEN
TULLY VALE
DRUID VALLEY
VALLEY DR
VALLEY CL
VALLEY W
VALLEY AVE
VALLEY WALK
KILBOGGET GRO
BEECH PK
SHANGANAGH VALE
FAIRVIEW LAWN
ROAD
N11
WILLOW PK
CRES
PL
AVENUE
WILLOW CT
LOUGHLINSTOWN RIVER
Tiknick
M50
BRIDES GLEN ROAD
HERONFORD LANE
RATHMICHAEL ROAD
R116
RATHMICHAEL HILL
RATHMICHAEL LANE
GROVEDALE
Dingle House
LOUGHLINSTOWN RIVER
ROAD
R116
BALLYCORUS ROAD
PUCK'S CASTLE LANE
Ballycorus
Church and Round Tower (ruins)
GRAVE YARD
Rathmichael
RATHMICHAEL HAVEN
RATHMICHAEL DALES
Puck's Castle (ruin)
MINE HILL LANE
LANE
FERNDALE
CASTLEGATE
Shankill Castle
SUTTON'S
Ballycorus House
Club House
PUCK'S CASTLE PAR 3 GOLF COURSE
Leadmines (disused)
Chimney
OLD RATHMICHAEL
FERNDALE
Knock Rose
SEAVIEW COTTAGES
QUARRY ROAD
A
B
C
1
2
3
4

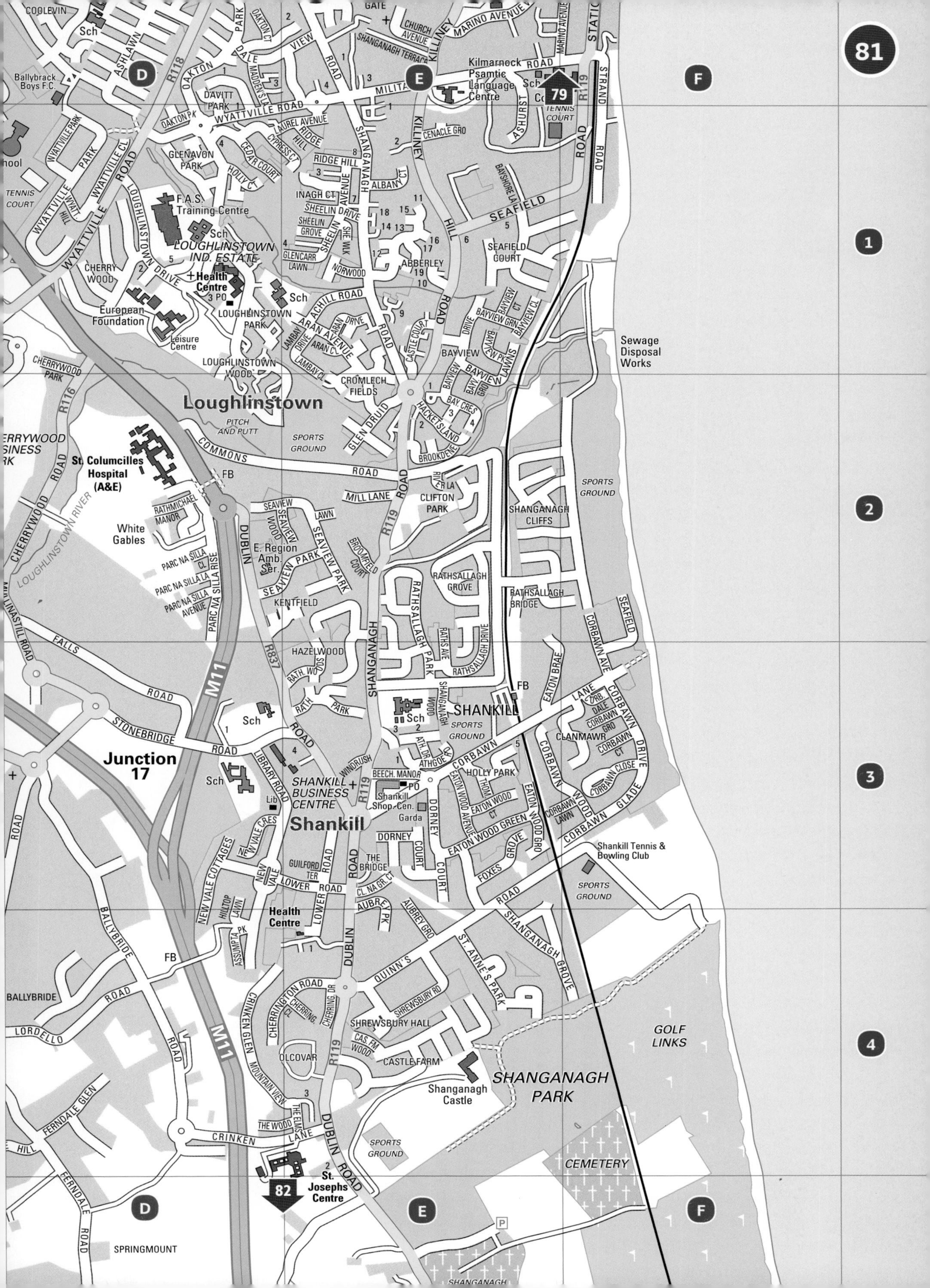
Loughlinstown
Shankill
Junction 17
SHANKILL
SHANGANAGH PARK
Shanganagh Castle
GOLF LINKS
CEMETERY
Sewage Disposal Works
St. Columcilles Hospital (A&E)
F.A.S. Training Centre
LOUGHLINSTOWN IND. ESTATE
Health Centre
European Foundation
Leisure Centre
Kilmarnock Psamtic Language Centre
Shankill Tennis & Bowling Club
SHANKILL BUSINESS CENTRE
Shankill Shop. Cen.
Garda
St. Josephs Centre
E. Region Amb. Ser.
White Gables
Ballybrack Boys F.C.
SPORTS GROUND
PITCH AND PUTT
LOUGHLINSTOWN RIVER
WYATTVILLE ROAD
LOUGHLINSTOWN DRIVE
COMMONS ROAD
SHANGANAGH ROAD
KILLINEY HILL ROAD
SEAFIELD ROAD
STATION ROAD
STRAND ROAD
DUBLIN ROAD
CORBAWN LANE
STONEBRIDGE ROAD
FALLS ROAD
CHERRYWOOD ROAD
BALLYBRIDE ROAD
LORDELLO ROAD
CRINKEN LANE
QUINN'S ROAD
LOWER ROAD
LIBRARY ROAD
MILL LANE
SPRINGMOUNT
BALLYBRIDE
COOLEVIN
M11
R119
R118
R116
R837
79
82
D
E
F
1
2
3
4

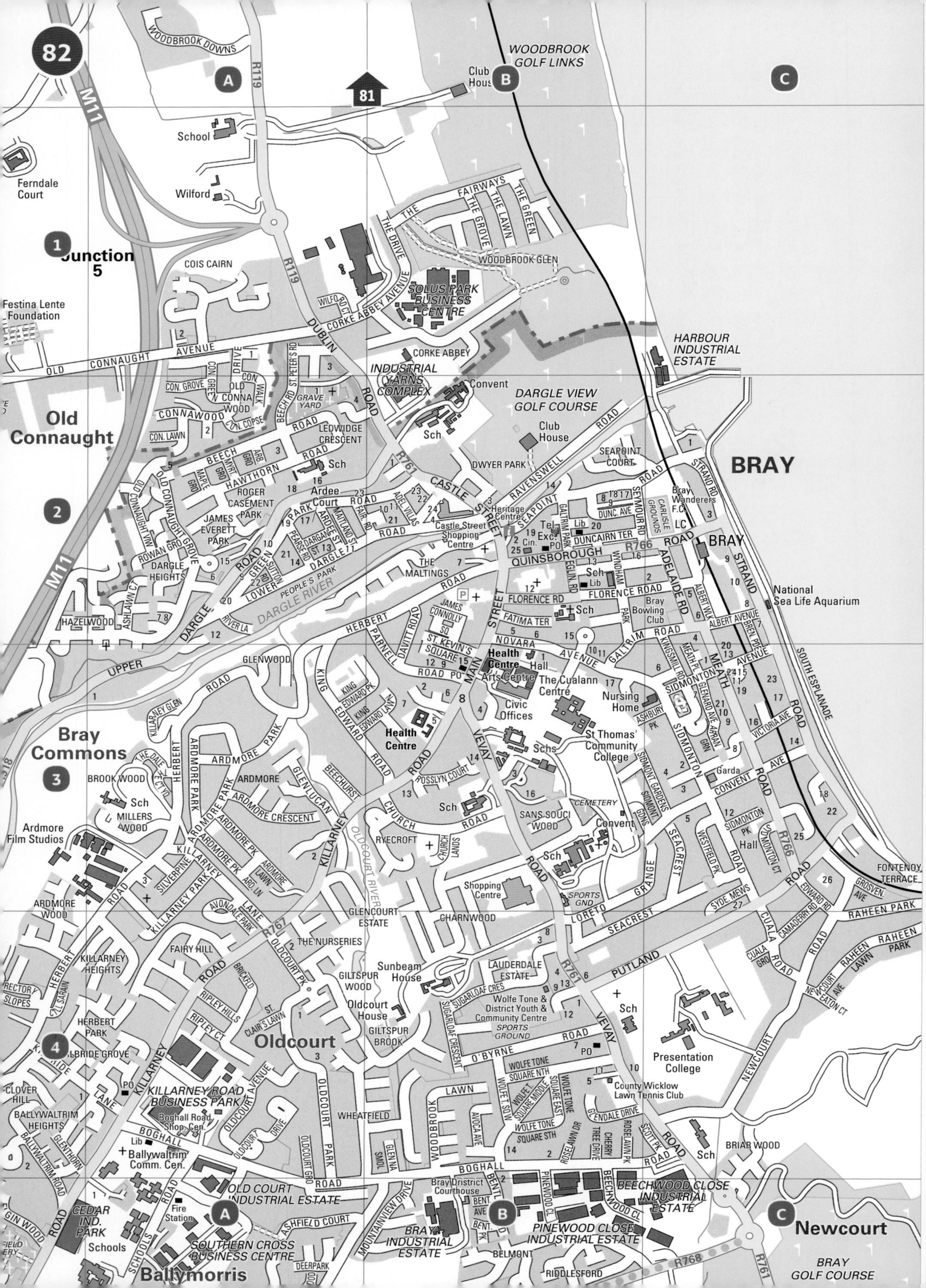
81
A
B
C
1
2
3
4
WOODBROOK DOWNS
WOODBROOK GOLF LINKS
Club House
R119
M11
School
Ferndale Court
Wilford
Junction 5
Festina Lente Foundation
COIS CAIRN
THE FAIRWAYS
THE GROVE
THE LAWN
THE GREEN
THE DRIVE
WOODBROOK GLEN
SOLUS PARK BUSINESS CENTRE
CORKE ABBEY AVENUE
WILFORD CT
DUBLIN ROAD
OLD CONNAUGHT AVENUE
CORKE ABBEY
INDUSTRIAL YARNS COMPLEX
Convent
HARBOUR INDUSTRIAL ESTATE
DARGLE VIEW GOLF COURSE
Club House
Old Connaught
CON. GROVE
CON. GREEN
OLD CONNA WOOD
CON. WALK
CON. COPSE
CONNAWOOD
CON. LAWN
GRAVE YARD
BEECH RD
ST. PETER'S RD
LEDWIDGE CRESCENT
Sch
BEECH
HAWTHORN
MAPLE GRO
ROGER CASEMENT PARK
JAMES EVERETT PARK
Ardee Court
CASTLE STREET
RAVENSWELL ROAD
DWYER PARK
SEAPOINT COURT
BRAY
Bray Wanderers F.C.
CARLISLE GROUNDS
DUNC. AVE
DUNCAIRN TER
Heritage Centre
Castle Street Shopping Centre
Tel. Exc.
PO
Cin.
Lib
QUINSBOROUGH ROAD
R766
ADELAIDE RD
SEYMOUR RD
STRAND RD
STRAND ROAD
LC
BRAY
National Sea Life Aquarium
OLD CONNAUGHT VW
OLD CONNAUGHT GROVE
ROWAN GRO
DARGLE HEIGHTS
DARGLE ROAD
PEOPLE'S PARK
LOWER DARGLE
DARGLE RIVER
THE MALTINGS
HAZELWOOD
ASHLAWN CT
RIVER LA
FLORENCE RD
FLORENCE ROAD
Bray Bowling Club
JAMES CONNOLLY SQ
FATIMA TER
HERBERT ROAD
ST. KEVIN'S SQUARE
MAIN STREET
NOVARA AVENUE
GALTRIM ROAD
ALBERT WALK
ALBERT AVENUE
MEATH ROAD
Health Centre
Hall
Arts Centre
The Cualann Centre
Nursing Home
SIDMONTON AVENUE
SOUTH ESPLANADE
UPPER
GLENWOOD
PARNELL ROAD
DAVITT ROAD
KING EDWARD PK
KING EDWARD LAWN
KING EDWARD ROAD
Civic Offices
Health Centre
St Thomas' Community College
VICTORIA AVE
Bray Commons
KILLARNEY GLEN
HERBERT
ARDMORE PARK
ARDMORE
THE DALE
BROOK WOOD
Sch
MILLERS WOOD
ARDMORE CRESCENT
GLENLUCAN
BEECHURST
ROSSLYN COURT
VEVAY ROAD
Schs
SIDMONTON GARDENS
SIDMONTON ROAD
CONVENT AVE
Garda
Ardmore Film Studios
KILLARNEY ROAD
OLDCOURT RIVER
CHURCH ROAD
RYECROFT
CHURCH LANDS
Sch
SANS SOUCI WOOD
CEMETERY
Convent
SEACREST
WESTFIELD PK
SIDMONTON PK
Hall
FONTENOY TERRACE
ARDMORE WOOD
SILVERPINE
KILLARNEY PARK
ARDMORE LAWN
AVONDALE PARK
KILLARNEY LANE
Shopping Centre
SPORTS GND
GRANGE
SYDE. MEWS
EDWARD RD
GROSVENOR AVE
RAHEEN PARK
GLENCOURT ESTATE
CHARNWOOD
LORETO
SEACREST
CUALA ROAD
CAMADERRY RD
R767
THE NURSERIES
FAIRY HILL
KILLARNEY HEIGHTS
RECTORY SLOPES
OLDCOURT PK
Sunbeam House
LAUDERDALE ESTATE
PUTLAND ROAD
R761
RAHEEN LAWN
RAHEEN PARK
NEWCOURT AVE
EATON CT
BRICKFIELD
RIPLEY HILLS
GILTSPUR WOOD
SUGARLOAF CRES
Wolfe Tone & District Youth & Community Centre
SPORTS GROUND
Sch
RIPLEY CT
ST. CLAIR'S LAWN
Oldcourt House
SUGARLOAF CRESCENT
HERBERT PARK
GILTSPUR BROOK
Oldcourt
O'BYRNE ROAD
PO
Presentation College
KILBRIDE GROVE
WOLFE TONE SQUARE NTH
WOLFE TONE SQUARE MIDDLE
WOLFE TONE SQUARE EAST
WOLFE T. SQ. W
County Wicklow Lawn Tennis Club
NEWCOURT
CLOVER HILL
KILLARNEY ROAD BUSINESS PARK
OLDCOURT AVENUE
LAWN
BALLYWALTRIM HEIGHTS
BALLYWALTRIM LANE
Boghall Road Shop. Cen.
OLDCOURT DRIVE
OLDCOURT PARK
WHEATFIELD
WOODBROOK
AVOCA AVE
GLENDALE DRIVE
ROSELAWN DR
TREE DRIVE
CHERRY
ROSELAWN RISE
SCOTT PK
Sch
BRIAR WOOD
GLENTHORN
Lib
Ballywaltrim Comm. Cen.
BOGHALL ROAD
WOLFE TONE SQUARE STH
GLEN NA SMOL
OLDCOURT GRO
BOGHALL ROAD
BENTL
Bray District Courthouse
PINEWOOD CL
BEECHWOOD CL
BEECHWOOD CLOSE INDUSTRIAL ESTATE
Newcourt
CEDAR IND. PARK
Fire Station
OLD COURT INDUSTRIAL ESTATE
ASHFIELD COURT
MOUNTAINVIEW DRIVE
BRAY INDUSTRIAL ESTATE
BENT. AVE
BENT. PK
PINEWOOD CLOSE INDUSTRIAL ESTATE
Schools
SCHOOLS ROAD
SOUTHERN CROSS BUSINESS CENTRE
DEERPARK
BELMONT
R768
RIDDLESFORD
BRAY GOLF COURSE
Ballymorris

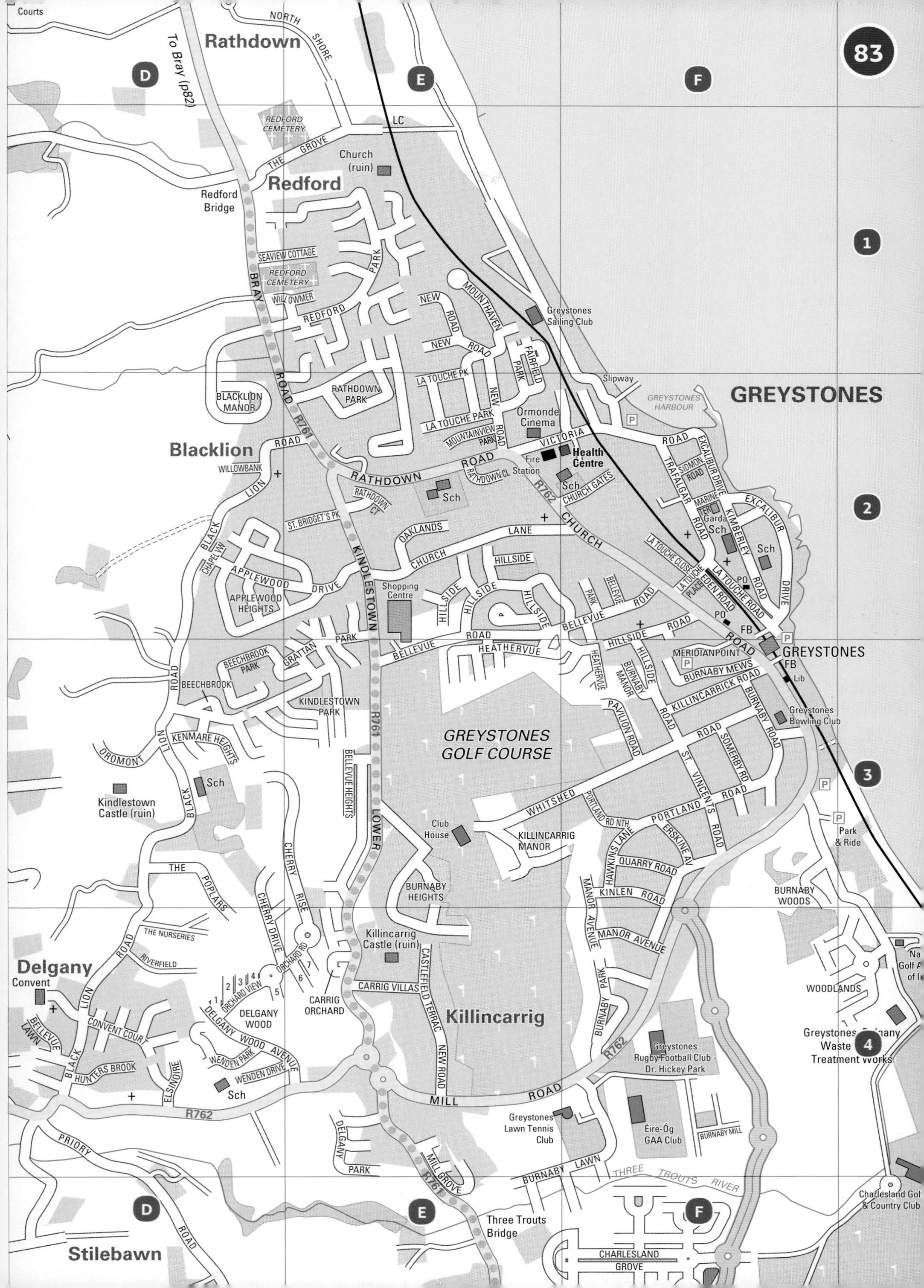
Courts
To Bray (p82)
Rathdown
NORTH SHORE
D
E
F
REDFORD CEMETERY
LC
THE GROVE
Church (ruin)
Redford
Redford Bridge
1
SEAVIEW COTTAGE
REDFORD CEMETERY
WILLOWMER
PARK
REDFORD
BRAY ROAD
MOUNTHAVEN
NEW ROAD
NEW ROAD
Greystones Sailing Club
FAIRFIELD PARK
LA TOUCHE PK
RATHDOWN PARK
BLACKLION MANOR
Slipway
GREYSTONES HARBOUR
GREYSTONES
P
NEW ROAD
Ormonde Cinema
LA TOUCHE PARK
MOUNTAINVIEW PARK
R761
Blacklion
ROAD
VICTORIA
ROAD
Fire Station
Health Centre
WILLOWBANK
RATHDOWN
RATHDOWN CL
R762
Sch
CHURCH GATES
TRAFALGAR ROAD
SIDMON ROAD
EXCALIBUR DRIVE
EXCALIBUR
MARINE TER
Garda
2
LION
Sch
RATHDOWN CT
CHURCH
ST. BRIDGET'S PK
KIMBERLEY
Sch
Sch
BLACK
OAKLANDS
LANE
CHAPELVW
CHURCH
HILLSIDE
LA TOUCHE CLOSE
LA TOUCHE PLACE
EDEN ROAD
LA TOUCHE ROAD
ROAD
DRIVE
PO
APPLEWOOD DRIVE
Shopping Centre
KINDLESTOWN
HILLSIDE
HILLSIDE
HILLSIDE
PARK
BELLEVUE
ROAD
APPLEWOOD HEIGHTS
BELLEVUE
PO
FB
PARK
ROAD
HILLSIDE
ROAD
ROAD
GREYSTONES
BEECHBROOK PARK
GRATTAN
BELLEVUE
HEATHERVUE
FB
MERIDIANPOINT
BURNABY MEWS
Lib
ROAD
BEECHBROOK
HEATHERVUE
BURNABY MANOR
HILLSIDE
KILLINCARRICK ROAD
KINDLESTOWN PARK
R761
PAVILION ROAD
ROAD
BURNABY ROAD
Greystones Bowling Club
KENMARE HEIGHTS
LION
ORMONT
GREYSTONES GOLF COURSE
ROAD
SOMERBY RD
BELLEVUE HEIGHTS
3
Sch
ST. VINCENTS ROAD
Kindlestown Castle (ruin)
BLACK
WHITSHED
PORTLAND RD NTH
PORTLAND
ROAD
P
LOWER
Club House
KILLINCARRIG MANOR
ERSKINE AV
Park & Ride
HAWKINS LANE
QUARRY ROAD
THE POPLARS
CHERRY RISE
BURNABY HEIGHTS
MANOR AVENUE
KINLEN ROAD
BURNABY WOODS
CHERRY DRIVE
THE NURSERIES
Killincarrig Castle (ruin)
MANOR AVENUE
ROAD
RIVERFIELD
ORCHARD RD
Delgany
Convent
ORCHARD VIEW
CARRIG VILLAS
CASTLEFIELD TERRACE
BURNABY PARK
WOODLANDS
LION
DELGANY WOOD
CARRIG ORCHARD
Killincarrig
BELLEVUE LAWN
CONVENT COURT
DELGANY WOOD AVENUE
NEW ROAD
R762
Greystones Rugby Football Club - Dr. Hickey Park
Greystones Delgany Waste Treatment Works
4
BLACK
HUNTERS BROOK
WENDEN PARK
WENDEN DRIVE
ELSINORE
Sch
MILL
ROAD
R762
Greystones Lawn Tennis Club
Éire-Óg GAA Club
BURNABY MILL
PRIORY
DELGANY
PARK
MILL GROVE
R761
BURNABY
LAWN
THREE TROUTS RIVER
Charlesland Golf & Country Club
D
E
F
Three Trouts Bridge
ROAD
Stilebawn
CHARLESLAND GROVE

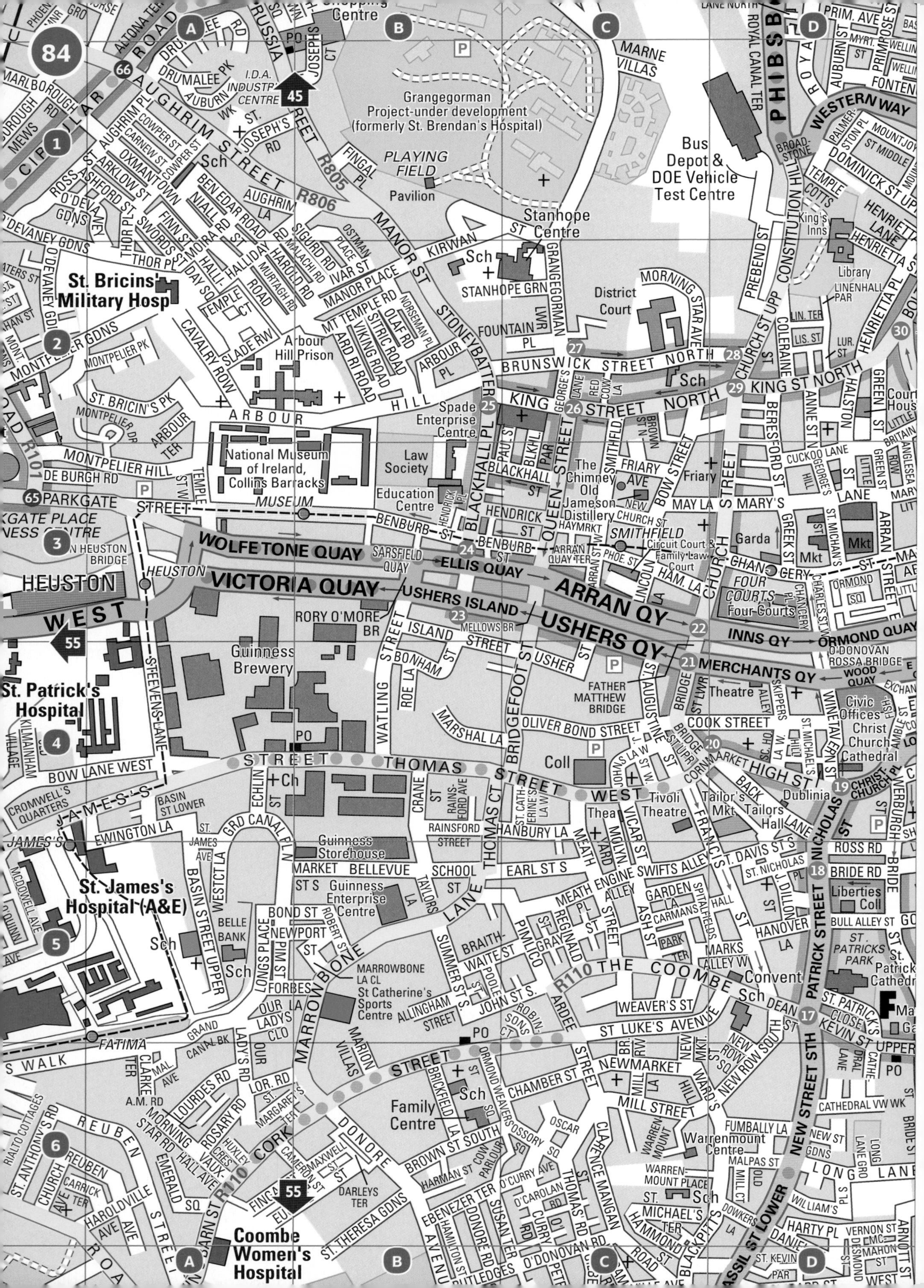
A
B
C
D
45
55
55
Grangegorman
Project-under development
(formerly St. Brendan's Hospital)
PLAYING
FIELD
Pavilion
I.D.A.
INDUSTRY
CENTRE
Bus
Depot &
DOE Vehicle
Test Centre
Stanhope
Centre
King's
Inns
Library
District
Court
St. Bricins
Military Hosp
Arbour
Hill Prison
Spade
Enterprise
Centre
Law
Society
Education
Centre
National Museum
of Ireland,
Collins Barracks
The
Chimney
Old
Jameson
Distillery
Friary
Garda
Mkt
Circuit Court &
Family Law
Court
FOUR
COURTS
Four Courts
HEUSTON
Guinness
Brewery
St. Patrick's
Hospital
Guinness
Storehouse
Guinness
Enterprise
Centre
St. James's
Hospital (A&E)
Coll
Tivoli
Theatre
Tailor's
Mkt
Tailors
Hall
Dublinia
Christ
Church
Cathedral
Civic
Offices
Theatre
Liberties
Coll
ST.
PATRICKS
PARK
St.
Patrick's
Cathedral
Convent
Warrenmount
Centre
Family
Centre
MARROWBONE
LA CL
St Catherine's
Sports
Centre
Coombe
Women's
Hospital
WOLFETONE QUAY
VICTORIA QUAY
ELLIS QUAY
ARRAN QY
USHERS QY
USHERS ISLAND
INNS QY
ORMOND QUAY
MERCHANTS QY
WOOD
QUAY
O'DONOVAN
ROSSA BRIDGE
FATHER
MATTHEW
BRIDGE
RORY O'MORE
BR
MELLOWS BR
SARSFIELD
QUAY
HEUSTON
BRIDGE
PARKGATE STREET
BENBURB ST
THOMAS STREET
THOMAS STREET WEST
JAMES'S ST
CORK STREET
THE COOMBE
R110
R805
R806
R101
AUGHRIM STREET
MANOR ST
STONEYBATTER
KING STREET NORTH
BRUNSWICK STREET NORTH
CHURCH ST
BOW STREET
SMITHFIELD
QUEEN STREET
BLACKHALL PL
ARBOUR HILL
MONTPELIER HILL
WATLING STREET
BRIDGEFOOT ST
OLIVER BOND STREET
HIGH ST
COOK STREET
PATRICK STREET
NEW STREET STH
CLANBRASSIL ST LOWER
MARROWBONE LANE
DONORE AVE
ST LUKE'S AVENUE
NEWMARKET
MILL STREET
WESTERN WAY
PHIBSBOROUGH
CONSTITUTION HILL
DOMINICK ST UPR
HENRIETTA ST
BOW LANE WEST
BASIN STREET UPPER
STEEVENS LANE
MUSEUM
HEUSTON
SMITHFIELD
FATIMA
JAMES'S

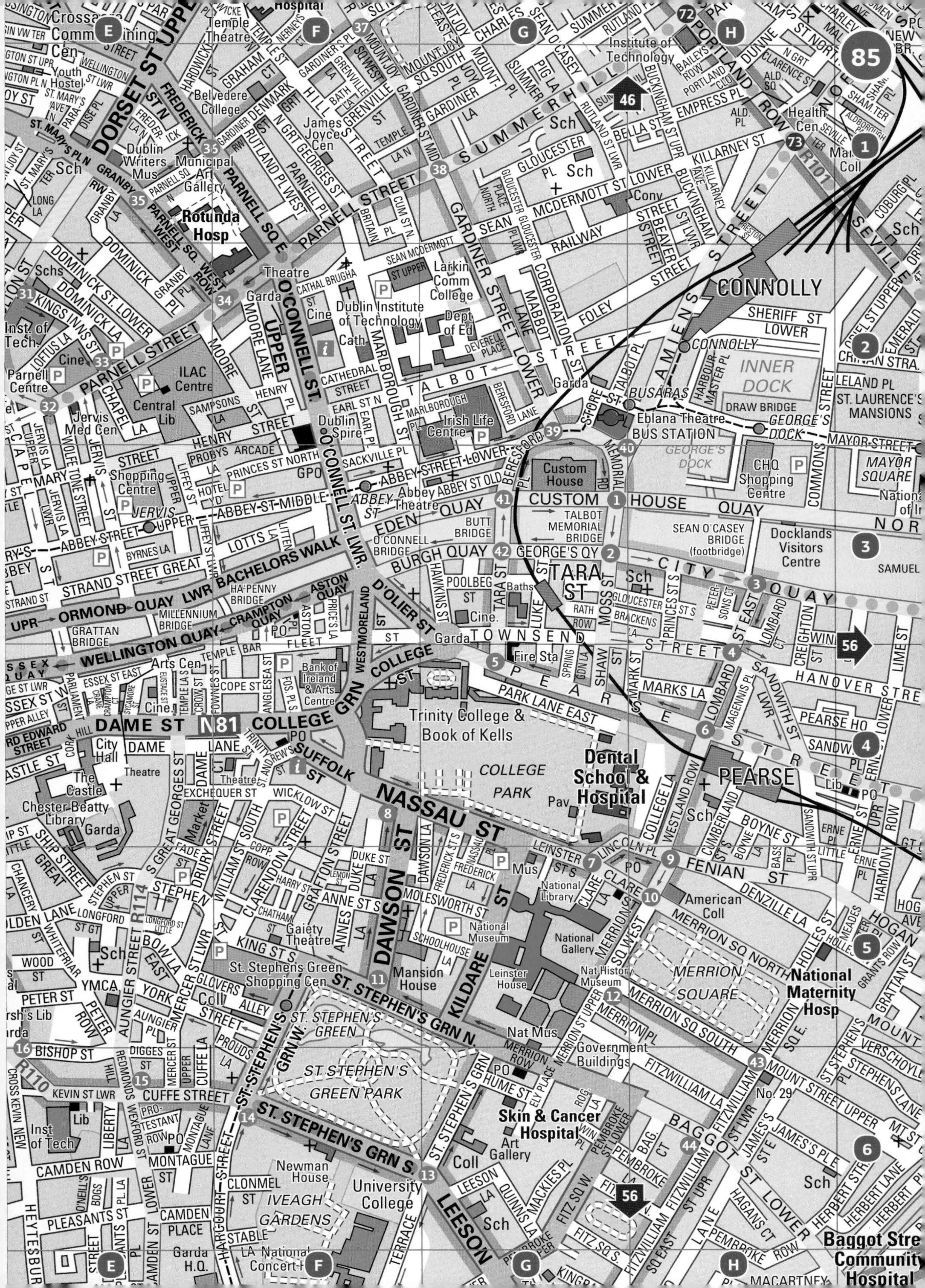
85
Crossair Community Training Cen
Youth Hostel
Temple Theatre
Hospital
Institute of Technology
46
Belvedere College
James Joyce Cen
Dublin Writers Mus
Municipal Art Gallery
Rotunda Hosp
Health Cen
Mater Coll
Larkin Comm College
Dublin Institute of Technology
Dept of Ed
Cath
Cine
Garda
Inst. of Tech.
Parnell Centre
ILAC Centre
Central Lib
Jervis Med Cen
Dublin Spire
Irish Life Centre
CONNOLLY
INNER DOCK
ST. LAURENCE'S MANSIONS
Eblana Theatre
BUS STATION
GEORGE'S DOCK
MAYOR SQUARE
CHQ Shopping Centre
Custom House
Abbey Theatre
Shopping Centre
GPO
Talbot Memorial Bridge
Sean O'Casey Bridge (footbridge)
Docklands Visitors Centre
Butt Bridge
O'Connell Bridge
Ha'penny Bridge
Millennium Bridge
Grattan Bridge
Baths
Fire Sta
Arts Cen
Bank of Ireland & Arts Centre
Trinity College & Book of Kells
COLLEGE PARK
Dental School & Hospital
Pav
City Hall
The Castle
Chester Beatty Library
Theatre
Market
Mus
National Library
American Coll
National Museum
National Gallery
Leinster House
Nat History Museum
MERRION SQUARE
National Maternity Hosp
Gaiety Theatre
Mansion House
St. Stephens Green Shopping Cen
YMCA
ST. STEPHEN'S GREEN
ST. STEPHEN'S GREEN PARK
Nat Mus
Government Buildings
No. 29
Skin & Cancer Hospital
Art Gallery
Newman House
University College
IVEAGH GARDENS
National Concert Hall
Garda H.Q.
Inst of Tech
Lib
56
Baggot Street Community Hospital
PEARSE
TARA ST
DAME ST
N81
COLLEGE GRN
NASSAU ST
DAWSON ST
KILDARE ST
GRAFTON STREET
O'CONNELL ST
PARNELL STREET
ORMOND QUAY
WELLINGTON QUAY
BACHELORS WALK
CUSTOM HOUSE QUAY
CITY QUAY
PEARSE STREET
ST. STEPHEN'S GRN N.
ST. STEPHEN'S GRN S.
LEESON
BAGGOT ST LOWER
MERRION SQ NORTH
MERRION SQ SOUTH
FITZWILLIAM ST
MOUNT STREET UPPER
HARCOURT STREET
CAMDEN ROW
CUFFE STREET
AUNGIER STREET
DORSET ST UPPER
GARDINER STREET LOWER
SUMMERHILL
TALBOT STREET
AMIENS STREET
SHERIFF ST LOWER
MAYOR STREET
R101
R114
R110
E
F
G
H
1
2
3
4
5
6

Index to place names

Index to street names

General abbreviations

All	Alley	Cotts	Cottages	Grd	Ground	N	North	St.	Saint
Apts	Apartments	Cres	Crescent	Grn	Green	No	Numbers	St	Street
Av	Avenue	Ct	Court	Gro	Grove	Off	Office	Sta	Station
Ave	Avenue	Dr	Drive	Ho	House	Par	Parade	Ter	Terrace
Bk	Bank	Dws	Dwellings	Hosp	Hospital	Pas	Passage	Vil	Villa, Villas
Bldgs	Buildings	E	East	Hts	Heights	Pk	Park	Vw	View
Boul	Boulevard	Ex	Exchange	Junct	Junction	Pl	Place	W	West
Br	Bridge	Ext	Extension	La	Lane	Prom	Promenade	Wd	Wood
Bri	Bridge	Fld	Field	Lo	Lodge	Rbt	Roundabout	Wds	Woods
Cem	Cemetery	Flds	Fields	Lwr	Lower	Rd	Road	Wk	Walk
Cen	Central, Centre	Fm	Farm	Mans	Mansions	Ri	Rise	Yd	Yard
Cl	Close	Gdn	Garden	Mkt	Market	S	South		
Clo	Close	Gdns	Gardens	Ms	Mews	Sch	School		
Coll	College	Gra	Grange	Mt	Mount	Sq	Square		

District abbreviations

Abb.	Abberley	Castle.	Castleknock	Dunb.	Dunboyne	Kins.	Kinsaley	Palm.	Palmerston
Ashb.	Ashbourne	Celbr.	Celbridge	Fox.	Foxrock	Leix.	Leixlip	Port.	Portmarnock
B'brack	Ballybrack	Clond.	Clondalkin	G'geary	Glenageary	Leo.	Leopardstown	R'coole	Rathcoole
Balg.	Balgriffin	Clons.	Clonsilla	Gra M.	Grange Manor	Lou.V.	Louisa Valley	Ronan.	Ronanstown
Black.	Blackrock	Collins.	Collinstown	Grey.	Greystones	Lough.	Loughlinstown	Sagg.	Saggart
Boot.	Booterstown	Cool.	Coolmine	Jobs.	Jobstown	Mala.	Malahide	Sally.	Sallynoggin
Cabin.	Cabinteely	Corn.	Cornelscourt	Kill.	Killiney	Manor.	Manorfields	Sandy.	Sandyford
Carp.	Carpenterstown	D'bate	Donabate	Kilt.	Kiltipper	Mayn.	Maynooth	Shank.	Shankill
Carrick.	Carrickmines	D.L.	Dún Laoghaire	Kings.	Kingswood	Mulh.	Mulhuddart	Still.	Stillorgan

Some streets are not named on the map due to insufficient space. In some of these cases the nearest street that does appear on the map is listed in italics. In other cases they are indicated on the map by a number which is listed here in **bold**.

A

Aideen Pl 63 D2
Aikenhead Ter 57 D2
Ailesbury 28 B3
Ailesbury Cl 65 D1
Ailesbury Dr 65 D1
Ailesbury Gdns 65 E1
Ailesbury Gro *Dublin 4* 65 D1
Ailesbury Gro *Dublin 16* 72 B2
Ailesbury Lawn 72 B2
Ailesbury Ms 65 F1
Ailesbury Pk 65 E1
Ailesbury Rd 65 D1
Ailsbury Gro 72 B2
Ailsbury Lawn 72 B2
Airfield Ct 65 D2
Airfield Manor 65 D2
Airfield Pk 65 D2
Airfield Rd 63 F2
Airfield Ter 65 D2
Airlie Hts 50 A1
Air Pk 70 C3
Airpark Av 70 C3
Airpark Cl 71 D3
Airport Business Pk 16 C2
Airport Ind Est 28 C1
Airside Business Pk 12 C3
Airside Retail Pk 12 C3
Airton Cl 69 E1
Airton Rd 69 D1
Airton Ter 69 E1
Airways Ind Est 28 C1
Albany Av 75 D3
Albany Ct 81 E1
Albany Rd 64 B1
Albert Av 82 C2
Albert Coll Av 28 A4
Albert Coll Cres 28 A4
Albert Coll Dr 28 A4
Albert Coll Lawn 28 A4
Albert Coll Pk 28 A4
Albert Coll Ter 28 A4
Albert Ct 78 A2
Albert Ct E 56 C2
Albert Pk 78 A2
Albert Pl *off Inchicore Rd* 54 C2
Albert Pl E 56 C2
Albert Pl W 56 A3
Albert Rd Lwr 78 A2
Albert Rd Upr 78 A3
Albert Ter *off Albert Pl W* 56 A3
Albert Vil *off Morehampton Rd* 56 C4
Albert Wk 82 C2
Albion Ter *off Inchicore Rd* 54 C2
Aldborough Par 46 C4
Aldborough Pl 85 H1
Aldborough Sq 85 H1
Aldemere 23 E4
Alden Dr 31 D4
Alden Pk 31 E4
Alden Rd 31 D4
Alderbrook Downs 8 C3
Alderbrook Glen 8 C3
Alderbrook Pk 8 C3
Alderbrook Ri 8 C3
Alderbrook Rd 8 C3
Alderbrook Vale 8 C3
Alder Ct **1** 19 F2
Alderpark Ct 68 C2
Alders, The 74 C3
Alderwood Av 68 C2
Alderwood Cl 68 C1
Alderwood Ct 68 C2
Alderwood Dr 68 C2
Alderwood Grn 68 C1
Alderwood Gro 68 C2
Alderwood Lawn 68 C1
Alderwood Pk 68 C2
Alderwood Ri 68 C1
Aldrin Wk 29 E3
Alexander Ter *Dublin 1* 56 C1
Alexander Ter *Dublin 8* 55 F3
Alexander Ter **1** *Bray* 82 B3
Alexandra Quay 57 E1
Alexandra Rd 57 D1
Alexandra Ter *Dublin 6* 63 F2
Alexandra Ter (Dundrum) *Dublin 14* 72 B1
Alfie Byrne Rd 47 D4
Allendale Cl 23 E3
Allendale Copse 23 E3
Allendale Ct 23 E3
Allendale Dr 23 E3
Allendale Elms 23 E3
Allendale Glen 23 E3
Allendale Grn 23 E3
Allendale Gro 23 E3
Allendale Heath 23 E3
Allendale Lawn 23 E3
Allendale Pl 23 E3
Allendale Ri 23 E3
Allendale Sq 23 E3
Allendale Ter 23 E3
Allendale Vw 23 E3
Allendale Wk 23 E3
Allen Pk Dr 73 F2
Allen Pk Rd 73 F2
Allenton Av 69 E4
Allenton Cres 69 E4
Allenton Dr 69 E4
Allenton Gdns 69 E4
Allenton Grn 69 E4
Allenton Lawns 69 E4
Allenton Pk 69 E3
Allenton Rd (Oldcourt) *Dublin 24* 69 E3
Allenton Rd (Tallaght) *Dublin 24* 69 E2
Allenton Way 69 E4
All Hallows Coll 46 B2
All Hallows La *off Drumcondra Rd Upr* 46 B2
Allied Ind Est 53 F3
Allingham St 84 B5
All Saints Dr 48 B2
All Saints Pk 48 B2
All Saints Rd 48 A2
Alma Pl 75 D3
Alma Rd 74 C2
Almeida Av *off Brookfield St* 55 D2
Almeida Ter *off Brookfield St* 55 D2
Alone Wk 47 F1
Alpine Hts 60 A1
Alpine Ri 60 B4
Altadore 77 F1
Altona Ter 84 A1
Alverno 47 E3
Amber Vale 68 B1
Amiens St 85 H2
Anastasia La 78 C3
Anfield Cl 42 A1
Anfield Ct 42 A2
Anfield Cres 42 A2
Anfield Dr 42 A2
Anfield Lawn **1** 42 A2
Anfield Vw **2** 42 A2
Anglesea Av 74 B2
Anglesea Br 65 D1
Anglesea Fruit Mkt *off Green St Little* 84 D3
Anglesea La 75 F3
Anglesea Pk 78 A4
Anglesea Rd 65 D1
Anglesea Row 84 D3
Anglesea St 85 F4
Anley Ct 41 E4
Annabeg **1** 77 F4
Annadale Av 46 C3
Annadale Cres 46 C2
Annadale Dr 46 C2
Annagh Ct 25 D3
Annaly Ct 23 E3
Annaly Gro 23 E3
Annaly Rd 45 E3
Annaly Ter 23 E3
Annamoe Dr 45 E3
Annamoe Par 45 E4
Annamoe Pk 45 E4
Annamoe Rd 45 E4
Annamoe Ter 45 E4
Anna Vil 64 B1
Annaville Av 74 B4
Annaville Gro 64 B4
Annaville Pk 64 B4
Annaville Ter *off Annaville Gro* 64 C4
Anne Devlin Av 71 D1
Anne Devlin Dr 71 D1
Anne Devlin Pk 71 D1
Anne Devlin Rd 71 D1
Anner Rd 54 C2
Annes La 85 F5
Annesley Av 46 C4
Annesley Br 46 C3
Annesley Br Rd 46 C3
Annesley Pk 64 B1
Annesley Pl 46 C3
Anne St N 84 D2
Anne St S 85 F5
Annsbrook 64 C3
Annville Dr 73 E2
Apollo Way 29 E3
Appian Way, The 56 B4
Apples Rd 73 D3
Applewood Dr 83 D2
Applewood Hts 83 D2
Aran Av 81 E1
Aran Cl 81 E1
Aran Dr 81 E1
Aranleigh Ct 71 F1
Aranleigh Dell 71 F2
Aranleigh Gdns 71 F1
Aranleigh Mt 71 E1
Aranleigh Pk 71 F1
Aranleigh Vale 71 F1
Áras An Uachtaráin 44 B3
Aras Naclunne 52 C4
Aravon Ct **8** 82 C3
Arbour Hill 84 A2
Arbour Pl 84 B2
Arbour Ter 84 A2
Arbutus Av 55 E4
Arbutus Gro 82 A2
Arbutus Pl 55 F3
Arcade 85 F3
Archerstown Rd 9 D2
Archers Wd 24 A1
Arches, The **11** *Lough.* 81 E1
Arches, The *Mayn.* 36 B2
Ardagh Av 74 B4
Ardagh Cl **1** 74 B4
Ardagh Ct 74 A4
Ardagh Cres 74 A4
Ardagh Dr 74 B4
Ardagh Gro 74 A4
Ardagh Pk 74 B4
Ardagh Pk Rd 74 B4
Ardagh Rd 55 D4
Ardara Av 30 C3
Ardbeg Cres 29 F4
Ardbeg Dr 29 F4
Ardbeg Pk 29 F4
Ardbeg Rd 29 F4
Ardbrugh Cl **1** 78 B4
Ardbrugh Rd 78 B4
Ardbrugh Vil **2** 78 B4
Ardcian Pk 12 B1
Ardcollum Av 29 E4
Ardee Gro 56 A4
Ardeen 40 C4
Ardee Rd 56 A4
Ardee St *Dublin 8* 84 C5
Ardee St *Bray* 82 A2
Ardeevin Av 40 C4
Ardeevin Ct 40 C4
Ardeevin Dr 40 C4
Ardeevin Rd 78 B3
Ardenza Pk *off Seapoint Av* 74 C2
Ardenza Ter 74 C2
Ardglas Est 72 C2
Ardilaun 19 F3
Ardilaun Rd 46 B4
Ardilea Downs 65 D4
Ardlea Rd 29 E4
Ard Lorcain 74 A4
Ard Lorcain Vil **1** 74 A4
Ardlui Pk 74 B4
Ardmeen Pk 74 B4
Ard Mhacha 69 D3
Ard Mhuire Pk 78 A4
Ard Mor Av 67 F2
Ard Mor Cl 67 F2
Ard Mor Ct 67 F2
Ard Mor Cres 67 F2
Ard Mor Dale 67 F2
Ard Mor Dr 67 F2
Ardmore 82 A3
Ardmore Av 45 E4
Ardmore Cl 29 D4
Ardmore Cres *Dublin 5* 29 E4
Ardmore Cres *Bray* 82 A3
Ardmore Dr 29 D4
Ardmore Gro 29 D4
Ardmore Lawn 82 A3
Ardmore Pk *Dublin 5* 29 E4
Ardmore Pk *Bray* 82 A3
Ardmore Pk *D.L.* 75 E4
Ard Mor Gdn 67 F2
Ard Mor La 67 F2
Ard Mor Pk 67 F2
Ard Mor Wk 67 F2
Ard Na Mara 14 B4
Ard Na Meala 28 A2
Ardpatrick Rd 44 C3
Ard Ri Pl *off Ard Ri Rd* 84 B2
Ard Ri Rd 84 B2
Ardtona Av 64 B4
Arena Rd 73 F4
Argyle Rd 56 C4
Arkendale Ct **1** 78 A3
Arkendale Rd 78 A2
Arkendale Wds **2** 78 A3
Arkle Hill 8 C3
Arkle Rd 73 E3
Arkle Sq **1** 73 F4
Arklow St 84 A1
Armagh Rd 62 C1
Armstrong St *off Harolds Cross Rd* 55 F4
Armstrong Wk 29 E3
Arnold Gro 77 F1
Arnold Pk 77 F2
Arnott St 84 D6
Arran Ct 25 D3
Arran Grn 82 C3
Arranmore Av 46 A3
Arranmore Rd 56 C4
Arran Quay 84 C3
Arran Quay Ter 84 C3
Arran Rd 46 B2
Arran St E 84 D3
Arran St W 84 C3
Arthur Griffith Pk 51 D1
Arundel 75 D3
Ascal An Charrain Chno (Nutgrove Av) 71 F1
Ascal Bhaile An Abba (Abbotstown Av) 26 B3
Ascal Bhaile Thuaidh (Ballyhoy Av) 48 B2
Ascal Dun Eanna (Ennafort Av) 48 A2
Ascal Measc (Mask Av) 29 F4
Ascal Phairc An Bhailtini (Villa Park Av) 44 C3
Ascal Ratabhachta (Ratoath Av) 26 B4
Asgard Pk 33 F3
Asgard Rd 33 F3
Ashberry 50 C2
Ashbourne Ind Pk 8 A1
Ashbrook *Dublin 3* 47 E2
Ashbrook *Dublin 7* 44 A2
Ashbrook *Leix.* 39 D3
Ashbury Pk 82 B3
Ashcroft 48 B1
Ashcroft Gro **1** 24 A2
Ashdale Av 63 E2
Ashdale Cl 13 E3
Ashdale Cres 8 C2
Ashdale Gdns 63 E2
Ashdale Pk 63 E2
Ashdale Rd *Dublin 6W* 63 E2
Ashdale Rd *Swords* 18 A1
Ashes, The 8 B1
Ashfield (Templeogue) 62 C4
Ashfield Av *Dublin 6* 64 B1
Ashfield Av *Dublin 24* 61 D3
Ashfield Cl *Dublin 6W off Ashfield* 62 C4
Ashfield Cl *Dublin 24* 61 D3
Ashfield Ct 24 A2
Ashfield Dr 61 D3
Ashfield Gdns 24 A2
Ashfield Grn 24 A1
Ashfield Gro 24 A1
Ashfield Lawn 24 A1
Ashfield Pk (Templeogue) *Dublin 6W off Ashfield* 62 C4
Ashfield Pk (Terenure) *Dublin 6W* 63 E2
Ashfield Pk *Dublin 24* 61 D3
Ashfield Pk *Boot.* 65 E3
Ashfield Pk **7** *Mulh.* 24 A2
Ashfield Rd (Ranelagh) 64 B1
Ashfield Way 24 A2
Ashford Cotts *off Ashford St* 84 A1
Ashford Pl *off Ashford St* 84 A1
Ashford St 84 A1
Ashgrove *Dublin 24* 68 C1
Ashgrove *Celbr.* 37 D2
Ashgrove *D.L.* 75 D4
Ashgrove Ind Est 75 D4
Ashgrove Lo 44 B2
Ashgrove Ter **1** 72 C1
Ashington Av 44 C2
Ashington Cl 44 B1
Ashington Ct 44 C2
Ashington Dale 44 C1
Ashington Gdns 44 C2
Ashington Grn 44 C2
Ashington Ms 44 C1
Ashington Pk 44 B2
Ashington Ri 44 B1
Ash Lawn *Dublin 16* 72 B2
Ashlawn *B'brack* 77 F4
Ashlawn Ct 82 A2
Ashleaf Shop Cen 62 B2
Ashleigh Grn 43 D1
Ashleigh Gro 25 D4
Ashleigh Lawn 19 D1
Ashley Av 13 D2
Ashley Dr **5** 13 D2
Ashley Gro **4** 13 D2
Ashley Hts **6** 82 A2
Ashley Ri 19 F2
Ashling Cl 55 D4
Ashling Hts 24 C3
Ash Pk Av 51 D2
Ash Pk Ct 51 E2
Ash Pk Gro 51 E1
Ash Pk Heath 51 E1
Ash St 84 C5
Ashton Av 70 C2
Ashton Cl 70 C2
Ashton Gro 70 C2
Ashton Lawn 70 C2
Ashton Pk 75 D3
Ashtown Br 25 F4
Ashtown Gate Rd 44 A2
Ashtown Gro 44 B2
Ashtown Rd 44 A1
Ashtown Sta 44 A1
Ashurst 81 E1
Ashville Cl 41 E4
Ashwood Av 51 F4
Ashwood Cl 51 F4
Ashwood Dr 52 A4
Ashwood Lawns 52 A4
Ashwood Pk 52 A4
Ashwood Rd 52 A4
Ashwood Way 52 A4
Aspen Dr 13 F3
Aspen Pk **1** *D.L.* 77 E1
Aspen Pk *Swords* 13 F3
Aspen Rd 13 E3
Aspen Wds 24 A4
Aspen Wds Av 24 A4
Aspen Wds Lawn 24 A4
Assumpta Pk 81 D4
Aston Pl 85 F3
Aston Quay 85 F3
Athgoe Dr 81 E3
Athgoe Rd 81 E3
Athlumney Vil 56 A4
Atmospheric Rd **3** 78 A3
Aubrey Gro 81 E3
Aubrey Pk 81 E3
Auburn Av *Dublin 4* 64 C1
Auburn Av *Dublin 15* 43 E2
Auburn Av *Cabin.* 77 E3
Auburn Cl *Dublin 15* 43 E1
Auburn Cl *Cabin.* 77 F3
Auburn Dr *Dublin 15* 43 E1
Auburn Dr *Cabin.* 77 E3
Auburn Grn 43 E1
Auburn Gro 18 B1
Auburn Pk 25 E4
Auburn Rd *Dublin 4 off Auburn Av* 64 C1
Auburn Rd *Cabin.* 77 E2
Auburn St 84 D1
Auburn Vil *Dublin 6* 63 F2
Auburn Vil **14** *Bray* 82 A2
Auburn Wk 84 A1
Aughavanagh Rd 55 E4
Aughrim La 84 A1
Aughrim Pl 84 A1

Aughrim St 84 A1
Aughrim Vil
off Aughrim St 84 A1
Augustine Vil **1** 82 C3
Aulden Gra 29 D2
Aungier Pl 85 E5
Aungier St 85 E5
Austins Cotts
off Annesley Pl 46 C3
Avalon **1** 76 B3
Ave Maria Rd 84 A6
Avenue, The *Dublin 6W* 62 C4
Avenue, The (Ballinteer)
Dublin 16 72 B3
Avenue, The (Ballyboden)
Dublin 16 70 C3
Avenue, The (Primrose Hill)
Celbr. 37 E4
Avenue, The (The Drive) *Celbr.* 37 E3
Avenue, The *Clons.* 23 D2
Avenue, The (Dunboyne Castle)
Dunb. 20 B3
Avenue, The (Lutterell Hall)
Dunb. 20 B1
Avenue, The (Plunkett Hall)
Dunb. 20 A1
Avenue, The *Gra M.* 51 D2
Avenue, The *Kins.* 13 E3
Avenue, The *Lou.V.* 39 E2
Avenue, The **4** *Mala.* 19 F1
Avenue, The *Manor.* 23 E2
Avenue, The *Mulh.* 24 A1
Avenue, The *Swords* 13 D1
Avenue Rd 55 F3
Avila Apts **2** 74 B4
Avila Pk 26 B3
Avoca Av *Black.* 74 A2
Avoca Av *Bray* 82 B4
Avoca Pk 74 A3
Avoca Pl 74 B2
Avoca Rd 74 A3
Avonbeg Ct **1** 69 E2
Avonbeg Dr 69 F2
Avonbeg Gdns 69 F2
Avonbeg Ind Est 53 F4
Avonbeg Pk 69 F2
Avonbeg Rd 69 F2
Avondale 39 F2
Avondale Av 45 F4
Avondale Business Pk 74 B2
Avondale Ct **4** 78 A2
Avondale Cres 78 A4
Avondale Lawn 74 B3
Avondale Lawn Ext 74 B3
Avondale Pk *Dublin 5* 48 C2
Avondale Pk *Bray* 82 A3
Avondale Pk *Dalkey* 78 A4
Avondale Rd *Dublin 7* 45 F3
Avondale Rd *Dalkey* 78 A4
Avondale Sq 20 B2
Avondale Ter 62 B2
Avonmore 76 A1
Avonmore Av **1** 69 F2
Avonmore Cl 69 F2
Avonmore Dr 69 F2
Avonmore Gro 69 F2
Avonmore Pk 69 F2
Avonmore Rd 69 F2
Aylesbury 69 E3
Ayrefield Av 30 A4
Ayrefield Ct 30 A4
Ayrefield Dr 30 A4
Ayrefield Gro 30 A4
Ayrefield Pl 30 A4

B

Bachelors Wk *Dublin 1* 85 F3
Bachelors Wk *Ashb.* 8 C3
Back La *Dublin 8* 84 D4
Back La *Dublin 13* 31 F3
Back La *Mayn.* 36 B1
Back Rd 18 C1
Baggot Cl
off Baggot St Lwr 85 G6
Baggot Ct 85 H6
Baggot La 56 C3
Baggot Rd 44 B3
Baggot St Lwr 85 H6
Baggot St Upr 56 C3
Baggot Ter
off Blackhorse Av 44 B3
Bailey, The 8 B3
Bailey Grn Rd 35 E3
Bailey's Row 85 H1
Bailey Vw 78 B2
Balally Av 73 D2
Balally Cl 73 D2
Balally Dr 72 C2
Balally Gro 73 D3
Balally Hill 73 D3
Balally Pk 73 D2
Balally Rd 72 C2
Balally Sta 72 C2
Balally Ter **1** 73 D3
Balbutcher Dr 27 F1
Balbutcher La 27 F2
Balbutcher Way 27 F1
Balcurris Cl 28 A2
Balcurris Gdns 28 A2
Balcurris Pk E 28 A2
Balcurris Pk W 27 F2
Balcurris Rd 27 F2
Baldara Ct 9 D4
Baldonnel Business Pk 67 D1
Baldoyle Ind Est 31 E4
Baldoyle Rd 32 A2
Balfe Av 62 B1
Balfe Rd 62 B1
Balfe Rd E 62 B1
Balfe St
off Chatham St 85 F5
Balgaddy Rd 51 F2
Balglass Est 33 E3
Balglass Rd 33 F3
Balgriffin Cotts 30 B2
Balgriffin Rd 30 B2
Balkill Pk 33 E3
Balkill Rd 33 F4
Ballawley Ct 72 C3
Ballinclea Hts 78 A4
Ballinclea Rd 77 F2
Ballinteer Av 72 B3
Ballinteer Cl 72 B3
Ballinteer Ct **2** 72 B3
Ballinteer Cres 72 B3
Ballinteer Dr 72 B3
Ballinteer Gdns 72 B3
Ballinteer Gro 72 B3
Ballinteer Pk 72 B3
Ballinteer Rd 72 B2
Ballinteer Shop Cen 72 B3
Ballintrane Wd 12 C2
Ballintyre Downs 72 B4
Ballintyre Heath 72 B4
Ballintyre Meadows 72 A4
Ballintyre Wk 72 B4
Ballintyre Wds **4** 72 B3
Balliskcourt 11 E2
Ball's Br 57 D4
Ballsbridge Av 57 D4
Ballsbridge Pk 57 D4
Ballsbridge Ter
off Ballsbridge Av 57 D4
Ballsbridge Wd 57 D3
Ballybin Rd 8 A2
Ballyboden Cres 71 D2
Ballyboden Rd *Dublin 14* 71 D2
Ballyboden Rd *Dublin 16* 71 D2
Ballyboden Way 70 C2
Ballyboggan Ind Est 44 C1
Ballyboggan Rd 45 D1
Ballybough Av
off Spring Gdn St 46 C4
Ballybough Br 46 C3
Ballybough Ct
off Spring Gdn St 46 C4
Ballybough Rd 46 B4
Ballybrack Shop Cen 77 F4
Ballybride 81 D4
Ballybride Rd 81 D3
Ballycoolin Business & Tech Pk 25 E1
Ballycoolin Rd 25 E2
Ballycullen Av 69 F3
Ballycullen Dr 70 A3
Ballydowd Dr 51 E1
Ballydowd Gro 41 E4
Ballydowd Manor 51 E1
Ballyfermot Av 53 F2
Ballyfermot Cres 53 F2
Ballyfermot Dr 53 E2
Ballyfermot Par 53 E2
Ballyfermot Rd
(Bothar Baile Thormod) 53 E2
Ballygall Av 27 E3
Ballygall Cres 27 D4
Ballygall Par 27 D4
Ballygall Pl 27 E4
Ballygall Rd E 27 F4
Ballygall Rd W 27 D4
Ballygihen Av 78 A2
Ballygihen Vil **5** 78 A2
Ballygoran Vw 37 D2
Ballyhoy Av
(Ascal Bhaile Thuaidh) 48 B2
Ballymace Grn 70 C1
Ballymadrough Rd 14 B1
Ballymanagin La **1** 52 B4
Ballymoss Par **2** 73 F4
Ballymoss Rd 73 E3
Ballymount Av *Dublin 12* 61 F3
Ballymount Av *Dublin 24* 61 F3
Ballymount Cross 61 E2
Ballymount Cross Ind Est 61 D2
Ballymount Dr 61 F2
Ballymount Ind Est 61 F2
Ballymount Lwr Rd 61 E2
Ballymount Rd 61 D3
Ballymount Rd Ind Est 61 F1
Ballymount Rd Upr 61 E2
Ballymount Trd Est 62 A2
Ballymun Ind Est 27 F1
Ballymun Rd 46 A1
Ballymun Rd N 28 A1
Ballymun Shop Cen 28 A2
Ballyneety Rd 54 A2
Ballyogan Av 76 A3
Ballyogan Cl 76 A4
Ballyogan Ct 76 A4
Ballyogan Cres 76 A4
Ballyogan Dr 76 A4
Ballyogan Grn 76 A3
Ballyogan Lawn 76 A3
Ballyogan Rd **1** 76 A4
Ballyogan Vale 76 B4
Ballyogan Wd 76 A4
Ballyolaf Manor **1** 72 C2
Ballyoulster Pk 37 F3
Ballyowen Av 41 F4
Ballyowen Castle Shop &
Med Cen 51 E1
Ballyowen Ct 41 F4
Ballyowen Cres 41 F4
Ballyowen Dr 41 F4
Ballyowen Grn 41 F4
Ballyowen Gro 41 F4
Ballyowen La 41 F4
Ballyowen Lawn 41 F4
Ballyowen Rd 41 F4
Ballyowen Vw 41 F4
Ballyowen Way 41 F4
Ballyroan Ct **1** 70 C1
Ballyroan Cres 71 D1
Ballyroan Hts 70 C2
Ballyroan Pk 70 C1
Ballyroan Rd 70 C1
Ballyshannon Av 29 D3
Ballyshannon Rd 29 D3
Ballytore Rd 63 F3
Balnagowan 64 B2
Balrothery Cotts 70 A1
Balrothery Est 69 F1
Balscadden Rd 33 F3
Bancroft Av 69 E1
Bancroft Cl 69 F1
Bancroft Gro 69 F1
Bancroft Pk 69 E1
Bancroft Rd 69 F1
Bangor Dr 55 D4
Bangor Rd 55 D4
Bank of Ireland 85 F4
Bankside Cotts 64 B3
Bannow Rd 45 D2
Bann Rd 45 D1
Bantry Rd 46 A1
Bantry Sq 25 D3
Banville Av 53 E3
Barclay Ct 74 B2
Bargy Rd 47 D4
Barnacoille Pk 78 B2
Barnamore Cres 45 D1
Barnamore Gro 45 D1
Barnamore Pk 45 D1
Barnewall Av 11 F1
Barnewall Cres 11 E1
Barnewall Dr 27 F2
Barnhall Dr 39 D3
Barnhill Av 78 A3
Barnhill Cross Rds 40 C4
Barnhill Gro 78 B3
Barnhill Lawn 78 B3
Barnhill Pk **4** 78 A3
Barnhill Rd 78 A3
Barnville Pk 52 C3
Barrack Ct 66 B3
Barren Hill Cross Rds 34 C3
Barrett St 75 E3
Barrow Rd 45 E2
Barrow Sta 56 C2
Barrow St 56 C2
Barry Av 26 C2
Barry Dr 26 C2
Barry Grn 26 C3
Barry La 23 D3
Barry Pk 26 C3
Barry Rd 26 C3
Barryscourt Rd 29 E3
Barton Av 71 E1
Barton Ct 72 A2
Barton Dr 71 E1
Barton Rd E 72 A2
Barton Rd Ext 71 F2
Barton Rd W (Willbrook) 71 E2
Bartra Rock **6** 78 B2
Basin St Lwr 84 A4
Basin St Upr 84 A5
Basin Vw Ter 45 F4
Baskin Cotts 18 A3
Baskin La 17 E2
Bass Pl 85 H5
Bath Av *Dublin 4* 57 D3
Bath Av *Mala.* 15 E4
Bath Av Gdns 57 D3
Bath Av Pl 57 D3
Bath La 85 F1
Bath Pl 74 B2
Bath St 57 D2
Bawn, The 19 D1
Bawn Gro, The 19 D1
Bawnlea Av 68 B2
Bawnlea Cl 68 A2
Bawnlea Cres 68 A2
Bawnlea Dr 68 A2
Bawnlea Grn 68 B2
Bawnogue Cotts **1** 59 F1
Bawnville Av 69 E3
Bawnville Cl 69 E3
Bawnville Dr 69 F2
Bawnville Pk 69 F2
Bawnville Rd 69 E2
Baymount Pk 48 B3
Bayshore La 81 E1
Bayside Boul N 31 E4
Bayside Boul S 31 E4
Bayside Pk 31 E4
Bayside Sq E 31 E4
Bayside Sq N 31 E4
Bayside Sq S 31 E4
Bayside Sq W 31 E4
Bayside Sta 31 F4
Bayside Wk 31 E4
Bayswater Ter **7** 78 B2
Bayview *Dublin 4*
off Pembroke St 57 D2
Bayview **2** *Bray* 82 B2
Bayview *Lough.* 81 E1
Bayview Av 46 C4
Bayview Cl 81 E1
Bayview Ct 81 E1
Bayview Cres 81 E2
Bayview Dr 81 E2
Bayview Glade **1** 81 E2
Bayview Glen **4** 81 E2
Bayview Grn 81 E1
Bayview Gro 81 E2
Bayview Lawn 81 E1
Bayview Pk 81 E1
Bayview Ri **3** 81 E2
Beach Av 57 E3
Beach Dr 57 E3
Beach Pk 19 F3
Beach Rd 57 E3
Beach Vw 49 E1
Beaconsfield Ct
off The Belfry 54 C2
Bearna Pk 73 D4
Beatty Gro 37 E2
Beatty Pk 37 D3
Beattys Av 57 D4
Beaufield 36 A3
Beaufield Ave 36 A3
Beaufield Cl 36 A3
Beaufield Cres 36 A3
Beaufield Dr 36 A3
Beaufield Gdns 36 A3
Beaufield Grn 36 A3
Beaufield Gro 36 A3
Beaufield Lawn 36 A3
Beaufield Manor 73 F1
Beaufield Pk 73 F1
Beaufort 78 A2
Beaufort Downs 71 E1
Beaumont Av 72 A1
Beaumont Cl 72 A1
Beaumont Cres 29 D4
Beaumont Dr 72 B1
Beaumont Gdns 74 A2
Beaumont Gro 28 C4
Beaumont Rd 28 C4
Beau Pk Av 31 D3
Beau Pk Cres 31 D3
Beau Pk Rd 31 D3
Beau Pk Row 31 D3
Beau Pk Sq 31 D3
Beau Pk St 31 D2
Beau Pk Ter 31 D3
Beauvale Pk 29 E4
Beaver Row 64 C2
Beaverstown Orchard 11 E1
Beaver St 85 H1
Beckett Way 52 C4
Bedford Row
off Temple Bar 85 F4
Beechbrook 83 D3
Beechbrook Gro **7** 30 C3
Beechbrook Pk 83 D3
Beechcourt 77 F3
Beechdale 20 C3
Beechdale Ms 64 A1
Beech Dr 72 B2
Beeches, The *Dublin 13* 30 C4
Beeches, The *Dublin 14* 71 E1
Beeches, The **12** *Abb.* 81 E1
Beeches, The *Black.* 75 D3
Beeches Pk 78 A3
Beeches Rd 73 D2
Beechfield 23 D1
Beechfield Av *Dublin 12* 62 B2
Beechfield Av *Dublin 24* 70 A4
Beechfield Cl *Dublin 12* 62 B2
Beechfield Cl *Dublin 24* 70 A4
Beechfield Cl **1** *Dunb.* 23 D1
Beechfield Ct *Dublin 24* 70 A4
Beechfield Ct **1** *Clons.* 23 D2
Beechfield Cres 70 A4
Beechfield Dr 23 D1
Beechfield Grn **2** 23 D1
Beechfield Haven **1** 81 E3
Beechfield Hts **2** 23 D2
Beechfield Lawn *Dublin 24* 70 A4
Beechfield Lawn **1** *Clons.* 23 E1
Beechfield Manor 81 E3
Beechfield Meadows 23 D1
Beechfield Pk **2** 70 A4
Beechfield Pl *Dublin 24* 70 A4
Beechfield Pl *Clons.* 23 E1
Beechfield Ri 23 E1
Beechfield Rd *Dublin 12* 62 B2
Beechfield Rd *Dublin 24* 70 A4
Beechfield Rd (Hartstown)
Clons. 23 D2
Beechfield Vw 23 D1
Beechfield Way *Dublin 24* 70 A4
Beechfield Way *Clons.* 23 D1
Beech Gro *Boot.* 65 F3
Beech Gro *Lucan* 41 D4
Beech Hill
off Beech Hill Rd 64 C2
Beech Hill Av 65 D1
Beech Hill Cres 65 D2
Beech Hill Dr 65 D1
Beech Hill Rd 64 C2
Beech Hill Ter 65 D2
Beech Hill Vil
off Beech Hill Ter 65 D2
Beech Lawn *Dublin 16* 72 A2
Beechlawn *Boot.* 65 F4
Beechlawn Av *Dublin 5* 29 F3
Beech Lawn Av *Dublin 16* 72 A2
Beechlawn Cl 29 F3
Beechlawn Grn 29 F3
Beechlawn Gro 29 F3
Beechlawn Ind Complex 62 A2
Beechmount Dr 64 C3
Beech Pk *Dublin 15* 43 E1
Beech Pk *Cabin.* 77 E4
Beech Pk *Lucan* 41 D4

Beech Pk Av *Dublin 5* 29 F3
Beech Pk Av *Dublin 15* 43 E1
Beech Pk Av *Deans Gra* 76 C1
Beechpark Ct 29 F3
Beech Pk Cres 43 E1
Beech Pk Dr 76 C2
Beech Pk Gro 76 C2
Beech Pk Lawn 43 E1
Beech Pk Rd 76 C1
Beech Rd *Dublin 12* 61 E1
Beech Rd *Bray* 82 A2
Beech Rd **3** *Shank.* 81 E4
Beech Row **3** *Clond.* 60 B1
Beech Row *Ronan.* 52 A3
Beechurst 82 A3
Beechview **1** 71 D3
Beech Wk 71 D3
Beechwood Av Lwr 64 B1
Beechwood Av Upr 64 B1
Beechwood Cl *Bray* 82 B4
Beechwood Cl *Manor.* 23 F2
Beechwood Ct 74 A4
Beechwood Downs 23 F2
Beechwood Gro **1** 75 F4
Beechwood Lawn 77 F2
Beechwood Lawns 66 B3
Beechwood Pk *Dublin 6* 64 A1
Beechwood Pk *D.L.* 75 F4
Beechwood Rd 64 B1
Beechwood Sta 64 B1
Belcamp Av 29 F2
Belcamp Cres 29 F1
Belcamp Gdns 29 F1
Belcamp Grn 30 A3
Belcamp Gro 30 A3
Belcamp La 30 A3
Belclare Av 27 F2
Belclare Cres 27 F2
Belclare Dr 27 F2
Belclare Grn 27 F2
Belclare Gro 27 F2
Belclare Lawns 27 F2
Belclare Pk 27 E2
Belclare Ter 27 E2
Belclare Way 27 F2
Belfield Cl 64 C3
Belfield Ct 65 D2
Belfield Downs 64 C4
Belfield Off Pk 64 C2
Belfry, The *Dublin 8* 54 C2
Belfry, The *Jobs.* 67 F3
Belfry Av 67 F3
Belfry Cl 67 F3
Belfry Dale 67 F3
Belfry Downs 67 F3
Belfry Dr 67 F3
Belfry Gdns 67 F3
Belfry Grn 67 F3
Belfry Gro 68 A3
Belfry Lawn 67 F3
Belfry Meadows 67 F3
Belfry Pk 67 F3
Belfry Pl 67 F3
Belfry Ri 67 F3
Belfry Rd 67 F3
Belfry Sq 67 F3
Belfry Ter 67 F3
Belfry Wk 67 F3
Belfry Way 67 F3
Belgard Cl **1** 61 D4
Belgard Grn 68 B1
Belgard Hts 60 C4
Belgard Ind Est 61 D4
Belgard Rd 61 D4
Belgard Sq E 69 D1
Belgard Sq N 68 C1
Belgard Sq S 69 D2
Belgard Sq W 68 C1
Belgard Sta 60 C4
Belgrave Av 64 A1
Belgrave Pl 64 A1
Belgrave Rd *Dublin 6* 64 A1
Belgrave Rd *Black.* 74 C2
Belgrave Sq E *Dublin 6* 64 A1
Belgrave Sq E *Black.* 75 D3
Belgrave Sq N *Dublin 6* 64 A1
Belgrave Sq N *Black.* 74 C2
Belgrave Sq S *Dublin 6* 64 A1
Belgrave Sq S *Black.* 74 C2
Belgrave Sq W *Dublin 6* 64 A1
Belgrave Sq W *Black.* 74 C2
Belgrave Ter *Black.*
off Belgrave Rd 74 C2
Belgrave Ter **9** *Bray* 82 C3
Belgrave Vil **10** 82 C3
Belgrove Lawn 43 F4
Belgrove Pk 53 F1
Belgrove Rd 47 F3
Bella Av
off Bella St 85 G1
Bella St 85 G1
Belle Bk 84 A5
Belleville 44 A2
Belleville Av 63 F2
Bellevue 84 B5
Bellevue Av *Boot.* 65 F2
Bellevue Av *Dalkey* 77 F1
Bellevue Copse 65 F2
Bellevue Ct 65 F2
Bellevue Hts 83 E3
Bellevue Lawn 83 D4
Bellevue Pk *Boot.* 65 E2
Bellevue Pk *Grey.* 83 F2
Bellevue Pk Av 65 F2
Bellevue Rd *Dalkey* 77 F2
Bellevue Rd *Grey.* 83 F2
Bellmans Wk
off Ferrymans Crossing 56 C1
Belmont 76 A1
Belmont Av 64 C1
Belmont Ct
off Belmont Av 64 C1
Belmont Gdns 64 C1
Belmont Grn 74 A4
Belmont Gro 74 A4
Belmont Lawn 74 A4
Belmont Pk *Dublin 4* 64 C1
Belmont Pk *Dublin 5* 48 C1
Belmont Vil 64 C1
Belton Pk Av 47 D1
Belton Pk Gdns 47 D1
Belton Pk Rd 47 D1
Belton Pk Vil 47 D1
Belton Ter **3** 82 B2
Belvidere Av 46 A4
Belvidere Ct 46 A4
Belvidere Pl 46 A4
Belvidere Rd 46 A3
Belview Bldgs
off School St 84 B5
Belvue 68 B1
Benbulbin Av 54 C4
Benbulbin Rd 54 C3
Benburb St 84 B3
Beneavin Ct 27 E4
Beneavin Dr 27 F4
Beneavin Pk 27 E3
Beneavin Rd 27 E3
Ben Edar Rd 84 A1
Bengal Ter 45 F2
Ben Inagh Pk 74 B1
Benmadigan Rd 54 C3
Benson St 57 D2
Benson St Enterprise Cen 56 C2
Bentley Rd 82 B4
Beresford 46 B2
Beresford Av 46 B2
Beresford La 85 G2
Beresford Lawn 46 B2
Beresford Pl 85 G3
Beresford St 84 D2
Berkeley Rd 45 F3
Berkeley St 46 A4
Berkeley Ter 56 C3
Berryfield 50 C2
Berryfield Cres 26 C4
Berryfield Dr 26 C4
Berryfield Rd 26 C4
Berwick 71 F1
Berwick Av 12 A1
Berwick Ct 12 A1
Berwick Cres 12 A1
Berwick Dr 12 A1
Berwick Gro 12 A1
Berwick Hall 71 F1
Berwick Lawn 12 A1
Berwick Pl 12 A1
Berwick Ri 12 A1
Berwick Vw 12 A1
Berwick Wk 12 A1
Berwick Way 12 A1
Berystede
off Leeson Pk 56 B4
Bessborough Av 46 C4
Bessborough Par 56 A4
Besser Dr 52 B3
Bethesda Pl
off Dorset St Upr 85 E1
Bettyglen 49 D2
Bettysford **7** 60 B1
Bettystown Av 48 B2
Beverly Av 70 B3
Beverly Cres 70 B3
Beverly Downs 70 B2
Beverly Dr 70 B2
Beverly Gro 70 B2
Beverly Hts 70 B3
Beverly Lawns 70 B3
Beverly Pk 70 B2
Beverly Ri 70 B3
Beverton Av 11 E1
Beverton Cl 11 E1
Beverton Cres 11 E1
Beverton Dr 11 E1
Beverton Grn 11 E1
Beverton Gro 11 E1
Beverton Lawn 11 E1
Beverton Pk 11 E1
Beverton Way 11 E1
Bewley 41 E4
Bewley Av 51 E1
Bewley Dr 41 E4
Bewley Gro 51 E1
Bewley Lawn 41 E4
Bianconi Av 67 E1
Big Br 63 E3
Bigger Rd 62 B1
Big La 37 E3
Binn Eadair Vw 32 A2
Binns Br 46 A3
Birch Av 73 E3
Birch Dale **2** *D.L.* 77 E1
Birch Dale **1** *Fox.* 76 B2
Birchdale Cl 13 F3
Birchdale Dr 13 F3
Birchdale Pk 13 F3
Birchdale Rd 13 F3
Birches, The 76 B2
Birches Rd 73 D2
Birchfield 73 D1
Birchgrove 75 D4
Birchs La 72 C1
Birchview Av 61 E4
Birchview Cl 61 E4
Birchview Ct
off Treepark Rd 61 E4
Birchview Dr 61 E4
Birchview Hts
off Birchview Dr 61 E4
Birchview Lawn
off Birchview Av 61 E4
Birchview Ri
off Birchview Dr 61 E4
Birchwood Cl 68 C1
Birchwood Dr 68 C1
Birchwood Hts 68 C1
Bird Av 64 C3
Biscayne 15 F4
Bishop St 85 E6
Bisset's Strand 14 C3
Black Av, The 40 A3
Blackberry La *Dublin 6* 56 A4
Blackberry La *Port.* 19 F3
Blackberry Ri 19 F3
Blackcourt Rd 24 C2
Blackditch Dr 53 D2
Blackditch Rd 53 E2
Blackhall Par 84 C3
Blackhall Pl 84 B3
Blackhall St 84 B3
Blackheath Av 47 F3
Blackheath Ct 48 A4
Blackheath Dr 47 F3
Blackheath Gdns 47 F3
Blackheath Gro 47 F3
Blackheath Pk 47 F3
Blackhorse Av 44 C3
Blackhorse Br 54 B3
Blackhorse Gro 45 D4
Blackhorse Ind Est 45 D4
Blackhorse Sta 54 B3
Blacklion Manor 83 D2
Black Lion Rd 83 D2
Blackpitts 55 F3
Blackrock Business Pk 74 B2
Blackrock Coll 74 A1
Blackrock Shop Cen 74 B1
Blackrock Sta 74 B1
Black St 55 D1
Blackthorn Av 73 E3
Blackthorn Cl *Port.* 19 F2
Blackthorn Cl **1** *Still.* 73 E3
Blackthorn Ct **3** 73 D3
Blackthorn Dr 73 D3
Blackthorne Hill 66 A3
Blackthorn Grn **4** 73 D3
Blackthorn Gro **2** 73 D3
Blackthorn Rd 73 E3
Blackwater Rd 45 E2
Blackwood 23 D2
Blackwood Cl 23 D3
Blackwood Cres 23 D2
Blackwood Dr 23 D2
Blackwood La 19 E2
Blackwood Lawn 23 D3
Blackwood Ms 23 D2
Blackwood Pk 23 D3
Blackwood Pl 23 D2
Blakesfield 23 F2
Blakestown Cotts 24 A3
Blakestown Dr 24 A2
Blakestown Rd 24 A3
Blakestown Way 24 B2
Blanchardstown Business & Tech Park 25 D2
Blanchardstown Bypass 24 C3
Blanchardstown Cen 24 B3
Blanchardstown Ind Pk 25 D1
Blanchardstown Rd N 24 C2
Blanchardstown Rd S 24 A4
Blarney Pk 63 D1
Blasket Sq 25 D3
Blessington Ct
off Blessington St 46 A4
Blessington Rd *Dublin 24* 69 D1
Blessington Rd *Jobs.* 68 B3
Blessington St 45 F4
Bloom Cotts 55 F3
Bloomfield Av (Donnybrook)
Dublin 4 56 B4
Bloomfield Av *Dublin 8* 55 F3
Bloomfield Pk 55 F4
Bluebell Av 53 F3
Bluebell Ind Est 53 E4
Bluebell Rd 54 A4
Bluebell Sta 54 A4
Blunden Dr 30 B3
Blythe Av
off Church Rd 56 C1
Boden Dale 71 E2
Boden Heath 71 D2
Boden Mill **2** 71 D3
Boden Pk 71 D2
Boden Wd 71 E1
Boeing Rd 28 C1
Boghall Rd 82 B4
Boghall Rd Shop Cen 82 A4
Boherboy Rd 67 D4
Bohernabreena Rd 69 E4
Bolbrook Av **2** 69 F2
Bolbrook Cl 69 F2
Bolbrook Dr **3** 69 F2
Bolbrook Enterprise Cen 70 A2
Bolbrook Gro 69 F2
Bolbrook Pk 69 F2
Bolbrook Vil 69 F2
Bolton St 84 D2
Bond Dr 57 E1
Bond Rd 47 D4
Bond St 84 A5
Bonham St 84 B4
Boolavogue Rd 57 D1
Booterstown Av 65 F3
Booterstown Pk 65 F4
Boot Rd 60 B2
Boroimhe Alder 12 B4
Boroimhe Ash 12 B4
Boroimhe Aspen 12 B3
Boroimhe Beech 12 B4
Boroimhe Birches 12 B3
Boroimhe Blackthorn 12 B3
Boroimhe Cedars 12 B3
Boroimhe Cherry 12 B3
Boroimhe Elms 12 C4
Boroimhe Hawthorns 12 B3
Boroimhe Hazel 12 C4
Boroimhe Laurels 12 B3
Boroimhe Maples 12 C4
Boroimhe Oaks 12 C4
Boroimhe Pines 12 C3
Boroimhe Poplars 12 C3
Boroimhe Willows 12 C3
Botanic Av 46 A2
Botanic Gdns 45 F2
Botanic Ms 45 F2
Botanic Pk 46 A2
Botanic Rd 45 F3
Botanic Vil
off Botanic Rd 46 A2
Bothar An Easa (Watermill Rd) 48 B2
Bothar Baile Thormod
(Ballyfermot Rd) 53 E2
Bothar Chille Na Manac
(Walkinstown Rd) 62 A1
Bothar Cloiginn (Cleggan Rd) 53 D2
Bothar Coilbeard (Con Colbert Rd)
Dublin 8 54 C2
Bothar Coilbeard (Con Colbert Rd)
Dublin 10 54 B2
Bothar Dhroichead Chiarduibh
(Cardiffsbridge Rd) 26 C3
Bothar Drom Finn
(Drumfinn Rd) 53 E2
Bothar Loch Con
(Lough Conn Rd) 53 E1
Bothar Phairc An Bhailtini
(Villa Park Rd) 44 C3
Bothar Raitleann (Rathland Rd) 63 D2
Boundary Rd 47 E4
Bourne Av 8 B3
Bourne Ct 8 B3
Bourne Vw 8 B3
Bow Br 55 D2
Bow La E 85 E5
Bow La W 55 D2
Bow St 84 C3
Boyne La 85 H5
Boyne Rd 45 D1
Boyne St 85 H4
Brabazon Cotts **4** 82 B2
Brabazon Row 84 C6
Brabazon Sq
off Gray St 84 C5
Brabazon St
off The Coombe 84 C5
Bracetown Business Pk 21 D1
Brackenbush Pk 77 F3
Brackenbush Rd 77 F4
Bracken Dr 19 F2
Bracken Hill 72 C4
Bracken Rd 73 E4
Brackens La 85 G3
Brackenstown Av 12 C2
Braemor Av 64 A4
Braemor Dr 64 A4
Braemor Gro 64 A4
Braemor Pk 64 A3
Braemor Rd 64 A4
Brainborough Ter
off South Circular Rd 55 E3
Braithwaite St 84 B5
Bramblefield 23 F1
Bramblefield Ct 23 F1
Bramblefield Cres 23 F1
Bramblefield Dr 23 F1
Bramblefield Pk 23 F1
Bramblefield Vw 24 A1
Bramblefield Wk 23 F1
Bramley Av 42 C2
Bramley Ct 42 C2
Bramley Cres 42 C2
Bramley Garth 42 C2
Bramley Grn 42 C1
Bramley Gro 42 C1
Bramley Heath 42 C2
Bramley Pk 42 B2
Bramley Rd 42 C1
Bramley Vw 42 C1
Bramley Wk 42 B1
Bramley Way 42 C2
Branch Rd N 57 F1
Branch Rd N Ext 57 F1
Branch Rd S 57 F1
Brandon Rd 54 B4
Bray Head Ter **1** 82 B4
Bray Rd *Cabin.* 77 E4
Bray Rd *Corn.* 76 C2
Bray Rd *Grey.* 83 D1
Bray Sta 82 C2
Breakwater Rd S 57 F1
Breffni Ter 78 B2
Breffni Gdns **1** 32 A1
Breffni Rd 78 B2
Breffni Ter 78 A2
Bregia Rd 45 E3
Brehon Fld Rd 72 A3

C

Coolmine Sta 42 B1
Coolmine Wds 24 B4
Coolnevaun 73 F2
Coolock Dr 29 F3
Coolock Ind Est 30 A4
Coolock La 28 C2
Coolock Village 29 F4
Coolrua Dr 28 C3
Coombe, The 84 C5
Copeland Av 47 D2
Copeland Gro 47 D2
Cope St 85 F4
Copper All 84 D4
Copper Beech Gro **7** 82 A2
Coppice, The 42 C4
Coppinger Cl 74 A3
Coppinger Glade 74 A3
Coppinger Row
off William St S 85 F5
Coppinger Wk 74 A3
Coppinger Wd 74 A3
Coppins, The *Celbr.* 37 E3
Coppins, The *Fox.* 76 B3
Corballis Row
off Kevin St Upr 84 D5
Corbally Av 67 F3
Corbally Cl 67 F3
Corbally Downs 67 E3
Corbally Dr 67 F3
Corbally Glade 67 E3
Corbally Grn 67 F3
Corbally Heath 67 E3
Corbally Lawn 67 E3
Corbally Pk 67 F3
Corbally Ri 67 E3
Corbally Sq 67 F3
Corbally Vale 67 F3
Corbally Way 67 F3
Corbawn Av 81 F2
Corbawn Cl 81 F3
Corbawn Ct 81 F3
Corbawn Dale 81 F3
Corbawn Dr 81 F3
Corbawn Glade 81 F3
Corbawn Gro 81 F3
Corbawn La 81 E3
Corbawn Lawn 81 E3
Corbawn Wd 81 E3
Corcaill 19 E2
Corduff Av 25 D2
Corduff Cl 25 D2
Corduff Cotts 24 C3
Corduff Cres 25 D2
Corduff Gdns 25 D2
Corduff Grn 25 D2
Corduff Gro 24 C2
Corduff Pk 24 C2
Corduff Pl 25 D2
Corduff Way 25 D2
Corkagh Vw 60 A2
Corke Abbey 82 B1
Corke Abbey Av 82 A1
Cork Hill 85 E4
Cork St 84 A6
Cormac Ter 63 E3
Cornelscourt Hill Rd 76 C3
Corn Ex Pl
off George's Quay 85 G3
Cornmarket 84 C4
Corporation St 85 G2
Corrib Rd 63 D2
Corrig Av 75 F4
Corrig Cl
off Lugaquilla Av 61 F3
Corrig Pk 75 F4
Corrig Rd *Dalkey* 78 B3
Corrig Rd *D.L.* 75 F4
Corrig Rd *Still.* 73 E3
Corrybeg 62 C4
Cottage Pl
off Portland Pl 46 A3
Coulson Av 63 F2
Coultry Av 28 B2
Coultry Cres 28 A2
Coultry Dr 28 A2
Coultry Gdns 28 A2
Coultry Gro 28 B2
Coultry Lawn 28 B2
Coultry Pk 28 B2
Coultry Rd 28 A2
Coultry Way 28 A2
Coundon Ct 77 F4
Court, The *Dublin 3*
off Clontarf Rd 47 E3
Court, The *Dublin 5* 48 C2
Court, The *Dublin 6W* 62 C4
Court, The *Dublin 9* 46 C1
Court, The *Dublin 13* 32 A2
Court, The *Dublin 16* 72 B3
Court, The (Cookstown)
Dublin 24 60 C4
Court, The (Kilnamanagh)
Dublin 24 61 D3
Court, The *Celbr.* 37 D3
Court, The (Dunboyne Castle)
Dunb. 20 B3
Court, The (Lutterell Hall) *Dunb.* 20 B2
Court, The (Plunkett Hall) *Dunb.* 20 A1
Court, The (Sadleir Hall) *Dunb.* 20 B2
Court, The (Ballyowen) *Lucan* 51 F1
Court, The **7** *Mala.* 19 F1
Court, The *Mulh.* 24 A1
Court, The *Swords* 13 D1
Courthill Dr 20 B2
Court Ho Sq **3** 36 B2
Courtlands 77 E3
Courtyard, The *Dublin 14* 63 F4
Courtyard, The *Bray* 82 A3
Courtyard, The *Celbr.* 37 D4
Courtyard, The *Cool.* 42 A1
Courtyard, The **6** *Fox.* 76 B1
Courtyard, The **1** *Mala.* 19 F1
Courtyard Business Pk, The 59 D1
Cove, The **1** 14 C3
Cowbooter La 33 F3
Cowley Pl 46 A3
Cow Parlour 84 B6
Cowper Downs 64 A2
Cowper Dr 64 B2
Cowper Gdns 64 B2
Cowper Rd 64 A2
Cowper Sta 64 B2
Cowper St 84 A1
Cowper Village 64 A2
Crag Av 52 B4
Crag Av Business Pk 52 B4
Crag Av Ind Cen 52 B4
Crag Cres 52 C3
Crag Ter 52 B4
Craigford Av 47 E1
Craigford Dr 47 E1
Craiglands **4** 78 C3
Craigmore Gdns 74 C2
Crampton Bldgs
off Temple Bar 85 E4
Crampton Ct 85 E4
Crampton Quay 85 F3
Crampton Rd 57 D3
Crane La 85 E4
Crane St 84 B4
Cranfield Pl 57 D3
Cranford Ct 65 E2
Cranmer La 56 C3
Crannagh 64 C2
Crannagh Castle 63 E4
Crannagh Ct 63 E4
Crannagh Gro 63 F4
Crannagh Pk 63 F4
Crannagh Rd 63 E4
Crannagh Way 63 F4
Crannoge Rd 27 F2
Crannogue Cl 27 F2
Crannogue Rd 27 F2
Crawford Av 46 A3
Creighton St 85 H4
Cremona Rd 53 E2
Cremore Av 45 F1
Cremore Cres 45 F1
Cremore Dr 45 F1
Cremore Hts
off Ballygall Rd E 27 F4
Cremore Lawn 45 F1
Cremore Pk 45 F1
Cremore Rd 45 F1
Cremorne *Dublin 6* 63 F2
Cremorne *Dublin 16* 70 C1
Crescent, The *Dublin 3* 47 D3
Crescent, The (Donnybrook)
Dublin 4 64 C1
Crescent, The (Beaumont)
Dublin 9 28 C4
Crescent, The (Whitehall)
Dublin 9 46 C1
Crescent, The *Dublin 13* 32 A2
Crescent, The (Ballinteer)
Dublin 16 72 B4
Crescent, The (Ballyboden)
Dublin 16 70 C3
Crescent, The *Dublin 24* 69 E2
Crescent, The (Cookstown)
Dublin 24 60 C4
Crescent, The (Kilnamanagh)
Dublin 24 61 D3
Crescent, The (Abbeyfarm)
Celbr. 37 D4
Crescent, The (Oldtown Mill)
Celbr. 37 D3
Crescent, The
(St. Wolstan's Abbey) *Celbr.* 37 E4
Crescent, The *Clons.* 23 D2
Crescent, The (Dunboyne Castle)
Dunb. 20 B3
Crescent, The (Lutterell Hall)
Dunb. 20 B2
Crescent, The (Plunkett Hall)
Dunb. 20 A1
Crescent, The *Gra M.* 51 D2
Crescent, The *Kins.* 13 E4
Crescent, The *Lucan* 40 B4
Crescent, The **5** *Mala.* 19 F1
Crescent, The **3** *Swords* 13 D2
Crescent, The (Seatown Pk)
Swords 13 D1
Crescent Gdns 46 C4
Crescent Pl 47 D3
Crescent Vil 46 A2
Crestfield Av 28 B4
Crestfield Cl 28 B4
Crestfield Dr 28 B4
Crestfield Pk
off Crestfield Cl 28 B4
Crestwood Av 8 B3
Crestwood Grn 8 B3
Crestwood Pk 8 B3
Crestwood Rd 8 B3
Crinan Strand 56 C1
Crinken Glen 81 D4
Crinken La 81 D4
Croaghpatrick Rd 44 C3
Crodaun Ct 37 D2
Crodaun Forest Pk 37 D1
Croft, The 37 E2
Crofton Av 75 E3
Crofton Rd 75 E2
Crofton Ter 75 E2
Croftwood Cres 53 D3
Croftwood Dr 53 D3
Croftwood Gdns 53 D3
Croftwood Grn 53 E3
Croftwood Gro 53 D3
Croftwood Pk 53 E3
Croke Pk Ind Est 46 B4
Cromcastle Av 29 E3
Cromcastle Dr 29 E3
Cromcastle Grn 29 E3
Cromcastle Pk 29 E3
Cromcastle Rd 29 E3
Cromlech Ct 27 F2
Cromlech Flds 81 E2
Cromwells Fort Rd 62 A1
Cromwells Quarters 55 D2
Cross & Passion Coll 46 C1
Cross Av *Boot.* 74 A1
Cross Av *D.L.* 75 E3
Crossbeg Ind Est 61 E2
Cross Guns Br 45 F3
Cross Kevin St 85 E6
Crosslands Ind Est 61 E2
Cross La 36 B1
Crosstrees 33 F3
Crosthwaite Pk E 75 F4
Crosthwaite Pk S 75 F4
Crosthwaite Pk W 75 F4
Crosthwaite Ter 75 F3
Crotty Av 62 B1
Crown All
off Temple Bar 85 E4
Crow St 85 E4
Croydon Gdns 46 C2
Croydon Grn 46 C3
Croydon Pk Av 46 C2
Croydon Ter 46 C2
Crumlin Pk 54 C4
Crumlin Rd 54 C4
Crumlin Shop Cen 55 D3
Cuala Gro 82 C4
Cuala Rd *Dublin 7* 45 E3
Cuala Rd *Bray* 82 C4
Cuckoo La 84 D3
Cuffe La 85 E6
Cuffe St 85 E6
Cullenswood Gdns 64 B1
Cullenswood Pk 64 B1
Culmore Pk 53 D1
Culmore Rd 53 D1
Cul Na Greine 69 D2
Cumberland Rd 56 B3
Cumberland St 75 E3
Cumberland St N 85 F1
Cumberland St S 85 H5
Cunningham Dr 78 B4
Cunningham Rd 78 B3
Curlew Rd 54 B4
Curved St
off Eustace St 85 E4
Curzon St 55 F3
Cushlawn Pk 68 C3
Custom Ho 85 G3
Custom Ho Quay 85 G3
Cymric Rd 57 E2
Cypress Av **3** 71 D3
Cypress Ct 81 D1
Cypress Downs 62 C4
Cypress Dr 62 C4
Cypress Garth 62 C4
Cypress Gro N 62 C4
Cypress Gro Rd 62 C4
Cypress Gro S 62 C4
Cypress Lawn 62 C4
Cypress Pk 62 C4
Cypress Rd 65 E4

D

Dakota Av 28 C1
Dalcassian Downs 45 F3
Dale, The (Cookstown)
Dublin 24 60 C4
Dale, The (Kilnamanagh)
Dublin 24 61 D3
Dale, The *Bray* 82 A3
Dale, The *Celbr.* 37 D3
Dale, The *Dunb.* 20 B1
Dale, The *Manor.* 23 E2
Dale Cl **1** 73 E2
Dale Dr 73 E1
Dalepark Rd 69 D3
Dale Rd 73 E1
Dale Tree 70 A4
Dale Tree Av 70 A4
Dale Tree Cres 70 A3
Dale Tree Dr 70 A4
Dale Tree Gro 70 A4
Dale Tree Pk 70 A4
Dale Tree Rd 70 A4
Dale Tree Vw 70 A3
Dale Vw 77 F4
Dale Vw Pk **3** 77 F4
Dale Vw Rd 12 B1
Dalkey Av 78 B4
Dalkey Ct 78 B3
Dalkey Gro 78 B3
Dalkey Pk 78 B3
Dalkey Rock 78 B4
Dalkey Sound 78 C3
Dalkey Sta 78 B3
Dal Riada 19 F1
Damastown Cl 24 A1
Damastown Grn 23 F1
Damastown Wk 21 F3
Damastown Way 24 A1
Dame Ct 85 E4
Dame La 85 E4
Dame St 85 E4
Dane Rd 27 F2
Danes Ct 48 B4
Danesfort 47 F3
Daneswell Rd 46 A2
Dangan Av 62 C2
Dangan Dr 62 C2
Dangan Pk 62 C2
Danieli Dr 47 F1
Danieli Rd 47 F1
Daniel St 84 D6
Dara Ct 37 E3
Dara Cres 37 E3
Dargan Ct **13** 82 C3
Dargan St 82 A2
Dargle Cres **8** 82 A2
Dargle Dr 71 F2
Dargle Hts 82 A2
Dargle Lo **1** 70 C2
Dargle Rd *Dublin 9* 46 A3
Dargle Rd *Black.* 74 B4
Dargle Valley 71 F2
Dargle Vw 72 A2
Dargle Wd 70 C2
Darley Cotts **3** 82 B3
Darleys Ter 84 B6
Darley St 55 F4
Darling Est 44 B2
Dartmouth Ho Ind Est 53 F3
Dartmouth La 56 B4
Dartmouth Pl 56 A4
Dartmouth Rd 56 A4
Dartmouth Sq 56 B4
Dartmouth Ter 56 A4
Dartmouth Wk
off Dartmouth Ter 56 A4
Dartry Cotts 64 A3
Dartry Pk 64 A2
Dartry Rd 64 A2
David Pk 46 A3
David Rd 46 A3
Davis Pl
off Thomas Davis St S 84 D5
Davitt Pk 77 F4
Davitt Rd *Dublin 12* 54 C3
Davitt Rd *Bray* 82 B3
Dawson Ct *Dublin 2*
off Stephen St 85 E5
Dawson Ct *Black.* 74 A2
Dawson La 85 G5
Dawson St 85 F5
Deans Ct **1** 76 C1
Deansgrange Business Pk 76 C1
Dean's Gra Rd 74 C4
Deansrath Av 51 E4
Deansrath Cres 51 E4
Deansrath Gro 51 E4
Deansrath Lawn 51 F4
Deansrath Pk 51 E4
Deansrath Rd 51 E4
Deanstown Av 26 B4
Deanstown Dr 26 C4
Deanstown Grn 26 C4
Deanstown Pk 26 C4
Deanstown Rd 26 C4
Dean St 84 D5
Dean Swift Grn 27 F4
Dean Swift Rd 27 F4
Dean Swift Sq
off Swifts All 84 C5
De Burgh Rd 55 D1
Decies Rd 53 E2
De Courcy Sq 45 F2
Deerhaven 23 F2
Deerhaven Av 23 F1
Deerhaven Cl 23 F1
Deerhaven Cres 23 F1
Deerhaven Grn 23 F2
Deerhaven Pk 23 F1
Deerhaven Vw 23 F1
Deerhaven Wk 23 F2
Deerpark 8 C3
Deerpark Av *Dublin 15* 43 F2
Deerpark Av *Kilt.* 68 C4
Deerpark Cl *Dublin 15* 43 F2
Deerpark Cl *Kilt.* 68 C4
Deerpark Downs 68 C4
Deerpark Dr *Dublin 15* 43 F2
Deerpark Dr *Kilt.* 69 D4
Deerpark Grn **9** 69 D4
Deerpark Lawn 43 F2
Deerpark Pl 69 D4
Deerpark Ri 69 D4
Deerpark Rd *Dublin 15* 43 F2
Deerpark Rd *Kilt.* 69 D4
Deerpark Rd *Still.* 65 E4
Deerpark Sq 68 C4
Deerpark Ter **10** 69 D4
Deerpark Way 69 D4
Deey Br 38 C2
Delaford Av 70 B2
Delaford Dr 70 B2
Delaford Gro 70 B2
Delaford Lawn 70 B2
Delaford Pk 70 B2
Delbrook Manor 72 C3
Delbrook Pk 72 C3
Delgany Pk 83 E4
Delgany Wd 83 D4
Delgany Wd Av 83 D4
Delhurst Av 23 D3
Delhurst Ct 23 D3
Delhurst Ms 23 D3
Delhurst Ter 23 D3

E

Edmondsbury Ct **1** 41 E4
Edmondstown Grn 71 D3
Edmondstown Pk 71 D3
Edmondstown Rd 71 D4
Edward Rd 82 C3
Edwards Ct 71 D3
Edwin Ct **5** 78 A3
Effra Rd 63 F1
Eglington Rd 82 B2
Eglinton Ct 64 C1
Eglinton Pk *Dublin 4* 64 C1
Eglinton Pk *D.L.* 75 E4
Eglinton Rd 64 C1
Eglinton Sq 64 C1
Eglinton Ter *Dublin 4* 64 C1
Eglinton Ter *Dublin 14* 72 C1
Eglinton Wd 64 C1
Elderberry 50 C2
Elderwood Rd 42 C4
Eldon Ter
off South Circular Rd 55 E3
Elgin Rd 56 C4
Elizabeth St 46 B3
Elkwood 70 C1
Ellenfield Rd 28 C4
Ellensborough 69 D4
Ellensborough Av 69 D4
Ellensborough Cl 69 D4
Ellensborough Copse 69 D4
Ellensborough Ct 69 D4
Ellensborough Cres 69 D4
Ellensborough Dale 69 D4
Ellensborough Downs 69 D4
Ellensborough Gra 69 D4
Ellensborough Grn 69 D4
Ellensborough Gro 69 D4
Ellensborough La 69 D4
Ellensborough Lo 69 D4
Ellensborough Meadows 69 D4
Ellensborough Pk 69 D4
Ellensborough Ri 69 D4
Ellensborough Vw 69 D4
Ellensborough Wk 69 D4
Ellesmere **1** 73 F3
Ellesmere Av 45 E4
Ellis Quay 84 B3
Ellis St
off Benburb St 84 B3
Elmbrook 51 E1
Elmbrook Cres 51 E1
Elmbrook Lawn 51 E1
Elmbrook Wk 51 E1
Elmcastle Cl 61 E4
Elmcastle Ct 61 E4
Elmcastle Dr 61 E4
Elmcastle Grn 61 E4
Elmcastle Pk 61 E4
Elmcastle Wk 61 E4
Elm Cl 51 E2
Elm Ct *Jobs.* 68 A3
Elm Ct *Lucan* 51 E2
Elmdale Cl 53 D2
Elmdale Cres 53 D2
Elmdale Dr 53 D2
Elmdale Pk 52 C2
Elm Dene 51 E2
Elm Dr *Jobs.* 68 A3
Elm Dr *Lucan* 51 E2
Elmfield Av 30 C3
Elmfield Cl **1** 30 C3
Elmfield Ct **4** 30 C3
Elmfield Cres 30 C3
Elmfield Dr **2** 30 C3
Elmfield Grn 30 C3
Elmfield Gro 30 C3
Elmfield Ind Est 52 B4
Elmfield Lawn 30 C3
Elmfield Pk
off Elmfield Av 30 C3
Elmfield Ri 30 C3
Elmfield Vale **3** 30 C3
Elmfield Wk 30 C3
Elmfield Way 30 C3
Elm Grn 51 D2
Elmgrove *B'brack* 77 F4
Elm Gro *Black.* 74 B3
Elm Gro *Jobs.* 68 A3
Elm Gro *Lucan* 51 E2
Elm Gro Cotts
off Blackhorse Av 44 C3
Elmgrove Ter **9** 82 B2
Elm Mt Av 47 D1
Elm Mt Cl 47 D1
Elm Mt Ct 47 E1
Elm Mt Cres 29 D4
Elm Mt Dr 47 D1
Elm Mt Gro 29 D4
Elm Mt Hts 29 D4
Elm Mt Lawn 29 D4
Elm Mt Pk 29 D4
Elm Mt Ri 29 D4
Elm Mt Rd 47 D1
Elm Mt Vw 29 D4
Elm Pk *Dublin 4* 65 E1
Elm Pk *Celbr.* 37 E3
Elmpark Av 56 B4
Elmpark Ter 63 E2
Elm Rd *Dublin 9* 47 D1
Elm Rd *Dublin 12* 61 E1
Elms, The *Dublin 4* 65 E2
Elms, The **14** *Abb.* 81 E1
Elms, The *Black.* 74 A2
Elms, The *Celbr.* 37 E2
Elms, The *Dunb.* 20 C2
Elms, The *Shank.* 81 E4
Elm Vale 51 E2
Elm Way *Dublin 16* 72 A3
Elm Way *Lucan* 51 E2
Elm Wd 51 E2
Elmwood Av Lwr 56 B4
Elmwood Av Upr
off Elmwood Av Lwr 64 B1
Elmwood Cl 23 E3
Elmwood Ct 12 B1
Elmwood Dr 12 B1
Elmwood Pk 12 B1
Elmwood Rd 12 B1
Elner Ct 19 F2
Elsinoire 83 D4
Elton Ct *Dublin 13*
off Elton Dr 30 B4
Elton Ct *Dunb.* 20 C2
Elton Ct *D.L.* 78 B2
Elton Ct *Leix.* 39 E3
Elton Dr *Dublin 13* 30 B4
Elton Dr *Dunb.* 20 C2
Elton Gro 20 C2
Elton Pk *Dublin 13* 30 B4
Elton Pk *D.L.* 78 A2
Elton Wk
off Elton Dr 30 B4
Ely Cres 69 F4
Ely Dr 69 F4
Ely Grn **1** 69 F4
Ely Gro 69 F4
Ely Manor 69 F4
Ely Pl 85 G6
Ely Pl Upr
off Ely Pl 85 G6
Ely Vw 69 F4
Embassy Lawn 64 C2
Emerald Cotts 56 C3
Emerald Pl
off Sheriff St Lwr 56 C1
Emerald Sq 84 A6
Emerald St 56 C1
Emily Pl
off Sheriff St Lwr 85 H2
Emmet Ct 54 B3
Emmet Rd 54 B2
Emmet Sq 74 A1
Emmet St *Dublin 1* 46 B4
Emmet St (Haroldscross)
Dublin 6 55 F4
Emmet St **1** *Sally.* 77 F1
Emor St 55 F3
Emorville Av 55 F3
Emorville Sq
off South Circular Rd 55 E3
Empress Pl 85 H1
Enaville Rd 46 C3
Engine All 84 C5
English Row 37 E4
Ennafort Av (Ascal Dun Eanna) 48 A2
Ennafort Ct 48 A2
Ennafort Dr (Ceide Dun Eanna) 48 A2
Ennafort Gro 48 A2
Ennafort Pk 48 A2
Ennafort Rd 48 A2
Ennel Av 48 A1
Ennel Ct **3** 81 E1
Ennel Dr 48 A1
Ennel Pk 48 A1
Ennis Gro 57 D3
Enniskerry Rd 45 F3
Erne Pl 56 C2
Erne Pl Little 85 H4
Erne St Lwr 56 C2
Erne St Upr 56 C2
Erne Ter Front
off Erne St Upr 56 C2
Erne Ter Rere
off Erne St Upr 56 C2
Errigal Gdns 54 B4
Errigal Rd 54 B4
Erris Rd 45 E3
Erskine Av 83 F3
Esker Dr 50 C1
Esker La (north) *Lucan* 41 E4
Esker La (south) *Lucan* 51 E1
Esker Lawns 41 D4
Esker Lo 51 E1
Esker Lo Av 51 E1
Esker Lo Cl 51 E1
Esker Lo Vw 51 E1
Esker Manor 51 D1
Esker Meadow 51 E1
Esker Meadow Cl 51 E1
Esker Meadow Ct 51 E1
Esker Meadow Grn 51 E1
Esker Meadow Gro 51 E1
Esker Meadow Lawn 51 E1
Esker Meadow Ri 51 E1
Esker Meadow Vw 51 E1
Esker Pk 51 E1
Esker Pines 41 E4
Esker Rd 51 D1
Esker S 51 D2
Esker Wds Ct 51 E1
Esker Wds Dr 51 E1
Esker Wds Gro 51 E1
Esker Wds Ri 51 E1
Esker Wds Vw 51 E1
Esker Wds Wk 51 E1
Esmond Av 46 C3
Esmonde Ter **10** 82 A2
Esplanade Ter **14** 82 C3
Esposito Rd 62 B1
Essex Quay 84 D4
Essex St E 85 E4
Essex St W 85 E4
Estate Av 65 F2
Estate Cotts 56 C3
Estuary Ct 13 D1
Estuary Rd 14 B4
Estuary Rbt 13 D1
Estuary Row 15 D3
Estuary Wk 14 B4
Eugene St 84 A6
Eustace St 85 E4
Everton Av 45 E4
Evora Cres 33 E3
Evora Pk 33 E3
Evora Ter
off St. Lawrence Rd 33 E3
Ewington La 84 A4
Excalibur Dr 83 F2
Exchange Ct
off Dame St 85 E4
Exchange St Lwr 84 D4
Exchange St Upr
off Lord Edward St 85 E4
Exchequer St 85 E4

F

Faber Gro **3** 75 D4
Fade St 85 E5
Fagan's La **1** 36 B2
Fairbrook Lawn 71 E1
Fairfield Av 46 C4
Fairfield Pk *Dublin 6* 63 F2
Fairfield Pk *Grey.* 83 E1
Fairfield Rd (Glasnevin) 46 A2
Fairgreen 67 D3
Fairgreen Ct **10** 82 B2
Fairgreen Rd 82 A2
Fairgreen Ter **11** 82 B2
Fair Haven **1** 15 D4
Fairlawn Pk
off Fairlawn Rd 27 D4
Fairlawn Rd 27 D4
Fairlawns 78 A3
Fairview 46 C3
Fairview Av (Irishtown) 57 D2
Fairview Av Lwr 46 C3
Fairview Av Upr 46 C3
Fairview Grn 46 C3
Fairview Lawn 80 C1
Fairview Pas
off Fairview Strand 46 C3
Fairview Strand 46 C3
Fairview Ter 46 C3
Fairways *Dublin 14* 63 D4
Fairways *D'bate* 11 F2
Fairways, The *Bray* 82 B1
Fairways, The *Port.* 19 D4
Fairways Av 27 E4
Fairways Grn 27 E4
Fairways Gro 27 E4
Fairways Pk 27 E4
Fairy Hill *Black.* 74 B4
Fairyhill *Bray* 82 A4
Faith Av 46 C4
Falcarragh Rd 28 B4
Falls Rd 81 D2
Farmhill Dr 64 C4
Farmhill Pk 73 D1
Farmhill Rd 64 C4
Farmleigh Av *Dublin 15* 43 E2
Farmleigh Av *Black.* 74 A4
Farmleigh Cl *Dublin 15* 43 E2
Farmleigh Cl *Black.* 74 A4
Farmleigh Ct 43 E2
Farmleigh Pk *Dublin 15* 43 E2
Farmleigh Pk *Black.* 74 A4
Farmleigh Vw 43 E2
Farmleigh Wds 43 E2
Farney Pk 57 E3
Farnham Cres 27 D4
Farnham Dr 27 D4
Farrenboley Cotts 64 B3
Farrenboley Pk 64 B3
Father Colohan Ter **4** 82 B3
Father Kitt Ct 62 C1
Father Matthew Br 84 C4
Fatima Mans 55 D3
Fatima Sta 84 A6
Fatima Ter 82 B2
Faughart Rd 63 D1
Faussagh Av 45 D2
Faussagh Rd 45 E3
Feltrim Hall 13 D3
Feltrim Ind Pk 13 E3
Feltrim Rd 18 A1
Fenian St 85 H5
Ferguson Rd 46 A2
Fergus Rd 63 E3
Fernbrook **2** 82 A1
Ferncourt Av 69 F4
Ferncourt Cl 69 F4
Ferncourt Cres **2** 69 F4
Ferncourt Dr **3** 69 F4
Ferncourt Grn 69 F4
Ferncourt Pk 69 F4
Ferncourt Vw 69 F4
Ferndale *Dublin 24* 69 D2
Ferndale *Manor.* 23 F2
Ferndale Av 27 E4
Ferndale Glen 81 D4
Ferndale Hill 80 C4
Ferndale Rd *Dublin 11* 27 E4
Ferndale Rd *Shank.* 81 D4
Fernhill Av 62 B3
Fernhill Pk 62 B3
Fernhill Rd 62 B3
Fernleigh 42 A2
Fernleigh Cl 42 A1
Fernleigh Ct 42 A2
Fernleigh Dale 42 A2
Fernleigh Dr 42 A1
Fernleigh Grn 42 A2
Fernleigh Gro 42 A2
Fernleigh Pk 42 A2
Fernleigh Pl **3** 42 A2
Fernleigh Vw 42 A2
Ferns Rd 63 D1
Fernvale Dr 54 B4
Fernwood Av 68 C1
Fernwood Cl 68 C2
Fernwood Ct 68 C1
Fernwood Lawn 68 C1
Fernwood Pk 68 C1
Fernwood Way 68 C2
Ferrard Rd 63 F2
Ferrycarrig Av 29 F2
Ferrycarrig Dr 29 F2
Ferrycarrig Grn **2** 29 F2
Ferrycarrig Pk 29 F2
Ferrycarrig Rd 29 F2
Ferrymans Crossing 56 C1
Fertullagh Rd 45 E3
Fettercairn Rd 68 B1
Fey Yerra **1** 76 A1
Fforester 51 E1
Fforester Cl 51 E1
Fforester Ct 51 E1
Fforester Lawn 51 E1
Fforester Pk 51 E1
Fforester Wk 51 E1
Fforester Way 51 E1
Field Av 62 B1
Fields Ter
off Ranelagh Rd 56 B4
Finches Ind Pk 54 A4
Findlater Pl
off Marlborough St 85 F2
Findlaters St 55 D1
Findlater St **14** 78 A2
Fingal Pl 84 B1
Fingal St 84 A6
Finglas Business Cen 27 D2
Finglas Business Pk 45 E1
Finglas Pk 27 E3
Finglas Pl 27 D4
Finglas Rd 45 E1
Finglas Rd Old 45 F1
Finglas Shop Cen 27 D3
Finglaswood Rd 26 C3
Finlay Sq 65 E4
Finneber Fort 27 D4
Finneber Fort Sq **1** 27 D4
Finnscourt 50 C3
Finnsgreen 50 C2
Finnsgrove 50 C2
Finnslawn 50 C3
Finnspark 50 C3
Finnstown Fairways 50 C2
Finn St 84 A1
Finnsvale 50 C2
Finnsview 50 C2
Finnswood 50 C3
Finsbury Grn 72 B1
Finsbury Pk 72 B1
Firgrove **1** 81 E1
Firhouse Rd *Dublin 16* 70 B1
Firhouse Rd *Dublin 24* 70 B1
Firhouse Rd W 69 D3
First Av *Dublin 1* 56 C1
First Av (Inchicore) *Dublin 10* 54 A2
First Av *Dublin 24* 60 C4
Fishamble St 84 D4
Fitzgerald Pk **2** 75 E4
Fitzgerald St 55 F4
Fitzgibbon La 46 B4
Fitzgibbon St 46 B4
Fitzmaurice Rd *Dublin 11* 27 F4
Fitzmaurice Rd *R'coole* 66 C2
Fitzroy Av 46 A3
Fitzwilliam Ct
off Pembroke St Upr 85 G6
Fitzwilliam La 85 H6
Fitzwilliam Pl 56 B3
Fitzwilliam Quay 57 D2
Fitzwilliam Sq E 56 B3
Fitzwilliam Sq N 85 G6
Fitzwilliam Sq S 85 G6
Fitzwilliam Sq W 85 G6
Fitzwilliam St (Ringsend) 57 D2
Fitzwilliam St Lwr 85 H6
Fitzwilliam St Upr 85 H6
Fleet St 85 F3
Fleming Pl 56 C3
Fleming Rd 46 A2
Flemings La
off Haddington Rd 56 C3
Flemingstown Pk 64 B4
Fleurville 74 B3
Floraville Av 60 B1
Floraville Dr 60 C2
Floraville Est 60 C1
Floraville Lawn 60 C1
Florence Rd 82 B2
Florence St
off Lennox St 56 A4
Florence Ter **2** 82 C2
Florence Vil **12** 82 B2
Flower Gro 77 F2
Foley St 85 G2
Fontenoy St 84 D1
Fontenoy Ter 82 C3
Fonthill Abbey **2** 71 E1
Fonthill Ct **3** 71 E1
Fonthill Pk 71 E1
Fonthill Retail Pk 52 A1
Fonthill Rd *Dublin 14* 71 E1
Fonthill Rd *Clond.* 52 A1

Fonthill Rd S 60 B2
Forbes La 84 A5
Forbes St 56 C2
Forest Av *Dublin 24* 61 E3
Forest Av *Swords* 12 B3
Forest Boul 12 A3
Forest Cl 61 E3
Forest Ct 12 A3
Forest Cres 12 B3
Forest Dale 12 B3
Forest Dr *Dublin 24* 61 E3
Forest Dr *Swords* 12 B3
Forest Flds Rd 12 B3
Forest Grn *Dublin 24* 61 E3
Forest Grn *Swords* 12 B3
Forest Gro 12 A3
Forest Hills 66 A3
Forest Lawn 61 E3
Forest Pk *Dublin 24* 61 E3
Forest Pk *Leix.* 39 E3
Forest Pk *Swords* 12 B3
Forest Rd 12 A4
Forest Vw **1** 12 B3
Forest Wk 12 B3
Forest Way **2** 12 B3
Forestwood Av 28 A2
Forestwood Cl 28 B2
Fortfield Av 63 D3
Fortfield Ct 63 D3
Fortfield Dr 63 D4
Fortfield Gdns 64 A2
Fortfield Gro 63 D3
Fortfield Pk 63 D4
Fortfield Rd 63 D3
Fortfield Sq 63 D3
Fortfield Ter 64 A2
Forth Rd 47 D4
Fortlawn 24 A3
Fortlawn Av 24 A3
Fortlawn Pk 24 A3
Fortlawns 78 A4
Fortrose Pk 62 C4
Fortunestown Cl 67 F2
Fortunestown Cres 67 F2
Fortunestown La 67 E2
Fortunestown Lawns 67 E2
Fortunestown Rd 68 A3
Fortunestown Wk 67 E2
Fosterbrook 65 F3
Foster Cotts
off Phibsborough Rd 45 F4
Foster Pl S 85 F4
Fosters, The 65 E4
Fosters Av 65 E4
Foster Ter 46 B4
Fountain Pl 84 B2
Fountain Rd 55 D1
Four Cts (Courts of Justice) 84 D3
Four Cts Sta 84 D3
Fourth Av *Dublin 1* 56 C1
Fourth Av *Dublin 24* 68 C1
Fownes St 85 F4
Foxborough Av 51 E2
Foxborough Cl 51 F2
Foxborough Ct 51 E3
Foxborough Cres **1** 51 E2
Foxborough Downes 51 E2
Foxborough Dr 51 E2
Foxborough Gdns 51 F2
Foxborough Glen 51 F2
Foxborough Grn 51 F2
Foxborough Gro 51 F2
Foxborough Hts 51 F2
Foxborough Hill 51 E2
Foxborough La 51 F2
Foxborough Lawn 51 F3
Foxborough Meadows 51 E2
Foxborough Pk 51 E2
Foxborough Pl 51 E2
Foxborough Ri 51 E2
Foxborough Rd 51 E3
Foxborough Row 51 F2
Foxborough Wk 51 F2
Foxborough Way 51 E2
Foxdene Av 51 F3
Foxdene Dr 52 A3
Foxdene Gdns 52 A2
Foxdene Grn 51 F2
Foxdene Gro 52 A2
Foxdene Pk 52 A2
Foxes Gro 81 E3
Foxfield 50 C2
Foxfield Av 48 C1
Foxfield Cres 49 D1
Foxfield Dr 49 D1
Foxfield Grn 49 D1
Foxfield Gro 48 C1
Foxfield Hts 48 C1
Foxfield Lawn 49 D1
Foxfield Pk 49 D1
Foxfield Rd 48 C1
Foxfield St. John 49 D1
Foxford 51 F1
Foxhill Av 30 B4
Foxhill Cl 30 B3
Foxhill Ct 30 B4
Foxhill Cres 30 B4
Foxhill Dr 30 B4
Foxhill Grn 30 B3
Foxhill Gro 30 B3
Foxhill Lawn 30 B4
Foxhill Pk 30 B4
Foxhill Way 30 B4
Foxpark 50 C2
Foxrock Av 76 B1
Foxrock Cl 76 C1
Foxrock Ct 76 B1
Foxrock Cres 76 C1
Foxrock Grn 76 C1
Foxrock Gro 76 C1
Foxrock Manor 76 A1
Foxrock Mt **1** 76 B1
Foxrock Pk 76 B1
Foxrock Wd 76 C1
Foxs La 49 D2
Foxwood *Lucan* 50 C2
Foxwood *Swords* 13 D2
Foyle Rd 46 C3
Francis St 84 C4
Frankfort 64 B4
Frankfort Av 63 F1
Frankfort Ct 63 F2
Frankfort Pk 64 B4
Frascati Pk 74 B2
Frascati Rd 74 B2
Frascati Shop Cen 74 B2
Frederick Ct
off Hardwicke St 85 E1
Frederick La 85 G5
Frederick La N 85 E1
Frederick St 8 B2
Frederick St N 85 E1
Frederick St S 85 G5
Frenchmans La
off Gardiner St Lwr 85 G2
Friarsland Av 64 C4
Friarsland Rd 64 C4
Friar's Wk **8** 60 B1
Friary Av 84 C3
Friel Av 53 E3
Fumbally La 84 D6
Furry Pk Ct 47 F2
Furry Pk Ind Est 28 B1
Furry Pk Rd 47 F2
Furze Rd *Dublin 8* 43 F3
Furze Rd *Sandy.* 73 E4

G

Gables, The *Clond.* 59 E1
Gables, The **4** *Fox.* 76 B2
Gaelic St 46 C4
Gailtrim Gra 19 D2
Gainsborough Av 14 B4
Gainsborough Cl **3** 14 B4
Gainsborough Ct 13 F3
Gainsborough Cres 13 F3
Gainsborough Downs 13 F3
Gainsborough Grn 13 F3
Gainsborough Lawn 13 F3
Gainsborough Pk 13 F3
Gairdini Sheinleasa 28 A3
Gallaun Rd 27 F2
Gallery, The 11 E2
Galloping Grn **3** 76 A1
Galmoy Rd 45 E3
Galtrim Pk 82 B2
Galtrim Rd 82 B3
Galtymore Cl 54 B3
Galtymore Dr 54 C3
Galtymore Pk 54 B4
Galtymore Rd 54 C3
Gandon Cl 55 F4
Gandon Ms 41 D4
Garden Croath 74 B3
Garden La 84 C5
Gardiner La 85 G1
Gardiner Row 85 F1
Gardiner's Pl 85 F1
Gardiner St Lwr 85 G1
Gardiner St Mid 85 F1
Gardiner St Upr 46 A4
Gardini Lein (Lein Gdns) 48 B2
Gardini Phairc An Bhailtini
(Villa Park Gdns) 44 C3
Garnett Hall 20 A2
Garnish Sq 25 D3
Garrynisk Cl 61 D4
Garrynisk Est 61 D4
Garrynure 64 B2
Garryowen Rd 53 F2
Gartan Av 46 A3
Gartan Ct 13 E1
Gartan Dr 13 E1
Garter La 67 D2
Garth, The *Dublin 24* 61 D3
Garth, The (Cookstown)
Dublin 24 60 C4
Garville Av 63 F2
Garville Av Upr 63 F2
Garville Rd 63 F2
Gas Yd La 15 D3
Gateway Ct **4** 28 A3
Gateway Cres 28 A3
Gateway Gdns **3** 28 A3
Gateway Ms **2** 28 A3
Gateway Pl **1** 28 A3
Gateway Vw **5** 28 A3
Gaybrook Lawns 14 B4
Geoffrey Keating Rd
off O'Curry Rd 84 C6
George's Av 74 B2
George's Hill 84 D3
George's La 84 C2
George's Pl *Dublin 1* 46 A4
George's Pl *Black.* 74 B2
George's Pl *D.L.* 75 E3
George's Quay 85 G3
Georges Rd 27 D3
George's St Lwr 75 E3
George's St Upr 75 F3
Georgian Hamlet 31 F3
Georgian Village 43 E2
Geraldine Ct **4** 36 B2
Geraldine St 45 F4
Geraldine Ter 64 B2
Geraldstown Wds 28 A2
Geraldstown Wds Apts **1** 28 A2
Gerald St 56 C2
Gertrude Ter **11** 82 A2
Gilbert Rd 55 F3
Gilford Av 57 E4
Gilford Ct 57 E4
Gilford Dr 57 E4
Gilford Pk 57 E4
Gilford Rd 57 E4
Giltspur Brook 82 B4
Giltspur Wd 82 A4
Glade, The *Dublin 16* 72 B3
Glade, The (Cookstown)
Dublin 24 60 C4
Glade, The (Oldtown Mill) *Celbr.* 37 D2
Glade, The (St. Wolstan's Abbey)
Celbr. 37 E4
Glade, The *Palm.* 42 C4
Glandore Pk 75 E4
Glandore Rd 46 C1
Glasanaon Ct
off Glasanaon Pk 27 E4
Glasanaon Pk 27 E4
Glasanaon Rd 27 E3
Glasaree Rd 27 E3
Glasilawn Av 27 F4
Glasilawn Rd 45 E1
Glasmeen Rd 45 E1
Glasmore Pk 12 B1
Glasnamana Pl 27 E4
Glasnamana Rd 45 E1
Glasnevin Av 27 E3
Glasnevin Br 45 F2
Glasnevin Business Pk 44 C1
Glasnevin Ct 45 E1
Glasnevin Downs 45 E1
Glasnevin Dr 27 F4
Glasnevin Hill 46 A1
Glasnevin Pk 27 F3
Glasnevin Wds 45 E1
Glasson Ct 64 B3
Glasthule Bldgs **15** 78 A2
Glasthule Rd 78 A2
Glaunsharoon 64 C1
Gleann Na Ri 80 C1
Gleann Na Smol *Dublin 24* 69 D2
Gleann Na Smol *D.L.* 74 C3
Glebe, The 51 D1
Glebe Vw 27 D3
Gledswood Av 64 C3
Gledswood Cl 64 C3
Gledswood Dr 64 C3
Gledswood Pk 64 C3
Glen, The (Ballinteer)
Dublin 16 72 B4
Glen, The (Ballyboden)
Dublin 16 71 D2
Glen, The **14** *D.L.* 75 F4
Glen, The *Lou.V.* 39 E2
Glenaan Rd 28 B4
Glen Abbey Complex 61 D4
Glenabbey Rd 73 E1
Glenageary Av 77 F1
Glenageary Ct 77 F1
Glenageary Hall 78 A3
Glenageary Lo 77 F1
Glenageary Off Pk 77 E1
Glenageary Pk 77 F1
Glenageary Rd Lwr 75 F4
Glenageary Rd Upr 75 E4
Glenageary Sta 75 F4
Glenageary Wds 75 E4
Glenalbyn Rd 74 A4
Glenalua Hts 79 E1
Glenalua Rd 79 E1
Glenalua Ter 79 E1
Glenamuck Rd 76 C4
Glenanne 63 D2
Glenard Av *Dublin 7* 45 E4
Glenard Av *Bray* 82 C3
Glenarm Av 46 B3
Glenarm Sq 46 A3
Glenarriff Rd 44 B2
Glenart Av 74 A3
Glenaulin 43 E4
Glenaulin Dr
(Ceide Glennaluinn) 53 E1
Glenaulin Grn 53 D1
Glenaulin Pk
(Pairc Gleannaluinn) 43 E4
Glenaulin Rd 53 D1
Glen Av 76 C3
Glenavon Pk 81 D1
Glenavy Pk 63 D2
Glenayle Rd 30 B4
Glenayr Rd 63 F3
Glenbeigh Pk 45 D4
Glenbeigh Rd 45 D4
Glenbourne Gro 76 A3
Glenbower Pk 72 B1
Glenbrook Pk 71 E1
Glenbrook Rd 44 B1
Glenburgh Ter **12** 82 A2
Glencairn 73 F4
Glencarr Ct **4** 81 E1
Glencarrig 32 C2
Glencarrig Ct 69 F3
Glencarrig Dr 69 F3
Glencarrig Grn 69 F3
Glencarr Lawn 81 E1
Glencar Rd 45 D4
Glen Cl 77 D3
Glencloy Rd 28 B4
Glencorp Rd 28 C4
Glencourt Est 82 B4
Glen Dale *Cabin.* 76 C3
Glendale *Leix.* 39 F2
Glendale Dr 82 B4
Glendale Meadows 40 A2
Glendale Pk 62 C3
Glendalough Rd 46 A2
Glendhu Pk 44 B1
Glendhu Rd 44 B1
Glendoher Av 71 E2
Glendoher Cl 71 D2
Glendoher Dr 71 E2
Glendoher Pk 71 E2
Glendoher Rd 71 D2
Glendoo Cl
off Lugaquilla Av 61 F3
Glendown Av 62 B3
Glendown Cl
off Glendown Gro 62 B3
Glendown Ct 62 B3
Glendown Cres 62 B3
Glendown Grn
off Glendown Gro 62 B3
Glendown Gro 62 B3
Glendown Lawn 62 C3
Glendown Pk 62 B3
Glendown Rd 62 B4
Glen Dr 77 D3
Glen Druid 81 E2
Glendun Rd 28 B4
Glenealy Downs 23 F2
Glenealy Rd 55 E4
Glen Easton 38 C2
Gleneaston Av 38 C3
Gleneaston Cl 39 D3
Gleneaston Ct 39 D3
Gleneaston Cres 39 D3
Gleneaston Dr 39 D3
Gleneaston Gdns 38 C2
Gleneaston Grn 39 D2
Gleneaston Gro 38 C3
Gleneaston Lawns 39 D3
Gleneaston Manor 39 D2
Gleneaston Pk 38 C3
Gleneaston Ri 38 C3
Gleneaston Sq 39 D3
Gleneaston Vw 39 D2
Gleneaston Way 39 D2
Gleneaston Wds 38 C2
Glen Ellan Cl 12 C1
Glen Ellan Ct 12 C1
Glen Ellan Cres 12 C1
Glenfarne Rd 30 A4
Glenfield Av 52 A1
Glenfield Cl 52 A1
Glenfield Dr 52 A1
Glenfield Gro 52 A1
Glenfield Pk 52 A1
Glengara Cl **4** 75 F4
Glengara Pk 75 F4
Glengariff Par 46 A3
Glen Garth 76 C3
Glen Gro 77 D3
Glenhill Av 27 E4
Glenhill Ct 27 E4
Glenhill Dr 27 D4
Glenhill Gro 27 E4
Glenhill Rd 27 D4
Glenhill Vil
off Glenhill Rd 27 D4
Glen Lawn Dr 76 C3
Glenlucan 82 A3
Glenlyon Cres 70 A3
Glenlyon Gro 70 A3
Glenlyon Pk 70 A3
Glenmalure Pk 55 D3
Glenmalure Sq 64 B2
Glenmaroon Pk 53 D1
Glenmaroon Rd 53 D1
Glenmore Ct 71 E3
Glenmore Pk 71 E3
Glenmore Rd 45 D4
Glen Na Smol 82 B4
Glenomena Gro 65 E3
Glenomena Pk 65 E2
Glenpark Cl 42 C4
Glenpark Dr 42 C4
Glenpark Rd 42 C4
Glenshane Cl 68 A2
Glenshane Cres 68 A2
Glenshane Gdns 68 A2
Glenshane Grn 68 A2
Glenshane Gro 68 B2
Glenshane Lawns 68 A2
Glenshane Pk 68 A2
Glenshesk Rd 28 C4
Glenside Vil **2** 43 D4
Glen Ter **16** 78 A2
Glenties Dr 26 C4
Glenties Pk 26 C4
Glentow Rd 28 B4
Glentworth Pk 30 B3
Glenvale 51 E2
Glenvara Pk 70 A3
Glenvar Pk 74 A2
Glenview 77 F2
Glenview Dr **4** 69 F2
Glenview Ind Est 55 D3
Glenview Lawn 70 A1
Glenview Pk 69 F1
Glenville Av 24 C4
Glenville Ct 42 B1
Glenville Dr 24 B4
Glenville Garth 24 B4
Glenville Grn 24 C4
Glenville Gro 24 C4

Glenville Ind Est 65 E4
Glenville Lawn 24 B4
Glenville Rd 42 B1
Glenville Way 24 C4
Glen Wk 76 C3
Glenwood 82 A3
Glenwood Rd 30 A4
Glin Av 29 F2
Glin Cres 29 F2
Glin Dr 29 F2
Glin Glen 29 F2
Glin Gro 29 F2
Glin Pk 29 F2
Glin Rd 29 F2
Gloucester La
off Sean McDermott St Lwr 85 G1
Gloucester Pl 85 G1
Gloucester Pl Lwr 85 G1
Gloucester Pl N 85 G1
Gloucester Pl Upr
off Gloucester Pl 85 G1
Gloucester St S 85 G3
Glovers All 85 E5
Goatstown Av 64 C4
Goatstown Rd 65 D4
Gofton Hall 27 D3
Golden Br 54 B2
Goldenbridge Av 54 C3
Goldenbridge Gdns 54 C3
Goldenbridge Sta 54 C3
Goldenbridge Ter
off Connolly Av 54 C3
Golden La 84 D5
Goldsmith St 45 F4
Goldsmith Ter **13** 82 B2
Golf La 76 B2
Golf Links Rd 19 F4
Gordon Av 76 C2
Gordon Pl
off Richmond St S 56 A3
Gordon St 56 C2
Gorsefield Ct 48 A1
Gortbeg Av 45 D1
Gortbeg Dr 45 D1
Gortbeg Pk 45 D1
Gortbeg Rd 45 D1
Gortmore Av 45 D1
Gortmore Dr 45 D1
Gortmore Pk
off Gortmore Rd 45 D1
Gortmore Rd 45 D1
Gort Na Mona Dr 76 C2
Gosworth Pk 78 A3
Government Bldgs 85 G5
Gowrie Pk 75 E4
Gracefield Av 48 A2
Gracefield Ct 47 F1
Gracefield Rd 29 F4
Grace O'Malley Dr 33 E3
Grace O'Malley Rd 33 E3
Grace Pk Av 46 B2
Grace Pk Ct 28 C4
Grace Pk Gdns 46 B2
Grace Pk Hts 46 C1
Grace Pk Meadows 47 D1
Grace Pk Rd 46 B2
Grace Pk Ter 46 C2
Grafton St 85 F5
Graham Ct 85 F1
Graigue Ct 27 F1
Granard Br 25 D4
Granby La 85 E1
Granby Pl 85 E2
Granby Row 85 E1
Grand Canal Bk *Dublin 8* 84 A5
Grand Canal Bk (Ranelagh)
Dublin 8 56 A4
Grand Canal Business Cen 54 A3
Grand Canal Harbour
off James's St 55 D2
Grand Canal Pl N 84 A4
Grand Canal Quay 56 C2
Grand Canal St Lwr 56 C2
Grand Canal St Upr 56 C3
Grand Canal Vw 54 C3
Grand Par 56 A4
Grange, The *Deans Gra* 77 D1
Grange, The *Still.* 74 A4
Grange Abbey Cres 31 D3
Grange Abbey Dr 31 D3
Grange Abbey Gro 31 D3
Grange Abbey Rd 31 D3
Grange Av 31 E3
Grange Brook 71 E3
Grangebrook Av 71 E3
Grangebrook Cl 71 E3
Grangebrook Pk 71 E3
Grangebrook Vale 71 E3
Grange Castle Int Business Park 51 D4
Grange Cl *Dublin 13* 31 E4
Grange Cl *Sally.* 77 E2
Grange Cotts **1** 74 C4
Grange Ct 71 F3
Grange Cres 77 D1
Grange Downs 71 F1
Grange Dr 31 E4
Grangefield 72 B4
Grangegorman Lwr 84 C2
Grangegorman Upr 45 E4
Grange Gro **2** 74 C4
Grange Hall 72 B4
Grange Lo Av 31 D3
Grange Manor 51 D2
Grange Manor Av 71 F2
Grange Manor Cl 71 F2
Grange Manor Dr 71 F2
Grange Manor Gro 71 F2
Grange Manor Rd 71 F2
Grangemore 30 C3
Grangemore Av 30 C3
Grangemore Ct 30 C3
Grangemore Cres 30 C3
Grangemore Dr 30 C3
Grangemore Gro 30 C3
Grangemore Lawn 30 C3
Grangemore Pk 30 C3
Grangemore Ri 30 C3
Grangemore Rd 30 C3
Grange Par 31 E4
Grange Pk *Dublin 13* 31 E3
Grange Pk *Dublin 14* 71 E1
Grange Pk *Corn.* 76 C1
Grange Pk Av 48 C1
Grange Pk Cl 48 C1
Grange Pk Cres 48 C1
Grange Pk Dr 48 C1
Grange Pk Grn 48 C1
Grange Pk Gro 48 C1
Grange Pk Par 48 C1
Grange Pk Ri 48 C1
Grange Pk Rd 48 C1
Grange Pk Wk 48 C1
Grange Ri 31 E3
Grange Rd *Dublin 13* 30 C4
Grange Rd (Baldoyle)
Dublin 13 31 D3
Grange Rd *Dublin 14* 63 E4
Grange Rd *Dublin 16* 71 E1
Grange Vw Cl 51 E4
Grange Vw Ct 51 E4
Grange Vw Grn 51 E4
Grange Vw Gro 51 E4
Grange Vw Lawn 59 E1
Grange Vw Pk 59 E1
Grange Vw Rd 51 E4
Grange Vw Wk 51 E4
Grange Vw Way 59 E1
Grange Vw Wd 51 E4
Grange Way 31 E4
Grange Wd *Dublin 16* 72 A3
Grangewood *D.L.* 77 D1
Granitefield 77 E2
Granite Hall **5** 75 F4
Granite Pl 57 D4
Granite Ter
off Inchicore Ter S 54 B2
Grantham Pl 56 A3
Grantham St 56 A3
Grants Av 58 A4
Grants Ct 58 A4
Grants Cres 58 A4
Grants Dr 66 A1
Grants Hill 58 A4
Grants La 66 A1
Grants Pk 66 A1
Grants Ri 58 A4
Grants Rd 66 A1
Grants Row *Dublin 2* 56 C2
Grants Row *Greenogue* 66 A1
Grants Vw 58 A4
Granville Cl 77 E3
Granville Cres 77 E3
Granville Pk 74 B4
Granville Rd *Cabin.* 77 E3
Granville Rd *Deans Gra* 76 B1
Grattan Br 85 E3
Grattan Ct E
off Grattan St 56 C2
Grattan Cres 54 B2
Grattan Hall 30 C3
Grattan Lo 30 C3
Grattan Par 46 A3
Grattan Pk 83 E3
Grattan Pl
off Grattan St 56 C2
Grattan St 56 C2
Gray Sq
off Gray St 84 C5
Gray St 84 C5
Great Clarence Pl 56 C2
Great Western Av
off North Circular Rd 45 F4
Great Western Sq 45 F4
Great Western Vil 45 F4
Greek St 84 D3
Green, The *Dublin 9* 29 D3
Green, The (Ballinteer)
Dublin 16 72 B3
Green, The (Ballyboden)
Dublin 16 70 C2
Green, The *Dublin 24* 61 D3
Green, The *Ashb.* 8 C3
Green, The *Bray* 82 B1
Green, The *Celbr.* 37 D3
Green, The (Dunboyne Castle)
Dunb. 20 B3
Green, The (Lutterell Hall)
Dunb. 20 B1
Green, The *Kins.* 13 E4
Green, The *Mala.* 15 D4
Green, The (Robswall) **2** *Mala.* 19 F1
Green, The *Manor.* 23 E2
Green, The *Mulh.* 24 A1
Green, The *Swords* 13 D1
Greenacre Ct 70 B1
Greencastle Av 29 F3
Greencastle Cres 29 F2
Greencastle Dr 29 F2
Greencastle Par 30 A4
Greencastle Pk 29 F2
Greencastle Rd 29 F2
Greendale Av 49 D1
Greendale Rd 49 D1
Greendale Shop Cen 49 D1
Greenfield Cl 36 A3
Greenfield Cres 65 D2
Greenfield Dr 36 B3
Greenfield Gro 8 C3
Greenfield Manor 65 D2
Greenfield Pk *Dublin 4* 65 D2
Greenfield Pk *Dublin 24* 70 A3
Greenfield Rd *Dublin 13* 32 B2
Greenfield Rd *Still.* 65 F4
Greenfort Av 52 A1
Greenfort Cl 52 B1
Greenfort Cres 52 B1
Greenfort Dr 52 A1
Greenfort Gdns 52 B1
Greenfort Lawns 52 B1
Greenfort Pk 52 A1
Greenhills Business Cen 61 F4
Greenhills Business Pk 69 F1
Greenhills Ind Est 62 A2
Greenhills Rd *Dublin 12* 61 F2
Greenhills Rd *Dublin 24* 61 F4
Green Isle Business Pk 60 A3
Green Isle Ct **1** 60 A3
Greenlands *Dublin 16* 73 D3
Greenlands, The *Dublin 14* 63 F4
Green La *Leix.* 39 E3
Green La *R'coole* 66 A4
Greenlawns **1** 29 F2
Greenlea Av 63 D3
Greenlea Dr 63 D3
Greenlea Gro 63 D3
Greenlea Pk 63 D3
Greenlea Rd 63 D3
Greenmount Av 55 F4
Greenmount Ct
off Greenmount Av 55 F4
Greenmount La 55 F4
Greenmount Lawns 63 E3
Greenmount Rd 63 F2
Greenmount Sq
off Greenmount La 55 F4
Greenogue Dr 66 B3
Greenore Ter
off Grattan St 56 C2
Green Pk 64 A3
Green Pk Rd *Bray* 82 A2
Greenpark Rd *Lucan* 50 B1
Greenridge Ct 24 C3
Green Rd *Black.* 74 A2
Green Rd, The *Dalkey* 78 C3
Green St 84 D2
Green St E 57 D2
Green St Little 84 D3
Greentrees Dr 62 B3
Greentrees Pk 62 B2
Greentrees Rd 62 B2
Greenview 19 D4
Greenville Av 55 F3
Greenville Rd 74 C3
Greenville Ter 55 F3
Greenwich Ct 64 A1
Greenwood Av 30 B3
Greenwood Cl 30 B3
Greenwood Ct 30 B3
Greenwood Dr 30 B3
Greenwood Lawn
off Greenwood Dr 30 B3
Greenwood Pk **2** 30 B3
Greenwood Wk 30 B3
Greenwood Way 30 B3
Grenville La 85 F1
Grenville St 85 F1
Greygates 65 F4
Greyhound Racing Stadium 55 F4
Greys La 33 F4
Greystones Sta 83 F3
Greythorn Pk 75 F4
Griffeen 51 E2
Griffeen Av 51 D2
Griffeen Glen Av 51 D2
Griffeen Glen Boul 51 E2
Griffeen Glen Chase 51 D2
Griffeen Glen Ct 51 E2
Griffeen Glen Cres 51 D2
Griffeen Glen Dale 51 D2
Griffeen Glen Dene 51 D2
Griffeen Glen Dr 51 E2
Griffeen Glen Grn 51 D2
Griffeen Glen Gro 51 E2
Griffeen Glen Lawn 51 D2
Griffeen Glen Pk 51 D2
Griffeen Glen Rd (east) *Lucan* 51 E2
Griffeen Glen Rd (west) *Lucan* 51 D2
Griffeen Glen Vale 51 E2
Griffeen Glen Vw 51 D2
Griffeen Glen Way 51 E2
Griffeen Rd 51 E2
Griffeen Way 51 E1
Griffin Rath Hall 36 B3
Griffin Rath Manor 36 B3
Griffin Rath Rd 36 B4
Griffith Av *Dublin 9* 46 B1
Griffith Av *Dublin 11* 45 F1
Griffith Br 54 C3
Griffith Cl 45 E1
Griffith Ct 46 C2
Griffith Downs 46 B1
Griffith Dr 27 E4
Griffith Hts 45 E1
Griffith Lawns 46 A1
Griffith Par 27 E4
Griffith Rd 27 E4
Griffith Sq
off Wesley Pl 55 F3
Griffith Sq S
off South Circular Rd 55 E3
Griffith Wk 46 C2
Grosvenor Av 82 C3
Grosvenor Ct *Dublin 3* 47 F2
Grosvenor Ct *Dublin 6W* 62 C3
Grosvenor Lo 63 F1
Grosvenor Pk 63 F1
Grosvenor Pl 63 F1
Grosvenor Rd 63 F1
Grosvenor Sq 55 F4
Grosvenor Ter **5** *Dalkey* 78 C3
Grosvenor Ter *D.L.* 75 E3
Grosvenor Vil 63 F1
Grotto Av 74 A1
Grotto Pl 65 F3
Grove, The *Dublin 5* 48 C2
Grove, The *Dublin 9* 46 C1
Grove, The (Ballinteer)
Dublin 16 72 B3
Grove, The (Meadow Mt)
Dublin 16 72 A2
Grove, The *Dublin 24* 69 E2
Grove, The (Cookstown)
Dublin 24 60 C4
Grove, The (Kilnamanagh)
Dublin 24 60 C3
Grove, The *Bray* 82 B1
Grove, The *Celbr.* 37 E4
Grove, The (Abbeyfarm) *Celbr.* 37 D4
Grove, The (Dunboyne Castle)
Dunb. 20 B3
Grove, The (Lutterell Hall) *Dunb.* 20 B1
Grove, The (Plunkett Hall) *Dunb.* 20 A1
Grove, The (Sadleir Hall) *Dunb.* 20 A2
Grove, The *Gra M.* 51 D2
Grove, The *Grey.* 83 D1
Grove, The *Kins.* 13 E4
Grove, The *Lou.V.* 39 E2
Grove Av *Dublin 6*
off Grove Rd 55 F4
Grove Av (Finglas) *Dublin 11* 27 E3
Grove Av *Black.* 74 A2
Grove Av *Mala.* 15 E4
Grove Ct **1** 12 A2
Grovedale 80 A3
Grove Ho 76 B3
Grove Ho Gdns 74 A3
Grove La 30 B3
Grove Lawn *Black.* 74 A3
Grove Lawn *Mala.* 15 E4
Grove Pk *Dublin 6* 55 F4
Grove Pk *Dublin 13* 30 B3
Grove Pk Av 27 E3
Grove Pk Cres 27 F3
Grove Pk Dr 27 E3
Grove Pk Rd 27 E3
Grove Rd (Rathmines) *Dublin 6* 55 F4
Grove Rd (Finglas) *Dublin 11* 27 E3
Grove Rd (Blanchardstown)
Dublin 15 24 B4
Grove Rd *Mala.* 15 D4
Grove Wd 27 E3
Guild St 56 C1
Guilford Ter 81 E3
Guinness Brewery 84 A4
Guinness Enterprise Cen 84 B5
Gulistan Cotts 56 A4
Gulistan Pl 56 A4
Gulistan Ter 56 A4
Gullivers Retail Pk 28 A1
Gurteen Av 53 E2
Gurteen Pk 53 E2
Gurteen Rd 53 E1

H

Hacketsland 81 E2
Haddington Lawns 78 A3
Haddington Pk **6** 78 A3
Haddington Pl 56 C3
Haddington Rd 56 C3
Haddinton Ter 75 F3
Haddon Pk
off Seaview Av N 47 E3
Haddon Rd 47 E3
Hadleigh Ct 43 E1
Hadleigh Grn 43 E1
Hadleigh Pk 43 E1
Hagans Ct 85 H6
Haigh Ter 75 F3
Hainault Dr 76 C3
Hainault Gro 76 C3
Hainault Lawn 76 C3
Hainault Pk 76 B3
Hainault Rd 76 B2
Halliday Rd 84 A2
Halliday Sq 84 A2
Halston St 84 D2
Hamilton Ct **1** 20 C2
Hamilton Hall 20 C3
Hamilton St 84 B6
Hammond La 84 C3
Hammond St 84 C6
Hampstead Av 28 A4
Hampstead Ct 28 A4
Hampstead Pk 46 A1
Hampton Ct 48 A3
Hampton Cres 65 F3
Hampton Grn 45 D3
Hampton Hermitage &
Theresian Trust 46 C2
Hampton Pk 65 F4
Hampton Wd Av 27 E1
Hampton Wd Ct 27 E1
Hampton Wd Cres 27 E1
Hampton Wd Dr 27 E1
Hampton Wd Grn 27 E1
Hampton Wd Lawn 27 E1

Hampton Wd Pk 27 E1
Hampton Wd Rd 27 E1
Hampton Wd Sq 27 E1
Hampton Wd Way 27 E1
Hanbury La *Dublin 8* 84 C4
Hanbury La **2** *Lucan* 40 C4
Hannaville Pk 63 E2
Hanover La 84 D5
Hanover Quay 56 C2
Hanover Sq W
off Hanover La 84 D5
Hanover St E 85 H4
Hanover St W
off Ash St 84 C5
Hansfield 23 E2
Hansfield Rd 23 D2
Hansted Cl **1** 50 C3
Hansted Cres 50 C3
Hansted Dale 50 C3
Hansted Pk 50 C3
Hansted Pl **2** 50 C3
Hansted Rd 50 C3
Hansted Way 50 C3
Ha'penny Br 85 F3
Harbour Ct
off Marlborough St 85 F3
Harbour Cres 78 B3
Harbour Ind Est 82 C1
Harbourmaster Pl 85 H2
Harbour Rd *Dublin 13* 33 E2
Harbour Rd *Dalkey* 78 B2
Harbour Rd *D.L.* 75 E2
Harbour Ter 75 E2
Harbour Vw
off St. Lawrence Rd 33 F3
Harcourt Grn 56 A3
Harcourt La
off Adelaide Rd 56 A3
Harcourt Rd 56 A3
Harcourt Sta 56 A3
Harcourt St 56 A3
Harcourt Ter 56 A3
Harcourt Ter La 56 B3
Hardbeck Av 62 A1
Hardiman Rd 46 A2
Hardwicke Pl 46 A4
Hardwicke St 85 E1
Harelawn Av 52 B2
Harelawn Cres 52 B2
Harelawn Dr 52 B1
Harelawn Grn 52 B2
Harelawn Gro 52 B1
Harelawn Pk 52 B2
Harlech Cres 65 D4
Harlech Downs 65 D4
Harlech Gro 65 D4
Harlech Vil 65 D4
Harman St 84 B6
Harmonstown Rd 48 A2
Harmonstown Sta 48 A2
Harmony Av 64 C1
Harmony Row 56 C2
Harold Rd 84 A2
Harolds Cross Rd 55 F4
Harold's Gra Rd 72 A4
Haroldville Av 84 A6
Harrington St 56 A3
Harrison Row 63 F2
Harry St 85 F5
Hartstown Rd 23 F3
Harty Av 62 B1
Harty Ct 62 B1
Harty Pl 84 D6
Harvard 65 D4
Hastings St 57 D2
Hastings Ter **17** 78 A2
Hatch La 56 A3
Hatch Pl
off Hatch La 56 B3
Hatch St Lwr 56 A3
Hatch St Upr 56 A3
Havelock Pl
off Bath Av 57 D3
Havelock Sq E 57 D3
Havelock Sq N 57 D3
Havelock Sq S 57 D3
Havelock Sq W 57 D3
Havelock Ter
off Bath Av 57 D3
Haven, The *Dublin 9* 46 A1
Haven, The *Mala.* 14 C3
Haven Vw **2** 14 C3
Haverty Rd 47 D3
Hawkins La 83 F3
Hawkins St 85 G3
Hawthorn Av 46 C4
Hawthorn Dr 72 B2
Hawthorn Lawn 43 E1
Hawthorn Lo 43 E1
Hawthorn Manor **1** 74 B3
Hawthorn Pk 12 C3
Hawthorn Rd *Dublin 12* 61 D1
Hawthorn Rd *Bray* 82 A2
Hawthorns, The **15** *Abb.* 81 E1
Hawthorns, The *Ashb.* 8 C2
Hawthorns Rd 73 D3
Hawthorn Ter 46 C4
Hawthorn Vw 37 D2
Hayden's La 50 C2
Haydens Pk 51 D3
Haydens Pk Av 51 D3
Haydens Pk Cl 51 D2
Haydens Pk Dale 51 D3
Haydens Pk Dr 51 D3
Haydens Pk Glade 51 D3
Haydens Pk Grn 51 D2
Haydens Pk Gro 51 D3
Haydens Pk Lawn 51 D3
Haydens Pk Vw 51 D3
Haydens Pk Wk 51 D2
Haydens Pk Way 51 D3
Hayden Sq 65 E4
Haymarket 84 C3
Hayworth Dr 23 D3
Hayworth Ms 23 D3
Hayworth Ter 23 D3
Hazel Av 73 E2
Hazelbrook Ct 63 E2
Hazelbrook Dr 63 D2
Hazelbrook Pk 61 F4
Hazelbrook Rd 63 D2
Hazelbury Grn 23 E1
Hazelbury Pk 23 E2
Hazel Ct **6** 19 E4
Hazelcroft Gdns 27 D4
Hazelcroft Pk 45 D1
Hazelcroft Rd 27 D4
Hazeldene 65 D1
Hazelgrove *Jobs.* 68 B3
Hazel Gro *Port.* 19 E4
Hazelgrove Ct 68 B3
Hazel Lawn (Blanchardstown)
Dublin 15 24 C4
Hazel Lawn **5** *D.L.* 77 E1
Hazel Pk 63 D2
Hazel Rd 47 D1
Hazel Vil 73 E2
Hazelwood *Bray* 82 A2
Hazelwood *D'bate* 11 E1
Hazelwood *Shank.* 81 E3
Hazelwood Av 23 F3
Hazelwood Cl 60 A2
Hazelwood Ct *Dublin 5* 29 E3
Hazelwood Ct *Clons.* 23 F3
Hazelwood Cres *Clond.* 60 A2
Hazelwood Cres *Clons.* 23 F3
Hazelwood Dr 29 E4
Hazelwood Grn 23 F3
Hazelwood Gro 29 E4
Hazelwood La 60 A2
Hazelwood Pk 29 E4
Hazelwood Vw 60 A2
Headford Gro 72 A1
Healthfield Rd 63 F2
Healy St
off Rutland Pl N 46 B4
Heaney Av 53 D3
Heany Av 78 C3
Hearse Rd 10 A3
Heath, The *Dublin 6W* 62 C4
Heath, The *Dublin 24* 60 C4
Heath Cres 44 B2
Heather Cl 72 A3
Heather Dr 72 A3
Heather Gro *Dublin 16* 72 A3
Heather Gro *Palm.* 52 C1
Heather Lawn 72 A3
Heather Pk 72 A3
Heather Rd *Dublin 16* 72 A3
Heather Rd *Sandy.* 73 E4
Heather Vw Av 69 D3
Heather Vw Cl 69 D3
Heather Vw Dr 69 D3
Heather Vw Lawn 69 D3
Heather Vw Pk 69 D3
Heather Vw Rd 69 D3
Heathervue 83 E3
Heathfield 75 D3
Heath Gro 44 C2
Hedgerows, The 76 B2
Heidelberg 65 D4
Heights, The *Dublin 16* 72 B4
Heights, The *Dunb.* 20 B3
Heights, The *Kins.* 13 E4
Heights, The *Mala.* 19 E1
Hellers Copse 74 A3
Hendrick La
off Benburb St 84 B3
Hendrick Pl 84 B3
Hendrick St 84 B3
Henley Ct 64 B4
Henley Pk 64 B4
Henley Vil 64 B4
Henrietta La 84 D1
Henrietta Pl 84 D2
Henrietta St 84 D2
Henry Pl 85 F2
Henry Rd 53 E3
Henry St 85 E2
Herbert Av 65 F2
Herbert Cotts 57 D4
Herbert Hill 72 C2
Herbert La 56 C3
Herberton Dr 55 D3
Herberton Pk 55 D3
Herberton Rd *Dublin 8* 55 D3
Herberton Rd *Dublin 12* 55 D3
Herbert Pk 56 C4
Herbert Pl 56 C3
Herbert Rd *Dublin 4* 57 D3
Herbert Rd (Blanchardstown)
Dublin 15 25 D4
Herbert Rd *Bray* 82 A2
Herbert St 85 H6
Herbert Vw **13** 82 A2
Hermitage Av 71 F2
Hermitage Cl 71 F2
Hermitage Ct 71 F2
Hermitage Cres 41 F4
Hermitage Downs 71 F2
Hermitage Dr 71 F2
Hermitage Gdn 41 F4
Hermitage Grn 41 F4
Hermitage Gro 71 F2
Hermitage Lawn 71 F2
Hermitage Manor 41 F4
Hermitage Pk *Dublin 16* 71 F2
Hermitage Pk *Lucan* 41 F4
Hermitage Pl 41 F4
Hermitage Rd 41 F4
Hermitage Valley 41 F4
Hermitage Vw 71 F2
Hermitage Way 41 F4
Heronford La 80 B2
Heuston Luas Sta 84 A3
Heuston Sta 55 D1
Hewardine Ter
off Killarney St 85 H1
Heytesbury La 56 C4
Heytesbury Pl
off Long La 84 D6
Heytesbury St 85 E6
Hibernian Av 46 C4
Hibernian Ind Est 69 E1
Hickey's La 8 C4
Highfield Av 71 F3
Highfield Cl 12 C2
Highfield Ct 63 F2
Highfield Cres 12 C2
Highfield Downs 12 C2
Highfield Dr 71 F3
Highfield Grn 12 C2
Highfield Gro 64 A2
Highfield Lawn 12 C2
Highfield Pk *Dublin 14* 64 B4
Highfield Pk *Leix.* 39 E3
Highfield Rd 63 F2
Highland Av 76 C3
Highland Gro 76 C3
Highland Lawn 76 C3
Highland Vw 76 C3
High Pk 46 C1
Highridge Grn 73 E2
High St *Dublin 8* 84 D4
High St *Dublin 24* 69 D1
Highthorn Pk 75 E4
Highthorn Wds **3** 75 E4
Hill, The *Dublin 16* 72 B4
Hill, The *Black.* 75 E3
Hill, The *Mala.* 19 D1
Hill, The **6** *Mulh.* 24 A2
Hill, The *Still.* 74 A3
Hillbrook Wds 24 A3
Hill Cotts **1** 79 F1
Hill Ct 19 F2
Hillcourt Pk 77 F1
Hillcourt Rd 77 F1
Hillcrest *Dublin 6W* 70 C1
Hillcrest *Lucan* 50 C1
Hillcrest (Mooretown) **1** *Swords* 14 B3
Hillcrest Av **2** *Grey.* 83 D4
Hillcrest Av *Lucan* 50 C1
Hillcrest Cl 50 B1
Hillcrest Ct 50 C1
Hillcrest Dr 50 C1
Hillcrest Grn 50 C1
Hillcrest Gro 50 C1
Hillcrest Hts 50 C1
Hillcrest Lawns 50 C1
Hillcrest Pk *Dublin 11* 27 F3
Hillcrest Pk *Lucan* 50 C1
Hillcrest Rd 50 C1
Hillcrest Vw 50 C1
Hillcrest Wk 50 C1
Hillcrest Way 50 C1
Hill Dr 19 D1
Hillsbrook Av 62 B2
Hillsbrook Cres 62 B2
Hillsbrook Dr 62 C2
Hillsbrook Gro 62 B2
Hillside *Dalkey* 78 B3
Hillside *Grey.* 83 E2
Hillside Dr 63 F4
Hillside Pk 71 D2
Hillside Rd 83 F3
Hillside Vw 49 E1
Hills Ind Est 41 D3
Hill St 85 F1
Hilltop Lawn 81 D4
Hilltop Shop Cen 48 B1
Hilltown Cl 12 B2
Hilltown Ct **4** 12 B2
Hilltown Grn **5** 12 B2
Hilltown Gro 12 B2
Hilltown Lawn 12 B2
Hilltown Pk 12 B2
Hilltown Rd 12 B2
Hilltown Way 12 B2
Hill Vw *Dublin 16* 72 A2
Hillview *R'coole* 66 A3
Hillview Cotts **3** 77 D2
Hillview Dr 77 D2
Hillview Glade **2** 72 A2
Hillview Gro 72 A2
Hillview Lawn 77 D2
Hilton Gdns 72 B3
Hoeys Ct
off Castle St 84 D4
Hogan Av 56 C2
Hogan Pl 56 C2
Hole In The Wall Rd, The 30 C3
Hole In Wall Rd, The 30 C2
Holles Row 85 H5
Holles St 85 H5
Hollows, The **7** 40 C4
Holly Av 73 E3
Hollybank Av 64 B1
Hollybank Rd 46 A2
Hollybrook Ct
off Hollybrook Rd 47 E3
Hollybrook Ct Dr 47 E3
Hollybrook Gro 47 D3
Hollybrook Pk 47 E3
Hollybrook Rd 47 E3
Holly Ct 81 D1
Holly Pk 81 E3
Holly Pk Av 74 B4
Holly Rd *Dublin 9* 47 D2
Holly Rd *Dublin 12* 61 D1
Hollyville Lawn 42 C4
Hollywell 27 E2
Hollywood Dr 73 D1
Hollywood Pk 73 D1
Holmston Av 75 F4
Holmwood 77 D4
Holycross Av 46 B3
Holy Cross Coll 46 B3
Holyrood Pk
off Sandymount Av 57 E4
Holywell 73 D2
Holywell Av *Dublin 13* 30 C4
Holywell Av *Swords* 13 D3
Holywell Ct **1** 13 D4
Holywell Cres *Dublin 13* 30 C4
Holywell Cres *Swords* 13 D4
Holywell Dr 13 D3
Holywell Gdns 13 D3
Holywell Glen 13 E4
Holywell Gro 13 E4
Holywell Pk 13 D4
Holywell Pl **2** 13 D4
Holywell Ri 13 D4
Holywell Rd *Dublin 13* 30 C4
Holywell Rd *Swords* 13 D4
Holywell Row 13 D4
Holywell Vw 13 E4
Holywell Wk 13 D4
Holywell Way 13 E4
Holywell Wd 13 D4
Home Fm Pk 46 B2
Home Fm Rd 46 A1
Homelawn Av 69 F2
Homelawn Dr 69 F2
Homelawn Gdns 69 F2
Homelawn Rd 69 F2
Homelawn Vil 69 E2
Homeleigh 42 B2
Home Vil 56 C4
Homeville *Dublin 6* 64 A1
Homeville, The *Dublin 24* 70 A2
Homeville Ct **4** 70 A2
Honey Pk **8** 77 E1
Hope Av 46 C4
Hope St 56 C2
Hopkins Sq 65 E4
Horseman's Row
off Parnell St 85 F1
Horton Ct 63 E3
Hospital Sta 68 C1
Hotel Yd 85 E3
House of Retreat 54 B3
House of St. John of God 74 A4
Howard St 56 C2
Howth Castle 33 D3
Howth Golf Course 33 D4
Howth Junct 31 D4
Howth Rd *Dublin 3* 47 D3
Howth Rd *Dublin 5* 48 A2
Howth Rd (Howth) *Dublin 13* 33 D2
Howth Sta 33 E2
Howth Vw Pk 30 C4
H.S. Reilly Br 44 C1
Huband Br 56 C3
Huband Rd 54 A4
Hudson Rd 78 A2
Hughes Rd E 62 B1
Hughes Rd N 62 B1
Hughes Rd S 62 B1
Hume Av 53 D4
Hume Cen 53 E3
Hume St 85 G6
Hunters Av 70 A4
Hunters Brook 83 D4
Hunters Ct 70 A4
Hunters Cres 70 A4
Hunters Grn 70 A4
Hunters Gro 70 A4
Hunters Hill 70 A4
Hunters La *Dublin 24* 70 A4
Hunters La *Ashb.* 8 C2
Hunters Meadow 70 A4
Hunters Par 70 A4
Hunters Pl 70 A4
Hunters Rd 70 A4
Hunter's Run 23 F1
Hunter's Run The Cl 23 F1
Hunter's Run The Dr 23 F1
Hunter's Run The Glade 23 F1
Hunter's Run The Gro 23 E1
Hunter's Run The Pk 23 F1
Hunter's Run The Ri 23 F2
Hunter's Run The Vw 23 F1
Hunter's Run The Way 23 F2
Hunters Wk 70 A4
Hunters Way 70 A4
Huntsgrove 8 C2
Huntstown Av 23 F2
Huntstown Cl 24 A2
Huntstown Ct 23 F2
Huntstown Dr 23 F2
Huntstown Glen 23 F2
Huntstown Grn 24 A2
Huntstown Gro 24 A2
Huntstown Lawn 24 A2
Huntstown Pk 24 A2
Huntstown Ri 24 A2

Mayne Rd 31 D1
Maynooth Business Campus 36 B4
Maynooth Pk 36 B3
Maynooth Rd 20 A3
Maynooth Sta 36 B2
Mayola Ct 64 B4
Mayor St Lwr 56 C1
Mayor St Upr 57 D1
May St 46 B3
Mayville Ter **1** 78 C3
Maywood Av 48 C2
Maywood Cl 48 C2
Maywood Cres 48 C2
Maywood Dr 48 C2
Maywood Gro 48 C2
Maywood La 48 C2
Maywood Pk 48 C2
Maywood Rd 48 C2
Meades Ter 56 C2
Meadow, The *Dublin 16* 72 B3
Meadow, The *Mala.* 19 F1
Meadow Av **2** 72 B2
Meadowbank 63 F3
Meadowbrook 36 A3
Meadowbrook Av *Dublin 13* 31 F4
Meadowbrook Av *Mayn.* 36 A3
Meadowbrook Cl 36 A3
Meadow Brook Ct *Ashb.* 8 C3
Meadowbrook Ct *Mayn.* 36 A3
Meadowbrook Cres 36 A3
Meadowbrook Dr 36 A3
Meadowbrook Lawn 31 F4
Meadowbrook Lawns 36 A3
Meadowbrook Pk 31 F4
Meadowbrook Rd 36 A3
Meadow Cl *Dublin 16* 72 A2
Meadow Cl *Black.* 74 B4
Meadow Copse 23 F2
Meadow Ct **1** *Grey.* 83 D4
Meadow Ct **1** *Lough.* 81 D1
Meadow Dale **1** 23 F2
Meadow Downs 23 F3
Meadow Dr 23 F2
Meadow Grn 23 F3
Meadow Gro 72 A2
Meadow Mt 72 A2
Meadow Pk 72 A2
Meadow Pk Av 72 A1
Meadows, The *Dublin 5* 48 A2
Meadows, The *Celbr.* 37 D2
Meadows, The *Dunb.* 20 B2
Meadows E, The 60 C4
Meadows W, The 60 C4
Meadow Vale 77 D2
Meadow Vw *Dublin 14* 72 A2
Meadow Vw *Dunb.* 20 B2
Meadowview Gro 50 B1
Meadow Vil **1** 72 A2
Meadow Way 23 F2
Meakstown Cotts 27 D1
Meath Pl *Dublin 8* 84 C5
Meath Pl *Bray* 82 C2
Meath Rd 82 C3
Meath Sq
off Gray St 84 C5
Meath St 84 C4
Meehan Sq 65 E3
Meetinghouse La
off Mary's Abbey 85 E3
Mellifont Av 75 F3
Mellowes Av 26 C3
Mellowes Ct 27 D3
Mellowes Cres 27 D3
Mellowes Pk 26 C3
Mellowes Rd 26 C3
Mellows Br 84 B3
Melrose Av *Dublin 3* 46 C3
Melrose Av *Clond.* 51 F4
Melrose Cres 51 F4
Melrose Grn 51 F4
Melrose Gro 51 F4
Melrose Lawn 51 F4
Melrose Pk *Clond.* 51 F4
Melrose Pk *Swords* 13 E4
Melrose Rd 51 F4
Melville Cl 27 E2
Melville Ct 27 D2
Melville Cres 27 D2
Melville Dr 27 D2
Melville Grn 27 D2
Melville Gro 27 E2
Melville Pk 27 D2
Melville Ter 27 D2
Melville Vw 27 D2
Melville Way 27 D2
Melvin Rd 63 E2
Memorial Rd 85 G3
Mercer St Lwr 85 E5
Mercer St Upr 85 E6
Merchamp 48 A4
Merchants Quay 84 C4
Merchants Rd 57 D1
Meretimo Vil **26** 82 C3
Meridianpoint 83 F3
Merlyn Dr 65 E1
Merlyn Pk 65 E1
Merlyn Rd 65 E1
Merrion Cres 65 F2
Merrion Gro 65 F3
Merrion Pk 65 F4
Merrion Pl 85 G5
Merrion Rd 57 D4
Merrion Row 85 G6
Merrion Shop Cen 65 E1
Merrion Sq E 85 H5
Merrion Sq N 85 H5
Merrion Sq S 85 H5
Merrion Sq W 85 G5
Merrion Strand 65 F1
Merrion St Lwr
off Clare St 85 H5
Merrion St Upr 85 G6
Merrion Vw Av 65 E1
Merrion Village 65 E1
Merrywell Ind Est 61 E2
Merton Av 55 E3
Merton Cres 64 B2
Merton Dr 64 B1
Merton Rd 64 B2
Merton Wk 64 B2
Merville Av *Dublin 3* 46 C3
Merville Av *Still.* 73 F2
Merville Rd 73 F2
Mespil Rd 56 B3
Mews, The *Dublin 3* 47 F3
Mews, The (Dollymount)
Dublin 3 48 B4
Mews, The **6** *Mala.* 19 F1
Mews, The *Sally.* 77 E2
Michael Collins Pk 52 A4
Middle III 47 F2
Milesian Av 13 E3
Milesian Ct 13 E3
Milesian Gro 13 E3
Milesian Lawn 13 E3
Milford 14 B3
Military Cem 44 C3
Military Rd (Rathmines)
Dublin 6 56 A4
Military Rd (Kilmainham)
Dublin 8 55 D2
Military Rd (Phoenix Pk)
Dublin 8 54 A1
Military Rd *Kill.* 79 E2
Millbank 19 E4
Millbourne Av 46 A2
Millbrook Av 30 B4
Millbrook Ct 55 D2
Millbrook Dr 30 C4
Millbrook Gro 30 B4
Millbrook Lawns 69 E2
Millbrook Rd 30 B4
Millbrook Village
off Prospect La 64 C2
Mill Cen 52 B4
Mill Ct Av 59 F1
Mill Ct Dr 59 F1
Mill Ct Way 59 F1
Millennium Br 85 E3
Millennium Business Pk 25 F1
Millers Wd 82 A3
Millfarm 20 C2
Millfield 19 E4
Millgate Dr 62 B3
Mill Gro 83 E4
Mill La *Dublin 8* 84 C6
Mill La *Dublin 15* 44 A1
Mill La *Dublin 20* 43 D4
Mill La *Leix.* 39 F3
Mill La *Lough.* 81 E2
Mill La Business Pk 40 A3
Millmount Av 46 A2
Millmount Gro 64 B3
Millmount Pl 46 B2
Millmount Ter (Drumcondra)
Dublin 9 off Millmount Av 46 B2
Millmount Ter (Dundrum)
Dublin 14 off Millmount Gro 64 B3
Millmount Vil 46 A2
Mill Pk 60 A1
Mill Pond Apts, The **4** 60 B1
Mill Race Av 66 C3
Millrace Cl 44 A2
Mill Race Ct 66 C3
Mill Race Cres 66 C3
Mill Race Dr 66 C3
Mill Race Gdn 66 C3
Mill Race Grn 67 D3
Mill Race Pk 66 C3
Millrace Rd 44 A2
Mill Race Vw 66 C3
Mill Race Wk 66 C3
Mill Rd *Dublin 15* 25 D4
Mill Rd *Grey.* 83 E4
Mill Rd *Sagg.* 66 C3
Millstead 25 D4
Millstream 19 E4
Millstream Rd 40 B4
Mill St 84 C6
Milltown Av 64 B2
Milltown Br 9 D3
Milltown Br Rd 64 B2
Milltown Dr 64 A4
Milltown Est 8 C3
Milltown Gro 64 A4
Milltown Hill
off Milltown Rd 64 B2
Milltown Path 64 B2
Milltown Rd *Dublin 6* 64 B2
Milltown Rd *Ashb.* 9 D3
Milltown Sta 64 B2
Millview Cl **1** 14 B4
Millview Ct 14 B4
Millview Lawns 14 B4
Millview Rd 14 B4
Millwood Pk 30 B4
Millwood Vil 30 B4
Milners Sq 28 B3
Milton Ter **14** 82 B2
Milward Ter **16** 82 C3
Mine Hill La 80 A4
Misery Hill 56 C2
Moatfield Av 30 A4
Moatfield Pk 30 A4
Moatfield Rd 30 A4
Moatview Av 29 F2
Moatview Ct 29 F1
Moatview Dr 29 F1
Moatview Gdns 29 F2
Moeran Rd 62 B1
Moira Rd 84 A2
Moland Pl
off Talbot St 85 G2
Molesworth Pl
off Molesworth St 85 G5
Molesworth St 85 F5
Molyneux Yd 84 C4
Monalea Dr 70 A2
Monalea Gro 70 A2
Monalea Pk 70 A2
Monalea Wd 70 A2
Monaloe Av 77 D3
Monaloe Ct **1** 77 D3
Monaloe Cres **2** 77 D2
Monaloe Dr 77 D2
Monaloe Pk 77 D2
Monaloe Pk Rd 77 D2
Monaloe Way 77 D2
Monarch Ind Est 69 D1
Monasterboice Rd 54 C4
Monastery Cres 60 C1
Monastery Dr 60 C1
Monastery Gate 61 D1
Monastery Gate Av 60 C1
Monastery Gate Cl 61 D1
Monastery Gate Copse 60 C1
Monastery Gate Grn 60 C1
Monastery Gate Lawns 61 D1
Monastery Gate Vil 60 C1
Monastery Heath 60 C1
Monastery Heath Av 60 C1
Monastery Heath Ct 60 C1
Monastery Heath Grn 60 C1
Monastery Heath Sq 60 C1
Monastery Hts **1** 60 C1
Monastery Pk 60 B1
Monastery Ri 60 B1
Monastery Rd 60 B1
Monastery Shop Cen 60 B1
Monastery Wk 60 C1
Monck Pl 45 F4
Monksfield 60 C1
Monksfield Ct 60 C1
Monksfield Downs 52 C4
Monksfield Gro 60 C1
Monksfield Hts 60 C1
Monksfield Lawn 52 C4
Monksfield Meadows 60 C1
Monksfield Wk 60 C1
Monkstown Av 75 D4
Monkstown Cres 75 D3
Monkstown Fm 75 D4
Monkstown Gate 75 E3
Monkstown Gro 75 D4
Monkstown Rd 74 C2
Monkstown Sq **4** 75 D4
Monkstown Valley 75 D3
Montague Ct
off Protestant Row 85 E6
Montague La 85 E6
Montague Pl
off Montague La 85 E6
Montague St 85 E6
Montebello Ter **17** 82 C3
Monte Vella **4** 78 B3
Montgommery Vw 13 E2
Montone Business Pk 53 D4
Montpelier Dr 55 D1
Montpelier Gdns 55 D1
Montpelier Hill 55 D1
Montpelier Par 74 C3
Montpelier Pk 84 A2
Montpelier Pl 74 C2
Montpelier Vw 68 A3
Montrose Av 29 D4
Montrose Cl 29 D4
Montrose Ct 29 D4
Montrose Cres 29 E3
Montrose Dr 29 D3
Montrose Gro 29 D4
Montrose Pk 29 D4
Moorefield 77 F4
Moore La 85 F2
Moore's Cotts **4** 74 B4
Moore St 85 F2
Mooretown Av 12 C1
Mooretown Gro 12 C1
Mooretown Pk 12 C1
Mooretown Rd 12 C1
Moorfield 52 A3
Moorfield Av 52 B3
Moorfield Cl **2** 52 B3
Moorfield Dr 52 B3
Moorfield Grn 52 B3
Moorfield Gro 52 A3
Moorfield Lawns 52 B3
Moorfield Par 52 B3
Moorfield Wk 52 A3
Moorings, The 15 E4
Moreen Av 73 D3
Moreen Cl 73 D4
Moreen Lawn **3** 73 D4
Moreen Pk 73 D4
Moreen Rd 73 D4
Moreen Wk 73 D4
Morehampton La 56 C4
Morehampton Rd 56 C4
Morehampton Sq 56 B4
Morehampton Ter 56 C4
Morgan Pl
off Inns Quay 84 D3
Morgan's Pl 43 F1
Morning Star Av 84 C2
Morning Star Rd 84 A6
Mornington Av 78 B2
Mornington Gro 29 F4
Mornington Rd 64 B1
Morrogh Ter 46 C2
Moss St 85 G3
Mountain Pk 69 E2
Mountain Vw 81 D4
Mountain Vw Apts **5** 82 B4
Mountain Vw Av
off Shamrock Vil 63 F1
Mountain Vw Cotts *Dublin 6* 64 B1
Mountain Vw Cotts *Castle.* 42 B2
Mountain Vw Dr 72 A1
Mountain Vw Pk *Dublin 14* 72 A1
Mountainview Pk *Grey.* 83 E2
Mountain Vw Rd *Dublin 6* 64 B1
Mountain Vw Rd **1** *Kill.* 79 E2
Mountain Vil **2** 79 E2
Mount Albany 74 B4
Mount Albion Rd 72 A1
Mount Albion Ter **1** 72 A1
Mount Alton 70 B2
Mount Alton Ct 70 B2
Mount Andrew 41 F4
Mount Andrew Av 42 A4
Mount Andrew Cl 42 A4
Mount Andrew Ct 41 F4
Mount Andrew Dale 42 A4
Mount Andrew Gro 42 A4
Mount Andrew Ri 42 A4
Mount Annville 73 E1
Mount Annville Conv 73 D1
Mount Annville Lawn 73 D1
Mount Annville Pk 73 E1
Mount Annville Rd 73 D1
Mount Annville Wd 73 E1
Mount Argus Cl 63 E1
Mount Argus Ct 63 E1
Mount Argus Cres 63 E1
Mount Argus Grn 63 E1
Mount Argus Gro 63 E1
Mount Argus Pk 63 E1
Mount Argus Rd 63 E1
Mount Argus Ter 63 E1
Mount Argus Vw 63 E1
Mount Argus Way 63 E1
Mount Auburn **1** 78 A4
Mount Bellew Cres **1** 51 F1
Mount Bellew Grn **2** 51 E1
Mount Bellew Ri **1** 51 E1
Mount Bellew Way 51 E1
Mount Brown 55 D2
Mount Carmel Av 64 C4
Mount Carmel Pk 70 A2
Mount Carmel Rd 64 C4
Mount Dillon Ct 29 F4
Mountdown Dr 62 B3
Mountdown Pk 62 B3
Mountdown Rd 62 B3
Mount Drinan Av 13 E4
Mount Drinan Cres 13 E4
Mount Drinan Gro **5** 13 E4
Mount Drinan Lawn **1** 18 A1
Mount Drinan Pk 13 E4
Mount Drinan Wk 13 E4
Mount Drummond Av 55 F4
Mount Drummond Sq 55 F4
Mount Eagle Dr 73 E4
Mount Eagle Grn 73 E4
Mount Eagle Gro 73 E4
Mount Eagle Lawn 73 E4
Mount Eagle Pk 73 E4
Mount Eagle Ri 73 E4
Mount Eagle Vw 73 E4
Mount Eagle Way 73 E4
Mount Eden Rd 64 C1
Mountfield 19 D1
Mount Gandon 40 C4
Mount Harold Ter 63 F1
Mounthaven 83 E1
Mount Jerome Cem 55 E4
Mountjoy Cotts 46 A3
Mountjoy Par
off North Circular Rd 46 B4
Mountjoy Pl 85 G1
Mountjoy Prison 46 A3
Mountjoy Prison Cotts
off Cowley Pl 46 A3
Mountjoy Sq E 46 B4
Mountjoy Sq N 46 A4
Mountjoy Sq S 85 F1
Mountjoy Sq W 46 A4
Mountjoy St 84 D1
Mountjoy St Mid 84 D1
Mount Merrion Av 65 F4
Mount Norris Vil **18** 82 C3
Mount Olive Gro 30 C4
Mount Olive Pk 30 C4
Mount Olive Rd 30 C4
Mountpleasant Av Lwr 56 A4
Mountpleasant Av Upr 56 A4
Mountpleasant Par
off Mountpleasant Pl 56 A4
Mountpleasant Pl 56 A4
Mountpleasant Sq 56 A4
Mountpleasant Vil **15** 82 A2
Mount Prospect Av 48 A4
Mount Prospect Dr 48 A3
Mount Prospect Gro 48 B3
Mount Prospect Lawns 48 A4
Mount Prospect Pk 48 A4
Mount Sackville Conv 43 E3

Mount Salus Rd 78 C4
Mountsandel 76 C4
Mount Sandford 64 C1
Mount Shannon Rd 55 D3
Mount St Cres 56 C3
Mount St Lwr 56 C2
Mount St Upr 85 H6
Mount Symon 23 E3
Mount Symon Av 23 F4
Mount Symon Cl 23 F3
Mount Symon Cres 23 E3
Mount Symon Dale 23 E3
Mount Symon Dr 23 F3
Mount Symon Grn 23 E4
Mount Symon Lawn 23 F4
Mount Symon Pk 23 F4
Mount Symon Ri 23 F3
Mount Tallant Av 63 E2
Mount Tallant Ter *off Harolds Cross Rd* 55 F4
Mount Temple Rd 84 B2
Mount Town Lwr 75 E4
Mounttown Pk **4** 75 E4
Mount Town Rd Upr 75 E3
Mount Vw Rd 24 A3
Mount Wd 75 E4
Mourne Rd 55 D3
Moyclare Av 31 F4
Moyclare Cl 31 F4
Moyclare Dr 31 F4
Moyclare Gdns 32 A2
Moyclare Pk 31 F4
Moyclare Rd 31 F4
Moycullen Rd 53 D2
Moy Elta Rd 46 C4
Moyglare Meadows 36 A1
Moyglare Rd 36 A1
Moyglare Village 36 A1
Moy Glas Av 51 E2
Moy Glas Chase 51 E2
Moy Glas Cl 51 E2
Moy Glas Ct 51 E2
Moy Glas Dale 51 E2
Moy Glas Dene 51 E2
Moy Glas Dr 51 E2
Moy Glas Glen 51 E2
Moy Glas Grn 51 E2
Moy Glas Gro 51 E2
Moy Glas Lawn 51 E2
Moy Glas Pk 51 E2
Moy Glas Rd 51 E2
Moy Glas Vale 51 E2
Moy Glas Vw 51 E2
Moy Glas Way 51 E2
Moy Glas Wd 51 E2
Moyle Cres 60 B1
Moyle Rd 45 D2
Moyne Pk 31 E2
Moyne Rd 64 B1
Moynihan Ct 69 F1
Moyville 71 D3
Moyville Lawns 71 D2
Muckross Av 62 B2
Muckross Cres 62 B2
Muckross Dr 62 C2
Muckross Grn 62 C2
Muckross Gro 62 B2
Muckross Par *off Killarney Par* 46 A3
Muckross Pk 62 B2
Muirfield Dr 54 A4
Mulally's La 66 B3
Mulberry Cres 42 C2
Mulberry Dr 42 C2
Mulberry Pk 42 C2
Mulcahy Keane Est 62 A2
Muldowney Ct 15 E4
Mulgrave St 75 F3
Mulgrave Ter 75 F4
Mulhuddart Wd 24 A1
Mullinastill Rd 81 D2
Mulroy Rd 45 E2
Mulvey Pk 64 C4
Munster St 45 F3
Munster Ter **3** 78 B2
Murphystown Rd 73 E4
Murrays Cotts *off Sarsfield Rd* 54 B2
Murtagh Rd 84 A2
Museum Sta 84 A3
Muskerry Rd 53 F2
Mygan Business Pk 27 D2
Mygan Pk Ind Est 27 D2
Myra Cotts 54 C2
Myra Manor 18 C2
Myrtle Av *Dublin 13* 31 E3
Myrtle Av **16** *D.L.* 75 F4
Myrtle Ct 31 E3
Myrtle Dr 31 E3
Myrtle Gro *Bray* 82 A2
Myrtle Gro *Still.* 73 F2
Myrtle Pk 75 F4
Myrtle Sq 31 E3
Myrtle St 84 D1
Méile An Rí Cres 51 F2
Méile An Rí Dr 51 F2
Méile An Rí Grn 51 F2
Méile An Rí Pk 51 F2
Méile An Rí Rd 51 F3

N

Naas Rd *Dublin 12* 61 E1
Naas Rd *Dublin 22* 61 D1
Naas Rd *R'coole* 66 A3
Naas Rd *Sagg.* 67 D1
Naas Rd Business Pk 54 A4
Naas Rd Ind Pk 54 A4
Nangor Cres **1** 60 A1
Nangor Pl **2** 59 F1
Nangor Rd *Dublin 12* 52 C4
Nangor Rd *Clond.* 60 A1
Nangor Rd Business Cen 53 D4
Nanikin Av 48 B2
Nash St 54 A3
Nashville Pk 33 F3
Nashville Rd 33 F3
Nassau Pl 85 G5
Nassau St 85 F4
National Mus *Dublin 2* 85 G5
National Mus (Collins Barracks) *Dublin 7* 84 A3
National Transport Mus 33 D3
Naul Rd 16 B1
Navan Rd *Dublin 7* 44 B2
Navan Rd *Dublin 15* 43 E1
Navan Rd (Blanchardstown) *Dublin 15* 24 B2
Navan Rd *Clonee* 23 E1
Navan Rd *Dunb.* 20 B2
Navan Rd *Mulh.* 23 F1
Neagh Rd 63 E2
Neillstown Av 52 B3
Neillstown Cres 52 B3
Neillstown Dr 52 B2
Neillstown Gdns 52 B3
Neillstown Pk 52 B3
Neilstown Cotts **2** 52 B4
Neillstown Rd 52 B2
Neilstown Shop Cen 52 A3
Neilstown Village Ct **1** 52 B3
Nelson St 46 A4
Nephin Rd 44 C3
Neptune Ter **4** 78 B2
Nerano Rd 78 C3
Nerneys Ct 46 A4
Neville Rd 64 A2
Nevinstown La 12 C4
New Bawn Dr 69 E2
New Bawn Pk 69 E2
New Bride St 85 E6
Newbridge Av *Dublin 4* 57 D3
Newbridge Av *D'bate* 11 E2
Newbridge Dr 57 D3
New Brighton Ter **9** 82 B3
Newbrook Av 31 D4
Newbrook Rd 31 D4
Newbury Av 29 E2
Newbury Dr 29 E2
Newbury Gro 29 E2
Newbury Lawns 29 E2
Newbury Pk 29 E2
Newbury Ter **1** 29 E2
Newcastle Business Cen 58 A1
Newcastle Rd *Lucan* 50 C1
Newcastle Rd *R'coole* 66 A2
New Ch St 84 C3
Newcomen Av 46 C4
Newcomen Br 46 C4
Newcomen Ct *off North Strand Rd* 46 C4
Newcourt 13 D1
Newcourt Av 82 C4
Newcourt Ms 13 D1
Newcourt Rd 82 C4
Newcourt Vil **6** 82 B4
New Gra Rd *Dublin 7* 45 E3
New Gra Rd *Black.* 74 B4
Newgrove Av 57 E3
New Gro Est 31 D3
Newhall Ct 68 A3
New Ireland Rd 55 D3
Newlands Av 60 C2
Newlands Business Cen 60 B2
Newlands Dr 60 B2
Newlands Manor 60 A3
Newlands Manor Ct 60 A3
Newlands Manor Dr 60 A3
Newlands Manor Fairway 60 A3
Newlands Manor Grn 60 A3
Newlands Manor Pk 60 A3
Newlands Pk 60 B2
Newlands Retail Cen 60 B2
Newlands Rd *Clond.* 60 B2
Newlands Rd *Lucan* 41 D4
Newlands Rd *Ronan.* 51 F2
New Lisburn St *off Coleraine St* 84 D2
New Lucan Rd 42 B4
Newman Pl 36 B2
Newmarket 84 C6
Newmarket St 84 C6
New Nangor Rd 52 A4
New Pk Lo **7** 76 B1
New Pk Rd 74 B4
Newport St 84 A5
New Rathmore Ter **16** 82 A2
New Ravenswell Row **17** 82 A2
New Rd (Inchicore) *Dublin 8* 54 A3
New Rd *Dublin 13* 33 F4
New Rd *Clond.* 60 B1
New Rd *Grey.* 83 E1
New Rd (Killincarrig) *Grey.* 83 E4
New Rd **1** *Swords* 13 D2
New Rd, The *Dublin 11* 25 F2
New Row S 84 D6
New Row Sq 84 D5
New St 15 D4
New St Gdns 84 D6
New St S 84 D6
Newtown 20 A2
Newtown Av *Dublin 17* 30 A3
Newtown Av *Black.* 74 C2
Newtown Cotts 30 A4
Newtown Dr 30 A4
Newtown Glendale 39 F2
Newtown Gro 36 A2
Newtown Ind Est 30 A3
Newtown Pk *Dublin 17* 30 A3
Newtown Pk *Dublin 24* 69 F1
Newtown Pk *Black.* 74 B4
Newtown Pk *Leix.* 39 F2
Newtownpark Av 74 B3
Newtown Pk Ct **5** 74 B4
Newtown Rd *Dublin 17* 30 A3
Newtown Rd *Celbr.* 37 E4
Newtownsmith 78 A1
Newtown Vil 74 C2
New Vale 81 D3
New Vale Cotts 81 D4
New Vale Cres 81 D3
New Wapping St 56 C1
Niall St 84 A1
Nicholas Av *off Church St* 84 D2
Nicholas Pl *off Patrick St* 84 D5
Nicholas St 84 D5
Ninth Lock Rd 60 B1
Nore Rd 45 D2
Norfolk Mkt *off Parnell St* 85 F1
Norfolk Rd 45 F3
Norseman Pl 84 B2
North Av 65 E4
Northbrook Av 56 B4
Northbrook Av Lwr *off North Strand Rd* 46 C4
Northbrook Av Upr 46 C4
Northbrook La 56 B4
Northbrook Rd 56 A4
Northbrook Ter 46 C4
Northbrook Vil *off Northbrook Rd* 56 A4
Northbrook Wk 56 B4
North Circular Rd *Dublin 1* 46 A4
North Circular Rd *Dublin 7* 46 A3
Northcote Av 75 E3
Northcote Pl 75 E3
North Dublin Docklands 57 E1
Northern Cl 29 F1
Northern Cross Business Pk 26 C2
North Gt Clarence St 85 H1
North Gt Georges St 85 F1
Northland Dr 45 E1
Northland Gro 45 E1
North Pk Business & Off Pk 26 C2
North Quay Ext 57 D1
North Rd *Dublin 8* 44 A2
North Rd *Dublin 11* 26 C2
North Rd Number 1 57 E1
Northside Shop Cen 29 E2
North Strand Rd *Dublin 1* 46 C4
North Strand Rd *Dublin 3* 46 C4
North St 13 D1
North St Business Pk 13 D1
Northumberland Av 75 F3
Northumberland Pk 75 F3
Northumberland Pl *off Northumberland Av* 75 F3
Northumberland Rd 56 C3
North Wall Quay 56 C1
Northway Est 26 C2
Nortons Av 45 F4
Norwood 81 E1
Norwood Pk 64 B1
Nottingham St 46 C4
Novara Av 82 B2
Novara Ms **15** 82 B2
Novara Pk **10** 82 B3
Novara Ter **11** 82 B3
Nugent Rd 72 A1
Nurney Lawn 30 C3
Nurseries, The **4** *B'brack* 79 E2
Nurseries, The *Bray* 82 A4
Nurseries, The *Grey.* 83 D4
Nurseries, The *Mulh.* 24 B1
Nurseries, The *Swords* 12 B3
Nutgrove Av (Ascal An Charrain Chno) 71 F1
Nutgrove Cres 72 A1
Nutgrove Enterprise Pk 72 A1
Nutgrove Off Pk 72 A1
Nutgrove Pk 64 C3
Nutgrove Shop Cen 72 A1
Nutgrove Way 72 A1
Nutley Av 65 D1
Nutley La 65 E2
Nutley Pk 65 E2
Nutley Rd 65 D1
Nutley Sq 65 D2

O

Oak Apple Grn 63 F2
Oak Av 28 C2
Oak Cl 53 D4
Oak Ct 28 C2
Oakcourt Av 53 D1
Oakcourt Cl 53 D1
Oakcourt Dr 53 D1
Oakcourt Gro 53 D1
Oakcourt Lawn 53 D1
Oakcourt Lawns 53 D1
Oakcourt Pk 53 D1
Oak Cres 28 C1
Oakdale Cl 70 A4
Oakdale Cres 69 F4
Oakdale Dr *Dublin 24* 70 A4
Oakdale Dr *Corn.* 77 E2
Oakdale Gro 70 A4
Oakdale Pk 69 F4
Oakdale Rd 69 F4
Oak Dene 78 A4
Oakdown Rd 72 A1
Oak Downs 60 A2
Oak Dr *Dublin 9* 28 C2
Oak Dr *Dublin 12* 61 D1
Oakfield 52 B4
Oakfield Ind Est 52 B4
Oakfield Pl 55 F3
Oak Grn 28 C2
Oak Gro 28 C2
Oaklands 83 E2
Oaklands Av 13 D2
Oaklands Cres 64 A2
Oaklands Dr *Dublin 4* 57 D4
Oaklands Dr *Dublin 6* 64 A2
Oaklands Pk *Dublin 4* 57 D4
Oaklands Pk *Swords* 13 D2
Oaklands Ter *Dublin 4* *off Serpentine Av* 57 D4
Oaklands Ter *Dublin 6* 63 F2
Oak Lawn *Dublin 9* 28 C2
Oak Lawn *Dublin 15* 43 D1
Oak Lawn *Castle.* 43 E1
Oaklawn *Leix.* 39 E3
Oaklawn Cl 39 E3
Oaklawn W 39 E2
Oakleigh 37 D4
Oakley Gro 74 B3
Oakley Pk *Dublin 3* 48 A4
Oakley Pk *Black.* 74 B3
Oakley Rd 56 B4
Oak Lo 43 E2
Oak Pk Av 28 C3
Oak Pk Cl 28 C3
Oak Pk Dr 28 C2
Oak Pk Gro 28 C2
Oak Ri *Dublin 9* 28 C2
Oak Ri *Clond.* 60 A2
Oak Rd *Dublin 9* 47 D2
Oak Rd *Dublin 12* 61 D1
Oak Rd Business Pk 53 D4
Oaks, The *Dublin 3* 48 B4
Oaks, The *Dublin 14* 72 B1
Oaks, The *Dublin 16* 72 B3
Oaks, The (Cookstown) *Dublin 24* 60 C4
Oaks, The **16** *Abb.* 81 E1
Oaks, The *Celbr.* 37 E3
Oaks, The **5** *Lough.* 81 D1
Oaks, The (Hilltown) *Swords* 12 B3
Oakton Ct 77 F4
Oakton Dr 77 F4
Oakton Grn **2** 77 F4
Oakton Pk 77 F4
Oaktree Av 42 C1
Oaktree Dr 42 C1
Oaktree Grn 42 C1
Oaktree Gro 42 C1
Oaktree Lawn 42 C1
Oaktree Rd 73 F3
Oak Vw 28 C2
Oakview Av 23 F3
Oakview Cl 23 F3
Oakview Ct 23 F3
Oakview Dr 23 F3
Oakview Gro **1** 23 F3
Oakview Lawn 23 F3
Oakview Pk 23 F3
Oakview Ri 23 F3
Oakview Wk 23 F3
Oakview Way 23 F3
Oak Way 60 A2
Oakwood Av *Dublin 11* 27 E3
Oakwood Av *Swords* 12 C2
Oakwood Cl 27 E2
Oakwood Gro Est 52 A4
Oakwood Pk 27 E2
Oakwood Rd 27 E2
Oatfield Av 52 B2
Oatfield Cl 52 B2
Oatfield Cres 52 B2
Oatfield Dr 52 B2
Oatfield Gro 52 B2
Oatfield Lawn 52 B2
Oatfield Pk 52 B2
Obelisk Ct **6** 74 B4
Obelisk Gro 74 B3
Obelisk Ri 74 B4
Obelisk Vw 74 A4
Obelisk Wk 74 B3
O'Brien Rd 62 B1
O'Brien's Inst 47 D2
O'Brien's Pl N 46 A2
O'Brien's Ter *off Prospect Rd* 45 F3
Observatory La 56 A4
O'Byrne Rd 82 B4
O'Byrne Vil **7** 82 B4
O'Carolan Rd 84 C6
Ocean Pier 57 E1
O'Connell Av 45 F4
O'Connell Br 85 F3
O'Connell Gdns 57 D3
O'Connell St Lwr 85 F2
O'Connell St Upr 85 F2
O'Curry Av 84 C6
O'Curry Rd 84 C6
O'Daly Rd 46 A1
Odd Lamp Rd 44 B3
O'Devaney Gdns 55 D1
O'Donnell Gdns **9** 75 F4
O'Donoghue St 54 A3
O'Donovan Rd 55 F3
O'Donovan Rossa Br *off Winetavern St* 84 D4

O'Dwyer Rd 62 B1
Offaly Rd 45 E3
Offington Av 32 C2
Offington Ct 32 C3
Offington Dr 32 C3
Offington Lawn 32 C3
Offington Pk 32 C2
O'Hanlon's La 15 D4
O'Hogan Rd 54 A2
Olaf Rd 84 B2
Olcovar 81 E4
Old Ballycullen Rd 70 A2
Old Bawn Av 69 D2
Old Bawn Cl 69 E3
Old Bawn Ct 69 E2
Old Bawn Dr 69 E2
Old Bawn Pk 69 D3
Old Bawn Rd 69 E2
Old Bawn Ter **1** 69 E3
Old Bawn Way 69 D2
Old Belgard Rd 60 C3
Old Belgard Rd Business Pk 60 C4
Oldbridge 51 D3
Oldbridge Cl 51 E2
Oldbridge Ct 51 D3
Oldbridge Glen 51 E3
Oldbridge Grn 51 E3
Oldbridge Gro 51 E3
Oldbridge Pk 51 D3
Old Br Rd 62 C4
Oldbridge Vw 51 E3
Oldbridge Wk 51 E2
Oldbridge Way 51 D3
Old Brighton Ter **12** 82 B3
Old Cabra Rd 45 D3
Old Camden St
off Harcourt Rd 56 A3
Old Castle Av 32 C4
Oldcastle Dr 59 E1
Oldcastlepark 59 E1
Oldcastlepark Cl 59 E1
Oldcastlepark Grn 59 E1
Oldcastlepark Gro 59 E1
Oldcastlepark Lawn 59 E1
Oldcastlepark Vw 59 E1
Oldchurch Av 59 F1
Oldchurch Cl 59 F1
Oldchurch Ct 59 F1
Oldchurch Cres 59 F1
Oldchurch Dr 59 F1
Oldchurch Gro 59 F1
Oldchurch Lawn 59 F1
Oldchurch Pk 59 F1
Oldchurch Way 59 F1
Old Connaught Gro 82 A2
Old Connaught Vw 82 A2
Old Conna Wd 82 A2
Old Corduff Rd 24 C3
Old Cornmill Rd 40 B4
Old Co Glen 55 D4
Old Co Rd 54 C4
Oldcourt Av *Dublin 24* 69 F4
Oldcourt Av *Bray* 82 A4
Oldcourt Cl 69 F3
Oldcourt Cotts 69 F4
Oldcourt Dr 82 A4
Oldcourt Fm 69 F3
Oldcourt Gro 82 A4
Oldcourt Lawn 69 E3
Oldcourt Lo 69 F3
Oldcourt Manor 69 F4
Oldcourt Pk 82 A4
Oldcourt Rd 70 A4
Oldcourt Ter **8** 82 B4
Oldcourt Vw 69 F3
Old Dublin Rd 73 F1
Old Dunleary 75 E3
Old Fairgreen 20 B2
Old Fm, The 73 D1
Old Forge, The 51 D3
Old Golf Links, The 15 E4
Old Greenfield 36 A2
Old Hill *Leix.* 39 E3
Old Hill, The *Lucan* 41 D4
Old Kilmainham 54 C2
Old Kilmainham Village 55 D2
Old Malahide Rd 29 F3
Old Mill Ct 84 D6
Old Mountpleasant
off Mountpleasant Pl 56 A4
Old Naas Rd *Dublin 12* 53 F4
Old Naas Rd *Kings.* 59 F4
Old Orchard 70 C1
Old Quarry 78 B3
Old Rathmichael 80 C4
Old Rathmore Ter **18** 82 A2
Old Ravenswell Row **19** 82 A2
Old Rectory 41 D4
Old Rectory Pk 72 C1
Old Rd 19 D4
Old Sawmills Ind Est 62 A2
Old St 15 D4
Oldtower Cres 52 A1
Oldtown Av 28 A3
Oldtown Cotts 37 D3
Oldtown Mill 37 D3
Oldtown Mill Rd 37 D3
Oldtown Pk 28 A3
Oldtown Rd 28 A3
Old Yellow Walls Rd 14 B3
O'Leary Rd 54 C3
Olivemount Gro 64 C3
Olivemount Rd 64 C3
Oliver Bond St 84 C4
Oliver Plunkett Av (Irishtown)
Dublin 4 57 D2
Oliver Plunkett Av *D.L.* 75 D4
Oliver Plunkett Rd 75 D4
Oliver Plunkett Sq **9** 75 D4
Oliver Plunkett Ter **10** 75 D4
Oliver Plunkett Vil **5** 75 D4
Olney Cres 63 E3
Omac Business Cen 60 B1
Omni Pk 28 B3
Omni Pk Shop Cen 28 B3
O'Moore Rd 54 A2
O'Neachtain Rd 46 A2
O'Neill Pk 36 B1
O'Neill's Bldgs 85 E6
Ongar Chase 22 C2
Ongar Grn 23 D3
Ongar Pk 23 E3
Ongar Village 23 D3
Ontario Ter 56 A4
Onward Cl 19 F2
Onward Wk 19 F2
Ophaly Ct 64 C4
O'Quinn Av 55 D2
O'Rahilly Par
off Moore St 85 F2
Oranmore Rd 53 D2
Orchard, The *Dublin 3* 46 C3
Orchard, The *Dublin 5* 47 F1
Orchard, The *Dublin 6W* 63 D2
Orchard, The *Dublin 13* 30 B3
Orchard, The *Black.* 74 B4
Orchard, The **3** *Cool.* 42 B1
Orchard, The *Palm.* 42 C4
Orchard Av *City W* 67 E1
Orchard Av *Clons.* 24 A4
Orchard Cl (Blanchardstown)
Dublin 15 24 B4
Orchard Cl *D'bate* 11 F1
Orchard Cotts **2** 74 B3
Orchard Ct 24 B4
Orchard Grn 24 B4
Orchard Gro (Blanchardstown) 24 B4
Orchard La *Dublin 6* 56 A4
Orchard La *Black.* 74 B4
Orchard Lawns 53 D2
Orchard Pk 27 F2
Orchard Rd *Dublin 3* 46 C3
Orchard Rd *Dublin 5* 49 D2
Orchard Rd *Dublin 6* 64 A2
Orchard Rd *Clond.* 60 B1
Orchard Rd *Grey.* 83 D4
Orchardston 71 D1
Orchardstown Av 71 D1
Orchardstown Dr 70 C1
Orchardstown Pk 71 D1
Orchardstown Vil 71 D1
Orchard Ter **9** 82 B4
Orchardton **1** 71 D2
Orchard Vw 83 D4
Ordnance Survey Off 43 F3
Ordnance Survey Rd 43 F3
O'Reilly's Av 55 D2
Oriel Pl 46 C4
Oriel St Lwr 56 C1
Oriel St Upr 56 C1
Orlagh Av 70 B3
Orlagh Cl 70 C3
Orlagh Ct 70 B3
Orlagh Cres 70 B3
Orlagh Downs 70 C3
Orlagh Gra 70 C3
Orlagh Grn 70 B3
Orlagh Gro 70 B3
Orlagh Lawn 70 B3
Orlagh Lo 70 C3
Orlagh Meadows 70 C3
Orlagh Pk 70 B3
Orlagh Pines 70 B3
Orlagh Ri 70 B3
Orlagh Vw 70 C3
Orlagh Way 70 B3
Orlagh Wd 70 C3
Ormeau Dr 78 B3
Ormeau St
off Gordon St 56 C2
Ormond Av 12 A1
Ormond Cl 12 A1
Ormond Cres 12 A1
Ormond Dr 12 A1
Ormond Gro 12 A1
Ormond Lawn 12 A1
Ormond Mkt Sq
off Ormond Quay Upr 84 D3
Ormond Quay Lwr 85 E3
Ormond Quay Upr 84 D3
Ormond Rd N 46 B2
Ormond Rd S (Rathmines) 64 A1
Ormond Sq 84 D3
Ormond St 84 B6
Ormond Vw 12 A1
Ormond Way 12 A1
Oromont 83 D3
O'Rourke Pk 77 E1
Orpen Cl 74 A3
Orpen Dale 74 A3
Orpen Grn 74 A4
Orpen Hill 74 A4
Orpen Ri 74 A4
Orwell Gdns 64 A3
Orwell Pk 64 A3
Orwell Pk Av 62 B4
Orwell Pk Cl 62 B4
Orwell Pk Cres 62 B4
Orwell Pk Dale 62 B4
Orwell Pk Dr 62 B4
Orwell Pk Glade 62 B4
Orwell Pk Glen 62 B4
Orwell Pk Grn 62 B4
Orwell Pk Gro 62 B4
Orwell Pk Hts 62 B4
Orwell Pk Lawns 62 B4
Orwell Pk Ri 62 B4
Orwell Pk Vw 62 B4
Orwell Pk Way 62 B4
Orwell Rd *Dublin 6* 63 F2
Orwell Rd *Dublin 6W* 62 B4
Orwell Rd *Dublin 14* 64 A3
Orwell Shop Cen 62 B4
Orwell Wk 64 A3
Orwell Wds 64 A3
Oscar Sq 84 C6
Oscar Traynor Rd 29 E2
O'Shea's Cotts **3** 77 D3
Osprey Av 62 A3
Osprey Dr 62 B4
Osprey Lawn 62 B3
Osprey Pk 62 A3
Osprey Rd 62 B4
Ossory Rd 46 C4
Ossory Sq 84 C6
Ostman Pl 84 B1
O'Sullivan Av 46 B3
Oswald Rd 57 E3
Otranto Pl 78 A2
Otterbrook 71 E1
Oulart 12 C3
Oulton Rd 47 F3
Our Ladys Cl 84 A5
Our Lady's Hospice 55 E4
Our Lady's Rd 84 A6
Oval, The 43 D4
Ovoca Rd 55 F3
Owendoher Haven 71 D2
Owendoher Lo 71 D2
Owendore Av 63 E4
Owendore Cres 63 E4
Owens Av 55 D2
Owenstown Pk 65 E4
Oxford Rd 56 A4
Oxford Ter *Dublin 3*
off Church Rd 56 C1
Oxford Ter *Dublin 6*
off Oxford Rd 56 A4
Oxmantown La
off Blackhall Pl 84 B3
Oxmantown Rd 84 A1
Oxmantown Rd Lwr
off Arbour Hill 84 A2

P

Pace Av 23 E1
Pace Cres 23 E1
Pacelli Av 49 E1
Pace Rd 23 E1
Pace Vw 23 E1
Packenham 75 E3
Paddock, The *Dublin 7* 44 A2
Paddock, The *Celbr.* 37 D2
Paddocks, The **4** *Clons.* 23 D2
Paddocks, The *Dalkey* 78 B2
Paddocks, The *Dunb.* 20 B2
Pairc Baile Munna 27 F3
Pairc Clearmont (Claremont Pk) 57 E3
Pairc Gleannaluinn
(Glenaulin Pk) 43 E4
Pairc Gleann Trasna 69 D4
Pairc Mhuire 67 D3
Pairc Na Cuilenn 27 F3
Pakenham Br 23 D4
Pakenham Rd 75 D3
Pakerton
off Sloperton 75 E3
Palace St
off Dame St 85 E4
Palmer Pk 71 E2
Palmers Av 52 C1
Palmers Cl 52 C1
Palmers Copse 52 C1
Palmers Ct 52 C1
Palmers Cres 52 C1
Palmers Dr 52 C1
Palmers Glade 52 C1
Palmers Gro 52 C1
Palmers Lawn 52 C1
Palmers Pk 52 C1
Palmers Rd 52 C1
Palmerston Av 53 D1
Palmerston Dr 43 D4
Palmerston Gdns 64 A2
Palmerston Gro 64 C2
Palmerston La 64 A2
Palmerston Pk *Dublin 6* 64 A2
Palmerston Pk *Palm.* 52 C1
Palmerston Pl 84 D1
Palmerston Rd 64 A1
Palmerston Vil 64 A2
Palmerstown Av 52 C1
Palmerstown Cl 52 C1
Palmerstown Ct 52 C1
Palmerstown Dr 43 D4
Palmerstown Grn 52 C1
Palmerstown Hts 52 C1
Palmerstown Lawn 52 C1
Palmerstown Manor 52 C1
Palmers Wk 52 C1
Palms, The 65 D4
Paradise Pl 85 E1
Parc Na Silla Av 81 D2
Parc Na Silla Cl 81 D2
Parc Na Silla La 81 D2
Parc Na Silla Ri 81 D2
Park, The *Dublin 9* 29 D4
Park, The *Dublin 24* 69 F2
Park, The (Greenhills)
Dublin 24 61 D3
Park, The (Oldtown Mill Rd)
Celbr. 37 D3
Park, The (Wolstan Haven Av)
Celbr. 37 D3
Park, The (Dunboyne Castle)
Dunb. 20 B3
Park, The (Lutterell Hall) *Dunb.* 20 B1
Park, The (Plunkett Hall) *Dunb.* 20 A1
Park, The *Gra M.* 51 D2
Park, The *Kins.* 13 E3
Park, The *Lou.V.* 39 E2
Park, The *Mala.* 19 F1
Park Av *Dublin 4* 57 E4
Park Av (Willbrook) *Dublin 14* 71 E2
Park Av *Dublin 15* 43 D2
Park Av *Dublin 16* 71 E1
Park Av *Deans Gra* 76 C1
Park Av (Hilltown) *Swords* 12 B2
Park Cl 77 F1
Park Ct 77 F1
Park Cres *Dublin 8* 44 C3
Park Cres *Dublin 12* 62 C2
Park Dr *Dublin 6* 64 B1
Park Dr *Cabin.* 76 C3
Park Dr Av 43 D1
Park Dr Cl 43 D1
Park Dr Ct 43 D1
Park Dr Cres 43 D1
Park Dr Grn 43 D2
Park Dr Gro 43 D1
Park Dr Lawn 43 D1
Parker Hill 56 A4
Parkgate Pl Business Cen 55 D1
Parkgate St 55 D1
Parkhill Av 61 D4
Parkhill Cl
off Parkhill Ri 61 D4
Parkhill Ct 61 D4
Parkhill Dr 61 D4
Parkhill Grn 61 D4
Parkhill Lawn 61 D4
Parkhill Ri 61 D4
Parkhill Rd 61 D4
Parkhill Way 61 E4
Parklands *Castle.* 43 D1
Parklands *Mayn.* 36 C2
Parklands, The *Dublin 14* 63 E4
Parklands Av 69 F3
Parklands Cl 36 B2
Parklands Ct *Dublin 24* 69 F3
Parklands Ct *Mayn.* 36 B2
Parklands Cres 36 B2
Parklands Dr 69 F4
Parklands Gro 36 C2
Parklands Lawns 36 B2
Parklands Ri 36 B2
Parklands Rd 70 A3
Parklands Sq 36 B2
Parklands Vw 69 F3
Parklands Way 36 B2
Park La *Dublin 4* 57 E4
Park La *Dublin 20* 53 F1
Park La E 85 G4
Park Lawn 48 B3
Park Lo 43 D1
Park Manor 42 C2
Parkmore 43 E1
Parkmore Dr 63 D3
Parkmore Ind Est 61 F1
Park Pl
off South Circular Rd 54 C1
Park Rd *Dublin 7* 44 B2
Park Rd *D.L.* 75 F3
Park Rd *Sally.* 77 F2
Park Shop Cen 45 E4
Park St 54 A2
Park Ter 84 C5
Parkvale *Dublin 13* 31 F4
Parkvale *Dublin 16* 72 C3
Parkview *Dublin 7* 45 D4
Park Vw *Dublin 15* 43 F2
Park Vw *Clons.* 24 A4
Park Vw *Mala.* 19 F1
Parkview *Port.* 19 F2
Parkview *Swords* 12 A2
Parkview Av (Haroldscross)
Dublin 6 63 F1
Park Vw Av (Rathmines)
Dublin 6 64 A1
Park Vw Lawns 60 A2
Parkview Ter **20** 82 A2
Park Vil *Dublin 15* 43 E1
Park Vil *Black.* 74 A3
Parkway Business Cen 61 E2
Park W Av *Dublin 10* 53 D4
Park W Av *Dublin 22* 53 D4
Park W Business Pk 53 D3
Park W Ind Pk 53 E3
Park W Rd 53 D3
Parkwood Av 69 E3
Parkwood Gro 69 E3
Parkwood Lawn 69 E3
Parkwood Rd **2** 69 E3
Parliament Row
off Fleet St 85 F3
Parliament St 85 E4
Parnell Av
off Parnell Rd 55 F4
Parnell Cotts 19 D1
Parnell Ct 55 F4
Parnell Pl 85 F1
Parnell Rd *Dublin 12* 55 E3
Parnell Rd *Bray* 82 B2
Parnell Sq E 85 F1
Parnell Sq N 85 E1
Parnell Sq W 85 E1

Parnell St *Dublin 1* 85 E2
Parnell St *Sally.* 77 F1
Parochial Av **2** 31 F3
Parslickstown Av 24 B1
Parslickstown Cl 24 B1
Parslickstown Ct 24 B1
Parslickstown Dr 24 B1
Parslickstown Gdns 24 A1
Parslickstown Grn 24 B1
Parson Ct 36 A2
Parson Lo 36 A2
Parson St 36 A2
Partridge Ter 54 A3
Patrician Pk **5** 75 E4
Patrician Vil 74 A3
Patrick Doyle Rd 64 B3
Patricks Row
off Carysfort Av 74 B2
Patrick St *Dublin 8* 84 D5
Patrick St *D.L.* 75 F3
Patrickswell Pl 27 D4
Patriotic Ter
off Brookfield Rd 55 D2
Paul St 84 C3
Pavilion Rd 83 F3
Pavilions Shop Cen, The 13 D2
Pavillion Gate **1** 76 C4
Pea Fld 74 A2
Pearse Av 77 E2
Pearse Brothers Pk 71 E2
Pearse Cl **9** 77 E1
Pearse Dr 77 E1
Pearse Gdns 77 E1
Pearse Grn **10** 77 E1
Pearse Gro
off Great Clarence Pl 56 C2
Pearse Ho 85 H4
Pearse Pk 77 E1
Pearse Rd *Bray* 82 A2
Pearse Rd *Sally.* 77 E1
Pearse Sq *Dublin 2* 56 C2
Pearse Sq **21** *Bray* 82 A2
Pearse Sta 85 H4
Pearse St *Dublin 2* 85 G4
Pearse St *Sally.* 77 E2
Pearse Vil 77 E2
Pear Tree Fld **3** 74 A4
Pebble Hill 36 B1
Pecks La 43 E1
Pelletstown Av 44 B1
Pembroke Cotts (Donnybrook)
Dublin 4 64 C1
Pembroke Cotts (Ringsend)
Dublin 4 57 D2
Pembroke Cotts (Dundrum)
Dublin 14 72 C1
Pembroke Cotts *Boot.* 65 F3
Pembroke Gdns 56 C3
Pembroke La *Dublin 2* 85 G6
Pembroke La *Dublin 4* 56 C3
Pembroke Pk 56 C4
Pembroke Pl
off Pembroke St Upr 56 B3
Pembroke Rd 56 C3
Pembroke Row 85 H6
Pembroke St 57 D2
Pembroke St Lwr 85 G6
Pembroke St Upr 56 B3
Penrose St 56 C2
Percy French Rd 62 B1
Percy La 56 C3
Percy Pl 56 C3
Peter Row 85 E5
Petersons Ct 85 H3
Peters Pl 56 A3
Peter St 85 E5
Petrie Rd 55 F3
Pheasant Run 23 F1
Pheasant Run The Dr 23 F1
Pheasant Run The Grn 23 F1
Pheasant Run The Gro 23 F1
Pheasant Run The Pk 23 F1
Phelan Av 44 C1
Phibsborough 45 F3
Phibsborough Av 45 F4
Phibsborough Pl 45 F4
Phibsborough Rd 84 D1
Philipsburgh Av 46 C3
Philipsburgh Ter 46 C2
Philomena Ter 57 D2
Phoenix Av 43 E1
Phoenix Ct *Dublin 7*
off Cavalry Row 84 A2
Phoenix Ct *Dublin 15* 43 E1
Phoenix Dr 43 E1
Phoenix Gdns 43 E1
Phoenix Manor 45 D4
Phoenix Pk Av 44 A2
Phoenix Pk Way 44 A2
Phoenix Pl 43 E1
Phoenix St *Dublin 7* 84 C3
Phoenix St *Dublin 10* 54 A2
Phoenix Ter 74 A1
Pigeon Ho Rd 57 D2
Pig La 85 G1
Piles Bldgs
off Golden La 84 D5
Piles Ter
off Sandwith St Upr 85 H4
Pilot Vw 78 B2
Pimlico 84 C5
Pimlico Sq
off The Coombe 84 C5
Pim St 84 A5
Pine Av 76 B2
Pinebrook 23 F2
Pinebrook Av 47 E1
Pinebrook Cl 23 F2
Pinebrook Cres
off Pinebrook Av 29 E4
Pinebrook Downs 23 F2
Pinebrook Glen 23 F2
Pinebrook Gro
off Pinebrook Rd 47 E1
Pinebrook Hts 23 F2
Pinebrook Lawn 24 A2
Pinebrook Ri 47 E1
Pinebrook Rd 47 E1
Pinebrook Vale 23 F2
Pinebrook Vw 23 F2
Pinebrook Way 23 F2
Pine Copse Rd 72 B2
Pine Ct *Black.* 74 B4
Pine Ct *Port.* 19 F3
Pine Gro 70 C1
Pine Gro Pk 12 B1
Pine Gro Rd 12 B1
Pine Haven 74 A1
Pine Hurst 45 D3
Pine Lawn *Dublin 24* 69 E2
Pine Lawn *Black.* 74 B4
Pine Rd 57 E2
Pines, The *Dublin 5* 47 F1
Pines, The *Dublin 14* 73 D2
Pines, The *Dublin 15* 43 E1
Pines, The *Dublin 16* 72 A4
Pines, The **3** *Bray* 82 A3
Pinetree Cres 61 D4
Pinetree Gro 61 D4
Pine Valley Av 72 A4
Pine Valley Dr 72 A4
Pine Valley Gro 72 A4
Pine Valley Pk 72 A4
Pine Valley Way 72 A4
Pineview Av 69 D3
Pineview Dr 69 D3
Pineview Gro 69 D3
Pineview Lawn 69 D3
Pineview Pk 69 E3
Pineview Ri 69 D3
Pineview Rd 69 D3
Pinewood 77 F4
Pinewood Av 27 F3
Pinewood Cl 82 B4
Pinewood Ct *Ashb.* 8 C3
Pinewood Ct *Mulh.* 24 A2
Pinewood Cres 27 F3
Pinewood Dr 27 F3
Pinewood Grn 27 F3
Pinewood Gro 27 F3
Pinewood Pk 71 D1
Pinewoods 60 A2
Pinewood Vil 27 F3
Pinnockhill Rbt 12 C3
Place, The 20 B3
Plaza Shop Cen, The 13 D2
Pleasants La 85 E6
Pleasants Pl 56 A3
Pleasants St 85 E6
Plums Rd 73 D3
Plunkett Av *Dublin 11* 26 C2
Plunkett Av *Fox.* 76 B2
Plunkett Cres 26 C2
Plunkett Dr 26 C2
Plunkett Grn 26 C2
Plunkett Gro 26 C2
Plunkett Hall 20 A1
Plunkett Rd 26 C3
Poddle Pk 63 D2
Polo Rd 44 C4
Poolbeg St 85 G3
Poole St 84 B5
Poplar Row 46 C3
Poplars, The *D.L.* 74 C3
Poplars, The *Grey.* 83 D3
Poppintree Ind Est 27 E2
Poppintree Pk La W 27 E2
Porters Av 24 B4
Portersfield 24 B4
Porters Gate 23 E4
Porters Gate Av 23 F4
Porters Gate Cl 23 E4
Porters Gate Ct 23 F4
Porters Gate Cres 23 E4
Porters Gate Dr 23 E4
Porters Gate Grn 23 E4
Porters Gate Gro 23 F4
Porters Gate Hts 23 F4
Porters Gate Ri 23 F4
Porters Gate Vw 23 E4
Porters Gate Way 23 F4
Porters Rd 24 A4
Porterstown Rd 24 A4
Portland Cl 85 H1
Portland Pl 46 A3
Portland Rd 83 F3
Portland Rd N 83 F3
Portland Row 46 B4
Portland St N 46 B4
Portmahon Dr 55 D3
Portmarnock Av **2** 19 F2
Portmarnock Br 19 E4
Portmarnock Cres 19 F2
Portmarnock Dr 19 F2
Portmarnock Gro 19 F2
Portmarnock Pk 19 F2
Portmarnock Ri 19 F3
Portmarnock Sta 19 D4
Portmarnock Wk 19 F2
Portobello Harbour 56 A4
Portobello Pl 56 A4
Portobello Rd 55 F4
Portobello Sq
off Clanbrassil St Upr 55 F4
Portraine Rd 11 F1
Portside Business Cen 47 D4
Port Side Ct 46 C4
Potato Mkt
off Green St Little 84 D3
Pottery Rd 77 D2
Pound La 36 A2
Pound Pk 36 A1
Pound St 39 F3
Powers Ct
off Warrington Pl 56 C3
Powers Sq
off John Dillon St 84 D5
Prebend St 84 D2
Preston St 85 H1
Price's La *Dublin 2* 85 F3
Prices La *Dublin 6* 56 A4
Priestfield Cotts 55 E3
Priestfield Dr
off Dolphin Av 55 E3
Priestfield Ter
off South Circular Rd 55 E3
Primrose Av 45 F4
Primrose Gate 37 F4
Primrose Gro 30 A3
Primrose Hill *Celbr.* 37 E4
Primrose Hill *D.L.* 75 E3
Primrose La 40 C4
Primrose St 84 D1
Prince Arthur Ter 64 A1
Prince of Wales Ter *Dublin 4* 57 D4
Prince Of Wales Ter **16** *Bray* 82 B2
Princes St N 85 F3
Princes St S 85 H3
Princeton 65 D4
Priorswood Rd 29 F2
Priory, The *Dublin 7* 44 C2
Priory, The *Dublin 16* 71 F2
Priory, The **4** *Mala.* 15 D4
Priory Av 74 A2
Priory Chase 37 D4
Priory Cl 37 D4
Priory Ct *Dublin 16* 71 F3
Priory Ct *Celbr.* 37 D4
Priory Cres 37 D4
Priory Dr *Black.* 73 F1
Priory Dr *Celbr.* 37 D4
Priory E 44 C2
Priory Grn 37 D4
Priory Gro *Black.* 73 F1
Priory Gro *Celbr.* 37 D4
Priory Hall *Dublin 12* 62 C3
Priory Hall *Black.* 73 F1
Priory Lo 37 D4
Priory N 44 C2
Priory Ri **3** 83 D4
Priory Rd *Dublin 6W* 63 E1
Priory Rd *Grey.* 83 D4
Priory Vw 37 D4
Priory Wk *Dublin 12* 62 C2
Priory Wk *Celbr.* 37 D4
Priory Way *Dublin 12* 62 C3
Priory Way *Celbr.* 37 D3
Priory Way **4** *Grey.* 83 D4
Priory W 44 C2
Proby Pk 78 A3
Probys La 85 E3
Proby Sq 74 B3
Promenade Rd 47 E4
Prospect Av *Dublin 9* 45 F2
Prospect Av *Dublin 16* 71 D3
Prospect Cem 45 F2
Prospect Ct 71 D4
Prospect Dr 71 D3
Prospect Glen 71 D4
Prospect Gro 71 D3
Prospect Heath 71 D3
Prospect Hts 71 D4
Prospect Hill 11 E2
Prospect La 64 C2
Prospect Lawn 77 D3
Prospect Meadows 71 D3
Prospect Rd 45 F3
Prospect Sq 45 F2
Prospect Ter (Sandymount)
off Beach Rd 57 E3
Prospect Vw 71 D3
Prospect Way 45 F2
Protestant Row 85 E6
Prouds La 85 F5
Prussia St 45 E4
Puck's Castle La 80 B3
Purley Pk 19 F2
Purser Gdns 64 A1
Putland Rd 82 B4
Putland Vil **10** 82 B4

Q

Quarry Dr 62 B2
Quarryfield Ct 60 C2
Quarry Rd (Cabra) *Dublin 7* 45 E3
Quarry Rd *Grey.* 83 F3
Queens Pk 74 C3
Queens Rd 75 F3
Queen St 84 C3
Quinns La 85 G6
Quinn's Rd 81 E4
Quinsborough Rd 82 B2

R

Racecourse Shop Cen 31 E3
Race Hill Cl 8 B2
Race Hill Cres 8 C2
Race Hill La 8 B1
Race Hill Lo 8 B1
Race Hill Manor 8 C1
Race Hill Pk 8 B1
Race Hill Rd 8 B2
Race Hill Vw 8 B2
Radlett Gro 19 F2
Rafters Av 54 C4
Rafters La 54 C4
Rafters Rd 54 C4
Raglan La 56 C4
Raglan Rd 56 C4
Raheen Av 68 B2
Raheen Cl 68 B2
Raheen Ct 68 B2
Raheen Cres 68 B2
Raheen Dr *Dublin 10* 53 E3
Raheen Dr *Dublin 24* 68 B2
Raheen Lawn 82 C4
Raheen Pk *Dublin 10* 53 E3
Raheen Pk *Dublin 24* 68 B2
Raheen Pk *Bray* 82 C4
Raheen Rd 68 B2
Raheny Pk 48 C2
Raheny Rd 48 B1
Raheny Sta 48 B2
Rail Pk 36 B3
Railway Av *Dublin 8*
off Tyrconnell Rd 54 B3
Railway Av (Inchicore) *Dublin 8* 54 A3
Railway Av *Dublin 13* 32 A2
Railway Av **3** *Mala.* 15 D4
Railway Cotts
off Serpentine Av 57 D4
Railway Ct **2** 15 D4
Railway Ms 31 D3
Railway Rd *Dublin 13* 31 E3
Railway Rd **5** *Dalkey* 78 B3
Railway St 85 G1
Railway Ter
off Grattan St 56 C2
Rainsford Av 84 B4
Rainsford La **3** 79 E2
Rainsford St 84 B4
Ralahine 77 F4
Raleigh Sq 54 C4
Ralph Sq **1** 39 F3
Ramillies Rd 53 F2
Ramleh Cl 64 C2
Ramleh Pk 64 C2
Ramleh Vil 64 B2
Ramor Pk 24 C4
Ranelagh Av 56 B4
Ranelagh Rd 56 A4
Ranelagh Sta 56 B4
Raphoe Rd 54 C4
Rathbeale Ct 12 C1
Rathbeale Cres 12 C1
Rathbeale Ri 12 C2
Rathbone Av 44 B1
Rathbone Cl 44 B1
Rathbone Dr 44 B1
Rathbone Pl 44 B1
Rathbone Way 44 B1
Rathclaren **2** 82 A3
Rathcoole Pk 66 B3
Rath Cross Rds 8 B1
Rathdown Av 63 E3
Rathdown Cl 83 E2
Rathdown Ct *Dublin 6W* 63 E2
Rathdown Ct *Grey.* 83 E2
Rathdown Cres 63 E3
Rathdown Dr 63 E3
Rathdown Gro **6** 73 D3
Rathdown Pk *Dublin 6W* 63 E3
Rathdown Pk *Grey.* 83 E2
Rathdown Rd *Dublin 7* 45 F4
Rathdown Rd *Grey.* 83 E2
Rathdown Sq 45 E4
Rathdown Ter **7** 73 D3
Rathdown Vil 63 E3
Rathdrum Rd 55 E4
Rathfarham Gate 63 E4
Rathfarnham Castle 63 E4
Rathfarnham Mill 63 E4
Rathfarnham Pk 63 E3
Rathfarnham Rd *Dublin 6W* 63 E3
Rathfarnham Rd *Dublin 14* 63 E3
Rathfarnham Shop Cen 63 D4
Rathfarnham Wd 63 F4
Rathgar Av 63 F1
Rathgar Pk 63 F2
Rathgar Rd 63 F2
Rathgar Vil 63 F2
Rathingle Rd 12 B3
Rathland Rd (Bothar Raitleann) 63 D2
Rathlawns 66 A3
Rathlin Rd 46 A1
Rath Lo 8 B1
Rathlyon 70 A3
Rathlyon Pk 70 A3
Rathmichael Dales 80 C3
Rathmichael Haven 80 C3
Rathmichael Hill 80 C3
Rathmichael La 80 C3
Rathmichael Manor 81 D2
Rathmichael Pk 81 E3
Rathmichael Rd 80 B3
Rathmichael Wds 81 E3
Rathmines Av 64 A1
Rathmines Cl 64 A2
Rathmines Pk 64 A1
Rathmines Rd Lwr 56 A4
Rathmines Rd Upr 64 A1
Rathmintan Cl **3** 68 A3
Rathmintan Ct 68 A3
Rathmintan Cres 68 A3
Rathmintan Dr 68 A3

Rathmore 19 E4
Rathmore Av 73 E2
Rathmore Pk 48 C2
Rathmore Vil 63 E2
Rath Row 85 G3
Rathsallagh Av 81 E2
Rathsallagh Br 81 E2
Rathsallagh Dr 81 E3
Rathsallagh Gro 81 E2
Rathsallagh Pk 81 E2
Rathvale Av 30 A4
Rathvale Dr 30 A4
Rathvale Gro
off Rathvale Av 30 A4
Rathvale Pk 30 A4
Rathvilly Dr 26 C4
Rathvilly Pk 26 C4
Rathvilly Rd 26 C4
Ratoath Av
(Ascal Ratabhachta) 26 B4
Ratoath Dr 26 B3
Ratoath Est 44 C2
Ratoath Rd *Dublin 7* 45 D3
Ratoath Rd *Dublin 11* 26 B4
Ratra Rd 44 B2
Ravens Ct 26 C3
Ravensdale Cl 63 D2
Ravensdale Pk 63 D2
Ravensdale Rd 47 D4
Ravens Rock Rd 73 E3
Ravenswell Rd 82 B2
Ravenswood 23 E2
Ravenswood Av 23 E3
Ravenswood Cres 23 E3
Ravenswood Dr 23 E3
Ravenswood Grn 23 E3
Ravenswood Lawn 23 E3
Ravenswood Ri 23 E2
Ravenswood Rd 23 E3
Ravenswood Vw 23 E3
Raverty Vil **3** 82 A2
Raymond St 55 F3
Red Arches Av 31 E3
Red Arches Dr 31 E3
Redberry 50 C2
Red Brick Ter **3** 74 B3
Redcourt Oaks 48 B4
Red Cow Business Pk 61 E1
Red Cow Cotts **3** 43 D4
Red Cow La 84 C2
Red Cow Sta 61 D2
Redesdale Cres 73 E1
Redesdale Rd 73 E1
Redfern Av 19 F2
Redford Br 83 D1
Redford Pk 83 E1
Redmonds Hill 85 E6
Redwood Av 61 E4
Redwood Cl
off Redwood Av 61 E4
Redwood Ct *Dublin 14* 64 A4
Redwood Ct *Dublin 24*
off Parkhill Rd 61 D4
Redwood Dr 61 D4
Redwood Gro 74 A2
Redwood Hts
off Redwood Pk 61 E4
Redwood Lawn 61 D4
Redwood Pk 61 E4
Redwood Ri
off Redwood Pk 61 E4
Redwood Vw
off Redwood Av 61 E4
Redwood Wk 61 D4
Reginald Sq
off Gray St 84 C5
Reginald St 84 C5
Rehoboth Av 55 E3
Rehoboth Pl 55 E3
Reillys Av
off Dolphin's Barn St 55 E3
Reuben Av 55 D3
Reuben St 84 A6
Rialto Br 55 D3
Rialto Bldgs
off Rialto Cotts 55 D3
Rialto Cotts 55 D3
Rialto Dr 55 D3
Rialto Sta 55 D3
Rialto St 55 D3
Ribh Av 48 A2
Ribh Rd 48 A2
Richelieu Pk 65 E1
Richmond 74 B4
Richmond Av 75 D3
Richmond Av N 46 C3
Richmond Av S 64 B2
Richmond Cotts *Dublin 1* 46 B4
Richmond Cotts (Inchicore)
Dublin 8 54 C2
Richmond Cotts N
off Richmond Cotts 46 B4
Richmond Ct 64 B3
Richmond Cres 46 B4
Richmond Est 46 C3
Richmond Grn 75 D3
Richmond Gro 75 D3
Richmond Hill *Dublin 6* 56 A4
Richmond Hill *Black.* 75 D3
Richmond La
off Russell St 46 B4
Richmond Ms 56 A4
Richmond Par 46 B4
Richmond Pk 75 D3
Richmond Pl 56 A4
Richmond Pl S
off Richmond St S 56 A4
Richmond Rd 46 B2
Richmond Row 56 A4
Richmond Row S
off Richmond St S 56 A3
Richmond St N 46 B4
Richmond St S 56 A3
Richmond Ter **19** 82 C3
Richview Off Pk 64 C2
Richview Pk 64 B2
Ridge Hill 81 E1
Ridgewood Av 12 A3
Ridgewood Cl 12 A3
Ridgewood Ct 12 A3
Ridgewood Grn 12 A4
Ridgewood Gro 12 B4
Ridgewood Pk 12 A3
Ridgewood Pl 12 A3
Ridgewood Sq 12 A3
Rinawade Av 39 D3
Rinawade Cl 39 D3
Rinawade Cres 39 D3
Rinawade Downs 39 D3
Rinawade Glade 39 D3
Rinawade Gro 39 D3
Rinawade Lawns 38 C3
Rinawade Pk 39 D3
Rinawade Ri 39 D3
Rinawade Vw 39 D3
Ringsend Br 57 D2
Ringsend Pk 57 D2
Ringsend Rd 56 C2
Ring St 54 A3
Ring Ter 54 B3
Ripley Ct 82 A4
Ripley Hills 82 A4
Rise, The (Drumcondra)
Dublin 9 46 A1
Rise, The (Ballinteer)
Dublin 16 72 B4
Rise, The (Ballyboden)
Dublin 16 71 D3
Rise, The (Cookstown)
Dublin 24 60 C4
Rise, The (Kilnamanagh)
Dublin 24 61 D3
Rise, The *Dalkey* 78 B3
Rise, The *Kins.* 13 E3
Rise, The *Leix.* 39 E2
Rise, The *Mala.* 15 D4
Rise, The (Robswall) **3** *Mala.* 19 F1
Rise, The *Manor.* 23 F2
Rise, The *Still.* 65 F4
Riverbank Hall 45 F1
River Cl **2** 81 E2
River Ct **1** 20 C3
Riverdale 39 F3
Riverfield 83 D4
River Forest 39 F2
River Forest Vw 39 E1
River Gdns 46 A1
River La *Bray* 82 A2
River La *Lough.* 81 E2
River Rd *Dublin 11* 44 B1
River Rd *Dublin 15* 24 D4
Riversdale 42 C4
Riversdale Av *Dublin 6* 63 F3
Riversdale Av *Clond.* 52 B4
Riversdale Av *Palm.* 42 C4
Riversdale Ct 42 C4
Riversdale Cres 52 B4
Riversdale Dr 52 B4
Riversdale Grn 52 B4
Riversdale Gro *Dublin 6W* 63 D2
Riversdale Gro *Palm.* 42 C4
Riversdale Ind Est 53 F4
Riversdale Pk *Clond.* 52 B4
Riversdale Pk *Palm.* 42 C4
Riversdale Rd 52 B4
Riverside **3** 52 B4
Riverside Av 29 E2
Riverside Cotts 63 D4
Riverside Cres 29 E2
Riverside Dr *Dublin 14* 63 F4
Riverside Dr *Dublin 17* 29 E2
Riverside Dr *Palm.* 42 C4
Riverside Gro 29 E2
Riverside Pk 29 E2
Riverside Rd 29 E2
Riverside Wk 64 C2
Riverston Abbey 44 C2
Rivervale Apts **1** 82 A3
River Valley Av 12 C2
River Valley Cl 12 B2
River Valley Ct 12 B2
River Valley Dr 12 B2
River Valley Gro 12 B3
River Valley Hts 12 B2
River Valley Lawn 12 C3
River Valley Pk 12 B3
River Valley Ri 12 B3
River Valley Rd 12 B2
River Valley Vw 12 B2
River Valley Way 12 B2
Riverview *Dublin 24* 69 E3
Riverview *Palm.* 43 D4
Riverview Business Cen 53 D4
Riverview Ct 53 F1
Riverwood Chase 42 A1
Riverwood Cl 42 B1
Riverwood Copse 42 A1
Riverwood Ct 42 B1
Riverwood Cres 42 B2
Riverwood Dale 42 B1
Riverwood Dene 42 A1
Riverwood Dr 42 B1
Riverwood Gdns 42 B2
Riverwood Glebe 42 A2
Riverwood Glen 42 B1
Riverwood Grn 42 B1
Riverwood Gro 42 B1
Riverwood Heath 42 A1
Riverwood Lawn 42 B1
Riverwood Pk 42 B1
Riverwood Pl 42 A2
Riverwood Rd 42 B1
Riverwood Ter 42 A1
Riverwood Vale 42 B1
Riverwood Vw 42 B1
Riverwood Way 42 B1
Road, The 23 F2
Road Number 1 57 E1
Road Number 2 57 E1
Road Number 3 57 E1
Robert Emmet Br 55 F4
Robert Pl
off Clonliffe Rd 46 B3
Robertstown Br 9 E4
Robert St *Dublin 3*
off Clonliffe Rd 46 B3
Robert St *Dublin 8* 84 B5
Robinhood Business Pk 61 E1
Robinhood Ind Est 61 F1
Robinhood Rd 61 F1
Robinsons Ct 84 C5
Robin Vil 43 D4
Robswall 19 F1
Rochestown Av 77 E2
Rochestown Pk 77 E2
Rochfort Av 51 F1
Rochfort Cl 51 F1
Rochfort Cres 51 F2
Rochfort Downs 51 F1
Rochfort Grn 51 F1
Rochfort Pk 51 F1
Rochfort Way 51 F2
Rock Br 37 D4
Rock Enterprise Cen 59 D4
Rockfield *Dublin 14* 72 C2
Rockfield *Lucan* 50 C2
Rockfield *Mayn.* 36 B3
Rockfield Av *Dublin 12* 62 B3
Rockfield Av *Mayn.* 36 B3
Rockfield Cl 42 B1
Rockfield Dr *Dublin 12* 62 C2
Rockfield Dr *Clond.* 60 B2
Rockfield Dr *Cool.* 42 B1
Rockfield Gdns 36 B2
Rockfield Grn 36 B2
Rockfield Lo 36 B3
Rockfield Manor 36 B3
Rockfield Pk *Clons.* 24 B4
Rockfield Pk *Mayn.* 36 B3
Rockfield Ri 36 B2
Rockfield Sq 36 B2
Rockfield Wk 36 B2
Rockford Pk 74 C3
Rockfort Av 78 C3
Rock Hill 74 B2
Rockingham Av 39 E2
Rockingham Grn 39 E2
Rockingham Gro 39 E2
Rockingham Pk 39 E2
Rocklands **2** 78 C2
Rock Lo 78 A4
Rock Rd 65 F2
Rockview 72 C4
Rockville Cres 74 C3
Rockville Dr 74 C3
Rockville Pk 74 C3
Rockville Rd 74 C3
Rockwood 50 C2
Rocwood 76 A1
Roebuck Av 65 F4
Roebuck Castle 65 D3
Roebuck Downs 64 C4
Roebuck Dr 62 B2
Roebuck Hall 65 D4
Roebuck Rd 64 C3
Roe La 84 B4
Roger Casement Pk 82 A2
Roger's La 85 G6
Rollins Ct **7** 77 E1
Rollins Vil 77 E1
Roncalli Rd 49 E1
Rookery, The 70 C2
Roosevelt Cotts 44 C3
Rooske Ct 20 B3
Rooske Rd 20 B3
Rope Wk Pl 57 D2
Rory O'Connor Pk 75 D4
Rory O'More Br 84 B3
Rosapenna Dr 30 C3
Rosary Gdns E 75 E3
Rosary Gdns W 75 E3
Rosary Rd 84 A6
Rosary Ter 57 D2
Rosbeg Ct 49 E1
Rosberry 51 D3
Rosberry Av 51 D3
Rosberry Ct 51 D3
Rosberry La 51 D3
Rosberry Pk 51 D3
Rosberry Pl 51 D3
Rosebank 69 E2
Rosedale (Hartstown) *Clons.* 23 D2
Rosedale *Dunb.* 20 B2
Rosedale Dr 23 D2
Rose Glen Av 49 D1
Rose Glen Rd 48 C1
Rosehaven **1** 42 B1
Rosehill **7** 74 B4
Roselawn 41 E4
Roselawn Av 24 C4
Roselawn Cl 25 D4
Roselawn Ct 25 D4
Roselawn Cres 24 C4
Roselawn Dr *Bray* 82 B4
Roselawn Dr *Castle.* 24 C4
Roselawn Glade 24 C4
Roselawn Gro 24 C4
Roselawn Pk 82 B4
Roselawn Rd 25 D4
Roselawn Vw 24 C4
Roselawn Wk 24 C4
Roselawn Way 25 D4
Rosemount 64 B4
Rosemount Av 47 F1
Rosemount Business Pk 25 F2
Rosemount Ct *Dublin 14* 72 C1
Rosemount Ct *Boot.* 65 F3
Rosemount Cres 64 C3
Rosemount Pk 64 C4
Rosemount Pk Rd 25 E2
Rosemount Rd 45 F4
Rosemount Ter 65 F3
Rose Pk 75 D4
Rosevale Ct
off Brookwood Glen 48 A2
Rosevale Mans 48 A2
Roseville Ct **4** 82 A2
Rosewood Gro 51 F2
Rosmeen Gdns 75 F3
Rosmeen Pk 75 F4
Rossecourt Av **2** 51 F2
Rossecourt Grn **6** 51 F2
Rossecourt Gro **1** 51 F2
Rossecourt La **5** 51 F2
Rossecourt Ri **8** 51 F2
Rossecourt Sq **4** 51 F2
Rossecourt Ter **7** 51 F2
Rossecourt Way **3** 51 F2
Rossfield Av 68 A1
Rossfield Cres 68 A2
Rossfield Dr 68 A1
Rossfield Gdns 68 A2
Rossfield Grn 68 A2
Rossfield Gro 68 A2
Rossfield Pk 68 A1
Rossfield Way 68 A2
Rosslyn **13** 82 B3
Rosslyn Ct 82 B3
Rosslyn Gro **14** 82 B3
Rossmore Av *Dublin 6W* 62 B4
Rossmore Av *Dublin 10* 53 E2
Rossmore Cl 70 B1
Rossmore Cres 62 B4
Rossmore Dr *Dublin 6W* 62 B4
Rossmore Dr *Dublin 10* 53 E1
Rossmore Gro 62 B4
Rossmore Lawns 62 B4
Rossmore Pk 70 B1
Rossmore Rd *Dublin 6W* 62 B4
Rossmore Rd *Dublin 10* 53 E1
Ross Rd 84 D5
Ross St 45 D4
Ross Vw 43 D4
Rostrevor Rd 63 F3
Rostrevor Ter 63 F3
Rothe Abbey 54 C3
Rowan Av 73 E3
Rowanbyrn 74 C3
Rowan Cl 37 E3
Rowan Gro 82 A2
Rowan Hall
off Prospect La 64 C2
Rowan Pk Av 74 C3
Rowans, The **17** 81 E1
Rowans Rd 73 D3
Rowlagh Av 52 A2
Rowlagh Cres 52 A2
Rowlagh Gdns 52 A2
Rowlagh Grn 52 A2
Rowlagh Pk 52 A2
Roxboro Cl 78 A4
Royal Canal Av 44 B1
Royal Canal Bk 84 D1
Royal Canal Ter 45 F4
Royal Hosp
(Museum of Modern Art) 55 D2
Royal Liver Retail Pk 53 F4
Royal Marine Ter **3** 82 C2
Royal Oak 28 C2
Royal Ter
off Inverness Rd 46 C3
Royal Ter E 75 F4
Royal Ter La **9** 75 E4
Royal Ter N **10** 75 F4
Royal Ter W 75 F4
Royse Rd 45 F3
Royston 62 C2
Ruby Hall 77 D1
Rugby Rd 56 A4
Rugby Vil
off Rugby Rd 56 A4
Rugged La 42 A2
Rushbrook 24 C4
Rushbrook Av 62 A4
Rushbrook Ct 62 B4
Rushbrook Dr 62 B4
Rushbrooke Cres 62 A4
Rushbrooke Rd 62 A4
Rushbrook Gro 62 B4
Rushbrook Pk 62 B4
Rushbrook Vw 62 A4
Rushbrook Way 62 B4
Rusheeney 23 E2
Rusheeney Av 23 F2
Rusheeney Cl 23 E2
Rusheeney Ct 23 F2

Rusheeney Cres 23 F2
Rusheeney Grn 23 F2
Rusheeney Gro 23 F2
Rusheeney Manor 23 E2
Rusheeney Pk 23 E2
Rusheeney Vw 23 F2
Rusheeney Way 23 F2
Rus-in-Urbe Ter **11** 75 F4
Russell Av *Dublin 3* 46 A3
Russell Av *Jobs.* 68 A2
Russell Av E 46 C4
Russell Cl 68 A2
Russell Ct 68 A2
Russell Cres 68 A2
Russell Downs 68 A2
Russell Dr 68 A2
Russell Grn 68 A2
Russell Gro 68 A2
Russell La 68 A2
Russell Lawns 68 A2
Russell Meadows 68 A2
Russell Pl 68 A2
Russell Ri 68 A2
Russell St 46 B4
Russell Vw 68 A2
Russell Wk 68 A2
Rutland Av 55 E4
Rutland Gro 55 E4
Rutland Pl
off Clontarf Rd 47 F4
Rutland Pl N 46 B4
Rutland Pl W 85 F1
Rutland St Lwr 85 G1
Rutledges Ter 55 E3
Ryders Row
off Parnell St 85 E2
Rye Br 39 F3
Ryecroft 82 B3
Ryemont Abbey 39 E2
Rye River 39 F2
Rye River Av 39 F3
Rye River Cl 39 F3
Rye River Ct 39 F3
Rye River Cres 39 F3
Rye River Gdns 39 F3
Rye River Gro 39 F3
Rye River Mall 39 F3
Rye River Pk 39 F3
Ryevale Lawns 39 F2

S

Sackville Av 46 B4
Sackville Gdns 46 B4
Sackville La
off O'Connell St Lwr 85 F2
Sackville Pl 85 F3
Saddlers Av 24 B2
Saddlers Cl 24 B2
Saddlers Cres 24 B2
Saddlers Dr **1** 24 B2
Saddlers Glade 24 B2
Saddlers Gro 24 B2
Saddlers Lawn 24 B2
Sadleir Hall 20 A2
Saggart Abbey 67 E3
St. Agnes Pk 62 C1
St. Agnes Rd 62 C1
St. Aidan's Dr 65 D4
St. Aidan's Pk 47 D3
St. Aidan's Pk Av 47 D3
St. Aidan's Pk Rd 47 D3
St. Aidan's Ter **20** 82 B2
St. Alban's Pk 65 F1
St. Alban's Rd 55 F3
St. Alphonsus Av 46 B3
St. Alphonsus Rd 46 A3
St. Andoens Ter
off Cook St 84 C4
St. Andrews 41 E4
St. Andrews Dr 41 F4
St. Andrews Fairway 51 F1
St. Andrews Grn 41 F4
St. Andrew's Gro 15 D4
St. Andrew's La
off Trinity St 85 F4
St. Andrews Pk 12 B1
St. Andrew's St 85 F4
St. Andrews Wd 41 F4
St. Annes 62 C2
St. Anne's Av 48 B2
St. Anne's Dr 48 B2
St. Anne's Pk 81 E4
St. Annes Rd 55 E3
St. Anne's Rd N 46 A3
St. Anne's Sq 74 B2
St. Anne's Ter 48 B2
St. Ann's Sq **5** 19 E4
St. Ann's Sq Lwr **4** 19 E4
St. Anthony's Av 60 B2
St. Anthony's Business Pk 61 D1
St. Anthony's Cres 62 A2
St. Anthony's Pl
off Temple St N 85 F1
St. Anthony's Rd 55 D3
St. Aongus Cres 61 F4
St. Aongus Grn 61 F4
St. Aongus Gro 61 F4
St. Aongus Lawn 61 F4
St. Aongus Rd 61 F4
St. Assam's Av 48 C2
St. Assam's Dr 48 C2
St. Assam's Pk 48 C1
St. Assam's Rd E 48 C2
St. Assam's Rd W 48 C2
St. Attracta Rd 45 E3
St. Aubyn's Ct **9** 81 E1
St. Audoens Ter
off School Ho La W 84 D4
St. Augustine's Pk 74 B4
St. Augustine St 84 C4
St. Barnabas Gdns 46 C4
St. Begnet's Vil 78 B3
St. Brendan's Av 29 F4
St. Brendan's Cotts 57 D2
St. Brendan's Cres 62 A3
St. Brendan's Dr 29 F4
St. Brendan's Pk 48 A1
St. Brendan's Ter *Dublin 5* 29 F3
St. Brendan's Ter *D.L.*
off Library Rd 75 E3
St. Bricin's Pk 84 A2
St. Bridget's Av 46 C4
St. Bridget's Dr 62 A2
St. Bridget's Pk 83 E2
St. Brigid's Av **3** 19 E4
St. Brigids Ch Rd 74 A4
St. Brigid's Cotts
(Blanchardstown) *Dublin 15* 25 D4
St. Brigids Cotts *Clond.* 60 C2
St. Brigid's Ct
off St. Brigid's Dr 47 F1
St. Brigid's Cres 29 F4
St. Brigid's Dr *Dublin 5* 47 F1
St. Brigid's Dr *Clond.* 60 B2
St. Brigids Flats 64 C2
St. Brigids Gdns 56 C1
St. Brigids Grn 47 F1
St. Brigids Gro 47 F1
St. Brigids Lawn 47 F1
St. Brigid's Pk (Blanchardstown)
Dublin 15 25 D4
St. Brigid's Pk **1** *Clond.* 60 B2
St. Brigid's Pk *Corn.* 76 C2
St. Brigid's Rd *Dublin 5* 29 F4
St. Brigid's Rd *Clond.* 60 B2
St. Brigid's Rd Lwr 46 A3
St. Brigid's Rd Upr 46 A3
St. Brigids Shop Mall 29 F4
St. Brigid's Ter **21** 82 B2
St. Broc's Cotts 64 C1
Saintbury Av 79 E2
St. Canice's Pk 27 F4
St. Canice's Rd 27 F4
St. Catherine's Av 55 E3
St. Catherines Gro **3** 59 F1
St. Catherine's La W 84 C4
St. Catherine's Pk *Dalkey* 78 A3
St. Catherine's Pk *D.L.* 78 A2
St. Catherine's Rd 78 A3
St. Clair's Lawn 82 A4
St. Clair's Ter **3** 82 A4
St. Clare's Av
off Harolds Cross Rd 55 F4
St. Clare's Home 27 F4
St. Clare's Ter
off Mount Drummond Av 55 F4
St. Clement's Rd 46 A3
St. Colmcilles Ct **1** 12 C2
St. Colmcille's Way 70 A3
St. Columbanus Av 64 B3
St. Columbanus Pl 64 B3
St. Columbanus Rd 64 B3
St. Columbas Hts 12 C2
St. Columbas Ri 12 C2
St. Columba's Rd 62 A2
St. Columba's Rd Lwr 46 A3
St. Columba's Rd Upr 46 A3
St. Columcille's Cres **2** 13 D2
St. Columcille's Dr 13 D2
St. Columcille's Ter **22** 82 B2
St. Columcills Pk 13 D2
St. Conleth's Rd 62 A2
St. Cronan's Av 12 B1
St. Cronan's Cl **1** 12 B2
St. Cronan's Ct 12 B1
St. Cronan's Gro 12 B1
St. Cronan's Lawn 12 B1
St. Cronan's Rd **23** 82 B2
St. Cronan's Vw **2** 12 B2
St. Cronan's Way **3** 12 B2
St. Davids 47 E1
St. Davids Pk 47 E1
St. David's Ter *Dublin 7*
off Blackhorse Av 45 D4
St. David's Ter (Glasnevin)
Dublin 9 46 A1
St. Davids Wd 46 A1
St. Declan Rd 46 C2
St. Declan Ter 47 D2
St. Dominic's Av 69 E2
St. Dominic's Cen 69 E2
St. Dominic's Ct **3** 69 E2
St. Dominic's Rd 69 E2
St. Dominic's Ter 69 E2
St. Donagh's Cres 30 C4
St. Donagh's Pk 31 D4
St. Donagh's Rd 30 C4
St. Edmunds 42 A4
St. Eithne Rd 45 E3
St. Elizabeth's Ct
off North Circular Rd 45 E4
St. Enda's Dr 71 E1
St. Enda's Pk 71 E1
St. Enda's Rd 63 E2
St. Finbar's Cl 62 A3
St. Finbar's Rd 45 D2
St. Finian's 51 D1
St. Finian's Av 51 D1
St. Finian's Cl 51 D1
St. Finian's Cres 51 D1
St. Finian's Gro 51 D1
St. Fintan Rd 45 E3
St. Fintan's Cres 32 C4
St. Fintan's Gro 32 C4
St. Fintan's Pk *Dublin 13* 32 C4
St. Fintan's Pk *Black.* 74 C4
St. Fintan's Rd 32 C4
St. Fintan's Ter **4** 43 D4
St. Fintan's Vil 74 C4
St. Fintan Ter 45 E2
St. Gabriel's 77 E3
St. Gabriels Ct 48 B4
St. Gabriel's Rd 48 B4
St. Gall Gdns N 64 B3
St. Gall Gdns S 64 B3
St. Gatien Ct 71 E2
St. Gatien Rd **2** 71 E2
St. George's Av *Dublin 3* 46 B3
St. George's Av *Kill.* 79 E1
St. Gerard's Rd 62 A2
St. Helena's Dr 27 D4
St. Helena's Rd 27 D4
St. Helen's 78 A2
St. Helen's Rd 65 F3
St. Helens Wd 65 F4
St. Ignatius Av 46 A3
St. Ignatius Rd 46 A3
St. Ita's Rd 46 A2
St. Ive's 15 D4
St. James Pl 54 B2
St. James's Av *Dublin 3* 46 B3
St. James's Av *Dublin 8* 84 A4
St. James's Pl
off Tyrconnell Rd 54 B3
St. James's Rd 62 A2
St. James's Ter 55 E3
St. James's Wk 55 D3
St. Jarlath Rd 45 E3
St. Johns 65 E1
St. John's Av *Dublin 8*
off John St S 84 C5
St. John's Av *Clond.* 60 A2
St. John's Cl 60 A2
St. John's Ct *Dublin 3* 47 E2
St. Johns Ct *Dublin 5* 29 E3
St. John's Ct *Clond.* 60 A2
St. John's Cres 60 A2
St. John's Dr 60 A2
St. John's Grn 60 A2
St. John's Lawn 60 A2
St. John's Pk *Clond.* 60 A2
St. John's Pk *D.L.* 75 E3
St. John's Pk W 60 A2
St. John's Rd *Dublin 4* 57 E4
St. John's Rd *Clond.* 60 A2
St. John's Rd W 54 C2
St. John St
off Blackpitts 84 C6
St. Johns Wd *Dublin 3* 47 F3
St. John's Wd *Clond.* 60 A1
St. Johns Wd Ct 8 B2
St. Johns Wd Dr 8 B2
St. Johns Wd Pk 8 B2
St. John's Wd W 60 A2
St. Joseph's 26 B4
St. Joseph's Av *Dublin 3* 46 B3
St. Joseph's Av *Dublin 9* 46 A3
St. Joseph's Conv 63 E2
St. Josephs Ct 84 B1
St. Josephs Gro 72 C1
St. Joseph's Par 46 A4
St. Joseph's Pl
off St. Joseph's Par 46 A4
St. Joseph's Rd *Dublin 7* 84 A1
St. Joseph's Rd *Dublin 12* 62 A2
St. Joseph's Sq
off Vernon Av 48 A4
St. Joseph's St
off Synnott Pl 46 A4
St. Joseph's Ter *Dublin 1*
off North Circular Rd 46 B4
St. Joseph's Ter *Dublin 3* 46 C3
St. Kevins Ct 64 A2
St. Kevins Gdns 64 A2
St. Kevin's Par 55 F3
St. Kevins Pk (Rathgar)
Dublin 6 64 A2
St. Kevin's Pk *Still.* 73 E2
St. Kevin's Rd 55 F4
St. Kevin's Sq 82 B2
St. Kevin's Ter **15** 82 B3
St. Kevin's Vil 75 E4
St. Killian's Av 61 F2
St. Killian's Pk **1** 60 B1
St. Laurence Gro 53 F1
St. Laurence Rd 53 F1
St. Laurence's Mans 56 C1
St. Laurences Pk 73 F1
St. Laurence's Ter **24** 82 B2
St. Laurence St N
off Sheriff St Lwr 85 H2
St. Lawrence Gro 47 E3
St. Lawrence O'toole Av **1** 19 E4
St. Lawrence Pl
off Sheriff St Lwr 85 H2
St. Lawrence Rd (Clontarf)
Dublin 3 47 E3
St. Lawrence Rd (Howth)
Dublin 13 33 E3
St. Lawrences Ct 47 E3
St. Lawrence St
off Sheriff St Lwr 85 H2
St. Lawrence Ter 33 F3
St. Lomans Rd 41 F4
St. Luke's Av 84 C5
St. Luke's Cres 64 B3
St. Maelruans Pk 69 E2
St. Magdalene Ter 57 D2
St. Malachy's Dr 62 A2
St. Malachy's Rd 46 A2
St. Margaret's Av *Dublin 5* 49 D1
St. Margaret's Av *Mala.* 15 D4
St. Margaret's Av N
off North Circular Rd 46 B4
St. Margaret's Business Pk 26 C2
St. Margaret's Cl **5** 78 B2
St. Margaret's Ct **1** 27 D2
St. Margaret's Halting Site 27 F1
St. Margaret's Pk 15 D4
St. Margaret's Rd *Dublin 11* 27 D2
St. Margaret's Rd *Mala.* 15 D4
St. Margaret's Ter 84 A6
St. Mark's Av 52 A1
St. Mark's Cres 52 A2
St. Mark's Dr 52 B2
St. Mark's Gdns 52 A2
St. Mark's Grn 52 A2
St. Mark's Gro 52 A2
St. Marnock's Av 19 E4
St. Martin's Dr 63 D2
St. Martin's Pk 63 D1
St. Mary's Av (Rathfarnham) 63 E4
St. Mary's Av N 85 E1
St. Mary's Av W 54 B2
St. Mary's Coll 56 A4
St. Mary's Cres 54 B4
St. Mary's Dr 54 B4
St. Mary's La 56 C3
St. Mary's Pk *Dublin 12* 62 B1
St. Mary's Pk *Dublin 15* 26 B4
St. Mary's Pk *Leix.* 39 F2
St. Mary's Pl
off Main St 33 F3
St. Mary's Pl N 85 E1
St. Mary's Rd *Dublin 3* 46 C4
St. Mary's Rd *Dublin 12* 62 B1
St. Mary's Rd *Dublin 13*
off Main St 33 F3
St. Mary's Rd N 46 C4
St. Mary's Rd S 56 C3
St. Mary's St 75 E3
St. Mary's Ter *Dublin 7* 85 E1
St. Marys Ter **22** *Bray* 82 C3
St. Mary's Ter **1** *Dunb.* 20 B2
St. Mel's Av 62 A3
St. Michael's Est 54 C3
St. Michael's Hill 84 D4
St. Michael's La
off High St 84 D4
St. Michael's Rd 46 A2
St. Michael's Ter 84 C6
St. Michan's St 84 D3
St. Mobhi Boithirin 46 A1
St. Mobhi Ct 46 A1
St. Mobhi Dr 46 A2
St. Mobhi Gro 46 A2
St. Mobhi Rd 46 A2
St. Mobhis Br 46 A2
St. Mochtas 42 B1
St. Mochtas Av 24 B4
St. Mochtas Chase 24 B4
St. Mochtas Dr 42 A1
St. Mochtas Grn 42 B1
St. Mochtas Gro 42 B1
St. Mochtas Lawn 24 A4
St. Mochtas Rd 42 A1
St. Mochtas Vale 24 B4
St. Nessan's Ter
off Tuckett's La 33 E3
St. Nicholas Pl 84 D5
St. Oliver's Pk 52 C3
St. Pappin Grn 27 F4
St. Pappin Rd 27 F4
St. Patrick Av
off North Strand Rd 46 C4
St. Patrick's Av **1** *Clond.* 52 A4
St. Patrick's Av **6** *Dalkey* 78 B3
St. Patrick's Av *Port.* 19 E4
St. Patrick's Cath 84 D5
St. Patrick's Cl *Dublin 8* 84 D5
St. Patrick's Cl **11** *D.L.* 75 D4
St. Patrick's Coll Maynooth 36 A2
St. Patrick's Cotts 71 E1
St. Patrick's Cres *D.L.* 75 D4
St. Patrick's Cres *R'coole* 66 A3
St. Patrick's Nat Sch 46 B2
St. Patrick's Par 46 A3
St. Patrick's Pk (Blanchardstown)
Dublin 15 24 C4
St. Patrick's Pk *Celbr.* 37 E3
St. Patrick's Pk *Clond.* 52 A4
St. Patricks Pk *D'bate* 11 F2
St. Patrick's Pk *Dunb.* 20 B2
St. Patrick's Rd *Dublin 9* 46 A3
St. Patrick's Rd *Dublin 12* 62 A2
St. Patrick's Rd *Clond.* 52 A4
St. Patrick's Rd *Dalkey* 78 B3
St. Patrick's Sq **1** *Bray* 82 B2
St. Patrick's Sq **7** *Dalkey* 78 B3
St. Patrick's Ter *Dublin 1*
off Russell St 46 B4
St. Patrick's Ter *Dublin 3*
off North Strand Rd 46 C4
St. Patrick's Ter *Dublin 8* 54 B2
St. Patricks Ter *D'bate* 11 F2
St. Patrick's Ter **6** *D.L.* 75 E4
St. Patrick's Vil 57 D2
St. Paul's Dr 62 B2
St. Paul's Ter **21** 78 A2
St. Peters Av 45 F3
St. Peters Cl 45 F4
St. Peter's Cres 62 B2
St. Peter's Dr 62 B2
St. Peter's Pk 20 B2
St. Peter's Rd *Dublin 7* 45 F3
St. Peter's Rd *Dublin 12* 62 A2

Wainsfort Rd 62 C3
Waldemar Ter 72 B1
Waldrons Br 64 A3
Walk, The *Dublin 6W* 62 C4
Walk, The *Dublin 16* 72 B4
Walk, The *Dublin 24* 69 E2
Walk, The *Celbr.* 37 D3
Walk, The *Dunb.* 20 B3
Walk, The *Kins.* 13 E4
Walk, The *Lou.V.* 39 E2
Walk, The *Mala.* 19 F1
Walk, The *Manor.* 23 E2
Walkinstown Av 62 A1
Walkinstown Cl 62 A1
Walkinstown Cres 62 A1
Walkinstown Cross 62 A1
Walkinstown Dr 62 A1
Walkinstown Grn 62 A1
Walkinstown Mall 62 A1
Walkinstown Par 62 A1
Walkinstown Pk 62 A1
Walkinstown Rd
(Bothar Chille Na Manac) 62 A1
Wallace Rd 62 B1
Walled Gdns, The 37 E2
Walnut Av *Dublin 9* 46 B1
Walnut Av *Dublin 24* 61 D3
Walnut Cl 61 D3
Walnut Ct 46 B1
Walnut Dr **2** 61 D3
Walnut Lawn 46 B1
Walnut Pk 46 B1
Walnut Ri 46 B1
Walnut Vw **5** 71 D3
Walsh Rd 46 A1
Waltersland Rd 73 F2
Waltham Ter 74 A2
Walworth Rd
off Victoria St 55 F4
Warburton Ter **24** 82 C3
Wards Hill 84 C6
Warners La 56 B3
Warren, The 14 B4
Warren Av 42 B2
Warren Cl 42 B2
Warren Cres 42 B2
Warren Grn *Dublin 13* 32 A2
Warren Grn *Carp.* 42 B2
Warrenhouse Rd 32 A1
Warrenmount 84 C6
Warrenmount Pl 84 C6
Warrenpoint 47 E3
Warrenstown 24 C2
Warrenstown Cl 24 C2
Warrenstown Ct 24 C2
Warrenstown Downs 24 C2
Warrenstown Dr 24 C1
Warrenstown Garth 24 B2
Warrenstown Grn 24 C2
Warrenstown Gro 24 C2
Warrenstown Lawn 24 C2
Warrenstown Pk 24 C2
Warrenstown Pl 24 B2
Warrenstown Ri 24 C2
Warrenstown Row 24 C2
Warrenstown Vale 24 C2
Warrenstown Vw 24 B2
Warrenstown Wk 24 C2
Warrenstown Way 24 C2
Warren St 56 A4
Warrington La
off Warrington Pl 56 C3
Warrington Pl 56 C3
Warwick Ter
off Sallymount Av 56 B4
Wasdale Gro 63 F3
Wasdale Pk 63 E3
Washington La 71 D1
Washington Pk 63 D4
Washington St 55 F3
Watercourse 62 B4
Waterfall Av 46 B3
Waterfall Rd 48 B2
Watergate Est 69 D2
Waterloo Av 46 C4
Waterloo La 56 B4
Waterloo Rd 56 C4
Watermeadow Dr 69 D2
Watermeadow Pk 69 D2
Watermill Av 48 B2
Watermill Cl 69 E3
Watermill Dr 48 B2
Watermill Gro 69 E3
Watermill Lawn *Dublin 5* 48 C2
Watermill Lawn *Dublin 24* 69 E3
Watermill Pk 48 B2
Watermill Rd (Bothar An Easa) 48 B2
Waterside Av 13 E3
Waterside Cl 13 E3
Waterside Ct 13 E3
Waterside Cres *Port.* 19 F2
Waterside Cres *Swords* 13 F3
Waterside Dr 13 E3
Waterside Grn 13 E3
Waterside Lawn 13 E3
Waterside Pk 13 E3
Waterside Ri **4** 13 E3
Waterside Rd **1** 13 E3
Waterside Wk 13 E3
Waterside Way **3** 13 E3
Waterstown Av 43 D4
Waterville Rd 25 D2
Waterville Row 24 C3
Waterville Ter 25 D3
Watery La *Clond.* 52 B4
Watery La *Swords* 12 C1
Watling St 84 B4
Watson Av 77 F3
Watson Dr 77 F3
Watson Pk 77 F3
Watson Rd 77 F3
Watson's Est 77 F3
Waverley Av 46 C3
Waverley Business Pk 53 F4
Waverley Ter *Dublin 6*
off Kenilworth Rd 63 F1
Waverley Ter **5** *Bray* 82 C2
Way, The 20 B3
Weatherwell Ind Est 52 B3
Weaver La
off Phibsborough Rd 45 F4
Weaver's Row 23 F4
Weavers Sq 84 C6
Weaver's St 84 C5
Wedgewood Est 73 D3
Weirview 40 C3
Weirview Dr 73 F2
Weldon's La **8** 31 F3
Wellesley Pl
off Russell St 46 B4
Wellfield Br 30 C2
Wellington Ct **17** 82 B3
Wellington La *Dublin 4* 56 C4
Wellington La *Dublin 6W* 62 B4
Wellington Monument 55 D1
Wellington Pk 62 B3
Wellington Pl (Donnybrook) 56 C4
Wellington Pl N 84 D1
Wellington Quay 85 E4
Wellington Rd *Dublin 4* 56 C4
Wellington Rd *Dublin 6W* 62 B4
Wellington Rd *Dublin 8* 54 C1
Wellington St 75 E3
Wellington St Lwr 85 E1
Wellington St Upr 84 D1
Wellmount Av 26 C4
Wellmount Ct 26 C4
Wellmount Cres 26 C4
Wellmount Dr 26 C4
Wellmount Grn 26 C4
Wellmount Par 26 C4
Wellmount Pk 26 C4
Wellmount Rd 26 C4
Wellpark Av 46 B1
Well Rd **2** 12 C2
Wellview Av 24 B1
Wellview Cres 24 B1
Wellview Pk 24 B1
Wendell Av 19 F2
Wenden Dr 83 D4
Wenden Pk 83 D4
Wentworth Ter
off Hogan Pl 56 C2
Werburgh St 84 D4
Wesbury 73 F2
Wesley Hts 72 C3
Wesley Lawns 72 C3
Wesley Pl 55 F3
Wesley Rd 63 F2
Westbourne 59 F1
Westbourne Av 59 F1
Westbourne Cl 59 F1
Westbourne Dr 59 F1
Westbourne Gro 59 F1
Westbourne Lo 70 B2
Westbourne Ri 59 E1
Westbourne Rd 63 E3
Westbourne Ter **25** 82 B2
Westbourne Vw 59 F1
Westbrook 62 C2
Westbrook Lawns 67 F3
Westbrook Pk 50 B1
Westbrook Rd 64 B4
Westbury 50 C1
Westbury Av 50 C1
Westbury Cl 50 C2
Westbury Dr 50 C1
Westbury Pk 50 C2
Westcourt
off Basin St Upr 84 A5
Westcourt La 84 A5
Westend Village 24 B3
Western Ind Est 61 E1
Western Parkway *Dublin 15* 42 C2
Western Parkway *Dublin 20* 52 C1
Western Parkway *Dublin 22* 61 D2
Western Parkway *Dublin 24* 61 D2
Western Parkway Business Cen 61 F2
Western Parkway Business Pk 61 F2
Western Rd 55 E3
Western Way 84 D1
Westerton Ri **5** 72 B2
Westfield Av 40 A4
Westfield Grn 8 B2
Westfield Pk 82 C3
Westfield Rd 63 E1
Westfield Vw 8 B2
Westgate Business Pk 61 E2
Westhampton Pl 63 E2
Westhaven 23 F2
Westland Ct
off Cumberland St S 85 H5
Westland Row 85 H4
Westlink Ind Est 53 F3
Westminster Ct **4** 76 B3
Westminster Lawns 76 A1
Westminster Pk 76 B1
Westminster Rd 76 B2
Westmoreland Pk 56 B4
Westmoreland St 85 F4
West Oil Jetty 57 F2
Weston Av 72 B1
Weston Cl *Dublin 14* 72 B1
Weston Cl *Lucan* 40 B4
Weston Ct 40 A4
Weston Cres 40 A4
Weston Dr 40 A4
Weston Grn 40 A4
Weston Gro 72 B1
Weston Hts 40 A4
Weston La 40 A4
Weston Lawn 40 A4
Weston Meadow 40 A4
Weston Pk *Dublin 14* 72 B1
Weston Pk *Lucan* 40 B4
Weston Rd 72 B1
Weston Ter 72 B1
Weston Way 40 A4
West Pk *Dublin 5* 48 A1
Westpark *Dublin 24* 69 E2
Westpark *R'coole* 66 B3
West Pk Dr 45 F1
Westpoint Business Pk 23 F1
Westpoint Ct Business Pk 53 F4
West Rd 46 C4
West Row 85 E2
West Ter 54 B2
Westview 8 B3
Westview Ter **6** 82 C2
Westway 25 D2
Westway Cl 25 D2
Westway Gro 25 D2
Westway Lawns
off Westway Gro 25 D2
Westway Pk 25 D2
Westway Ri 25 D2
Westway Vw 25 D2
Westwood Av 26 B4
Westwood Rd 26 B4
Wexford St 85 E6
Wharton Ter
off Harolds Cross Rd 55 F4
Whately Pl 73 F2
Wheatfield 82 B4
Wheatfield Gro 19 F2
Wheatfield Rd *Dublin 20* 53 D1
Wheatfield Rd *Port.* 19 F2
Wheatfields Av 52 B2
Wheatfields Cl 52 B2
Wheatfields Ct 52 B2
Wheatfields Cres 52 B2
Wheatfields Dr 52 B2
Wheatfields Gro 52 B2
Wheatfields Pk 52 B2
Whiteacre Ct 28 B3
Whiteacre Cres 28 B3
Whitebank Rd 57 F2
Whitebarn Rd 64 A4
Whitebeam Av 64 C2
Whitebeam Rd 64 C2
Whitebeams Rd 73 D3
Whitebrook Pk 68 B2
Whitechapel Av 24 A3
Whitechapel Ct 24 A3
Whitechapel Cres 24 A3
Whitechapel Grn 24 A3
Whitechapel Lawn 24 A3
Whitechapel Pk 24 A3
Whitechapel Rd 24 A3
Whitechurch 71 E3
Whitechurch Abbey **7** 71 E1
Whitechurch Av 71 E3
Whitechurch Cl 71 E3
Whitechurch Ct 71 E3
Whitechurch Cres 71 E3
Whitechurch Dr 71 E3
Whitechurch Grn 71 E3
Whitechurch Gro 71 E3
Whitechurch Hill 71 E4
Whitechurch Lawn 71 E3
Whitechurch Pk 71 E3
Whitechurch Pines 71 E1
Whitechurch Pl 71 E3
Whitechurch Rd *Dublin 14* 71 E1
Whitechurch Rd *Dublin 16* 71 E1
Whitechurch Stream **5** 71 E1
Whitechurch Vw 71 E3
Whitechurch Wk 71 E3
Whitechurch Way 71 E3
Whitecliff 71 E2
Whitefriar Pl
off Peter Row 85 E5
Whitefriar St 85 E5
White Hall 60 C3
Whitehall Cl 62 B3
Whitehall Gdns 62 C2
Whitehall Ms 76 B2
Whitehall Pk 62 B3
Whitehall Rd (Rathfarnham) 72 A1
Whitehall Rd E 62 B3
Whitehall Rd W 62 B3
White Oak 64 C3
Whites La N 45 F4
Whites Rd 43 E3
Whitestown 24 B2
Whitestown Av 24 B2
Whitestown Business Pk 68 C3
Whitestown Cres 24 B2
Whitestown Dr *Dublin 24* 68 C2
Whitestown Dr *Mulh.* 24 A2
Whitestown Gdns 24 B3
Whitestown Grn 24 B2
Whitestown Gro 24 B2
Whitestown Pk 24 B2
Whitestown Rd 68 C2
Whitestown Wk 24 B3
Whitestown Way 69 D2
White's Vil 78 B3
Whitethorn 52 C2
Whitethorn Av 29 E4
Whitethorn Cl 29 D4
Whitethorn Cres *Dublin 5* 29 E4
Whitethorn Cres *Dublin 10* 52 C2
Whitethorn Dr 52 C2
Whitethorn Gdns 52 C2
Whitethorn Gro 29 E4
Whitethorn La
off Thorncastle St 57 D2
Whitethorn Pk *Dublin 5* 29 E4
Whitethorn Pk *Dublin 10* 52 C2
Whitethorn Ri 29 E4
Whitethorn Rd *Dublin 5* 29 D4
Whitethorn Rd *Dublin 14* 64 C2
Whitethorn Wk **1** *D.L.* 77 D1
Whitethorn Wk **2** *Fox.* 76 B2
Whitethorn Way 52 C2
Whitshed Rd 83 E3
Whitton Rd 63 E2
Whitworth Av
off Whitworth Pl 46 A3
Whitworth Pl 46 A3
Whitworth Rd *Dublin 1*
off Seville Pl 46 C4
Whitworth Rd *Dublin 9* 45 F3
Whyteleaf Gro 30 C3
Wicklow La
off Wicklow St 85 F4
Wicklow St 85 F4
Wigan Rd 46 A3
Wilderwood Gro 62 B4
Wilfield 57 E4
Wilfield Rd 57 E4
Wilford Ct 82 A1
Wilfrid Rd 63 F1
Willans Av 23 D3
Willans Dr 23 D3
Willans Grn 23 D3
Willans Ri 23 D3
Willans Row 23 D3
Willans Way 23 D3
Willbrook 71 E2
Willbrook Downs 71 E2
Willbrook Gro 71 E1
Willbrook Lawn 71 E1
Willbrook Pk 71 E1
Willbrook Rd 71 E1
Willbrook St 71 E1
Willfield Pk 57 E4
William's La
off Princes St N 85 F3
William's Pk 56 A4
William's Pl S 84 D6
William's Pl Upr 46 A3
William's Row
off Abbey St Mid 85 F3
William St N 46 B4
William St S 85 F5
Willie Nolan Rd 31 F3
Willington Av 62 B3
Willington Ct 62 B3
Willington Cres 62 B4
Willington Dr 62 B4
Willington Grn 62 B3
Willington Gro 62 B4
Willington Pk
off Willington Gro 62 B4
Willmont Av 78 A2
Willow Av *Celbr.* 37 F4
Willow Av *Clond.* 60 A2
Willow Av *Lough.* 80 C1
Willowbank *Dublin 16* 72 C2
Willow Bk *D.L.* 75 E3
Willowbank *Grey.* 83 D2
Willowbank Dr 71 E2
Willowbank Pk 71 D1
Willow Brook *Celbr.* 37 F4
Willowbrook *D'bate* 11 F1
Willowbrook Gro 37 D3
Willowbrook Lawns 37 D3
Willowbrook Lo 37 D2
Willowbrook Pk 37 D2
Willow Business Pk 53 E4
Willow Cl 37 F4
Willow Ct *Clond.* 60 A2
Willow Ct *Lough.* 80 C1
Willow Cres *Celbr.* 37 F4
Willow Cres *Lough.* 80 C1
Willow Dr *Celbr.* 37 F4
Willow Dr *Clond.* 60 A2
Willowfield 57 E4
Willowfield Av 65 D4
Willowfield Pk 65 D4
Willow Gate 72 B2
Willow Grn 37 F4
Willow Gro *Clond.* 60 A2
Willow Gro *Corn.* 76 C2
Willow Gro **4** *D.L.* 77 E1
Willow Lawn 37 F4
Willowmere 83 D1
Willow Ms 65 F1
Willow Par 37 F4
Willow Pk *Dunb.* 20 C2
Willow Pk **5** *Fox.* 76 B1
Willow Pk *Lough.* 80 C1
Willow Pk Av 27 F3
Willow Pk Cl 27 F3
Willow Pk Cres 27 E3
Willow Pk Dr 27 F3
Willow Pk Gro 27 F3
Willow Pk Lawn 27 F3
Willow Pk Rd 27 F3
Willow Pl *Boot.* 74 A1
Willow Pl *Lough.* 80 C1
Willow Ri 37 F4
Willow Rd *Dublin 12* 53 D4
Willow Rd *Dublin 16* 72 B2